third edition

The Community College Experience

Amy Baldwin
Pulaski Technical College

PEARSON

Boston • Columbus • Indianapolis • New York • San Francisco • Upper Saddle River
Amsterdam • Cape Town • Dubai • London • Madrid • Milan • Munich • Paris • Montreal • Toronto
Delhi • Mexico City • São Paulo • Sydney • Hong Kong • Seoul • Singapore • Taipei • Tokyo

Editor-in-Chief: Jodi McPherson
Editor: Katie Mahan
Development Editor: Elana Dolberg
Editorial Assistant: Clara Ciminelli
Executive Marketing Manager: Amy Judd
Production Editor: Annette Joseph
Editorial Production Service: Electronic Publishing Services Inc.
Manufacturing Buyer: Megan Cochran
Electronic Composition: Jouve
Interior Design: Electronic Publishing Services Inc.
Photo Researcher: Annie Fuller
Cover Designer: Diane Lorenzo

Credits and acknowledgments borrowed from other sources and reproduced, with permission, in this textbook appear on the appropriate page within text.

Library of Congress Cataloging-in-Publication Data

Baldwin, Amy
   The community college experience / Amy Baldwin.—3rd ed.
        p.   cm.
   ISBN-13: 978-0-13-281987-9 (pbk.)
   ISBN-10: 0-13-281987-2 (pbk.)
   1. College student orientation—United States.   2. Community colleges—United
States.   3. College students—Conduct of life.   I. Title.
   LB2343.32.B24 2013
   378.1'543—dc23
                                                                    2011044898

10   9   8   7   6   5   4   3   2   1

ISBN 10: 0-13-281987-2
ISBN 13: 978-0-13-281987-9

AMY BALDWIN, M.A., is an instructor of writing, literature, and college success at Pulaski Technical College in North Little Rock, Arkansas. Since 1996, she has served the college in various roles, including self-study editor, distance education coordinator, and professional development coordinator. She is also the author of four student success textbooks that were the first on the market to address the special needs of students: *The Community College Experience,* Brief Edition, third edition (Pearson, 2012), *The First-Generation College Experience* (Pearson, 2012), *The Community College Experience,* third edition (Pearson, 2013), and *The College Experience* (Pearson, 2013). She has also facilitated over 120 workshops and breakout sessions all over the country—at community colleges, K–12 professional days, and national conferences—on teaching and learning issues such as transitioning to college, student engagement practices, and active learning. Amy will complete her doctorate of higher education from the University of Arkansas at Little Rock in December 2012. The focus of her dissertation is student engagement, retention, and success for African American males in college. She is also serving as the project manager for the Complete College America initiative for the state of Arkansas.

BRIEF CONTENTS

CONTENTS

CHAPTER 1   College Culture and the Campus   1

CHAPTER 2   Goal Setting, Motivation, and Learning Styles   25

CHAPTER 9 Writing, Presenting, and Information Literacy 177

CHAPTER 10 Studying and Taking Tests 203

CHAPTER 11   Planning for Your Degree   227

CHAPTER 12   Preparing for a Career and a Life   253

You have heard all of the clichés about college being a great time to discover who you are and who you want to be, while enjoying yourself during the process, but for many—myself included—starting college was a time filled with nervousness and anxiety. Fortunately, I had enrolled in a college that understood first-year student issues and helped me navigate the first few weeks and subsequent semesters with less fear so that I became more confident that I could complete a degree.

It is with that memory of what it was like to be a new student that this book has been written. It has you in mind. You are the one who had good grades in high school, and now you have entered a new environment away from home, but you need to know how college really is. You are the one who didn't do as well as you wanted to in high school, and you are now committed to staying focused and getting your degree, but you could use a little help with honing your study skills. You are the one who is returning to college after taking some time off to work and build a life, but you could use some help meeting your college's expectations.

No matter where you come from and how excited you are about being in college for the first time—or again after some time away—things will be different, and any help you can get mastering the new "rules" of college will help you more quickly get a firm footing. This book has been written to help you do just that. As a community college student, your time is valuable. To that end, each chapter provides "just-in-time" information to help you master the key concepts of student success, and each feature within the chapters has been designed for real-world relevance. Think of this book as a resource manual for your first semesters and beyond.

ACKNOWLEDGMENTS

A very special thank you to the following people for helping me during the process of writing this book: Kyle, Emily, and Will; Brian Tietje, a true collaborator and colleague, for his work on rethinking and reshaping this edition; Jodi McPherson and Elana Dolberg; Amy Judd; and the instructors and administrators who provided valuable feedback during the process.

Thanks also to the reviewers for this edition: Gabriel Adona, San Diego Mesa College; Pamela Bilton Beard, Houston Community College Southwest; Mei Mei Burr, Northern Kentucky University; Donna Colondres, Chaffey College; Lory Conrad, University of Arkansas–Fort Smith; Christine Crowe, Suffolk Community College; Raven Davenport, Houston Community College; Luke E. Faust, Indiana University of Pennsylvania; Shirley Flor, San Diego Mesa College; Alonzo Flowers, Blinn College; Kim Forcier, University of Texas–San Antonio; Barry Foster, Brazosport Community College; Patricia S. Foster, Stephen F. Austin State University; Altheria Gaston; Monique Gilchrist, Community College of Philadelphia; Mary Gumlia, Solano Community College; Linda M. Hensen-Jackson, Arkansas Tech University; Lauren Hensley, The Ohio State University; Robert Irizarry, Brazosport College; Kimberly Koledoye, Houston Community College Northwest; Rula Mourad Koudsia, Ivy Tech Community College Northeast; Alice Lanning, University of Oklahoma; Catherine Lee, Cape Fear Community College; Rhonda Lee Meadows, West Virginia University; Shannon E. McCasland, Aims Community College; Cynthia Pascal, The Art Institute of Washington; Melissa Rathburn, University of South Florida; Jacqueline Robinson, Milwaukee Area Technical College; Amy Skeens, West Virginia University; Leigh Smith, Lamar Institute of Technology; Ellen Stohl, California State University–Northridge; Margaret A. Soucy, Western New Mexico University; Victoria Washington, Houston Community College; Cornelia Wills, Middle Tennessee State University; and Jennifer Woltjen, Broome Community College.

INTRODUCTION FOR FACULTY

As a professor, you know that student success doesn't just happen. Instead, it is a combination of motivation, preparation, persistence, and relationships. You also know that no matter how prepared some students are for the academic challenges of college, they may not always be ready for the cultural challenges, including understanding professors' expectations and navigating the financial issues that are part of the community college experience. So much of what we expect students to know about being a successful student are what we call "hidden rules," and the rest is new information about how college works. If students don't know the "unwritten rules" for college success, how might it impact them? *The Community College Experience* meets students where they are and helps them develop a plan to handle any situation.

Student success is determined by motivation, preparation, knowledge, persistence, and relationships, the outcome largely measured by performance in other courses from the first term throughout the college career. Students are often not prepared for the social and cultural challenges, such as meeting expectations, managing pressures on time, and navigating financial issues. Many of the standards for college success are indeed those "unwritten rules" that require an experienced perspective to anticipate, understand, and overcome. This text covers the topics students need to make the transition into a university culture, become active learners, and make intelligent choices. Course materials are realistic and supportive. They resonate with diverse student backgrounds, including first-generation college students, students of color, returning adults, and others. Once students know the "rules"— written and unwritten—they can adapt their plan for a more successful college experience.

To that end, each chapter contains the following features with the focus on the "unwritten rules" or the "what, where, and when" for being successful in college.

"WHAT" WILL SUPPORT STUDENTS

60-Second Pause. In a fast-paced, consumer-driven world, it is helpful to provide soft stops for students to pause, think, and reflect on what they have read so far. This feature provides the student with a question to consider before moving on to the rest of the chapter content.

Buzz Boxes. There are times when students have special questions that are not always answered in the content. This feature allows for those kinds of questions and honest, expert responses.

Technology Tips. This feature provides information Web resources students can access easily to help reinforce or explore further the concepts from the chapter.

Your Terms for Success. Because many new students are unfamiliar with the terms that are unique to the university setting, this feature provides a handy overview of common words they will encounter, as well as meanings.

Integrity Matters. Integrity plays a major role in a student's academic life. This feature provides an opportunity to reflect on integrity issues that are academic and personal.

"WHERE" CAN STUDENTS APPLY WHAT IS BEING LEARNED

It's in the Syllabus. This feature reminds students to review one of the most important documents in college—the "contract" between their instructors and themselves—by asking them a few questions about the document.

Opening Stories. This feature runs throughout the book and presents four characters on their journey as first-time-in-college students. The stories provide opportunities for your students to relate to their situations.

From College to University and From College to Career. These features provide a connection for students, whether they choose to transfer to a four-year university or choose to move into the world of work right after college.

End of Chapter Exercises. Based on Bloom's taxonomy, all exercises in the book are designed to build on students' understanding of the material, help them synthesize the concepts, and apply them to their own college situations. Rubrics for the exercises are available in the Instructor's Resource Manual to help faculty track student outcomes.

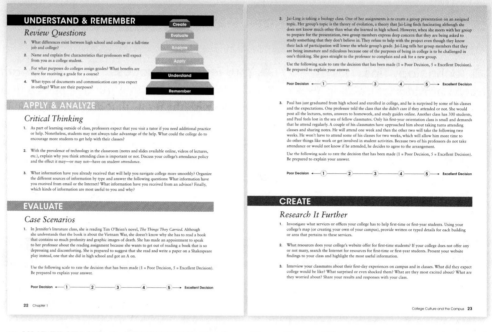

■ **UNDERSTAND & REMEMBER: Review Questions.** These questions are designed to help students review what they have learned by reading the chapter. Each question is designed to take 2–5 minutes to complete, depending on how well the student has read and understood the chapter. An answer key is provided in the Instructor's Resource Manual.

■ **APPLY & ANALYZE: Critical Thinking.** These questions are designed to challenge students to apply what they have learned from the chapter in new and unique situations. They are designed to take 5–10 minutes each to complete. A critical thinking rubric is included in the Instructor's Resource Manual.

■ **EVALUATE: Case Scenarios.** These scenarios are intended to provide students with an example situation in which a fictional student makes an important decision. They are then asked to rate the effectiveness of the fictional student's decision based on a provided scale. These questions are designed to take 3–5 minutes to complete individually or 5–7 minutes if completed with a partner. A decision making rubric is included in the Instructor's Resource Manual.

■ **CREATE: Research It Further.** These activities are designed to challenge students to create new knowledge by researching additional sources of information and synthesizing the new research findings with the content provided in the chapter through a questionnaire/survey of fellow student opinion, compilation of campus resources, and Internet research. They will take 30 minutes to 3 hours to complete. An information literacy grading checklist is included in the Instructor's Resource Manual.

INTRODUCTION FOR STUDENTS

You made it! You have taken the first steps toward a college education, and for that, you should feel a sense of accomplishment. It is no easy task to apply for admission, enroll in classes, and find your way around campus, but you have obviously completed those steps successfully. Getting your course supplies, such as textbooks and notebooks, too, is a feat worth congratulations. Now is the time to take a moment and think about why you are here and what you hope to achieve.

W. Edwards Deming, professor and industrial consultant, once said, "It's not enough to do your best. You must know what to do and then do your best." Obviously from your commitment to take the first step into college, you have the desire to do your best. Now you just need the tools to help you know what to do so that you can do your best in college, in a career, and in your life. With that thought in mind, this book is designed to help you learn what you need to do to accomplish your goals by providing you with the basic information about college expectations, academic strategies, and life management skills.

The student stories that begin each chapter allow you to consider what life will be like for you now that you are in college. You will meet and get to know Juanita, who is 18 and dependent on her family for support; Laura, a single parent, who is 31 and has a learning disability; Michael, who is 42 with an accomplished military career but no formal education; and Evan, who is 20 and has many ambitions but no clear path to success. These stories will help you see how you can meet the challenges you will surely face as a new student, and they will help you see how others may experience college for the first time.

Other features that you may find helpful as a first-time student include "Your Terms for Success," which provides a list of terms you may not be familiar with as a first-time student, but knowing them will help you navigate your way through college. The "Buzz" question and answer feature provides a real-life student question and the answer to help you, too, be successful. Then, the "60-Second Pause" activity allows you to "breathe" at certain times during the chapter so that you can reflect on what you have read so far. "Technology Tips" provides you with easy-to-access information about how technology can and will be used in college. Whether you are technologically savvy or a beginner, you will benefit from seeing how technology can be applied to help you succeed.

"Integrity Matters" will remind you of one of the core values of higher education—integrity, or doing what is right even if no one is watching—and will offer opportunities to explore acting with integrity, a good habit to acquire during college. "It's in the Syllabus" helps to demystify that handout that you get from each of your professors; with this feature, you will be able to turn it from a piece of paper to a tool that helps you succeed. "From College to University" will help you see how the same issues will be important at a four-year university, and "From College to Career" will help you connect concepts you are learning to be a successful student in life after college, whatever path you take after your current college experience.

The entire book has been written with your best interests in mind. May it serve you well as you take those first steps toward your future!

Supplemental Resources

INSTRUCTOR SUPPORT – Resources to simplify your life and support your students.

Book Specific

Online Instructor's Manual – This manual is intended to give professors a framework or blueprint of ideas and suggestions that may assist them in providing their students with activities, journal writing, thought-provoking situations, and group activities. This supplement is available for download from the Instructor's Resource Center at www.pearsonhighered.com/irc

Online PowerPoint Presentation – A comprehensive set of PowerPoint slides that can be used by instructors for class presentations or by students for lecture preview or review. The PowerPoint Presentation includes bullet point slides for each chapter, as well as all of the graphs and tables found in the textbook. These slides highlight the important points of each chapter to help students understand the concepts within each chapter. Instructors may download these PowerPoint presentations from the Instructor's Resource Center at www.pearsonhighered.com/irc

MyTest Test Bank – Pearson MyTest offers instructors a secure online environment and quality assessments to easily create print exams, study guide questions, and quizzes from any computer with an Internet connection.

Premium Assessment Content
- Draw from a rich library of question testbanks that complement the textbook and course learning objectives.
- Edit questions or tests to fit specific teaching needs.

Instructor Friendly Features
- Easily create and store questions, including images, diagrams, and charts using simple drag-and-drop and Word-like controls.
- Use additional information provided by Pearson, such as the question's difficulty level or learning objective, to help quickly build a test.

Time-Saving Enhancements
- Add headers or footers and easily scramble questions and answer choices all from one simple toolbar.
- Quickly create multiple versions of a test or answer key, and when ready, simply save to Word or PDF format and print!
- Export exams for import to Blackboard 6.0, CE (WebCT), or Vista (WebCT)!
  Additional information available at www.pearsonmytest.com

Instruct 4 Success – This online teacher training course supports instructors at all experience levels implement our best-selling franchises: Baldwin Experience, Carter Keys, and Sherfield Cornerstones. Boosts student engagement by helping instructors improve facilitation techniques, learn first hand how to implement active based learning practices, navigate potential pitfalls, acquire new activities from authors and peers - and connect more with our students. This multi-dimensional training tool offers the practical resources instructors rely on – teaching techniques, PowerPoint, etc. – as well as the 'best of' video, active learning exercises, and technology tips from nationally recognized authors and experts. All with the extreme flexibility of use whenever you like, as often as you please, from wherever you choose. How inspiring! Contact your Pearson representative for access information. For instructors reaching students - *'Inspiring you to inspire them.'*

MyStudentSuccessLab – Are you teaching online, in a hybrid setting, or looking to infuse technology into your classroom for the first time? It is an online solution designed to help students build the skills they need to succeed for ongoing personal and professional development at www.mystudentsuccesslab.com

Other Resources

"Easy access to online, book-specific teaching support is now just a click away!"

Instructor Resource Center – Register. Redeem. Login. Three easy steps that open the door to a variety of print and media resources in downloadable, digital format, available to instructors exclusively through the Pearson 'IRC'. www.pearsonhighered.com/irc

"Provide information highlights on the most critical topics for student success!"

Success Tips is a 6-panel laminate with topics that include MyStudentSuccessLab, Time Management, Resources All Around You, Now You're Thinking, Maintaining Your Financial Sanity, and Building Your Professional Image. Other choices are available upon request. This essential supplement can be packaged with any student success text to add value with 'just in time' information for students.

Supplemental Resources

Other Resources

"Infuse student success into any program with our "IDentity" Series booklets!" - Written by national subject matter experts, the material contains strategies and activities for immediate application. Choices include:

- Financial Literacy (Farnoosh Torabi)
- Financial Responsibility (Clearpoint Financial)
- Now You're Thinking about Student Success (Judy Chartrand et.al.)
- Now You're Thinking about Career Success (Judy Chartrand et.al.)
- Ownership (Megan Stone)
- Identity (Stedman Graham).

"Through partnership opportunities, we offer a variety of assessment options!"
LASSI– The LASSI is a 10-scale, 80-item assessment of students' awareness about and use of learning and study strategies. Addressing skill, will and self-regulation, the focus is on both covert and overt thoughts, behaviors, attitudes and beliefs that relate to successful learning and that can be altered through educational interventions. Available in two formats: Paper ISBN: 0131723154 or Online ISBN: 0131723162 (access card).

Robbins Self Assessment Library – This compilation teaches students to create a portfolio of skills. S.A.L. is a self-contained, interactive, library of 49 behavioral questionnaires that help students discover new ideas about themselves, their attitudes, and their personal strengths and weaknesses. Available in Paper, CD-Rom, and Online (Access Card) formats.

"For a truly tailored solution that fosters campus connections and increases retention, talk with us about custom publishing."
Pearson Custom Publishing – We are the largest custom provider for print and media shaped to your course's needs. Please visit us at www.pearsoncustom.com to learn more.

STUDENT SUPPORT – Tools to help make the grade now, and excel in school later.

"Now there's a Smart way for students to save money."
CourseSmart is an exciting new choice for students looking to save money. As an alternative to purchasing the printed textbook, students can purchase an electronic version of the same content. With a CourseSmart eTextbook, students can search the text, make notes online, print out reading assignments that incorporate lecture notes, and bookmark important passages for later review. For more information, or to purchase access to the CourseSmart eTextbook, visit www.coursesmart.com

"Today's students are more inclined than ever to use technology to enhance their learning."
MyStudentSuccessLab will engage students through relevant YouTube videos with 'how to' videos selected 'by students, for students' and help build the skills they need to succeed for ongoing personal and professional development. www.mystudentsuccesslab.com

"Time management is the #1 challenge students face."
Premier Annual Planner - This specially designed, annual 4-color collegiate planner includes an academic planning/resources section, monthly planning section (2 pages/month), weekly planning section (48 weeks; July start date), which facilitate short-term as well as long term planning. Spiral bound, 6x9.

"Journaling activities promote self-discovery and self-awareness."
Student Reflection Journal - Through this vehicle, students are encouraged to track their progress and share their insights, thoughts, and concerns. 8½ × 11. 90 pages.

MyStudentSuccessLab

Start Strong. Finish Stronger.
www.MyStudentSuccessLab.com

MyStudentSuccessLab is an online solution designed to help students acquire the skills they need to succeed for ongoing personal and professional development. They will have access to peer-led video interviews and develop core skills through interactive practice exercises and activities that provide academic, life, and professionalism skills that will transfer to ANY course.

It can accompany any Student Success text or used as a stand-alone course offering.

How will MyStudentSuccessLab make a difference?

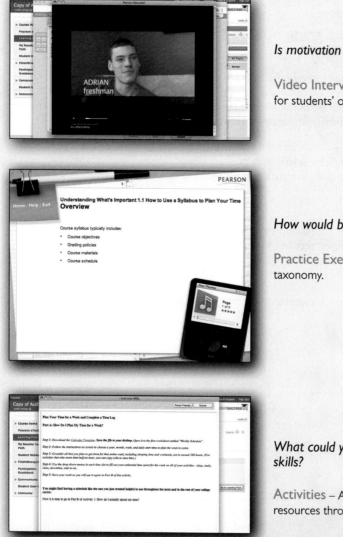

Is motivation a challenge, and if so, how do you deal with it?

Video Interviews – Experience peer led video 'by students, for students' of all ages and stages.

How would better class preparation improve the learning experience?

Practice Exercises – Practice skills for each topic - leveled by Bloom's taxonomy.

What could you gain by building critical thinking and problem-solving skills?

Activities – Apply what is being learned to create 'personally relevant' resources through enhanced communication and self-reflection.

MyStudentSuccessLab

Start Strong. Finish Stronger.
www.MyStudentSuccessLab.com

As an instructor, how much easier would it be to assign and assess on MyStudentSuccessLab if you had a Learning Path Diagnostic that reported to the grade book?

Learning Path Diagnostic

- For the **course**, 65 Pre-Course questions (Levels I & II Bloom's) and 65 Post-Course questions (Levels III & IV Bloom's) that link to key learning objectives in each topic.

- For each **topic**, 20 Pre-Test questions (Levels I & II Bloom's) and 20 Post-Test questions (Levels III & IV Bloom's) that link to all learning objectives in the topic.

As a student, how much more engaged would you be if you had access to relevant YouTube videos within MyStudentSuccessLab?

Student Resources

A wealth of resources like our FinishStrong247 YouTube channel with 'just in time' videos selected 'by students, for students'.

MyStudentSuccessLab Topic List -

1. A First Step: Goal Setting
2. Communication
3. Critical Thinking
4. Financial Literacy
5. Information Literacy

6. Learning Preferences
7. Listening and Taking Notes in Class
8. Majors and Careers
9. Memory and Studying
10. Problem Solving

11. Professionalism
12. Reading and Annotating
13. Stress Management
14. Test Taking Skills
15. Time Management

MyStudentSuccessLab Feature set

Learning Path Diagnostic: 65 Pre-Course (Levels I & II Bloom's) and 65 Post-Course (Levels III & IV Bloom's)/Pre-Test (Levels I & II Bloom's) and Post-Test (Levels III & IV Bloom's).

Topic Overview: Module objectives.

Video Interviews: Real video interviews 'by students, for students' on key issues.

Practice Exercises: Skill-building exercises per topic provide interactive experience and practice.

Activities: Apply what is being learned to create 'personally relevant' resources through enhanced communication and self-reflection.

Student Resources: Pearson Students Facebook page, FinishStrong247 YouTube channel, MySearchLab, Online Dictionary, Plagiarism Guide, Student Planner, and Student Reflection Journal.

Implementation Guide: Grading rubric to support instruction with Overview, Time on Task, Suggested grading, etc.

PEARSON

Pearson Success Tips, I/e

ISBN-10: 0132788071 • ISBN-13: 9780132788076

Success Tips is a 6-panel laminate that provides students with information highlights on the most critical topics for student success. These topics include MyStudentSuccessLab, Time Management, Resources All Around You, Now You're Thinking, Maintaining Your Financial Sanity, and Building Your Professional Image. Other choices are available upon request via our www.pearsoncustomlibrary.com program, as well as traditional custom publishing. This essential supplement can packaged with any student success text to add value with 'just in time' information for students.

Features

- **MyStudentSuccessLab** — Helps students 'Start strong, Finish stronger' by getting the most out of this technology with their book.

- **Time Management** — Everyone begins with the same 24 hours in the day, but how well students use their time varies.

- **Resources All Around You** — Builds awareness for the types of resources available on campus for students to take advantage of.

- **Now You're Thinking** — Learning to think critically is imperative to student success.

- **Maintaining Your Financial Sanity** — Paying attention to savings, spending, and borrowing choices is more important than ever.

- **Building Your Professional Image** — Students are motivated by preparing for their future careers through online and in person professionalism tips, self-branding, and image tips.

- **Additional Topics** — Topics above are 'default.' These topics include MyStudentSuccessLab, Time Management, Resources All Around You, Now You're Thinking, Maintaining Your Financial Sanity, and Building Your Professional Image. Other choices are available upon request via our www.pearsoncustomlibrary.com program, as well as traditional custom publishing. This essential supplement can be packaged with any student success text to add value with 'just in time' information for students.

Topic List

- MyStudentSuccessLab*
- Time Management*
- Resources All Around You*
- Now You're Thinking*
- Maintaining Your Financial Sanity*
- Building Your Professional Image*
- Get Ready for Workplace Success
- Civility Paves the Way Toward Success

- Succeeding in Your Diverse World
- Information Literacy is Essential to Success
- Protect Your Personal Data
- Create Your Personal Brand
- Service Learning
- Stay Well and Manage Stress
- Get Things Done with Virtual Teams
- Welcome to Blackboard!

- Welcome to Moodle!
- Welcome to eCollege!
- Set and Achieve Your Goals
- Prepare for Test Success
- Good Notes Are Your Best Study Tool
- Veterans/Military Returning Students

NOTE: those with asterisks are 'default' options; topic selection can be made through Pearson Custom Library at www.pearsoncustomlibrary.com, as well as traditional custom publishing.

PERSONALIZE THE EXPERIENCE WITH

PEARSON LEARNING SOLUTIONS

FOR STUDENT SUCCESS AND CAREER DEVELOPMENT

The Pearson Custom Library Catalog

With Pearson Custom Library, you can create a custom book by selecting content from our course-specific collections. The collections consist of chapters from Pearson titles like this one, and carefully selected, copyright cleared, third-party content, and pedagogy. The finished product is a print-on-demand custom book that students can purchase in the same way they purchase other course materials.

Custom Media

Pearson Learning Solutions works with you to create a customized technology solution specific to your course requirements and needs. We specialize in a number of best practices including custom websites and portals, animation and simulations, and content conversions and customizations.

Custom Publications

We can develop your original material and create a textbook that meets your course goals. Pearson Learning Solutions works with you on your original manuscript to help refine and strengthen it, ensuring that it meets and exceeds market standards. Pearson Learning Solutions will work with you to select already published content and sequence it to follow your course goals.

Online Education

Pearson Learning Solutions offers customizable online course content for your distance learning classes, hybrid courses, or to enhance the learning experience of your traditional in-classroom students. Courses include a fully developed syllabus, media-rich lecture presentations, audio lectures, a wide variety of assessments, discussion board questions, and a strong instructor resource package.

In the end, the finished product reflects your insight into what your students need to succeed, and puts it into practice.
Visit us on the web to learn more at www.pearsoncustom.com/studentsuccess or call 800-777-6872

ALWAYS LEARNING

PEARSON

Introducing CourseSmart, The world's largest online marketplace for digital texts and course materials

A Smarter Way for Instructors

▶ **CourseSmart saves time.** Instructors can review and compare textbooks and course materials from multiple publishers at one easy-to-navigate, secure website.

▶ **CourseSmart is environmentally sound.** When instructors use CourseSmart, they help reduce the time, cost, and environmental impact of mailing print exam copies.

▶ **CourseSmart reduces student costs.** Instructors can offer students a lower-cost alternative to traditional print textbooks.

▶ **"Add this overview to your syllabus today!"**
REQUIRED COURSE MATERIALS - ALTERNATE VERSION AVAILABLE:

CourseSmart is an exciting new choice for students looking to save money. As an alternative to purchasing the printed textbook, students can purchase an electronic version of the same content. With a CourseSmart eTextbook, students can search the text, make notes online, print out reading assignments that incorporate lecture notes, and bookmark important passages for later review.

A Smarter Way for Students

▶ **CourseSmart is convenient.** Students have instant access to exactly the materials their instructor assigns.

▶ **CourseSmart offers choice.** With CourseSmart, students have a high-quality alternative to the print textbook.

▶ **CourseSmart saves money.** CourseSmart digital solutions can be purchased for up to 50% less than traditional print textbooks.

▶ **CourseSmart offers education value.** Students receive the same content offered in the print textbook enhanced by the search, note-taking, and printing tools of a web application.

CourseSmart is the Smarter Way

To learn for yourself, visit www.coursesmart.com

This is an access-protected site and you will need a password provided to you by a representative from a publishing partner.

1 College Culture and the Campus

"Destination: Degree," the travel-themed orientation, is winding down after an afternoon of skits, presentations, and door prizes.

"If everyone will score their inventories, we will explain how learning style preference affects your study habits," says Jason, an orientation leader who is wearing an orange "Ask me!" T-shirt.

"Hey, I am 'kinesthetic.' That kind of makes sense. I teach kickboxing and learned how to do it by working out almost every day," Evan says.

"I thought I would be more of a social learner, but my learning style preference is 'individual,'" says Michael as he rubs his head. "I spent so much time leading troops when I was in the military."

"I am definitely 'aural,'" Laura says to the group. "I got through all my classes in high school by listening to the lectures. I rarely took notes because I liked to listen."

"Yeah, I can see that. You talked during every presentation!" Evan jokes.

"Will you be able to do that in college, just listen?" Juanita, the youngest of the group, asks. "I mean, I have heard that the professors expect so much more of you when it comes to being in class."

"I am sure you will," says Michael. "My girlfriend graduated last year with a degree in nursing. All she did was read for class and then study her notes every night."

"Yeah, that makes sense. If anyone needs someone to study with, let me know," Juanita says.

"If you want to learn a few kickboxing moves in exchange for help taking notes, let me know," Evan says to Juanita.

"Sounds good!" Juanita laughs.

"If anyone wants to exchange a home-cooked meal for some babysitting while I study, let me know," says Laura.

"I know Laura is the talkative one, but give me a call if you ever need anything. Good luck to everyone!" Michael says.

YOUR GOALS FOR THIS CHAPTER

Just as these four students have been oriented to college life, the purpose of this chapter is to introduce you to this new culture, to reveal the truths about higher education, to debunk the myths, and to prepare you for meeting the challenges that you will inevitably face. At the end of this chapter you will be able to do the following:

- Recognize the transitional issues of going to college
- Anticipate the expectations of college
- Adjust to the rhythm of college
- Locate and utilize resources on campus

MyStudentSuccessLab (www.mystudentsuccesslab.com) is an online solution designed to help you 'Start strong, Finish stronger' by building skills for ongoing personal and professional development.

This is an exciting time for you as you transition into college life. The definition of *transition* is a change or modification, and you will find that going to college will create a change in you—and not just in your schedule and your workload. You will find that your concept of yourself will change, your relationships will change, and your outlook on your future will change. All of these changes will require an investment of your time for reflection to make the transition successfully. At the end of your college experience, you will find yourself *transformed* into a new person. You will most likely be more thoughtful and more confident about your abilities; most certainly, you will be more aware of what it takes to earn a degree. However, this transformation won't be easy; the following section on transitioning from where you are now to where you want to be will give you a better understanding of what you need to do to make the transition successfully.

Your Terms for SUCCESS

WHEN YOU SEE . . .	IT MEANS . . .
Academic integrity	Doing honest work on all assignments and tests
Core curriculum	Also called general education requirements or basic courses; the common courses that almost all students who earn an associate's degree complete
Corequisite	A course that can be taken at the same time as another course
Course content	The material that will be covered in a course
Course objectives	The goals of a course
Credit hour	The unit of measurement that colleges use that usually equals the amount of time you are in class each week during a 16-week semester
Degree plan	A list of classes that you must successfully complete in order to be awarded a degree
Disability accommodation policy	A policy that states how accommodations for documented disabilities will be handled
FERPA	Family Educational Rights and Privacy Act; federal law that regulates the communication and dissemination of your educational records
GPA	Grade point average; each grade that is earned is awarded grade points that are multiplied by the number of credit hours taken, resulting in the grade point average
Grading criteria	The standards by which an assignment is graded
Prerequisite	A course that must be taken before one can take another course
Quality points	The points determined by a grade point multiplied by the credit hours for a course; e.g., an A (4 grade points) in a writing class (3 credit hours) will equal 12 quality points; used to calculate grade point average
Syllabus	The contract between an instructor and a student; provides information about the course content, course objectives, grading criteria, and course schedule

Transitioning from High School or from Work Offers Distinct Challenges

For some students, the move from high school to college seems fairly simple—both require reading, writing, testing, and attending class. Students who are taking the step from work to school may also see some similarities between their jobs and their classroom work—both require working hard, keeping yourself motivated, and following the rules. If the differences between high school or work and college are that minor, then why do so many college students have difficulty making a successful transition?

The answer to that question can be given by the instructors who see smart, competent students have trouble adjusting to the climate and culture of college because they do not understand what is expected of them. In other words, in order to be successful, students must know what is expected of them beyond the questions on the next test. Students need to know how college works and how to navigate through not only their courses, but also the common challenges that they will face as they work toward a degree.

The Biggest Change Involves Personal Responsibility

Exhibit 1.1 illustrates some of the differences and similarities among high school, a full-time job, and college. As you take a look at the column labeled "College" in Exhibit 1.1, you'll notice that a pattern emerges—compared to their high school or full-time job, college students experience a dramatic increase in the amount of personal

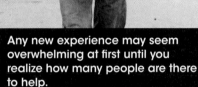

Any new experience may seem overwhelming at first until you realize how many people are there to help.

©JUPITER IMAGES / GETTY IMAGES

responsibility they must handle. In high school, teachers, counselors, and coaches provide significant oversight and direction to students, and carefully manage everything from school lunches to study hall. In the workplace, employers oversee their employees using timesheets, employee policy manuals, and supervisors. High school teachers and job supervisors provide clear guidance, both about expectations and how to achieve them. In college, however, the student is responsible for understanding the expectations for academic and career success, and developing a strategy for meeting those expectations.

There have probably been some times during your high school or work experience when you wished that you had more freedom to make your own decisions and pursue your own interests. As you step into college, these wishes indeed come true. The range of opportunities and alternatives that lie before you is so broad and diverse that you'll find yourself making important decisions every day. Which general education (GE) courses will you take next semester? Do you want to take classes primarily in the morning or later in the day? Where do you want to live and with whom? Do you want to join a student club or organization? Would you be able to participate in a study-abroad program? What kind of career advice and support will there be? The list of questions, decisions, and responsibilities that you face affords you tremendous freedom to chart your own course in college and your future career. This broad range of personal responsibility is exciting, but it can also become overwhelming at times, and you can find yourself suffering significant consequences for poor decisions along the way. It's important, then, to develop a personal approach that you can use as you step into an experience that offers so much personal responsibility and autonomy.

EXHIBIT  **1.1** Differences among High School, Full-Time Work, and College

High School	Full-Time Work	College
Attendance is mandatory in order to meet requirements	Attendance is mandatory in order to stay employed	Attendance may not be mandatory
At least 6 continuous hours spent in class each day	At least 8 continuous hours spent at work each day	Different amounts of time spent in class and between classes each day
Very little choice in what classes you take and when you take them	May have little choice in work assignments and when the work is to be completed	More flexibility in when you work on assignments and how soon you complete them before the due date
Moderate to no outside work necessary to be successful	Moderate to no overtime work necessary to complete job duties	Substantial amount of outside work to complete assignments and to be successful
Teachers check homework and keep you up-to-date on progress; they will inform you if you are not completing assignments and progressing well	Supervisors check completion and quality of work at regular intervals; they will inform you if you are not meeting the standards for the position	Professors may not check all homework or provide feedback on progress at regular intervals; they may not inform you if you are not meeting the standards of the course
Teachers go over material and expect you to remember facts and information	Employers provide basic information, expect you to use it to complete the job effectively	Professors provide concepts and theories and expect you to evaluate the ideas, synthesize the ideas with other concepts you have learned, and develop new theories
Frequent tests over small amounts of material allow for grades to be raised if needed	Supervisors create employee improvement plans to allow you to improve your ratings if needed	Professors provide the standards and grading criteria but often allow only a few chances (through infrequent testing/assignments) to meet them

Make a Plan for Exercising Your New Freedom

Before you start making a lot of important decisions that affect your academics, social life, and physical and psychological health, take some time to consider how you want to approach these decisions so that you exercise good judgment. One consideration is with whom you will consult when you encounter important decisions and

personal freedoms. Identify individuals in your life who can help you think through important decisions and consider all the important factors. Your family, friends, classmates, advisors, professors, and mentors may come to mind. Seek their counsel and input as you explore your alternatives in college. Another consideration is what personal values or principles you want to uphold in your life. It's important to keep those values in your sights as you experience a range of new opportunities and diversions that might either reinforce your values or undermine them. Finally, give careful consideration to how your decisions will affect others. Although we refer to this topic as "personal" responsibility, it's important to recognize that every decision you make will affect not only your life, but others as well. For example, a decision to miss a meeting for a group project in a class not only affects your performance in the class, but your team members' performance, also.

Having greater personal freedom is an exciting component of the college experience, and it's an important part of your transformation. The advice we've offered is intended to help you navigate this wider road with success and good judgment.

USING TECHNOLOGY TO GET AHEAD

There are numerous websites that provide information about succeeding in college, including websites devoted to transitioning into college successfully.

RECOMMENDED SITES

- http://www.gonorth.org/start/highschl.htm: This website provides a guide for making the transition from high school to college.
- http://www.unt.edu/pais/howtochoose/glossary.htm: This site provides an exhaustive list of common college terms.
- http://www.back2college.com/gpa.htm: This website provides a handy GPA calculator that allows you to put in your grades and determine what GPA you have made.

Given the circumstances of your own life to date, what are some of the most significant changes you expect as you step into college? What's your plan for handling this transition successfully?

HIGHER EDUCATION BRINGS HIGH EXPECTATIONS

A marathon is a 26.2 mile run, and regardless of whether a participant runs full speed or walks, it's an event that is challenging for everyone. Similarly, college is a demanding experience—there is no way to avoid that reality. Regardless of the national or international reputation of your college, your college experience will challenge you mentally, physically, and emotionally. We don't tell you this to intimidate or discourage you, but to help you get into the right mindset for success. New students can fall prey to rumors and suggestions that college is easy, or that one college is easier than another. Don't fall for these myths! If you start college with the expectation that it will be easy, you'll run the risk of stumbling during your very first semester in college, and you'll have to work even harder to recover.

A typical associate's degree requires 60 semester credit hours, and many students take three, four, or even five years to finish their degrees. Along the way, you'll be expected to attend four or five classes every semester, study several hours outside of class each week, meet with team members, participate in cocurricular and extracurricular events, and perhaps even work part-time or full-time to pay for school. Even though your professors know that you face all of these responsibilities, all of them will expect you to give your very best effort and quality of work to their classes. Because of their experience in teaching hundreds if not thousands of students over time, professors know that students can succeed and perform extremely well when they are challenged. Here, we offer some tips for getting yourself in shape, so to speak, for a successful and challenging college experience. We build our recommendations around the four Cs: (1) computers and supplies, (2) classroom preparation, attendance, and behavior, (3) constructive criticism, and (4) controversial content.

Computers and Supplies

In high school, books and course materials are provided for each student, but in college, you will be responsible for obtaining and purchasing your own materials—and you will need to do that before or at the very beginning of the semester. Here's a quick list of "the right stuff" that you will likely need:

- *Access to a computer and a working knowledge of how to use one.* Most colleges provide computer labs, email accounts, and printers for student use, but their hours may be limited, they may be crowded at busy times during the semester, and you may have to pay for the pages that you print. Having the necessary computer skills as well as regular access to a computer will be integral to your success, and if you need some help honing those skills, your college may offer computer classes.

- *Textbooks and course materials.* Usually, an exact list of course materials is included in your syllabus; if not, the bookstore may have this information. If you find yourself unable to acquire or buy your materials, then you will need to talk to your professor immediately to ask about alternative arrangements. For example, some professors put a copy of the textbook "on reserve" in the library, which means that students can borrow the book for limited periods of time.

- *Writing materials.* This includes notebooks (one for each class), computer printer paper, pens, highlighters, and #2 pencils.

- *Scientific calculator.* Depending on the type of math, engineering, or science classes, you will probably need a scientific calculator. Check with your professor first for any requirements or recommendations before purchasing one.

- *A good, sturdy backpack.* Since you will not have a locker or place to store your things between classes, you will have to find a bag that holds up to the task of carrying all your books and notebooks.

- *A portable storage device.* Thumb drives, also known as flash drives and pin drives, are increasingly popular because they hold a large amount of files and because they are easy to carry, allowing you to access your computer files at any computer. Use a permanent marker or tape to put your name on the drive, and save a Word file on the drive labeled "If found, please contact," and include your contact information. College computer labs have hundreds of these thumb drives that were misplaced by students in just one semester.

Classroom Preparation, Attendance, and Behavior

In addition to your supplies, knowing and meeting your professor's expectations in the classroom will make a great foundation for success. One essential expectation that professors have is preparation—yours. You should prepare *before* you get to class by reading the assigned pages or completing the homework. Professors who assign reading or homework expect students to be prepared—they may even administer quizzes to ensure that students have prepared—and to ask questions about anything they did not understand. Professors assume that if you don't ask questions or participate in a discussion, you understand the assignment. They may also hold you accountable for the assigned reading on exams even though it was not discussed in class.

Another expectation is that out-of-class assignments must be typed; in fact, unless otherwise stated, assume that all outside assignments should be typed, because they are easier to read and they look more professional. If you don't know how to create written documents on a computer, now is the time to learn; relying on others to create these documents will put you at a disadvantage. You may not be able to control when the person can complete the work, which can make you miss important due dates.

Professors also expect that college students are able to access technology regularly and use it competently. What this means is that your professors will assume and expect that you have consistent access to a computer and the Internet. They will also believe that you have an email account and can send emails—even messages with attachments—successfully. If these are skills and equipment that you do not have, you will need to find out where you can access a computer on campus or off campus and make sure that you have the ability to use it properly.

Finally, instructors expect you to use their office hours—the time when they are formally available to meet with students—to meet with them if you have any questions or need anything. This is a time not only to address any concerns you may have about your progress, but it is also a wonderful time to get to know your professors better. Professors typically post their office hours in their syllabi, on their course websites, and on the doors of their offices.

Regular attendance in your classes is crucial so that you can obtain information and guidance about assignments, tests, and grading. Especially in courses that build on concepts (such as math, foreign languages, and writing), regular attendance is essential to help you overcome problems with challenging assignments and prepare for tests. If you are receiving financial aid through grants or loans, your attendance may be a requirement for you to continue to receive funds in the future.

If you miss a class or intend to miss a class, you should contact your professor in writing. You may need a doctor's excuse if you miss an exam or assignment, and if your absence isn't due to a medical situation, you should be prepared to justify your absence. Most professors, though, may not care why you were absent or may not distinguish between excused or unexcused absences. Instead, they use your attendance as an indication of your effort and contribution to the class. Many professors base a portion of their grades on attendance and/or class participation. Since you can't participate in a class discussion while absent, your attendance will likely have a direct impact on your grade.

Attending class is just part of the effort you will put forth; you will also need to produce quality work. Writing a paper and turning it in is only part of the requirement. You also have to adhere to the standards of the course. If your professor asks for a 10-page paper that argues a contemporary topic and uses five sources, you must follow those guidelines. In some instances, you may receive no credit for completing an assignment if you have not followed the requirements.

The more time you work to complete an assignment *usually* translates to better quality, but this is not always the case. For example, someone who types 30 words a minute will need less time to produce the same typographical error–free assignments as someone who "hunts and pecks" at the keyboard. The quality of your work is what you will be graded on, not the number of hours you spend doing it.

No doubt you already juggle numerous responsibilities, and going to class and studying are just more tasks that you must complete each week. Handling your responsibilities skillfully will take a positive attitude, self-respect, and maturity. If you recall Laura from this chapter's opening dialogue, Laura knows the importance of being responsible for her son and her. She has had many years of relying on herself and a few family members to meet her responsibilities. Obviously, as a student, she has the responsibility to take notes, study for tests, and attend classes regularly. But she also has the responsibility to ask questions when she doesn't understand to resolve any conflict that may occur.

With responsibility also comes maturity, which is the foundation for many of the other components of college culture. Without a mature attitude and outlook, the other parts are unattainable. There are, however, less obvious actions that can help you present yourself as a dedicated, mature student. The first one is paying attention during lectures, presentations, talks by guest speakers, and videos. Although this sounds obvious, it is sometimes forgotten after the first few weeks of the semester. Work on looking at the front of the room and avoiding distractions. A common barrier to paying attention, besides staring out the window, is doing homework in class. Instructors frown on students who use class time to study for other classes or complete assignments that were due at the beginning of class. Just remember that the instructor sees that you are not paying attention and will make note of it.

Small but equally important actions that convey maturity and readiness to meet college expectations include staying for the duration of the class, limiting off-topic conversations with classmates, refraining from eating or participating in distracting activities, and getting ready to exit class only after the instructor has dismissed everyone. One small activity that causes big problems in class is the use of cell phones, headsets, and other electronic communication devices. In some classes, such as a chemistry lab, the distraction can be dangerous. Some colleges have strict policies forbidding the use of cell phones in class. There may be exceptions, however. For example, if you work in a field that requires your immediate attention in the event of an emergency or if you have a gravely ill family member, ask if you may leave these electronic devices turned on. If your college does not have a policy, turn off your cell phone in class anyway. Students who answer social calls in class appear immature and unconcerned about their education.

Constructive Criticism

Another important way to demonstrate maturity in college is to understand and appreciate constructive criticism from your professors. Your professors will provide feedback on your assignments, exams, projects, and presentations, both in writing and verbally, and sometimes the feedback will be challenging. Because professors are busy, because they work with a lot of students each semester, and because they have high expectations for student work, they may deliver feedback in a way that can be tough to hear. For example, your professor might return your term paper covered in red ink with numerous comments and corrections throughout the document. If you get this kind of feedback, don't take it personally, and don't jump to the conclusion that your work was poor. Getting a lot of feedback and response from your professor is actually a really positive opportunity. Your professor's intention is to help you learn and improve your performance. Read the professor's feedback carefully, identify the lessons you can learn from the feedback to improve the quality of future assignments, and, if the feedback triggers an emotional response, give yourself a day or two before you respond to it. Even better, share the professor's feedback with a trusted classmate or friend and invite that person's advice about how you can best learn from the feedback and the experience. Some of you may have experienced athletic coaches or high school teachers who were tough on their students in a well-intentioned manner that brought out the best in student performance. Professors who provide challenging feedback are similarly effective at facilitating high performance among students, especially for students who are open to constructive criticism and who view it as an opportunity to learn and grow.

Controversial Content

For the most part, college will be a straightforward experience—you will learn the expectations, and when you meet them, you will be successful. There are, though, other aspects of college culture that may be uncomfortable or even shocking to you. All colleges value diversity, both in the student body population and in the backgrounds of its faculty. Most definitely, you will find diversity in ideas and theories among the subjects that are offered that may challenge your beliefs and values. Still other subjects may contain material that you find disrespectful, offensive, distasteful, or disturbing. Besides the reading and discussing of controversial issues, your college may produce student and faculty work that contains language, images, or situations that you find offensive.

What should you do if you encounter college "culture shock"? First, remember that the purpose of college is to provide you with a wider worldview and understanding of diversity—even if that diversity involves different ideas and theories. Second, remember that you have the right to an opinion and a feeling about what you encounter in college. There is no reason you should hide your feelings or attitudes about what you are learning and encountering. With this said, the third point to remember is that with your right to an opinion, you also have an obligation as a college student to examine your previously held beliefs and evaluate how they are being challenged in your courses or as you participate in college activities. You also have the obligation to appreciate that there is more than one way to view an "offensive" idea or image. Exhibit 1.2 provides a list of possible subjects that could be controversial to you or other students.

You will learn about diversity and relationships in depth in another chapter, but it is worth mentioning here that dealing with diversity, conflict, and controversy takes a certain level of maturity. Effectively meeting any challenge to your belief system or values will demand that you act

FOTOLIA

Getting familiar with library services and other services on campus and online will be essential to your transitioning smoothly.

EXHIBIT 1.2 A Sample of Possible Controversial Subjects

The existence of God, higher being	The theory of extraterrestrial life
Conservatism and liberalism	Evolution
Nudity in art, photography	The beginning of life
Sexuality, including homosexuality and adultery	Scientific investigation and experimentation (stem cells, cloning)
The creation of the universe	Socioeconomic theory

with integrity and openness. Because the purpose of getting an education is to stretch your mind and expand your ideas, you will need maturity to help you put all that new information into perspective.

60-second PAUSE

Besides your grades, what are some practical ways you can monitor yourself to gauge how well you are meeting the high expectations of college?

THE COLLEGE EXPERIENCE HAS A RHYTHM

Now you know what to expect and what is expected of you in college, but understanding a few other customary practices will help you go from being a "tourist" to a "native." One of the characteristics of a college environment that you'll start to notice over time is that there's a rhythm, or recurring pattern, that drives the pace and intensity of the college experience. In the same way that a 24-hour period in your life tends to have variations in what you're doing and how intense your schedule is, the college experience has predictable variations that you can expect and anticipate.

Schedules

First, it is helpful to note that colleges organize their annual calendar around semesters, terms, or quarters, which can be as short as four weeks during the summer, or as long as 16 weeks. Many colleges have at least four semesters: fall, spring, first summer term, and second summer term, with the summer terms being shorter than the fall and spring terms. Other colleges organize the academic calendar around 10- or 11-week quarters. If you are unsure how many weeks the semester is, count the number of weeks from the first day of class until the last day of finals. You can also find the information in the college catalog or in the course outline of your syllabus.

No matter how many weeks in the term, classes are scheduled at different days during the week. This arrangement may differ significantly from your high school schedule. In college, you may take classes once a week, as is the case in evening or night classes, or you may take them on Mondays, Wednesdays, and Fridays, or just Tuesdays and Thursdays. Usually, colleges do not offer classes on Friday nights, so if you take classes in the evening, you will take them either once a week or twice a week, Mondays through Thursdays.

Exceptions to this schedule occur during shortened terms, such as summer semesters or intersession terms, in which you may go every day during the week. Also, you may have a lab or special class that meets only once a week, but is tied to another class such as biology or chemistry. The best advice for new students is to read the schedule of classes carefully before registering, and as always, ask an advisor, counselor, professor, or fellow student if you have trouble reading your schedule.

Colleges award credit hours (remember this term from earlier in the chapter?) based on how many hours a week you are in class during a regular semester (summer or intersession terms will double or quadruple the number of hours a week as compared to a regular semester). Thus, a 3-credit-hour class will require that you spend about three hours in class per week—some classes may last only 50 minutes, three times a week. Exceptions do exist: Labs are often worth 1 credit hour, but they may meet for more than one hour, one day a week.

Exhibit 1.3 shows a typical schedule of a full-time student. Notice the "TR" under the "Days" column: "T" stands for Tuesday and "R" stands for Thursday. Thus, the biology class meets both Tuesday and Thursday, while the lab meets on Thursday only. Labs and other special classes may meet for more than one hour a week, but they are usually worth only 1 credit hour. Although the classes in this schedule meet two-and-a-half hours each week, they are given 3 credit hours. Three hours is often an approximation of the time spent in class.

If the schedule in Exhibit 1.3 reflects a 16-week semester, this student will spend over 40 hours in class for the semester. During summer or intersession terms, you will

EXHIBIT 1.3   Sixteen-Week Class Schedule

FALL 2012 (16-WEEK) SCHEDULE				
COURSE ID	**COURSE NAME**	**DAYS**	**TIME**	**CREDIT HOURS**
Engl 030	Composition Fundamentals	M W F	8:00–8:50 A.M.	3.0
Biol 110	Biology	T R	8:00–9:15 A.M.	3.0
Biol 112	Biology Lab	R	9:25–11:25 A.M.	1.0
Math 034	Intermediate Algebra	M W F	10:00–10:50 A.M.	3.0
Coll 101	Freshman Seminar	T R	12:15–1:30 P.M.	3.0
TOTAL HOURS				**13.0**

EXHIBIT **1.4** Four-Week Class Schedule

SUMMER 2012 (4-WEEK) CLASS SCHEDULE				
COURSE ID	**COURSE NAME**	**DAYS**	**TIME**	**CREDIT HOURS**
MATH 101	College Algebra	M T W R F	8:00–10:00 A.M.	3.0
Engl 101	Composition I	M T W R F	10:10–12:10 P.M.	3.0
TOTAL HOURS				**6.0**

spend about the same number of hours in class, but you will attend class more often and for longer periods of time.

Because Exhibit 1.4 is a schedule for a four-week term, the classes meet for more than three hours a week. In this case, students meet for 10 hours a week for four weeks, which will equal 40 hours or the equivalent of the total number of hours a 3-credit-hour class will meet during a 16-week term.

As you build your schedule each semester, here are a few tips to consider:

- Identify the courses you need to make progress toward a degree. Meet with your advisor well in advance of when you need to formally enroll in the next semester, and make sure you know what GE courses you should take next, and what required and elective courses you should be taking for your major. Don't build your schedule around classes that are interesting or fit the time of day when you want to attend class—focus on the courses you need to move closer to graduation.

- Have a contingency plan, or alternative courses in mind. Depending on the balance between student demand and the supply of courses at your college, you may encounter situations in which the classes you want to take are either not being offered next term (not every class listed in the college catalog is offered every term) or are already full by the time you register for classes. For that reason, identify courses that could be appropriate second options for you. For example, some GE requirements provide several options. Your top choice might be a popular culture class that you know you would really enjoy, but it's a good idea to identify another suitable GE course that you could take if that class is full or not scheduled.

- Don't make your schedule a popularity contest. If you rely on fellow classmates to tell you when you should take class and which professor you should choose, you'll find yourself competing against everyone else for the same classes. This doesn't always work in your favor. Sometimes an "unpopular" 7 A.M. class may be your best option because it fits your schedule well, and you may discover that you think most clearly in the morning. You might also discover that a professor is "unpopular" simply because he or she challenges students to work hard, and you actually learn a lot in the course. Select courses for the right reasons, not the popular reasons.

- Build in time for individual study and to meet with study groups. As you build your schedule, insert blocks of time when you can go to the library or other study space to review lecture notes, read the textbook, and complete homework and assignments. Also, set time aside for study group meetings and team projects.

There are other factors you'll want to consider when you build your schedule—such as your part- or full-time job, eating, exercising, sleeping, and social activities—so take time to build a complete schedule before you have to officially enroll in the next term. The schedule you build will determine the rhythm of each term, and you want that rhythm to fit you well.

Grades

What is a discussion about college expectations without mentioning grades? Grades are an important part of your education, but they aren't the only measure of your learning and success. Grades are important because they reflect your level of achievement on an assignment or in a course, they are often used for obtaining and maintaining scholarships and financial aid, and they are a relevant piece of news to family, friends, and employers who may be supporting you financially and emotionally. Many people view grades as a reflection of a level of success. For instance, most of the people you ask would view a student who has straight A's as someone who is smart and successful. Earning good grades can motivate you to do your best and give you more confidence as you earn them.

Although good grades feel great when you earn them, grades are not always an indication of your success or lack of success in mastering a subject. Banner and Cannon assert that grades have limitations: "Grades are evaluations of your work, not of your character or intelligence. You may be a wonderful person but a failure as a biologist. You may find it impossible to do satisfactory work in history but may excel in all other subjects" (Banner & Cannon, 1999, p. 160). They are a necessary part of evaluation, much as you are evaluated on your job. However, as Banner and Cannon point out, grades do not show the whole picture of who you are. Grades, then, are only part of the story of your education. Grades are important because they are a way to describe the work you have done in a class. However, grades alone are not the magic carpet to success in college; they are only part of the story of your achievements. Your goal should be to strike a balance between caring about your grades and caring about improving your skills and increasing your knowledge.

As stated earlier, college professors grade a student on his or her ability to meet the standards of the course or of a particular assignment. Effort is definitely a necessary part of earning good grades—and you will earn the respect of your professor and fellow students by demonstrating an intense effort to master the concepts of a class—but it is

BUZZ

Q My roommate told me about a website that provides student comments about professors. He uses it to pick which professors to take. Should I?

A Students' ratings and comments about professors may provide some useful information about a professor, but don't rely on this information alone. Here are some tips for getting accurate information about your professors:

- Take time to review the professor's syllabus, professional qualifications, and experience.

- Ask upperclassmen who have been very successful in college. They will often point you to professors who are challenging and difficult, even though it means you won't get an automatic A.

- Talk to the professors directly to get a sense of who they are and how they teach.

EXHIBIT **1.5** Grading Criteria for an A Paper

An excellent introduction with engaging hooks, setup, plan for essay, and/or main idea

An original, significant thesis that offers insightful interpretation or thought

An inventive and logical organizational plan

Smooth and varied transitional expressions, phrases, and sentences that provide unity and coherence

Strong conclusion that ends the essay effectively

Expressive, clear style with sophisticated sentence structure and word choice

No more than three major grammatical errors

only one part of achieving success in a course. College professors expect that you also meet the standards, sometimes called grading criteria, of the course. Exhibit 1.5 shows a potential set of criteria for a college-level paper. In this case, these criteria must be met to receive a grade of A on the paper.

Knowing how your college assesses student performance is a start to improving your overall outlook on grading. The following is a typical grading scale in college:

100–90 A   89–80 B   79–70 C   69–60 D   59–0 F

Some colleges may use a + or − next to a letter grade, such as A− or C+. Colleges that allow for +'s and −'s will usually alter the grading scale to designate the different grades. Here is an example of a grading scale that includes +'s and −'s:

100–94 A   93–90 A−   89–87 B+   86–84 B   83–80 B−

Each semester, the registrar, the person who keeps your academic records at your college, will calculate your grade point average, or GPA, and post it to your transcript, or your list of classes and grades. Because the calculation of your GPA requires a little mathematical skill, it is important to know how your registrar figures it. Hours are the number of hours you are in class each week. As discussed, classes are usually 3 credit hours. Science or specialized classes that have labs usually carry 4 credit hours. Depending on the course and the program, credit hours can be as many as 6 or as few as 1. To know how many hours a course carries, check the description in the college catalog, because some classes meet for more hours a week than they are worth in terms of credit.

Letter grades carry point values called quality points. Exhibit 1.6 shows how many quality points each letter grade is worth.

Courses that are designated as developmental or remedial usually do not figure into your grade point average, so they do not carry any quality points. If you audit a course or receive AP or CLEP credit for a course, you will not receive quality points either. In other words, while you receive credit on your transcript for taking the course or taking an equivalent of the course, the course will not factor into your grade point average. Before you figure your GPA, you will need to figure your grade points for each class (see Exhibit 1.6). You arrive at your grade points by multiplying the quality points for the grade you received by the number of hours the class is worth. For instance, if you took a 4-credit-hour class and you made a B, then you will multiply 4 (hours) by 3 (quality points for a B).

Evan is taking 15 hours (five 3-credit-hour courses) this semester; if he receives an A, a B, and three C's, then his grade would be calculated as shown in Exhibit 1.7.

1.6 **Grades and Quality Points**

Letter Grade	Quality Points
A	4
B	3
C	2
D	1
F	0

EXHIBIT **1.7** **GPA Calculation Table**

Hours	Grade (Quality Points)	Grade Points (Hours × Quality Points)
3	A (4)	3 × 4 = 12
3	B (3)	3 × 3 = 9
3	C (2)	3 × 2 = 6
3	C (2)	3 × 2 = 6
3	C (2)	3 × 2 = 6
15 Hours		39 Grade Points

Finally, divide the total grade points by the total hours (39/15). Evan's GPA would be 2.6.

Building your schedule every term and tracking your grades will establish a regular rhythm for your college experience. Other activities may be part of this rhythm as well, such as club or Greek life responsibilities, intramural sports, academic competitions, career fairs and workshops, and on-campus events such as concerts and sporting events. Over time, you'll adapt to the ebbs and flows of these activities and the intensity of your work to meet all of the expectations and responsibilities that you face. As you learn to anticipate these variations in intensity and pace, you'll be able to prepare for them and succeed.

60-second PAUSE

Reflect on your own schedule and how you'd like to arrange it each semester to best suit your own personal circumstances and preferences. Besides classes, what other activities will fill your schedule?

INTEGRITY *Matters*

Your college transcript, which includes your grade point average, can reveal more than just the grades you earned in your courses. For example, some colleges make notations on students' transcripts if they have failed a class because of plagiarism or cheating. These marks can be evidence that a student did not follow academic integrity policies. In some cases, these marks can be deleted from transcripts if the student successfully completes an academic integrity workshop.

YOUR TURN

In approximately 250 words, discuss the specifics of your college's academic integrity policy. Describe how your college records failing grades that are due to academic integrity violations. Also include in your discussion whether there are any programs at your college to help students understand and follow the academic integrity policy.

YOUR COLLEGE IS A COMMUNITY OF RESOURCES

Now that you have a better understanding of college culture and what is expected of you, it is time to examine how your college looks. Getting to know the layout of the campus and the people who work there is important to understanding the culture and getting the help you need to support your success. For example, knowing where to go when you need to use a computer will make your ability to complete an assignment a little easier. Finding your professor's office may save you time and stress when you need to talk to him or her about an upcoming test. The more you are on campus, the easier it will be for you to find the people and places that will help you no matter what you need, but it will help if you take some time to study your campus so you know where to look.

Explore Your Campus

Find a map of your campus and study it for a few minutes. How many buildings does it have? How much parking space? How much "green" space, or landscaping? Are there any unique features to your campus that make it an inviting and exciting place? Familiarizing yourself with your campus is probably the first activity you did when you enrolled in classes. If you have not taken a tour or simply walked around the campus, do so within the first few weeks of the semester. Locate the library, the student center, student parking, the bookstore, the business office, and the registrar's office—just to name a few important destinations.

The more you know about your campus's layout, the easier it will be to find what you are looking for when you need it most. Using your map of the campus or your memory and Exhibit 1.8, check off the types of buildings or departments within buildings that you know are present at your college.

If your college has more than one campus, familiarize yourself with the layout of other college property. You may have to travel to a satellite campus to take a test or to pick up materials for a class. If you have the time and the other campus is not too far away, ask for a tour. At the very least, familiarize yourself with any of the items you marked "not sure" in Exhibit 1.8.

EXHIBIT 1.8 Campus Layout Checklist

Building or Area	At My College	Not Sure
Student center or union		
Library		
Bookstore		
Administration building		
Theater or auditorium		
Snack bars, food courts, and other dining facilities		
Athletic training facilities (indoor or outdoor)		
Science labs		
Computer labs		
Individual colleges and departments (such as business, psychology, engineering, and graphic communication)		
Student parking		
Benches and tables for meeting outside		
Quiet study space inside		
Disability Resource Center		
Health Center		
Cashier's Office		
Housing Office		
Registrar's Office		

Locate Information about Campus Resources

Knowing where to go to find services and people is only part of learning about your college. Another important aspect is finding and using the information that the college produces for students. College publications are a great place to find information about courses, programs, scholarships, activities, and policy changes. It is important that you regularly read these publications in order to stay up-to-date with what is going on.

College Catalog

The college catalog is an essential document during your academic career. All the information that you need to apply for financial aid, to choose courses, and to graduate is contained in the catalog. You will also find out what you are required to do to complete a degree. The academic calendar is usually placed at the beginning of the catalog. There you will find the dates for registering, dropping courses, and taking final exams.

It is important to read and keep your college catalog, because if the college changes any requirements of your degree program, you will be able to follow the guidelines

Students who have "the right stuff"—such as access to a computer, textbooks, and other materials and equipment that are required for classes—are much more likely to be successful.

© PATRICK WHITE/MERRILL

that were published the year you began the program. For instance, if you are working on a psychology degree and you have taken three semesters of courses so far, you will not necessarily have to adhere to new requirements that are made at a later date.

Student Handbook

The student handbook, which provides you with specific information about student conduct, academic standards, and services, is another valuable publication. The handbook usually contains descriptions of career services, the bookstore, computer labs, and financial aid offices. Academic information, including probation and suspension for misconduct and qualifications for making the dean's list, can also be found in the student handbook. Most schools view the student handbook as a legal document that outlines what students can do in certain situations, so be sure to read it closely and keep a copy at home or in your book bag.

College Newspaper

College newspapers differ from the college catalog and student handbook in that students are usually the ones who are responsible for the content. Within a college newspaper, you will find articles about upcoming events; reports on changes on the college campus; editorials on important student issues; profiles of programs; and advertisements for used books, performances by musical groups, and anything else that students want to announce. The college newspaper is also a forum to explore controversial topics and to discuss sensitive issues.

Newspapers always need students to interview, write, edit, and publish. If you are interested in working for the newspaper, contact the editor or visit a journalism or composition professor.

Bulletin Boards

Even with the increased use of the Internet, the bulletin board is still an important way to get a message to students. Found all over campus, bulletin boards usually advertise used books, needs for roommates and part-time jobs, and upcoming campus events. Bulletin boards within academic buildings often announce study abroad opportunities, summer workshops, special events, and other types of notable activities.

It's in the Syllabus

Anything that professors hand out in class is a communication tool. The syllabus is one of the most important documents that you will receive in class, so be sure to read it carefully. In the syllabus, you will usually find the following information:

- instructor's name; office location, phone number, and hours open to students; and email address
- prerequisites for the course
- course description from the catalog
- textbook information

- course objectives, or what you will accomplish by the time you finish the class
- course content, or what topics will be covered throughout the semester
- assignments and due dates
- grading criteria
- attendance and late-work policies
- academic integrity statement (which also appears in the student handbook)
- disability accommodations policy
- general policies for classroom conduct

The syllabus is considered a contract between the student and the instructor. This means that not only will the syllabus contain what is expected of you during class, but it will also contain what you can expect from the professor. Both of you—the student and the professor—will be bound by what is stated in the document. Reading the syllabus closely and following it regularly will keep you on top of the policies, expectations, and assignments.

Other essential information that is handed out in class includes directions for assignments, photocopied readings, study questions, and notes. Regard anything that is given to you by the instructor as important, even if you are told "This won't be on the test."

You should also consider the grades and written comments you receive as communication from your instructors. Be sure to read any comments or suggestions that are written on papers and exams, ask questions if you don't understand them or they are illegible, and save all feedback until the semester is over.

BUZZ

Q I feel lost on my college campus. It seems as though everyone knows what is going on—from how to pick classes to when and where parties are—but I don't know anything.

A It is normal to feel a little bit like an outsider when you first step on campus. Here are some tips to get "in the know" about the activities and events on your campus.

- Read the bulletin boards. They usually contain information about local bands, parties, and student functions.

- Pick up a student newspaper or college newsletter. You will get an idea of future events as well as current happenings.

- Talk with staff in the student center about how to get involved on campus

- Check the college's website for additional current information.

Online Resources

The college's website is where you can find the most current information about classes, academic programs, and contact information for professors. It is easier to update information on a website because it doesn't involve printing and distribution, so it is more likely to provide the most accurate information. College websites usually list phone numbers and email addresses of professors and deans, which makes contacting them easier.

In addition to general information about degrees and departments, your college's website may give you access to professors' syllabi and assignments. This provides a good opportunity to investigate what courses you want to take based on the course objectives and activities and information about the professor.

Most professors establish a course website, either as a standalone site, or within a learning management system such as Blackboard or Moodle. Once you're enrolled in a course, you will gain special access to the course website, and you need to visit this site often. Professors use course websites to post announcements; distribute the syllabus, assignments, and reading materials; facilitate discussion boards; track grades; collect electronic versions of projects and assignments; and even administer online quizzes and tests.

Campus Organizations

Campus organizations and student groups are another part of college life you will want to learn more about. Depending on how large your college is and how involved the students are, you may find a variety of student organizations and clubs in which to participate. Even if your time is limited, consider getting involved in some way, because these activities can enhance your college experience, and employers value extracurricular leadership experience when they recruit potential employees. Campus organizations include, but are not limited to, student clubs, student government, student leadership programs, and clubs focused on certain interests (e.g., gay, lesbian, bisexual, and transgendered issues; political action; community service; academic honors and distinctions; religious or spiritual development; and career exploration). Getting involved will help your transition to the college and provide immediate connections with students, faculty, and staff. You can learn about these opportunities on the college website, through on-campus club fairs and information sessions, and by asking upperclassmen about their own experiences.

College is an exciting place with a wide variety of activities and experiences that can enrich your life and help you succeed. Because there are many options for how you can get involved, you'll need to gather information about them and carefully choose the best opportunities in which you'll invest time and effort. It's a common mistake among students to get excited about all these opportunities and then overcommit. This leads to avoidable disappointment and failure. As you begin your college career, carefully select only one or two extracurricular activities until you can gain experience with your academic responsibilities and determine what capacity you have for commitments outside the classroom.

How well do you know your campus already? What are some steps you could take this week to become more familiar with the resources and opportunities mentioned in this section?

from COLLEGE
to UNIVERSITY

The Changes in Culture and College Services

If you are moving from your community college to a larger, more diverse university, you may experience a slight culture shock despite the semesters you already have under your belt. In addition to a bigger campus with more buildings to find and more students to meet, you may find that a university seems more impersonal. Transfer students also note that expectations are higher—and their grades are lower—especially as they move into their majors and begin working toward a career.

All in all, the culture shock you experience when transferring to a four-year university will depend on how much bigger and how much more different the school is from your community college. Just remember that whatever differences you notice, there are people at the four-year school who can help you deal with the adjustment. Seek out counselors, advisors, faculty, and students to help make your transition smoother.

from COLLEGE
to CAREER

How the Culture Will Change Again

When starting your first job out of college, you will experience a period of getting used to the way the office or business works. You will encounter new terms, new methods of doing things, and new people. In addition, you will experience working in groups or teams to accomplish tasks, and you will be expected to communicate orally and in writing. There will be less supervision and more expectation that you will do the work you say you will do.

Paying attention to how others act on the job can alleviate any anxiety that you may feel. Just as you made friends and found mentors in college, you should look for others who can offer guidance and help as you learn the ropes of a new career. Also, think about how you adjusted to college, and use the same strategies to make your new working environment seem less foreign and more comfortable.

UNDERSTAND & REMEMBER

Review Questions

1. What differences exist between high school and college or a full-time job and college?

2. Name and explain five characteristics that professors will expect from you as a college student.

3. For what purposes do colleges assign grades? What benefits are there for receiving a grade for a course?

4. What types of documents and communication can you expect in college? What are their purposes?

Create

Evaluate

Analyze

Apply

Understand

Remember

APPLY & ANALYZE

Critical Thinking

1. As part of learning outside of class, professors expect that you visit a tutor if you need additional practice or help. Nonetheless, students may not always take advantage of the help. What could the college do to encourage more students to get help with their classes?

2. With the prevalence of technology in the classroom (notes and slides available online, videos of lectures, etc.), explain why you think attending class is important or not. Discuss your college's attendance policy and the effect it may—or may not—have on student attendance.

3. What information have you already received that will help you navigate college more smoothly? Organize the different sources of information by type and answer the following questions: What information have you received from email or the Internet? What information have you received from an advisor? Finally, which kinds of information are most useful to you and why?

EVALUATE

Case Scenarios

1. In Jennifer's literature class, she is reading Tim O'Brien's novel, *The Things They Carried*. Although she understands that the book is about the Vietnam War, she doesn't know why she has to read a book that contains so much profanity and graphic images of death. She has made an appointment to speak to her professor about the reading assignment because she wants to get out of reading a book that is so depressing and discomforting. She is prepared to suggest that she read and write a paper on a Shakespeare play instead, one that she did in high school and got an A on.

   Use the following scale to rate the decision that has been made (1 = Poor Decision, 5 = Excellent Decision). Be prepared to explain your answer.

Poor Decision ← ①——②——③——④——⑤ → Excellent Decision

2. Jai-Ling is taking a biology class. One of her assignments is to create a group presentation on an assigned topic. Her group's topic is the theory of evolution, a theory that Jai-Ling finds fascinating although she does not know much other than what she learned in high school. However, when she meets with her group to prepare for the presentation, two group members express deep concern that they are being asked to study something that they don't believe in. They refuse to help with the project even though they know their lack of participation will lower the whole group's grade. Jai-Ling tells her group members that they are being immature and ridiculous because one of the purposes of being in college is to be challenged in one's thinking. She goes straight to the professor to complain and ask for a new group.

Use the following scale to rate the decision that has been made (1 = Poor Decision, 5 = Excellent Decision). Be prepared to explain your answer.

Poor Decision ← ①——②——③——④——⑤ → Excellent Decision

3. Paul has just graduated from high school and enrolled in college, and he is surprised by some of his classes and the expectations. One professor told the class that she didn't care if they attended or not. She would post all the lectures, notes, answers to homework, and study guides online. Another class has 300 students, and Paul feels lost in the sea of fellow classmates. Only his first-year orientation class is small and demands that he attend regularly. A couple of his classmates have approached him about taking turns attending classes and sharing notes. He will attend one week and then the other two will take the following two weeks. He won't have to attend some of his classes for two weeks, which will allow him more time to do other things like work or get involved in student activities. Because two of his professors do not take attendance or would not know if he attended, he decides to agree to the arrangement.

Use the following scale to rate the decision that has been made (1 = Poor Decision, 5 = Excellent Decision). Be prepared to explain your answer.

Poor Decision ← ①——②——③——④——⑤ → Excellent Decision

CREATE

Research It Further

1. Investigate what services or offices your college has to help first-time or first-year students. Using your college's map (or creating your own of your campus), provide written or typed details for each building or area that pertains to these services.

2. What resources does your college's website offer for first-time students? If your college does not offer any or not many, search the Internet for resources for first-time or first-year students. Present your website findings to your class and highlight the most useful information.

3. Interview your classmates about their first-day experiences on campus and in classes. What did they expect college would be like? What surprised or even shocked them? What are they most excited about? What are they worried about? Share your results and responses with your class.

Based on the goals we set at the beginning of this chapter, here's how you can take this learning with you toward college success:

■ Recognize the differences between high school and college that affect your habits and mindset.

■ Familiarize yourself with the various resources on campus now, before you need them.

■ Anticipate the expectations of college and use the resources you have available to meet those expectations.

■ Adjust to the rhythm of college by getting plugged into important events and deadlines during the semester.

REFERENCES AND RECOMMENDED READINGS

Banner, J. M., & Cannon, H. C. (1999). *The elements of learning.* New Haven, CT: Yale University Press.

College Board. (2008). *Succeeding in college: What it means and how to make it happen.* Plano, TX: College Board.

Dabbah. M. (2009). *Latinos in college: Your guide to success.* Scarborough, NY: Consultare.

Newport, C. (2005). *How to win at college: Surprising secrets for success from the country's top students.* New York, NY: Broadway.

Nist-Olejnik, S., & Patrick Holschuh, J. (2007). *College rules!: How to study, survive, and succeed in college.* Berkeley, CA: Ten Speed Press.

Watkins, B. D. (2004). *Everything you ever wanted to know about college: A guide for minority students.* Camillus, NY: Blue Boy.

MyStudentSuccessLab

MyStudentSuccessLab (www.mystudentsuccesslab.com) is an online solution designed to help you 'Start strong, Finish stronger' by building skills for ongoing personal and professional development.

2 Goal Setting, Motivation, and Learning Styles

Juanita calls her mother for the second time in two hours. She just created her schedule, visited with her advisor, and now is looking for where her classes will be. "Call me," she texts to her mother. Juanita's mom calls immediately.

"Do you think I can do this?"

"Juanita," her mother says with softness and fatigue in her voice, "you always overthink these things. I know you like to be prepared, but things will be different, including how you are going to manage getting to classes in different buildings. It's not high school."

The classes seem different from the dual-enrollment classes Juanita took in high school.

"Yeah, but I didn't have to make a life decision in high school. It made me nervous when my advisor asked me to choose a degree plan," she replies.

"You did choose electrical engineering, just like we talked about, right?" her mother asks.

"Well, I wanted to talk to you about that. I saw a flyer about careers in the health field. I could make a really good salary right after I graduate," Juanita says.

"But you don't like working with people who are sick, Juanita. Don't you want to build things instead? You were always building things in the backyard," her mother replies. Because of the classes she has taken in her high school's dual-enrollment program, Juanita could graduate earlier than her classmates who started this fall, but she knows even with those extra credits she earned, it will still take a lot of money to do it.

"I will be proud of you whatever you decide, but make a choice and stick with it," her mother says.

Juanita knows her mother is right. She has a goal of getting a degree, but she is not sure how to make the right decisions today and the day she graduates.

YOUR GOALS FOR THIS CHAPTER

You are now a college student, and your journey will be an exciting one, but you will also find yourself changing, growing, and defining or redefining who you are and who you want to be. This chapter will start you on that part of the journey by helping you

- Discover your story
- Develop a personal strategy for achieving your goals and fulfilling your dreams
- Develop your support system
- Determine your learning style preference

MyStudentSuccessLab (www.mystudentsuccesslab.com) is an online solution designed to help you 'Start strong, Finish stronger' by building skills for ongoing personal and professional development.

The question "Who are you?" sounds easy to answer. You may start by listing a variety of characteristics. For example, you are male, age 25, married, father of a son, an electrician, and a Native American. Or, you are a single female, age 19, part-time sales assistant, full-time student, and mountain climber. But what are you beyond those labels? Where have you been? What are you doing now? Where are you going and where do you want to be? Now the questions get a little more difficult and take more time and thought to answer. The point is that you need to have some idea of who you are, or at least an idea of where you want to be, when you begin college.

Maybe you can say that you don't know who you are yet, but you hope that enrolling in classes and pursuing a degree will help you come to a better understanding of who you are. Don't worry, though, if you cannot immediately articulate the essence of you. This question—"Who are you?"—and the possible answers have been intriguing human beings for thousands of years. The ultimate goal is to know yourself and your environment well enough to reach your goals.

Of course, who you are will change, maybe dramatically, as you take classes, encounter new subjects, and research interesting topics. But taking the time now to think and reflect about yourself will help you map your course throughout your community college experience and beyond—from returning to work, to raising a family, to attending another college, to having a fulfilling career. This chapter assists you in understanding who you are by helping you identify what you know and how you learn. This chapter also aids in your decisions about who and what you want to be while helping you make the transition into college.

Your Background is the First Chapter of Your Story

To discover your story—and to write your future—you will need to consider where you have come from. Your background, which includes your family, your culture, and your

Your Terms for SUCCESS

WHEN YOU SEE . . .	IT MEANS . . .
Background	The experiences that you have had that make up who you are
Learning style preference	The learning style that you prefer or the one in which you learn best
Long-term goal	A goal that will take a month, a semester, a year, or several years to complete
Mission statement	A statement in which you describe how your values and goals will create your life's mission
Motivation	What keeps you moving toward your goal
Multiple Intelligences	Areas of intellectual strength, or "intelligences," for example, bodily/kinesthetic, intrapersonal, and naturalistic
Priority	Something that is important at that moment
Short-term goal	A goal that takes an hour, a day, or a week to complete
Value	What you believe in
VARK	Learning style preferences that include Visual, Aural, Read/Write, and Kinesthetic

experiences, will serve as a foundation for creating a life. Think about what experiences you have had and how they have shaped who you are. Also, consider how your family has influenced you as well—What beliefs have they instilled in you? What is their attitude toward your college aspirations?

Who you are and how you have developed will be part of your value system as well as part of the foundation for setting goals for future achievements. If you have had great support and good educational experiences, the prospect of completing your degree may seem relatively easy and attainable. However, if you have had more challenges as part of your life history, you may need more support and resources to see that you can indeed be successful. No matter what your background, your college experience will give you the chance to write a life story that includes a college degree.

Your Values Drive Your Goals

Part of your life story will include your value system. Values can be inherited from your parents, or they can come from what your culture, religion, or ethnicity regard as important. Values can also be formed from both positive and negative experiences. For example, a value of yours may be honesty, which means that you try to be truthful and straightforward in most situations and that you expect others to be honest with you. If you value hard work, then you strive to do your best in your life. If a friend has treated you with compassion, you may value sensitivity to others. On the other hand, if you have been discriminated against in the past, you may now value open-mindedness in others.

The importance of knowing and understanding your values is that this knowledge can help you set realistic goals. If you value a satisfying career, for instance, you will set goals that support that value. Therefore, you will probably investigate careers and fields that are challenging and interesting. If you value a stable financial future, you will set goals that enable you to earn enough money to provide for your needs and wants. If you value your family, you will make spending time with them a priority. Your values should be a true reflection of who *you* are and what *you* believe.

Think about Juanita's conversation with her mother. Her mother wants Juanita to consider electrical engineering, perhaps because she values financial stability and success or career prestige. What if one reason Juanita hesitates at choosing a major and career path is that she values a career that helps the human condition? What if she also wants to learn more about how we recover from illness? If she decides to adopt her mother's values and ignore her own, what kind of future can you envision for her? Although her mother's intentions may be well meaning, Juanita will have to compromise herself in order to meet her parents' goals for her, and she will probably suffer some regret in the future.

Does this example mean that you should ignore others who have helped you figure out what you want to be? Certainly not. But you should pay attention to what you want when you do get help with your educational and career goals. Be open to others' suggestions, but make sure that your final decisions are consistent with

©FOTOLIA

If you value an education and it is part of your overall goal to graduate with a degree, then studying will be one way to achieve your goal and support your values.

Staying true to your values is part of integrity. If you try to please others or adopt their values when you do not completely agree with them, you will lack integrity.

For example, you may have been raised with the value of staying true to your ethnic or cultural heritage, even at the expense of meeting someone new or experiencing a new culture. Now that you are in college, you may find that you are exposed to a variety of ethnicities and cultures and that you enjoy and appreciate learning more about others.

YOUR TURN

In approximately 250 words, discuss a time in which you took on someone else's values. Discuss your motivations for doing so as well as the outcome. Finally, explain what you learned in the process.

your own values. Those who truly want you to succeed will be proud of you when they know you have achieved your heart's desire, not theirs.

Your Dreams Are Worth Pursuing

As you consider your goals, you will also want to think about your dreams. Dreams are the big ideas and bold achievements that you sometimes imagine and for which you secretly hope. What do you want to do or achieve that you have not written down because you feel it is too far-fetched? There are many stories of people who ignored their dreams and took jobs that provided them with financial security and prestige, only to discover that their lives were not fulfilled because they regretted giving up on their dreams. There are also many exciting stories about people who never forgot their dreams and who eventually achieve them through hard work and determination.

Why don't more people follow their dreams? First, they may not know what their dreams are. Sometimes day-to-day life takes up so much of our time, attention, and energy that we don't take time to reflect on our lives and consider our dreams. Second, these same people may be scared. Pursuing your dreams is a risky proposition, and there's always the chance that circumstances or events could bring disappointment and failure in this pursuit. Third, some people need to make the "safe" choice first before they feel confident that they can pursue their dreams. Personal responsibilities and family obligations may dictate that you need to choose a path that provides a predictable source of income and security for now, with the hope that you will have a chance to pursue your dreams sometime in the future.

Although you may not be able to fulfill your dreams in the immediate future, don't lose sight of them. Your life experiences and personal background, your values, and your dreams all shape who you are and who you can become.

60-second PAUSE

What are some of the most important qualities of your background, values, and dreams that are influencing your decision to pursue a college degree?

YOUR PERSONAL STRATEGY CAN BRING YOUR DREAMS TO LIFE

The fact that you are reading this book is evidence that you are someone who not only has a purpose, but also is willing to take action to fulfill that purpose. These two elements—defining your purpose and taking action—are important components of something we'll call your personal strategy. Your personal strategy is what you can plan and implement to fulfill the dreams that you've imagined and achieve the goals that you have set for your life.

The first step in developing a personal strategy is to define your mission statement. Your personal mission statement describes your purpose in life. We'll cover that first in the next section. Once you've defined your mission statement, you can develop specific goals that, if they are achieved, would bring your mission statement to life. Goals set a standard for you to know how well you're staying on track to live out your mission statement. With a mission statement and goals in place, your next step is to develop a strategy—a course of decisions and actions that you can implement to achieve your goals and fulfill your mission statement. Your strategy starts with some big-picture action items and decisions and narrows to more tactical elements, such as day-to-day activities and short-term decisions. These building blocks—mission statement, goals, and strategy—will help you live a purposeful life that you can examine each hour, day, month, and year and say to yourself, "I'm on my way to living my dreams."

Along the way, you will encounter obstacles, some of which may threaten to knock you off course. Flexibility and determination are the keys to achieving your goals despite setbacks. Your ability to adapt to and endure setbacks and adversity will shape your character and help you become a strong, resilient, confident person who is capable of tremendous success and accomplishment in life.

Your Mission Statement Defines Your Purpose

Mission statements are statements of purpose. Most companies develop a mission statement for themselves because it defines their purpose and answers the crucial questions—Why do I exist? and What is my purpose? Your personal mission statement, therefore, should explain your purpose in life from a very broad perspective. Your personal values are the foundation of your mission statement. Once you've identified your values and what is most important to you, your next step is to describe your mission statement to establish your purpose.

As you meet your goals and learn new things, your mission will likely change and your mission statement will need to be revised. The following is an example of a mission statement that you can use as a model for writing your own.

Sample Personal Mission Statement

My mission is to have a fulfilling personal and professional life that allows me to meet new people, take on new challenges, and have flexibility in my schedule. As a mother and wife, I want to have a close relationship with my family, acting both as a caregiver and as a role model. As a teacher, I will be dedicated to providing students with the best education that will prepare them for a four-year university curriculum as well as for the demands of the world of work.

Your Goals Set the Bar for Achievement

To build upon your mission statement—and to fulfill that mission in the process—you will need to set goals that you can achieve. A goal is something that you work toward—it may be to learn how to cook macaroni and cheese, to quit a bad habit, or to write a novel. Whatever your goals, they should be reasonable and attainable in the time frame that you have assigned. For instance, if you want to lose 10 pounds in one week, you may need to rethink the time in which you would like to achieve your goal. A more reasonable goal would be to lose 10 pounds in four months. Reasonable goals are more likely to be met.

As you begin to think about your goals, consider dividing them into long-term goals and short-term goals. Certainly, one of your long-term goals is to earn a degree. This goal may take one year or more, depending on how many degree requirements you need to complete or how many other responsibilities you may have.

When you make a list of your goals, follow the SMAC acronym. Your goals should be specific, measurable, achievable, and challenging:

- Specific: Write goals that are specific to a particular outcome. For example, "losing weight" is a specific goal about your health, which is more specific than a goal such as "become a healthier person."

- Measurable: Write goals that you can measure so that you can know whether you've achieved them. "Lose 10 pounds by next June," for example, is measurable both in terms of how much weight you want to lose and the timeline when you want to achieve the weight loss. If you only set a generic goal to "lose weight," on the other hand, you won't have a clear timetable or measure to use to determine whether or when you've achieved the goal.

- Achievable: Set goals that you can realistically achieve, given the amount of time you're giving yourself and the scope of the accomplishment that you're committing to. If you set goals that are too difficult to achieve, you can get discouraged and lose your motivation to pursue the goal. If it's a goal that you have a reasonable chance of achieving, however, you'll be able to press on, even when you face obstacles or setbacks.

- Challenging: While your goals should be achievable, they should also challenge and stretch you. "Wake up every morning before noon" may be an achievable goal, but unless you're working the night shift, sleeping until noon isn't going to challenge you to do your best. Goals are about self-improvement, and that means setting goals that take you beyond your present achievements and capacity.

Because it is difficult to plan 10 years into the future, make a list of goals that are tied to the near future. For instance, if you want to own your own business in the next 10 years, think about structuring your short-term and long-term goals this way:

Ten-Year Goals
- Establish a successful landscape design firm with at least $100,000 in annual income.
- Help others by providing landscaping services for low-income properties.

Five-Year Goals
- Obtain full-time employment with a landscape design firm.
- Engage in at least 10 hours of community service-related landscape activities every week.

Three-Year Goals
- Complete my bachelor's degree in landscape design and management.
- Perform an average of two hours of community service work each week.

One-Year Goals

- Complete two semesters of landscape design classes.
- Continue working at the garden center.
- Plant and maintain my own flower and vegetable garden.

Here are a few other tips for writing effective goals:

- Write your goals. No matter what you want to achieve, be sure that you write down all your goals and review them every few months to assess your progress. Henriette Anne Klauser has made a career of helping people write down their dreams and goals so that they can finally realize them. "Writing down your dreams and aspirations is like hanging up a sign that says 'Open for Business.' . . . Putting it on paper alerts the part in your brain known as the reticular activating system to join you in the play" (Klauser, 2001, p. 33). In other words, the process of writing down your goals tells your brain to start paying attention to your ambitions and makes you aware of opportunities to achieve them.

- Break larger goals into smaller goals that will lead to fulfillment. You'll see from the earlier example how we broke the larger 10-year goal of running a successful landscape design firm into smaller goals with shorter time periods that contributed to the larger goal.

- Regularly review your goals and make changes as necessary. Circumstances will occur beyond your control that will require you to adjust your plans. Or, you may set goals now that change over time as you discover new things about yourself or learn about new career and personal opportunities.

- Reach out to others who care about you to help you achieve your goals. Once you have written down your goals, communicate them to your coworkers, family, and friends. Enlist them to help you meet your goals, especially if you need to schedule time to study and complete assignments. For example, tell them that you must have the evenings free of distractions, or make arrangements with them to have a weekend or weekday to yourself to study. Don't assume that because they *know* you are in school, they will also *know* you need extra time and personal space to get your work finished. Managing your time will be much easier if your priorities and goals are concrete, realistic, and communicated to those around you.

- Identify habits or challenges that could interfere with your goals. As you work toward your goals, make an effort to eliminate anything that keeps you from focusing on your goals. If you think you don't have time to accomplish two short-term goals during the week, examine where you have been spending your time and eliminate the activities that do not contribute to your goals. If you watch seven hours of television a week, and you aren't achieving the sought-after short-term goal of becoming more informed or of relaxing, then spend that time doing something that does contribute to your goal. In addition to meaningless activities, anything that distracts you and is unnecessary in your life should be eliminated, including a habit that is destructive or dangerous, such as taking drugs. In fact, making a goal of staying healthy (e.g., eating right, exercising, de-stressing your life) is not only a good goal to have, but achieving the goal will help you achieve your other goals. If you are unsure whether your activities contribute to your goals, take a few minutes to list what you have done this week and determine how each activity has supported or not supported one of your goals. Exhibit 2.1 gives some examples.

EXHIBIT 2.1 Activities That Contribute to and Distract from Your Goals

Activities That Contribute to Your Goals	Activities That May Distract You from Your Goals
Practicing car maintenance allows you to get to school and work safely.	Socializing excessively depletes the time and energy you have to focus on your goals.
Exercising allows you to remain healthy and reduce stress.	Mindlessly watching TV may not contribute to learning.
Eating well and getting enough sleep keeps you healthy and reduces stress regularly.	Using drugs and alcohol keeps you from focusing on goals and is dangerous.
Reading the newspaper keeps you informed, helps improve reading skills, and contributes to learning	Sleeping and eating irregularly creates stress, which inhibits the ability to reach goals..

Your Strategy Is Your Action Plan

With a mission statement that reflects your values, and long-term and short-term goals that set the bar for your achievement, you can now move into the most exciting part of your personal strategy—strategic implementation. The word *implementation* means to put something into action and to commit to certain decisions. The word *strategic* means that your decisions and actions are consistent with a course of action, which you've defined in terms of your mission statement and goals. If you enjoy board games like Monopoly, for example, your decisions to purchase certain properties will be guided by a particular goal, like owning all the utilities or the most expensive hotels. When you have a clear mission statement and goals that meet the SMAC criteria, you will have clear guidance for your decisions and actions on a day-to-day, week-to-week, semester-to-semester, and year-to-year basis.

If you've written your goals effectively, the action plan that you need to implement to achieve those goals should be relatively clear. For example, if one of your goals is to achieve your bachelor's degree in landscape design in four years, your action plan will consist of taking (and passing) the courses you need to fulfill those degree requirements. If another goal is to lose 10 pounds in the next four months, your action plan will include proper nutrition and exercise, and a plan to set time aside each day to prepare healthy meals and work out. Sometimes it won't be entirely clear where your goals end and your strategies begin, but that distinction isn't as important as defining what you want to accomplish and making decisions and performing activities that move you forward toward those accomplishments. Some people are really good at setting goals, but they struggle with the actual behaviors and decisions that are necessary to reach those goals. Other individuals are really good at taking action and making decisions, but their actions and decisions aren't consistent with a cohesive strategy. The balance between goals and actions will shift over time, but just keep your eyes on both, and you'll find yourself making progress over time.

Perhaps the most important benefit of having a strategy and specific action steps is that you can pursue really big goals—and the dreams they fulfill—by breaking them down into achievable steps. Becoming a highly successful business owner is a wonderful goal and an exciting aspiration. If you're in the first semester of a bachelor's degree, however, that goal may seem so far away. Setting mid-range and shorter-term goals that lead up to your 10-year goal can help, but the most important activity that can build your confidence and hope is to start making decisions and performing activities that move you toward that 10-year goal. Growing your own garden to develop your knowledge and understanding of plants is an example. Volunteering for community service will give you relevant experience and confidence that you'll need someday to become a major contributor to your community's well-being. During each day of your life, you'll encounter decisions and responsibilities that may seem relatively unimportant by themselves, but they add up every day to put you on a path toward achieving major goals in your life and fulfilling your dreams.

Another benefit of having a strategy is that you'll be able to identify the alternatives and activities around you that are *not* good options for your life. Your college experience will be full of many opportunities, and almost all of them have some desirable qualities or apparent benefits. For example, in addition to pursuing a major, some students choose to also earn a minor while they are in college, or even a double-major. Student clubs, Greek organizations (fraternities and sororities), study-abroad programs, weekend road trips, and Spring Break vacations are all examples of activities that may sound appealing and offer great opportunities for new experiences. However, not all of these opportunities are going to help you achieve your goals and fulfill your dreams. In fact, your decision to pursue some of these opportunities might actually distract you or hinder you from achieving the more important goals in your life. If you take time to develop a personal mission statement, establish long-term and short-term goals, and develop an action plan for achieving those goals, you'll find yourself making far better decisions over time and feeling a sense of purpose and accomplishment each day.

USING TECHNOLOGY TO GET AHEAD

Goal setting is much easier when you have techniques or processes for deciding what to achieve and for creating a pathway to success.

RECOMMENDED SITES

- http://www.motivateus.com: Motivate Us is a site that provides numerous quotes and stories that can inspire you when you feel you cannot take another step forward.

- http://www.goal-setting-guide.com/goal-setting -tutorials/smart-goal-setting: Goal Setting Guide reminds us that goals must be SMART.

- http://www.maryannsmialek.com/resources/ articles/roadblocks.html: This site offers another perspective as to why we encounter roadblocks on the way to achieving our goals.

Priorities Determine Your Next Steps

A discussion of values and goals cannot be complete without also talking about priorities. Simply stated, a priority is something that is important at the moment. Today, your top priority could be studying for an exam, but later in the day, it could be taking care of a sick child, which means that studying will have to come second, if at all. Priorities, by their very nature, can change weekly, if not daily or even hourly.

Your actions also reflect your priorities. If you say that your first priority is to pass your classes this semester but you spend all your spare time playing basketball with friends, then your social life, as well as a little exercise, is really your top priority. You must make sure you know what your priorities are and take action to satisfy them. You may also need to express to others what your priorities are so that they can help you stick to them.

© SHUTTERSTOCK

Celebrate when you complete your goals.

Maintain Your Motivation

One of the hardest parts of setting goals is maintaining the momentum to achieve them. There will be times in your academic career when you will feel overwhelmed by the responsibilities you have, and you will feel unsure of your ability to handle them all. When you feel weighed down by all that you have to accomplish for a particular week or day, try to calm down first. If you can, talk with a friend, an instructor, or a counselor and explain your frustration and stress. Sometimes, if an instructor knows you are feeling overwhelmed by expectations in a course, he or she will assist you by helping you find resources that will keep you on track. A friend may also volunteer to help by studying with you.

To stay motivated and to resist the temptation to give up because of the stress, review your short-term and long-term goals. Is there anything that you can change that will make your goals more reasonable or attainable? Have you allowed enough time to achieve them? Revising your goals or your timeline may be necessary to keep yourself on track.

Finally, think positively about yourself and your progress. Many students before you have successfully juggled a job, classes, and a family. That is not to say that they did not doubt themselves along the way or suffer any setbacks. The difference between these students and those who were not successful is that they persevered because they believed in themselves more often than not. Tell yourself that you *can* get through stressful times.

Q I can't seem to get motivated this semester. I was really excited when I started, but I have lost any enthusiasm to work toward my goals to get a degree. What can I do?

A It is hard to sustain high motivation all the time, but there are some things that you can do to get your motivation back:

- Review and revise your goals and your timeline for achieving them. Reading through them again may give you the boost you need.

- Make a list of reasons you should continue to work toward your goals.

- Create a visual of what life will be like when you reach your goals.

Get your calendar out and schedule at least two 2-hour "appointments" with yourself to develop your personal strategy, including a mission statement, goals, and a strategic implementation plan. If you will need some information or materials to help you develop your plan, create a list of those items and make a plan to compile them before that first appointment.

YOUR SUPPORT SYSTEM IS A KEY TO SUCCESS

Even the most dedicated student cannot do it all alone. In fact, behind every successful college graduate is a good support system, usually comprised of family, friends, and community members. It is no secret that succeeding in college will take more than just studying hard—you will need to surround yourself with people who encourage you to do your best. There will be times when you need others for academic, emotional, and even financial support. Recognizing who in your circle of friends, family, and contacts will be the best resources for you is part of the process of creating a support system that will inevitably be part of your college success.

Your Family

Whether you live with your parents, you are a parent, or you are somewhere in between, your family is an important part of who you are and what you will become. Your family has influenced your values and beliefs, and your family members may be a part of the reason you have enrolled in college. For many students, their ability to stay in college and be successful depends on the support of their family. If your family will be an important part of your life as you pursue a degree, then you will need to consider how they will support you and what you need to communicate with them about what to expect when you have to spend more time studying and taking classes than strengthening relationships with them. Questions to ask yourself as you begin your first semester in college include:

- Who in my family will support my decision to attend college?
- What kinds of financial support can I expect?
- What kinds of emotional support can I expect?
- How may my relationships change with my family?
- What can I do to communicate my needs while I am in college?

Answering these questions early and communicating your responses at the beginning of the semester will make it easier for you to keep the lines of communication open in the long run. If you don't feel comfortable talking face-to-face with your loved ones, you could write a letter. At the very least, getting your thoughts down on paper first can help you polish what you want to say before you say it.

Your Friends

Another important part of your support system is your friends. While you may not be able to choose your family members, you will have more choice as to which friends will be positive influences on your college experience. If you have friends who have also attended or are attending college, you will have a great opportunity to connect with each other on this common pursuit. Even if you do not attend the same college, you can develop a support system with them since you will all be having similar experiences. You can share advice and study strategies as well as have a shoulder to lean on when you feel stressed. Knowing that a friend is having a similar experience can often give you the motivation to continue working hard.

©THINKSTOCK

You may find yourself away from family and friends more often than normal as you begin to work toward your degree.

While friends, especially those who are also in college, can provide a solid support system, not all friends, just as not all of your family members, will be a positive influence as you work toward your degree. Those who are not supportive may be very open about their anger, jealousy, or disappointment that you are pursuing a different path than the ones that they have chosen; others will be more subtle. Still other friends may fear that you will not have enough time for them or will find new friends to replace them. In some cases, you may discover that your values no longer match your friends' values, which may signal a time to reduce your contact with them.

For sure, you will be busier than when you were not in college, and keeping in touch will be more difficult for you. Letting these friends know that you may not be able to give them as much time as you did in the past can help you distance yourself from them. Of course, there is always the option of being upfront and honest about their lack of support. Telling these friends that you need positive relationships while you are in college may be the message they need to hear to change their attitudes toward your exciting endeavor. If they still don't get the message, it may be time to eliminate them from daily contact.

Your Roommates

If you've chosen to live with others during your college career, you'll discover that your roommates can be either very helpful or, unfortunately, very destructive influences on your life. Roommates who share the same goals and values as you and who are equally committed to being successful in college as you are can provide a strong support system for you. They can offer encouragement when you're feeling discouraged, or companionship when you're feeling lonely. You can provide the same support to them. It will be important for you to have study habits and a personal strategy of your own, but at times you'll benefit greatly from sharing the college experience with your roommates, with whom you may share meals, social activities, and household chores.

Your Community

There are other places you can look for support as you make your way through college. Your community may offer support to college students. Check out your local community center to see if it offers workshops on time management or study skills; the local library may sponsor book clubs or study groups. Area churches, temples, and synagogues may provide financial support for students in need. Most communities support their residents' goals to go to college and earn a degree, because as more residents have college degrees, the more the community improves. A gesture as simple as a local store offering a discount for college students is a sign that the area businesses recognize and value a student's hard work in college. Local community leaders may be willing to provide internships or mentoring sessions for students who could use extra advice and guidance throughout college. See what your community has to offer, or start your own community support group.

Create a list of people who you would consider to be important members of your support system to help you succeed in college. What are some regular activities or commitments you can put in place to maintain and build this support system throughout your college years?

Take a Learning Style Preference Inventory

Knowing your learning style preferences provides a foundation for understanding yourself in other aspects of your life. Information about what you like and dislike, how you relate to others, and how to work productively will help you achieve your goals. As Gordon Lawrence (1995) states in his book, *People Types and Tiger Stripes*, knowing your learning style helps you make "dramatic improvements in the effectiveness of [your] work" (p. 5). The following section offers Neil Fleming's VARK learning styles inventory, which focuses on four learning style preferences: Visual, Aural, Read/Write, and Kinesthetic. Consider the results of the inventory as information about a part of who you are. Your values, dreams, mission statement, goals, and learning style work together to create a more complete picture of who you are and how to get where you want to go.

Although learning preferences are not necessarily directly linked to college majors or careers, you can easily see that your learning style preference will come into play when you choose your major and your career. Kinesthetic learners, for example, may be drawn to majors or careers that allow them to move about or use their bodies to complete tasks. Landscape design, theater, culinary arts, and nursing are just a few college degree programs that would appeal to kinesthetic learners. Review Exhibit 2.2, which lists possible majors and careers for some of the learning style preferences, but note that it is not considered an exhaustive list. Also, some majors and careers may speak to more than one learning style preference; for example, an advertising executive who writes, edits, and directs commercials may rely on almost all the learning style preferences on a daily basis as she creates commercials and ads for clients. For sure, she will need to work individually, with peers, and with her boss on different aspects of a project, and she may find that she needs to complete tasks at different times of the day, even late at night when filming continues long after the typical workday ends.

There Are Different Types of Intelligence

Harvard psychologist Howard Gardner is well known for his theory of multiple intelligences, which is a term for "what we know, understand, and learn about our world" (Lazear, 1991, p. xiv). Gardner has created eight categories of how we can know and learn.

Verbal/linguistic intelligence is evident in people who can use language with ease. People who demonstrate the verbal/linguistic intelligence enjoy reading and writing and may be journalists, novelists, playwrights, or comedians. Logical/mathematical intelligence is demonstrated by an ease and enjoyment with numbers and logic problems. People who have a strong leaning in the logical/mathematical intelligence like to solve problems, find patterns, discover relationships between objects, and follow steps. Career choices for logical/mathematical people include science, computer technology, math, and engineering.

Visual/spatial is an intelligence that is characterized by anything visual—paintings, photographs, maps, and architecture. People who have a strong visual/spatial sense are usually good at design, architecture, painting and sculpture, and map making. Bodily/kinesthetic is an intelligence that focuses on body movement. Bodily/kinesthetic people enjoy using their bodies to express themselves. Obvious career choices for this intelligence include dancing, sports, and dramatic arts. Musical/rhythmic intelligence encompasses the mind's proficiency with the rhythms of music and hearing tones and beats. People who have strong musical/rhythmic intelligence may use musical instruments or the human voice to express themselves. Career choices for this intelligence include all types of musical performers.

How you relate to others and yourself is part of the interpersonal and intrapersonal intelligences. People with strong interpersonal intelligence relate well with others. They read others' feelings well and act with others in mind. Intrapersonal intelligence is centered around the ability to understand oneself. People who possess intrapersonal intelligence know how and why they do what they do. Naturalistic, the eighth intelligence, refers to people who enjoy and work well in an outdoor environment. Naturalistic people find peace in nature and enjoy having natural elements around them.

Different Theories Provide Unique Insights

There are numerous ways to see yourself and understand your behavior in certain situations, and many education specialists and psychologists have provided theories on how we take in and process information. They have developed different inventories and personality profiles to enhance your understanding of yourself. As you will discover, the learning process is somewhat complex; it involves more than just our preferences in how we create knowledge, because there are many factors that affect our ability to take in and process information.

Theories about the two hemispheres of our brain, known as the left brain and the right brain, have given us insight into how people think, learn, and see the world. People who have strong left-brain tendencies are more likely to be logical, to see the parts rather than the whole, and to prefer to do activities step by step. They are also more analytical, realistic, and verbal than their right-brained companions. The right-brain preference is to see the whole picture rather than the details, to work out of sequence, and to bring ideas together.

The Myers-Briggs Type Indicator® (MBTI), on the other hand, is a personality assessment that provides you with information about how you prefer to think and act. For example, one dimension of the personality test asks you how outgoing, or extroverted, you are in certain situations or how reserved, or introverted, you are in social settings. These questions indicate whether you are Extroverted (E) or Introverted (I). Both left-brain/right-brain inventories, or samples of the complete inventories, as well as the MBTI, can be found in books and online sources.

Other inventories, such as the Dunn and Dunn Learning Styles Assessment and the PEPS Learning Styles Inventory, focus not only on how a person prefers to take in information, but also on a person's social and environmental learning preferences. These types of inventories provide a thorough view of how you prefer to learn, including the temperature of the room, the amount of light and sound, or the preference for moving about as you learn.

Regardless of which learning theory leads you to greater personal insight, as stand-alone models they are somewhat insignificant unless you *use* the

Kinesthetic learning involves using your hands or body to master a concept.

©FOTOLIA

information to benefit your situation. The purpose of this learning plan inventory is to provide you with a basic understanding of the factors that impact your learning preferences so that you can use this information to create an individualized and flexible learning plan for the various tasks and assignments that you will experience while you are in college. Ultimately, greater personal understanding and self-knowledge leads to action, and this learning plan inventory provides you with not only information about how you prefer to learn but also the road-map for the journey to completing tasks and goals successfully.

There are many ways of analyzing yourself and creating a plan of action for your work in college, but no single inventory, assessment, or work plan will completely reflect the exceptional person you are or your unique circumstances; in other words, no matter what inventory you take or what you learn about how you prefer to learn, the results are not the final verdict on your abilities and potential.

The goal, then, of this learning plan is to provide you with an adaptable, flexible model for putting your learning style preference into action. It also gives you a roadmap for accomplishing the many goals that you will set for yourself. Additionally, it can serve as a place to start when faced with situations that require you to work outside your learning preference comfort zone. For example, what will you do, as a morning learner, when faced with completing an important project late at night? Or how will you, as an individual learner, fare when required to collaborate with classmates on an assignment?

As you read about the characters whose stories begin each chapter, reflect on how you would act in the same situation and consider how you would meet similar challenges—this is one way to move outside your learning preference comfort zone. For example, you have already met Juanita and have learned more about her relationship with her family. In the previous chapter, you read about all four characters and their experience with orientation.

Although the characters are fictional, representative of many different college students, their stories ring true because they are based on real-life situations that you may face. Reflecting on who you are and how you will get where you want to go will help you create your own story of success.

It's in the SYLLABUS

Your professors' syllabi contain clues about how the content will address learning style preferences. For example, a syllabus for biology may include a description of a kinesthetic class project that will involve creating a 3-D model of DNA replication.

- What learning styles will be addressed through the assignments in your classes this semester?

- Which assignments do you think will be the most challenging for you to complete?

- Which assignments are the most intriguing? Why?

BUZZ

Q My learning style preferences are kinesthetic and visual, but most of my classes seem to benefit students whose preferences are read/write and aural. I feel as though my professors should provide more opportunities for students like me. What can I do?

A Your professors will teach you in the manner that they believe is most effective for learning the content, so it is best to find ways to adapt your preference to their teaching styles. Here are a few more tips for making your preference work for you:

- Find a classmate who complements your learning style preference and study together.

- "Translate" the material into your learning style preference. For example, if your professor lectures on the Kreb's cycle, it may be helpful to find or create diagrams and other visual representations of the material to be included in your written notes.

- Be open to developing your least preferred learning styles by embracing the way your professor teaches.

EXHIBIT 2.2 Learning Style Preferences, Majors, and Careers

Learning Style Preference	College Majors	Careers
VISUAL	Art, graphic design, architecture, video production	Art teacher, artist, graphic designer, architect, interior designer, video producer
AURAL	Music, communications, counseling	Musician, music educator, marketing director, public relations director, counselor
READ/WRITE	English, writing, journalism, communications, public relations, marketing	Copy editor, writer, journalist, public relations director, grant writer, policy writer
KINESTHETIC	Sciences, sociology, computer technology, culinary arts, theater	Nurse, doctor, therapist, networking specialist, computer technician, thespian, director

Learning Styles Relate to Career Choices

Discovering your learning style preference and your personality type will definitely help you set realistic short-term and long-term goals. For example, confirming that you have a read/write learning preference and you work well with deadlines and stay organized may help you realize that your long-term goal of being a writer will work well with who you are and how you learn and work. However, identifying your style and type should not limit your choices or keep you from working on areas of your learning style and personality that may be weaker or get less attention. If you are a strong visual learner, but you are taking a class that relies on listening effectively and critically, you should use that opportunity to become a better listener and improve your aural learning style by following the listening tips that are discussed in another chapter. Likewise, if you work better alone and have a strong kinesthetic learning style preference, choosing a career as a computer technician may play to your strengths, but you may also find yourself working with others collaboratively and communicating frequently in writing and verbally. See Exhibit 2.2 for examples of careers and majors as they connect to learning style preferences.

Whatever your learning style strength and personality preferences are, consider how other styles and types will factor into your short-term and long-term educational goals. Then, look for opportunities to strengthen those less-developed sides of your learning style and personality so that you are more comfortable in a variety of situations and so that you are a well-rounded person.

The VARK Questionnnaire (Version 7.1)

Copyright Version 7.1 (2011) is held by Neil D. Fleming, Christchurch, New Zealand. Used with permission.

The following inventory allows you to answer the question that Neil Fleming asks: "How do you learn best?" When completing the inventory, choose the answer which best explains your preference and circle the letter(s) next to it. Circle more than one if a single answer does not match your perception. Leave blank any question that does not apply.

1. You are helping someone who wants to go to your airport, town center, or railway station. You would:
   A. go with her.
   B. tell her the directions.
   C. write down the directions.
   D. draw or give her a map.

2. You are not sure whether a word should be spelled 'dependent' or 'dependant'. You would:
   A. see the words in your mind and choose by the way they look.
   B. think about how each word sounds and choose one.
   C. find it in a dictionary.
   D. write both words on paper and choose one.

3. You are planning a holiday for a group. You want some feedback from them about the plan. You would:
   A. describe some of the highlights.
   B. use a map or website to show them the places.
   C. give them a copy of the printed itinerary.
   D. phone, text, or email them.

4. You are going to cook something as a special treat for your family. You would:
   A. cook something you know without the need for instructions.
   B. ask friends for suggestions.
   C. look through the cookbook for ideas from the pictures.
   D. use a cookbook where you know there is a good recipe.

5. A group of tourists want to learn about the parks or wildlife reserves in your area. You would:
   A. talk about, or arrange a talk for them about parks or wildlife reserves.
   B. show them internet pictures, photographs, or picture books.
   C. take them to a park or wildlife reserve and walk with them.
   D. give them a book or pamphlets about the parks or wildlife reserves.

6. You are about to purchase a digital camera or mobile phone. Other than price, what would most influence your decision?
   A. Trying or testing it.
   B. Reading the details about its features.
   C. It is a modern design and looks good.
   D. The salesperson telling me about its features.

7. Remember a time when you learned how to do something new. Try to avoid choosing a physical skill, e.g., riding a bike. You learned best by:
   A. watching a demonstration.
   B. listening to somebody explaining it and asking questions.
   C. diagrams and charts—visual clues.
   D. written instructions—e.g,. a manual or textbook.

8. You have a problem with your heart. You would prefer that the doctor:
   A. gave you a something to read to explain what was wrong.
   B. used a plastic model to show what was wrong.
   C. described what was wrong.
   D. showed you a diagram of what was wrong.

9. You want to learn a new program, skill or game on a computer. You would:
   A. read the written instructions that came with the program.
   B. talk with people who know about the program.
   C. use the controls or keyboard.
   D. follow the diagrams in the book that came with it.

10. I like websites that have:
   A. things I can click on, shift, or try.
   B. interesting design and visual features.
   C. interesting written descriptions, lists, and explanations.
   D. audio channels where I can hear music, radio programs, or interviews.

11. Other than price, what would most influence your decision to buy a new non-fiction book?
   A. The way it looks is appealing.
   B. Quickly reading parts of it.
   C. A friend talks about it and recommends it.
   D. It has real-life stories, experiences, and examples.

12. You are using a book, CD, or website to learn how to take photos with your new digital camera. You would like to have:
   A. a chance to ask questions and talk about the camera and its features.
   B. clear, written instructions with lists and bullet points about what to do.
   C. diagrams showing the camera and what each part does.
   D. many examples of good and poor photos and how to improve them.

13. Do you prefer a teacher or a presenter who uses:
   A. demonstrations, models, or practical sessions.
   B. question and answer, talk, group discussion, or guest speakers.
   C. handouts, books, or readings.
   D. diagrams, charts, or graphs.

14. You have finished a competition or test and would like some feedback. You would like to have feedback:
   A. using examples from what you have done.
   B. using a written description of your results.
   C. from somebody who talks it through with you.
   D. using graphs showing what you had achieved.

15. You are going to choose food at a restaurant or cafe. You would:
   A. choose something that you have had there before.
   B. listen to the waiter or ask friends to recommend choices.
   C. choose from the descriptions in the menu.
   D. look at what others are eating or look at pictures of each dish.

16. You have to make an important speech at a conference or special occasion. You would:
   A. make diagrams or get graphs to help explain things.
   B. write a few key words and practice saying your speech over and over.
   C. write out your speech and learn from reading it over several times.
   D. gather many examples and stories to make the talk real and practical.

The VARK Questionnaire Scoring Chart

Use the following scoring chart to find the VARK category that each of your answers corresponds to. Circle the letters that correspond to your answers. For example, if you answered B and C for question 3, circle V and R in the question 3 row.

Question	A Category	B Category	C Category	D Category
3	K	(V)	(R)	A

Scoring Chart

Question	A Category	B Category	C Category	D Category
1	K	A	R	V
2	V	A	R	K
3	K	V	R	A
4	K	A	V	R
5	A	V	K	R
6	K	R	V	A
7	K	A	V	R
8	R	K	A	V
9	R	A	K	V
10	K	V	R	A
11	V	R	A	K
12	A	R	V	K
13	K	A	R	V
14	K	R	A	V
15	K	A	R	V
16	V	A	R	K

Calculating Your Scores

Count the number of each of the VARK letters you have circled to get your score for each VARK category.

Total number of Vs circled =	
Total number of As circled =	
Total number of Rs circled =	
Total number of Ks circled =	

60-second
PAUSE

After completing the learning style inventory and considering the different theories about intelligences and learning preferences, what are some learning-related insights that you have discovered about yourself? How can you apply these insights to your college experience?

from COLLEGE
to UNIVERSITY

What You Know and How You Learn Will Change

If your beliefs, goals, and values remain relatively unchanged during your community college experience, then your move to a four-year university should be easy, right? The transition can be relatively smooth if you are willing to apply some of the ideas in this chapter to your new environment and your new challenges.

Your definition of who you are will change when you transfer, perhaps dramatically. You will likely be more confident in your abilities, and you will be better able to handle the stress of juggling numerous responsibilities. Your values may also change after your transfer; if you were unsure of what you valued before, you may finally have a clearer picture of your belief system. No matter what shape your values are in by the time you transfer, you will find support as you struggle to make sense of it all at both the community college and the four-year university.

from COLLEGE
to CAREER

Goals and a Mission Will Help You Succeed

Many businesses rely on creating mission statements, strategic plans (long-term goals), and operational plans (short-term goals) to chart a course for their success. Because you have experience writing your own mission and goals, you will be able to contribute to your company's planning. You will be able to do this because you understand how the company's values underlie its mission and how its goals create its roadmap to success. Your experience in goal setting will also help you to write departmental or personal goals. If you understand how values, mission, and goals fit together, you will be better able to create goals that are explicitly linked to the focus of your workplace.

45

UNDERSTAND & REMEMBER

Review Questions

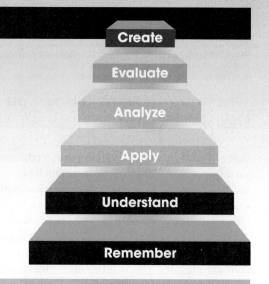

1. How do your values and background affect your goal setting?

2. Why do some people have trouble reaching their goals?

3. What steps can you take to manage your priorities effectively?

4. How do your learning style and personality preferences affect goal setting?

Create
Evaluate
Analyze
Apply
Understand
Remember

APPLY & ANALYZE

Critical Thinking

1. What is the dream that has brought you to college? How will earning a college certificate or degree help you achieve that dream?

2. Working within a small group, exchange mission statements with each other. Using a classmate's mission statement, write down two long-term goals and four short-term goals that you think the classmate would have based on his or her mission statement. Share your predictions with your group, and discuss how well they matched your classmate's actual goals.

3. Who is part of your support system so far? Are they mostly family and friends? Make a list of those people, and describe what kinds of support they provide. Be sure to include people who provide academic, professional, personal, financial, and spiritual support.

EVALUATE

Case Scenarios

1. Peter has started college, but he is not entirely sure what he wants to do. In fact, he is afraid to tell his parents that he wants to be a dental hygienist because his parents want him to take over the family business. Neither of his parents went to college, and they don't understand why any of their children would want to work outside the family business. Peter values loyalty to his family—he has been through many challenges that have strengthened his relationship with his parents—but he also has a strong interest in working in the health field. Peter's ultimate goal is to be a dentist, but he thinks that working as a hygienist first would be a way to make sure that he has what it takes. Without talking with an advisor about his long-term plans, he applies for and gets accepted into a partnering program for dental hygienists on his college campus that links college students to technical programs, allowing them to complete a bachelor's degree after they complete their program requirements. He has not told his parents about his decision despite their funding half of his tuition.

   Use the following scale to rate the decision that has been made (1 = Poor Decision, 5 = Excellent Decision). Be prepared to explain your answer.

   Poor Decision ← ①———②———③———④———⑤ → Excellent Decision

2. Serena, a single parent, has started her first semester in college, but she also works full-time in a law office. Her sister keeps Serena's twin boys while she works, but she sometimes has to miss work when her sister cannot look after them. Serena wants to complete a degree in psychology and eventually go to law school, but she feels as though it will take too long if she doesn't start now. She is motivated by time and money. She wants to hurry and get her degree, and she wants to be financially independent so that she can take care of her boys. She works very hard, but she doesn't have any other family or friends who can help her. To add to her obstacles, her sister is not supportive of Serena's desire to get a degree and improve her life. Serena's sister thinks that she has all she needs and shouldn't "mess it up by going to college and getting all kinds of crazy ideas." In fact, her sister has threatened to stop supporting Serena by caring for her children if she continues. Serena decides to continue.

Use the following scale to rate the decision that has been made (1 = Poor Decision, 5 = Excellent Decision). Be prepared to explain your answer.

Poor Decision ← ①——②——③——④——⑤ → Excellent Decision

3. Horatio took a learning style inventory that said he is a kinesthetic learner, prefers mornings, and works best in groups. He has registered for a visual art appreciation class in the late afternoon—the only one that was offered and he really needed the class. So far, he has enjoyed the class, especially the historical parts, but he is having a hard time taking notes and keeping up with all the different artists, styles, and media because his professor lectures while showing slides of works of art. There is one group project that will require Horatio to work with others to present the works and themes of a selected artist from the 21st century. Because he doesn't feel that this class really connects with his learning style preferences and is not sure what to do to get a better grasp on the concepts, he has decided to focus on his other classes, which are more rewarding and match his learning style preference better. He decides that not every class will be an opportunity to do his best.

Use the following scale to rate the decision that has been made (1 = Poor Decision, 5 = Excellent Decision). Be prepared to explain your answer.

Poor Decision ← ①——②——③——④——⑤ → Excellent Decision

CREATE

Research It Further

1. Create a survey for your classmates about their reasons for enrolling in college. Create a list of possible reasons (e.g., to learn more about other cultures), and then tally the results and report them back to your class. Be sure to discuss why you think one reason was more frequently cited than another.

2. Search the Internet for tips on setting and achieving goals. Look for video, audio, images, and text. Then, compile the top five ideas about how to effectively set, measure, and complete goals. Report the information to your classmates.

3. What is your college's mission statement? Locate it on the website or in the catalog, and then determine what you think the institution's values and goals are. Finally, identify five activities or resources that your college provides that support its mission statement, and report your results to your class.

TAKE THIS WITH YOU

Based on the goals we set at the beginning of this chapter, here's how you can take this learning with you toward college success:

- Keep writing your story. What do you want the next chapter to be?

- Write down your personal strategy, review it regularly, and update it as you learn new ideas and opportunities.

- Begin to build your support system with people who support your goals to get an education.

- Take the inventory and determine your learning style preference; then, be aware of how your learning style preference can help you succeed.

REFERENCES AND RECOMMENDED READINGS

Beals, M. P. (1994). *Warriors don't cry.* New York, NY: Pocket Books.

Dickerson, D. J. (2000). *An American story.* New York, NY: Anchor Books.

Fleming, N. (2011). VARK Learning Style Preferences. Retrieved from www.vark-learn.com

Glass, L. (1997). *Toxic people: 10 ways of dealing with people who make your life miserable.* New York, NY: St. Martin's.

Godwin, M. (2000). *Who are you? 101 ways of seeing yourself.* New York, NY: Penguin.

Klauser, H. A. (2001). *Write it down, make it happen: Knowing what you want and getting it!* New York, NY: Simon & Schuster.

Lawrence, G. (1995). *People types and tiger stripes* (3rd ed.). Gainesville, FL: CAPT.

Lazear, D. (1991). *Seven ways of teaching: The artistry of teaching with multiple intelligences.* Palatine, IL: Skylight.

Myers-Briggs Type Indicator. (2008). Retrieved from http://www.myersbriggstypeindicator .co.uk

Rodriguez, R. (1982). *Hunger of memory: The education of Richard Rodriguez.* New York, NY: Dial Press.

Smiley, T. (2006). *What I know for sure: My story of growing up in America.* New York, NY: Anchor Books.

MyStudentSuccessLab

MyStudentSuccessLab (www.mystudentsuccesslab.com) is an online solution designed to help you 'Start strong, Finish stronger' by building skills for ongoing personal and professional development.

3 Relationships and Diversity

"Evan, are you going to be around later today? I may need some help," Michael asks. Michael stayed after orientation to exchange numbers with Evan and, since then, they have talked a few times on campus. One reason Michael felt an instant connection with Evan that first day they met was that Evan is a lot like him—athletic, driven, and still unsure of himself as a college student.

"Sure, man," Evan says. "Maybe you can help me, too. You think you can lend me a hand with some furniture?"

"Are you sure you can use help from an old man like me?" Michael asks. Michael has never thought much about being 42 until recently, when some students he was working with on a group project said something about him being "too old" to work with.

"You may be old, man, but I'm pretty sure you can bench press more than me," Evan says as he laughs.

"Maybe when I was your age, but not anymore," Michael says. "Seriously, though, I have this group project, and, well, my group keeps meeting without me, and I have to do well on this."

"Ah, c'mon," Evan says. "I would make you the leader of my group. I've heard you debate others and win! You are fierce in an argument."

"I think that is part of the problem, too. I ran into a guy in the class, and he said he saw two people in my group meeting in the library," Michael says. "I don't know, maybe I come on too strong, offend people."

"So what do you need from me? Need some boxing tips?" Evan asks.

"Do you think if I talked to the professor that she would reassign me to another group or tell me to deal with it?" asks Michael.

"Man, what do you have to lose by asking?" Evan replies.

YOUR GOALS FOR THIS CHAPTER

As Michael will discover, getting to know those around you is essential to your well-being and happiness while you are working on your degree. After reading this chapter, you will be able to:

- Describe the different types of people on your campus, and understand the benefits of cultivating relationships in college
- Recognize the importance of diversity and cultural competence
- Explain how stereotyping, prejudice, and discrimination are related
- Describe the process of resolving conflict in relationships

MyStudentSuccessLab (www.mystudentsuccesslab.com) is an online solution designed to help you 'Start strong, Finish stronger' by building skills for ongoing personal and professional development.

Research has shown that getting to know at least one person, no matter who it is, on your campus will increase the likelihood that you will stay in college and complete your degree (Kuh et al., 2006). Whether it is the janitor or a career counselor, getting to know someone beyond just her name, title, and face is to your advantage while you are in college.

You have probably noticed already that there are many people who work at a college—and most of them are there to support and guide you through your college experience. Knowing who does what on your campus is just as important as knowing where buildings and services are located. It saves you time when you know, for example, that to get copies of your transcript will involve speaking with someone in the registrar's office, or that checking on loan applications will include contact with a financial aid officer. All of these people are charged with the task of helping you succeed each semester you are in college, and it will make your transition into college much easier if you are familiar with the various common jobs on campus.

Your Terms for SUCCESS

WHEN YOU SEE . . .	IT MEANS . . .
Administrator	A person at your college who manages staff at the college
Advisor	A person who works with students to provide guidance and planning for a degree
Ageism	Discrimination against a person in a certain age group
Counselor	A person who advises students on personal, academic, or career matters
Diversity	A state of difference; variety
Due process	Formal procedures designed to protect a person's rights
Faculty	A person or persons who teach
Homophobia	Irrational fear of homosexuals
Instructor	A person who teaches
Mentor	A person who provides advice or guidance
Peer mentor/peer leader	A person of equal status who provides advice or guidance
Racism	Hatred of a race; discrimination against a person of a certain race
Sexism	Hatred of a gender; discrimination against a certain gender
Sexual harassment	Unwanted or offensive sexual advances, usually by a person in a superior position
Tutor	A person who provides academic support

Get to Know Your Professors

There may be no one more important to your college and possible future career success than a professor. She does not just provide you with access to the content and challenge you to think critically about the subject matter; she also can be a mentor and a resource as you complete your degree and start your career. One way to start out on the right path to a good relationship is to greet your professor with a smile and a "hello" when you see her in and out of class. College professors see their relationships with their students outside of class as part of their advising and mentoring duties. For many instructors, their students are not only people in their classes, but they are also potential graduates from their programs and lifelong acquaintances. Being friendly in and outside of class is a great way to start on the path to a strong, valuable relationship during your college career (and maybe even after!).

Review your syllabus and determine what information is provided that will help you strengthen your relationship with your professor.

- What are your professors' office hours?
- Where are their offices located?
- How do they prefer to be contacted when you have a question?
- What are the expectations regarding meeting with your professors? Should you only meet with them when you have a problem?
- What other reasons would you have to meet with your professors?

Another way to start developing meaningful relationships with your professors is to appreciate the diversity of disciplines, personality types, and teaching styles among them. For sure, you will not love every class, every teaching style, and every personality that you will encounter in college (although we professors wish you could). When you take pleasure in the class and the instructor, enjoy every minute of it; when you don't, use the experience to keep focused on what you want: a college degree. Also realize, however, that what you don't like at first may just be a first impression that will not necessarily be your feelings at the end of the course. Sometimes students' initial experiences in a class are uncomfortable, but those same experiences may be ones that they reflect on as the most meaningful because they learned something about the course topic as well as themselves.

Each instructor's expectations in terms of class preparation and policies regarding attendance, late work, and make-up exams will differ, so be mindful that rules that apply in one class may be different in another. Relationships built on acknowledgement of others' boundaries (in this case, professors' expectations and policies) as well as respect and integrity are strong and authentic. To cultivate a solid relationship with your professor, make the most of his office hours. Office hours are best used for questions about material that was previously covered, assignments and policies that were previously explained, and anything else that does not pertain to the day's lecture or in-class activity. Sometimes students only see office hours as a time to discuss a problem; office hours should be used for positive visits as well—stopping by to say "Hello!" or to follow up on an idea that sparked your interest in class are great ways to strengthen your relationship with your professor.

It would be a perfect world if there were no conflicts in your relationship with your professor. However, there may be a time in your college career when you don't feel as though you have a strong, respectful relationship. If you experience conflict with a professor, be sure to discuss the issue as soon as possible—and in private. Use "I" statements to explain your perspective rather than "you" statements. For example, saying "I am confused about what our exam will cover" is better than saying "You were confusing when you talked about the exam." Using "I" statements also underscores your control over your actions and reactions during the conflict. Look, too, for common ground that can help you manage the conflict maturely and respectfully.

A good relationship for its own sake is perfectly acceptable, but also remember that professors can provide a link to other opportunities beyond the classroom. You will most likely turn to a professor when you need a recommendation letter for student activities, scholarships, internships, and jobs. Getting to know at least one professor well will give you an advantage when you want to move forward in your college career. Professors in your major are usually tied closely to the business and industry in which they teach. Thus, a good relationship with a professor in mechanical engineering, for example, may lead to a job opportunity in the field.

Although a good relationship with your professor is a key to enjoying your education experience, remember that your professor is not an equal in the relationship and still must challenge you to learn and stretch your concept of yourself and others, as well as evaluate you during and at the end of the term. Creating boundaries in relationships is discussed later in the chapter.

Advisors, Counselors, and Staff Work Hard for Your Success

In addition to professors, some of the most important relationships that you will forge during college will be with people whose sole job is to help you succeed. Counselors and advisors will be key people in your academic career, so be sure to take the time to get to know these individuals. College administrators also play an important role.

Advisors

Your advisor may be the first person you encounter at college. An advisor explains to you what courses you should take, how many hours you should take a semester, and how to plan remaining semesters. You may be lucky enough to have the same advisor throughout your college career, in which case, regular contact with your advisor will help keep the lines of communication open. If you have a different advisor each semester, you may wish to find one person who can act as a regular advisor. That person may be a former professor or a counselor who has advised you in the past. The goal is to find someone on campus who has an interest in your education beyond one semester, and who is knowledgeable about your degree requirements to help you stay on track toward graduation.

Counselors

You should take the opportunity to get to know at least one counselor on your campus. Whether it is a career counselor or a disability counselor, make it a point to schedule an appointment with one while you are in college. Getting to know counselors is a great way to obtain more information about the school and its services. For example, a career counselor may inform you of a career fair or recruiting day. He can also help you prepare a resume and practice interviewing. Counselors who deal with students who have personal issues are another valuable resource for you. Even if you do not need personal counseling, you may benefit from a relationship with one. This type of counselor can give you tips for managing stress and dealing with difficult people, just to name a few experiences you may have in college.

Administrators

During your college experience, you may have an opportunity to meet or work with administrators—individuals with titles such as "Dean," "Provost," and even "President." Many administrators were or still are professors themselves, so they understand the college experience very well. Although they may not spend time in the classroom any longer, their sole focus is on student success, and they provide the leadership to your institution to make sure that everyone stays focused on that goal. If you have a chance to spend time with an administrator, share your ideas about student success and take time to learn about the work they're doing to support it.

Tutors, Mentors, and Student Leaders

In addition to the key staff you will encounter in college, there are a variety of other people who work or volunteer their time to help you achieve your academic, career, and personal goals, including tutors in a learning assistance lab. Working one-on-one with a tutor provides you with a unique relationship where the tutor can really get to know what your learning needs are and how to help you fulfill them. A tutor can be a great resource for understanding the material for a class because he is often a student himself or has just recently taken the class.

Student or peer mentors are other key people you will find on your college campus who can be instrumental in keeping you on track to success. Peer mentors are usually current students who have been successful in their classes and who are willing to provide support to new students who may need extra encouragement to navigate the choppy waters of the first few semesters. Peer mentors may give you advice for studying, for choosing a degree, or for balancing family, work, and college. And just think—if you are also successful, you may be a great peer mentor for a student who was just like you when you started!

One final group of people with whom you may come in contact is student leaders. You may find them in special clubs, associations, or student government. Unlike peer mentors, whose primary role is to work one-on-one with a student, student leaders work with both students and the college or organization to provide leadership in certain areas. For example, a student government representative may ask college officials to provide more family-friendly activities so that more students can attend with their children. If administrators agree, then the Student Government Association may work with students to find out what types of activities are best and may organize an event to get more students involved.

Classmates

Last, but certainly not least, getting to know your classmates can be the difference between struggling all alone and meeting new challenges with a like-minded support group. Who else can relate to the challenge of studying for a chemistry final exam than the students in the class with you? Think about it: Your classmates will be the majority of the people who populate a college campus. You may get to know only three or four professors well throughout your college career, but you have the potential of meeting and working with hundreds of students.

In addition to sharing experiences with your fellow students, you can also rely on them as study partners or emergency note-takers if you can't be in class. Another benefit to making friends with classmates is that you can learn about other classes, instructors, and degree programs from them. Their firsthand knowledge could help you choose the best classes and the most promising programs.

©FOTOLIA

Getting along with classmates will be essential to your success both in and out of the classroom.

INTEGRITY *Matters*

Integrity is related to trust. If you can trust others, then you will be better able to learn and grow. If you do not have trust, then you may shut yourself off from others and experiences that are new to you. Give people reasons to trust you and then deliver on your promises.

Trust is also reliability, or doing what you say you will do. If your classmate asks you to take notes for him and you fail to do so each time, then you lack reliability.

YOUR TURN

In approximately 250 words, describe a time in which you have demonstrated you are trustworthy. Discuss the effects of the experience and how you felt about it. Then, describe how you plan to achieve greater trust.

Getting to know your classmates can be relatively simple, especially since you will be sitting close to them during each class. Here are a few tips for creating lasting relationships with fellow students:

- Introduce yourself to those sitting around you. It may be easier to arrive early and start conversations with other students.
- Exchange phone numbers or email addresses with classmates who seem reliable and trustworthy. You may need to call someone if you miss class.
- Offer to study with someone. Not only will you help a classmate, but you will also help yourself learn the material.
- Keep in contact with friends even after the semester is over. While you may not share classes any more, you still may be able to study together and offer support to one another.

Family and Friends

Entering college will be a new experience not only for you, but also for your family and friends, especially if they have not gone to college. Communication will be the key to weathering any changes in your relationships—they need to know how you feel about going to college, and they need to be aware that you will be going through changes while you are there. You will surely be experiencing changes in your outlook on life, your belief in yourself, and your attitude toward the future.

When these changes occur, people around you may react differently. Some will be supportive and excited that you have created personal goals and are achieving them. A few, however, may react negatively. These people may be jealous of your success or your new "lease on life," because they did not have the same opportunities or because they squandered the opportunities that they did have. Others who react negatively may be insecure about themselves and feel "dumb" around a person in college; these same people often fear that once the college student graduates, he or she will leave them for a "better" spouse or friend. Also, there are parents who do not want to acknowledge that their children are grown adults who are and should be making decisions on their own; parents are also often worried that their children will be exposed to value systems and beliefs that are very different from what they taught them.

Whatever the reactions that the people around you have to the changes you experience, be comforted by the fact that you will survive, and better yet, you will have more of an understanding of the *diversity* of opinions that you will encounter. Learning how to deal with different people in college will allow you to apply what you learn to your personal relationships.

Create a relationship "inventory" that lists the people you already know at your college. What are some ways that you can maintain and strengthen the relationships you already have? What are some action items you can put in place this week to start building relationships that you may be lacking?

VALUE DIVERSITY AND DEVELOP YOUR CULTURAL COMPETENCE

An exciting part of college is that you will meet and work with people from all ages and backgrounds. Universities attract individuals from a wide variety of backgrounds, with a broad spectrum of opinions and beliefs. Your college experience offers a great opportunity for you to learn how to live, learn, and work with other people who may be very different from you in some ways, but who share similarities with you as well. The benefits of experiencing diversity in college are many: "Students learn better in . . . [a diverse] environment and are better prepared to become active participants in our pluralistic, democratic society once they leave school. In fact, patterns of racial segregation and separation historically rooted in our national life can be broken by diversity experiences in higher education" (Gurin, 1999).

A simple definition of diversity is "difference" or "variety." Another term heard when "diversity" is discussed in a college setting is *multiculturalism*. Although the two words have different implications, they often have the same motivation—to expose the community to a variety of ideas, cultures, viewpoints, beliefs, and backgrounds.

When people talk about diversity, they usually mean race, gender, ethnicity, age, and religion. Colleges that want to promote diversity on their campuses often look for opportunities to hire and enroll people who have different backgrounds than the majority of the campus population. They do this with the belief that diversity enriches the educational experience for all, because it exposes faculty, staff, and students to new ideas and challenges our preconceived notions of the world around us.

Recognize and Appreciate Gender and Sexual Orientation Diversity

The latest educational statistics show that over half of the college student population across the country is female (Knapp, Kelly-Reid, & Ginder, 2011). In the past few decades, women have enrolled in college in record numbers. It may seem strange to think that several decades ago, there were far fewer women in college, especially in law school and medical school. You will encounter gender diversity at your college, and what this means for you is that you will have plenty of opportunities to work with both men and women and explore any preconceptions you may have about the differences between the sexes. You may have to pay more attention to society's assumptions about gender and be more attuned to how language, art, and sciences, among other disciplines, perpetuate gender stereotypes.

Sexual orientation is another type of diversity that you will more than likely encounter in college, if you have not already. Homosexuality and bisexuality are just two categories of sexual orientation diversity. Organizations such as the Human Rights Campaign (www.hrc.org) strive to educate others about discrimination that can—and does—occur because of the stereotypes and prejudice that exist regarding sexual orientation. Why should you know more about sexual orientation as a part of diversity? Sexuality is part of the human experience, and one purpose of higher education is to help you better understand and appreciate your and others' human experience. Recognizing sexual orientation as a category of diversity gives you a more complete picture of humankind.

Understand and Avoid Sexual Harassment

Colleges and universities, as well as the workforce, have been working hard to educate students and employees about the definitions and prevention of sexual harassment for decades. Sexual harassment, by legal definition, refers to a superior, or a person in power, harassing a subordinate, or a person with less power than the harasser. College and employee policies often broaden the definition, however, to include any unwanted sexual advances that create an uncomfortable situation or hostile environment. This broader definition means that, in college, a student can sexually harass another student or a student can sexually harass a professor—or any other scenario that involves students, prospective students, and employees and guests of the college. To further round out the definition, women can sexually harass men and people can experience sexual harassment from someone of the same sex.

Despite educational programs for new students and required seminars for employees, colleges—like any place in which people live and work—are not immune to instances of sexual harassment. According to Katz (2005), when the American Psychological Association surveyed female graduate students about their experiences in college, the survey results found that 12.7% of female students experienced sexual harassment, and 21% avoided taking certain classes for fear of being sexually harassed. Surveys about sexual harassment in the workplace paint a dimmer picture, with 31% of female employees and 7% of male employees claiming to be sexually harassed at work.

Educating yourself about the seriousness of sexual harassment, your college's policy on sexual harassment, and the common behaviors that are often considered sexual harassment are steps in the right direction to minimizing incidents. Sexual harassment is no laughing matter, and a review of your college's statement on the issue will reveal to what lengths the college will go to discipline those who sexually harass others. Some college policies list the following behaviors as sexual harassment:

- Offensive jokes or comments of a sexual nature
- Requests or demands for sexual favors in return for favorable treatment or rewards (e.g., a good grade)
- Unwanted physical contact or assault
- Showing or distributing sexually explicit materials to others
- Posting sexually explicit images or websites in college-owned online course management systems or emailing those images or websites from college-owned computers

Although it may not be considered sexual harassment if it is not distributed to others, accessing sexually explicit websites with college-owned computer hardware and software may be prohibited conduct that will result in disciplinary action on the part of the college and possible criminal charges.

As with all forms of diversity and possible problems that can arise, be sensitive to others; treat everyone you meet on campus with respect; and be honest with others if you feel uncomfortable in a situation or with certain conversational topics.

Racial, Ethnic, and Cultural Diversity Enables Cultural Competence

The demographic profile of our planet is changing in dramatic ways that affect you wherever you live. The population growth among countries like China and India, the increase in the U.S. Hispanic population, and the growth of the world's Muslim population are just a few examples of demographic trends that will affect not only your college experience, but also your career and personal life well beyond college. Learning to communicate and work well with individuals who have a different demographic profile than your own is a critical skill for lifelong learning. Exhibit 3.1 provides you with activities that you can do to better appreciate diversity.

While diversity is a characteristic of the student or geographic population in which you live, *cultural competence* (or cultural competency) is the learned ability to interact effectively with people of a different race, ethnicity, or culture than your own. You could be attending a very diverse campus, but you might not have a well-developed cultural competence. In the same way, you may have cultural competence but attend a campus that is not particularly diverse. Because of the importance of cultural competence for your short-term and long-term success, your college will provide courses, activities, and resources to help you become culturally competent. For example, your campus might host a multicultural event or include a cultural pluralism course in its general education requirements. The college environment also provides the ideal place for you to meet people of diverse cultures and backgrounds. Be proactive and seek out these opportunities whenever possible. It may seem intimidating at first, especially if you recognize that you're lacking in certain aspects of cultural competence. But, just as

---

EXHIBIT 3.1 Tips for Appreciating Racial, Ethnic, and Cultural Diversity

Work to eliminate all racial, ethnic, and cultural stereotypes and slurs from your thoughts and vocabulary. Stop yourself before you speak and ask, "Is this a stereotype or could it be offensive to some?"

Racial, ethnic, and cultural jokes, images, and cartoons are insensitive at best, harassment at worst. Avoid making fun of others' heritages. Be sensitive to others' backgrounds.

Learn more about your heritage and culture.

Strive to learn more about cultures that are new and different to you.

Participate in college and community cultural celebrations.

Attend seminars, guest lecturers, and artistic performances about different cultures and countries.

Do not tolerate others who exhibit racial and cultural insensitivity. If you don't feel comfortable saying something to them, then avoid them and similar situations in the future.

Q All of this talk about diversity and cultural competence makes me nervous, because I'm afraid of saying or doing something wrong when I'm with people who are really different from me.

A The fact that you're nervous is a really positive indication that it's important to you to treat others with respect and understanding. Here are some tips for communicating sensitively with others:

- Be transparent. If you find yourself in a group or a setting that is unfamiliar to you, let others know that this is a new experience for you, and that you'd like their help in knowing what's customary and expected.

- Ask for your new friends and colleagues to explain the customs and unwritten etiquette in certain situations. They will admire your willingness to learn new things, and they'll gladly help you become more comfortable with their customs.

- Keep an open mind. Encounter any new experiences with curiosity and appreciation.

the citizens of a foreign country appreciate it when a visitor attempts to speak in their language—even if it's done somewhat poorly—the people of different cultures with whom you engage will welcome and appreciate your efforts to learn more about them and their perspectives.

Generational Diversity

The idea that our parents' generation is vastly different from our own, which will be greatly different from our children's generation, is considered a fact of life. One unifying viewpoint among the generations is that different generations view the world differently.

You will, no doubt, encounter generational diversity at your college and in the world of work—more so than in generations past. A *generational cohort* is a group of the population that was born within a certain period of time, that mark some of the same world events as important, and that hold certain common values (Zemke et al., 2000; see Exhibit 3.2). Generational cohorts hold certain values that influence how they work with others and how they achieve personal success. During your college experience, you will have classmates, professors, employers, employees, or friends from a different generation than your own, and this creates a wonderful opportunity to learn how to work with someone who has a different perspective on life than you do. Your differences with this person may be a source of misunderstanding, miscommunication, and conflict at times, but as you work through these issues you will develop valuable skills and perspectives that will serve you well throughout your lifetime. There are many movies that depict both the challenges and wonderful rewards that occur from generational diversity, including *Finding Forrester* with Sean Connery, and *Flipped* with Callan McAuliffe. The key with generational diversity—as with all types of diversity—is to learn more about yourself and others and appreciate the differences. See Exhibit 3.2 on generational diversity.

EXHIBIT 3.2 Generations, Birth Years, and Core Values

Generation	Birth Years	Core Values
Veterans	1922–1943	Dedication, sacrifice, patience, respect for authority
Baby Boomers	1943–1960	Health and wellness, optimism, personal growth
Generation Xers	1960–1980	Diversity, fun, self-reliance, global thinking
Nexters or Millenials	1980–present	Civic duty, morality, street smarts

Socioeconomic Diversity Shouldn't Be Overlooked

The forms of diversity we've discussed so far—gender, ethnic, racial, cultural, and generational—tend to be observable characteristics that we recognize about people when we meet them. However, there are other forms of diversity that are less visible, but no less important, such as socioeconomic diversity. Students, faculty, staff, and administrators who gather within the college community come from a wide variety of social and economic backgrounds, and this variety provides yet another enrichment opportunity for your college experience.

Because of differences in socioeconomic background, the student sitting next to you may have a very different set of beliefs, attitudes, abilities, experiences, and motivations than you do. These differences may have little to do with his physical characteristics that you can observe, and far more to do with his childhood experiences in a relatively poor or wealthy family, or a family from a different socioeconomic class than your own. As you meet people, take time to listen to their life stories. You'll come to appreciate the challenges and obstacles they've overcome, the goals they are trying to achieve, and the beliefs they hold true because of their experiences. To help you explore this dimension of diversity even more, we encourage you to take a look at the book *Bridges Out of Poverty* by Ruby K. Payne, Philip DeVol, and Terie Dreussi Smith.

Look for Other Kinds of Diversity

Dealing successfully with diversity includes more than working well with people from different nations, different religious or political backgrounds, and different disabilities; you will also need to consider the diversity of attitudes and work ethics. For example, not everyone you meet in college or in your career will value the same things you do. What will you do if you work with others whose values conflict with your own? What will you do if the difference between your and others' work ethics cause conflict?

You will get the opportunity to work with others in class when you are assigned a group project or presentation. Even if you are all the same gender, race, religion, and age, you will still find that each of you is different and has different expectations and opinions of the assignment. Being able to work with others, regardless of their learning and work styles, is a vital skill. The more you are exposed to diversity, the more you will be able to handle and appreciate the differences between you and everyone you meet.

Teaching Styles Will Also Be Diverse

You will encounter many different teaching styles. It has been said that most professors teach the way they learn best, but there are college instructors who use a variety of teaching methods to encourage student learning. You will be more successful if you can identify each teaching style and what you need to do to adapt to it. Gone are the days of saying "I just can't learn in her class. She doesn't teach the way I need her to." Like the people who must work together in groups and be sensitive to one another's personalities, you, too, will need to recognize what

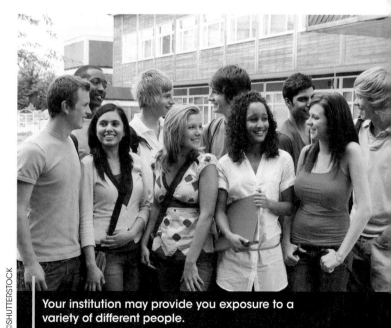

Your institution may provide you exposure to a variety of different people.

EXHIBIT **3.3** Teaching Styles

Teaching Style	Description	Tips for Success
Lecture	Professor talks for the majority of the class; a brief outline may be included; questions are limited or discouraged; usually very structured	Practice good listening skills; record lectures with permission; take good notes during class and review them frequently
Discussion	Professor poses a question and requires students in the class to answer and build on an idea or theme	Practice good listening skills; record theme or question for the discussion; note repeated ideas; record essence of each person's contribution; participate in discussion
Project	Professor bases class learning on projects; provides instruction for assignment; assigns roles; monitors progress	Make connection between project assignment and course objectives; ask for feedback during project to make sure you are progressing; refer to course materials for extra help
Problem solving	Professor poses or writes a problem on the board, then walks through solving the problem	Break process down into steps; identify any step that is unclear; ask for extra practice and feedback if needed

your learning style is and how it will fit into your professor's teaching style. In some cases, your instructor will adapt his course to appeal to different learning styles, but not everyone you encounter in college will vary his teaching style to meet your needs. Your best bet is to be ready to learn no matter what the teaching style. This is, by the way, great preparation for the world of work, in which you will likely encounter supervisors and bosses with different management styles. Rarely will managers adjust to you; they will expect you to adjust to them and their organizational culture.

To help you recognize the different methods of teaching, Exhibit 3.3 contains a description of each and tips for making the most of the different types of classroom instruction.

60-second PAUSE

From your observations of your own campus so far, what types of diversity have you observed? What opportunities does this diversity offer for you? What challenges or limitations will you need to overcome to take advantage of these opportunities?

STEREOTYPING, PREJUDICE, AND DISCRIMINATION ARE PROBLEMS WE FACE

To understand what a problem hate is in our world, all you have to do is open a newspaper or click on the latest news story online. Hatred for others because of their skin color, their religious beliefs, or their sexual orientation has fueled violence and discrimination all over the world. Whether it is as large as millions of people being slaughtered in a Third World country or as small as a person being beaten up for his beliefs, the remedy to begin to combat hatred is the same: learning to understand others and appreciate diversity. To do that, we must confront the very ideas and processes that lead people to greater acts of hatred.

Stereotypes

A discussion of diversity is not complete without mentioning some common problems. Stereotyping is an oversimplified opinion of someone or something. We often use stereotypes to make quick decisions every day. When choosing a checkout line, we may make a quick decision as to which is the fastest based on the people in line and what they have in their carts. When playing outfield on a softball team, we may stereotype the smaller players as weaker hitters, which will cause us to move closer to the infield. Parents also encourage children, who have difficulty making complex decisions, to stereotype strangers in order to protect them. Although these stereotypes are not necessarily harmful, they can create problems for us. We may get in a line we think will be shorter, but we end up standing in line for a longer time; we may move so close to the infield that the smaller player hits the ball over our heads; we may confuse children about the characteristics of a stranger, making it difficult for them to trust adults.

Stereotypes can serve a purpose in the short run, but as the examples above illustrate, stereotypes do not take into consideration all the facts. For the most part, stereotypes keep us from having to think about the complexity of issues, and often, we are then unable to appreciate the beauty of diversity. In essence, stereotypes are shorthand for evaluating situations and making decisions, but if used repeatedly, they can become prejudice and discrimination.

Prejudice

Prejudice is literally "pre-judging" a person or situation without knowing the facts. Prejudice is often based on stereotyping, which is one of the dangers of stereotyping in the first place. Let's take a seemingly harmless example of stereotyping that can result in prejudice: If you assume that all smaller softball players are weak hitters, then you may take that stereotype a bit further by disliking playing with smaller players because they don't make the game very challenging.

Like stereotyping, prejudice is a judgment based on little or no information or misinformation about a person or thing. In other words, it is based on ignorance or lack of correct information. This is why education is so important—you can avoid pre-judging people and things by learning about them and making decisions about them based on *knowledge* rather than ignorance. Although we cannot always avoid stereotyping, we can eliminate prejudice and subsequently eradicate discrimination by making the decision to learn about others.

As you have just read, there are a variety of ways we can categorize and classify ourselves and others. When used as one way of understanding ourselves better, these types of diversity are useful tools. If they are used to stereotype and then make judgments about people based on these stereotypes, then the categories become means of discrimination.

Sexist Attitudes

The increased number of women in college has changed the culture to be more sensitive and inclusive of women, but stereotypes and prejudice about females still exist. However, sexism is not limited to prejudice against women. Men, too, can suffer from sexist attitudes that are based on stereotypes.

Homophobia

Sexual orientation prejudice is often in the form of homophobia, or fear of homosexuals. Homophobia is sometimes born out of ignorance of sexual orientation diversity, and it can come from a person's own background and values.

Racist Attitudes

Racist attitudes can be obvious or subtle. People can hold racist views, like all other prejudices, and not realize that they are being intolerant of others. Asking people of other races what kinds of racism they experience is one way to understand what they perceive as prejudice. Monitoring your own words, actions, and attitudes is another way to be more sensitive to other races and cultures. You may think you don't mean any harm by what you say or do, but the recipients of racism don't always agree.

Ageist Attitudes

As you read earlier in the chapter, different generations have different values and viewpoints. An environment in which people from different generations work closely together can be exciting or tense, depending on how much people are willing to recognize, understand, and appreciate their generational differences. Problems arise, though, when people have prejudicial attitudes about a certain age group. We usually think of ageist attitudes as ones that stereotype people older than us, but people can hold prejudicial views against those who are younger, also.

Discrimination

Discrimination occurs when an action is taken on the basis of the prejudice. If, for instance, you decide that you do not want to play softball with teams with smaller players because you believe they are not as fun as teams with bigger players, then you have discriminated against smaller players and their teams. Because of recent laws and lawsuits, colleges and other places of business are sensitive to discrimination issues and spend a large amount of time and resources educating employees. Sexism, racism, and ageism are types of discrimination that are most common in the workplace. It will be an important part of your education to understand how and why people discriminate so that you can avoid similar problems that stem from discrimination. That is why this chapter spends a considerable amount of time on this subject.

Even though most workplaces strive hard to eliminate sexual, racial, and age discrimination, there are still other types of discrimination that can appear in everyday situations. For example, a coworker may declare that she won't hire anyone from a certain college because she believes that all its graduates are more interested in partying than working. Your boss may state his disdain for people from a certain part of the country and then refuse to promote an employee who is originally from that area. Although you may not be able to change everyone's mind, you should be attuned to these more subtle, and sometimes accepted, forms of discrimination and make an effort to eliminate them.

Think of an example from your own life in which the connection among stereotypes, prejudice, and discrimination was apparent. How can that experience help you become more aware of your own use of stereotypes and how they influence your judgment?

CONFLICT IN COLLEGE WILL HAPPEN, BUT YOU CAN RESOLVE IT

While you are in college, you may find yourself in a conflict that must be resolved in order for you to be successful and satisfied. The conflict can arise between you and a family member, you and a classmate, or even you and a professor. How you handle the conflict may have long-term consequences that directly affect your ability to complete a degree. Often, a minor conflict, such as miscommunication or a misunderstanding, can easily be resolved. Other times, the disagreement may be larger than you can handle with a calm conversation.

Boundaries Provide Healthy Limits

Because you will be surrounded by a diverse group of people, it may be difficult for you to create and maintain the traditional boundaries that exist between students and their counselors, professors, administrators, and learning support staff. It almost seems contradictory, but boundaries may be necessary at the same time that you are getting to know others. Why should

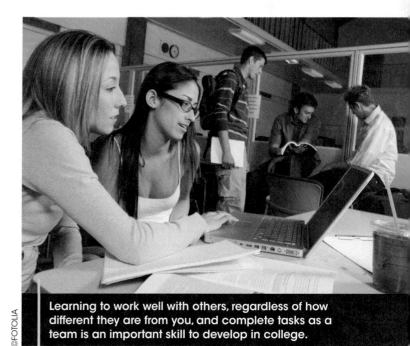

©FOTOLIA

Learning to work well with others, regardless of how different they are from you, and complete tasks as a team is an important skill to develop in college.

Q I have a conflict with one of my professors who gave me a failing grade on a paper, but said I could rewrite it for a higher grade. I really feel she is being unfair with her grading, so I really have no incentive to take her up on her offer.

A Conflict is a natural part of any relationship, but there are some tips for managing it effectively. Here are some tips to help you in this situation:

- Review your paper first and make sure you clearly understand what you did to fail it.

- Make an appointment with your professor during her office hours as soon as you can so that you can resolve this and move forward.

- Use "I" statements when conveying your thoughts about the situation.

- Listen to what she has to say about how to improve your paper.

- Take her up on her offer to let you revise.

- Remember, your professor is "on your team" and wants you to do your best.

you refrain from close relationships with professors and advisors when you need them to get to know you if you are to ask for a referral or recommendation?

For one, some colleges discourage intimately personal relationships between professors and students, just as many companies prohibit the same type of overly friendly relationships between supervisors and their employees, because such relationships can be problematic. One possible problem is that intimate relationships can result in perceived or actual unfair evaluation or treatment. Because a professor is considered a superior, the college views the professor's role as one of authority and power. Many sexual harassment policies and laws are built on the imbalance of power between a person in authority and a subordinate.

Another possible problem is that other students may see the relationship as favoritism and feel as though they are being treated unfairly. Additionally, there is the possibility of a sexual relationship, which is sometimes strictly prohibited at colleges. If you have not already done so, check your student handbook regarding your college's policy about relationships between students and faculty. Ultimately, you will need to make the decision that is best for you and the situation as to how friendly you should be with faculty and other college officials.

If you get along well with a professor and genuinely enjoy his or her company, then your best move is to respect the professor–student relationship while you are in class. You can do this by meeting your professor during his or her office hours on campus and keeping conversations focused on your progress in your classes and your career plans. You can then continue the friendship after you have finished the semester and have no intentions of taking another class with that professor again. Some friendships between professors and students are long lasting, so consider cultivating them once the class is over.

Problems Require Procedures

A time may arise when you have a problem in one of your classes. If it does, you can be assured that the college's employees will work with you to resolve it. There are, however, rules and procedures regarding how to resolve a problem at a college. Knowing and following these procedures will ensure that a problem is handled appropriately and quickly.

The first step in resolving a conflict in class is to define the problem. Is it a communication problem? Is it a problem with the course material? Is it a problem with the course standards? Once you have defined the problem, your next step is to discuss the problem with the person directly. If the problem is with your instructor, make an appointment during office hours to discuss the issue. If you are emotional—angry, upset, nervous— wait until you have calmed down to discuss the problem. Your goal in meeting with the instructor is to resolve the conflict.

For the process of conflict resolution to work, you will need to complete these first two steps. If you are not satisfied with the result or if you feel the problem has gotten worse, not better, move to the next step: talking to the department chair or dean. You will no doubt be asked if you have met with the instructor. Again, your goal at this step is to resolve the issue. Occasionally, the instructor may be called in to help resolve the issue. Staying calm and focused on resolving the conflict will be to your advantage. In the event that the problem is not solved at this level, your last stop is with the Dean of Students or Vice President for Academic Affairs. Starting at the top will only delay resolution. See Exhibit 3.4 for common issues that can cause conflict for college students.

EXHIBIT 3.4 Potential Conflict Issues

Potential Conflict Issues	Tips for Managing Conflict
Conflicts with Professors	
Grades	Make sure you read the syllabus, assignment directions, and grading criteria, and request an appointment if you have questions about what you have earned.
Deadlines	If you have any issue with a deadline, speak to your professor before the due date. If you have an emergency that prevents you from completing an assignment, contact your professor as soon as possible.
Controversial topics	Remember that your university courses are supposed to challenge your thinking. Think about how the controversial topic can enrich your understanding of others and yourself. Always speak to your professor privately for serious concerns.
Conflicts with Other Students	
Workload on team projects	Communication is key to managing conflict with group work. Be sure to clearly communicate individual expectations and responsibilities throughout the entire project, and work through conflict immediately.
Dating/personal relationships	Work through any conflict while dating with honesty and communication, but seek out help from a counselor if the conflict is more than you can manage.
Roommates	Roommate conflict may be best managed with clear expectations and immediate communication about issues. A resident advisor can help with tools for keeping communication lines clear.
Conflict with University Staff	
Financial aid	Manage conflict with financial aid when you are calm and level-headed. Focus on what you need and what you can do to move forward rather than rehash the issues that led to the conflict.

Lasting Relationships Need Time and Attention

It can be a challenge to cultivate friendships because of busy schedules and competing priorities. Despite these challenges, what can you do to forge relationships in college?

Leave time in your schedule to talk with friends and meet with professors. If you must leave directly after class to get to work, you will not be as successful in cultivating important relationships. One way to ensure that you connect with your professors is to make appointments with them during the semester to ask questions or get feedback on your progress. Your ulterior motive is to cultivate relationships with them. Also, be sure to approach conflict as an opportunity to learn more about yourself, and always act with integrity. Lasting relationships are ones that are built on trust and doing what is right.

Recall the last time that you encountered some type of relational conflict. How did you handle it, and was it resolved? What did you learn from this section that you could apply to future conflicts that may arise?

from COLLEGE

The Relationships You Foster Now Will Open Doors after Transfer

Your relationships with advisors, counselors, and professors should yield more contacts at your new school. Advisors and counselors will be able to recommend certain programs and administrators. Professors will be able to put in a good word with the people they know at your transfer school, which may mean extra consideration for admission into a program or for a scholarship.

Those same relationships may also prove fruitful if your advisors, counselors, or professors have inside knowledge of little-known internships and aid, or if they know about deadline extensions and special transfer scholarships. The closer the relationships you have, the more you will be able to use your connections to make a smooth transfer. Advisors, counselors, and professors can also provide advice about the particular challenges you may face once you have completed the move.

©SHUTTERSTOCK

from COLLEGE
to CAREER

Dealing with Diversity Is a Key to Success on the Job

©ISTOCKPHOTO

We sometimes think that once we reach our ultimate educational goal and have started our dream career, we will be magically transported to a world in which everyone gets along. Unfortunately, we are brought back down from the clouds as early as the first day on the job.

Certainly, you will never stop needing to make positive connections with others or to redefine the relationships you already have. You will also encounter diversity on a daily basis and will have to rely on what you have learned in college (and in life in general) in order to consider others' feelings, beliefs, and attitudes. What you have learned in college about other cultures, time periods, and philosophical and political ideas should provide you with a well-rounded view and will make it easier to work with and appreciate your diverse coworkers.

UNDERSTAND & REMEMBER

Review Questions

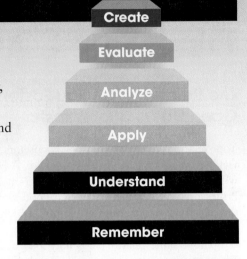

1. What are the advantages of cultivating relationships with faculty, advisors, and classmates?

2. What four categories of diversity will you encounter in college and in the world of work?

3. What is the connection among stereotyping, prejudging, and discriminating?

4. What is the process for resolving conflict? What steps do you need to take to resolve issues effectively?

APPLY & ANALYZE

Critical Thinking

1. From what you have learned about diversity, how can you make changes in your interactions with others that will show that you value and appreciate diverse peoples and situations?

2. There are some communities and groups around the world that believe a "pure" (no diversity) group, race, or community is ideal. What would be the benefits of being a part of a group that valued "sameness"? What would be the drawbacks to such a group?

3. Choose one of the types of prejudice listed in the chapter, and discuss how the college or the community can help people appreciate this type of diversity. What events could help the community learn more about fighting hate or more about celebrating diversity?

EVALUATE

Case Scenarios

1. Jonathan has been raised in a very religious household. He believes that homosexuality is wrong, and he is struggling with an assignment in one of his classes in which he must write about the issue from a sociological perspective. The professor cautioned the students that they must be objective in their papers, but Jonathan doesn't think he can. He decides to write an argumentative paper condemning homosexuality and uses both unscholarly sociological research and religious doctrines to support his arguments.

   Use the following scale to rate the decision that has been made (1 = Poor Decision, 5 = Excellent Decision). Be prepared to explain your answer.

   Poor Decision ← ①——————②——————③——————④——————⑤ → Excellent Decision

2. Marie has been married for 14 years. She and her husband have twin girls who are 12. Since Marie started college, she has noticed that her husband seems less interested in her and what she is learning in her classes. He has started belittling her desire to earn a degree. Although he first encouraged her to enroll at the nearby community college branch in their town, he now seems to be against her continuing her education there. Marie has been discouraged by his reaction and has decided not to enroll next semester. In fact, she has missed the deadline for continuing students to register and apply for financial aid.

Use the following scale to rate the decision that has been made (1 = Poor Decision, 5 = Excellent Decision). Be prepared to explain your answer.

Poor Decision ← 1 —— 2 —— 3 —— 4 —— 5 → Excellent Decision

3. One of Willis's professors has missed three night classes in a row without telling the students beforehand, and without providing a plan to make up the missed material. Willis really needs this class for his major in business, and he is worried that he won't be successful in subsequent classes. He is also worried that if he complains to the instructor, his grade will be lowered in retaliation. He decides to stick it out and not complain about the course and hope that he earns a grade good enough to pass.

Use the following scale to rate the decision that has been made (1 = Poor Decision, 5 = Excellent Decision). Be prepared to explain your answer.

Poor Decision ← 1 —— 2 —— 3 —— 4 —— 5 → Excellent Decision

CREATE

Research It Further

1. Visit the website for the "Implicit Association Test," a research methodology, at https://implicit.harvard .edu/implicit/demo, and take one of the demonstration tests relating to implicit associations we may have that lead to stereotypes, prejudice, and discrimination. Provide a summary of the results, and describe your reaction to the test and the results.

2. What does your college do to promote cultural appreciation on the campus? Interview faculty, staff, and students to find out what your institution does currently and what it could do for future events. Also, collect examples of the college's promotion of multiculturalism, and determine what, if anything, the college could do to enhance racial, ethnic, and cultural sensitivity and understanding. Report your findings to your class.

3. What is your college's policy regarding relationships between students and faculty? In addition to reviewing your student handbook, survey your classmates and fellow students about their opinions regarding faculty–student friendships and intimate relationships. Provide a summary or tally of the results.

TAKE THIS WITH YOU

Based on the goals we set at the beginning of this chapter, here's how you can take this learning with you toward college success:

- Start investing in the relationships that are available to you on campus. Schedule time to meet with your professors; build your schedule so you have some time after class to talk with your classmates.

- Reflect on your own cultural competence, and identify opportunities on your campus to interact with people whose backgrounds and cultures are different from your own. Intentionally look for opportunities that take you out of your typical comfort zone.

- Explore the stereotyping, prejudice, and discrimination that may have occurred in your own life, or what you observe around you. Add more information and knowledge to those areas in your life where you seem most prone to rely on stereotypes to make judgments about people.

- Anticipate the types of conflicts that might occur this semester with professors, roommates, classmates, friends, and family. In advance of the conflict, develop your own plan of how you want to handle conflict when it occurs.

REFERENCES AND RECOMMENDED READINGS

Gurin, P. (1999). New research on the benefits of diversity in college and beyond: An empirical analysis. Retrieved from http://www.diversityweb.org/digest/sp99/benefits.html

Katz, N. (2005). Sexual harassment statistics in the workplace and in education. Retrieved from http://womenissues.about.com/cs/sexdiscrimination/a/sexharassstats.htm

Knapp, L. G., Kelly-Reid, J. E., and Ginder, S. A. (2011). Enrollment in Postsecondary Institutions, Fall 2009; Graduation Rates, 2003 & 2006 Cohorts; and Financial Statistics, Fiscal Year 2009 (NCES 2011-230). U.S. Department of Education. Washington, DC: National Center for Education Statistics. Retrieved from http://nces.ed.gov/pubsearc

Kuh, G. D., et al. (2006). Commissioned Report for the National Symposium on Postsecondary Student Success: Spearheading a Dialog on Student Success. National Postsecondary Education Cooperative. Retrieved from http://nces.ed.gov/npec/pdf/kuh_team_report.pdf

Zemke, R., Raines, C., & Filipczak, B. (2000). *Generations at work: Managing the clash of veterans, boomers, xers, and nexters in your workplace.* New York, NY: Amacom.

MyStudentSuccessLab

MyStudentSuccessLab (www.mystudentsuccesslab.com) is an online solution designed to help you 'Start strong, Finish stronger' by building skills for ongoing personal and professional development

4 Time and Money

Pouring her fourth cup of coffee at 11:00 P.M. Laura searches for her history paper assignment that she copied from the board. It's due at 9 A.M. tomorrow. She sinks into her chair at the kitchen table to go through her backpack one more time and debates whether to call a classmate for help. Is it too late to call?

Laura doesn't normally procrastinate about her school work, but her middle child has been sick for two days and she's been home caring for him and taking him to doctor's appointments.

Three hours later, Laura's paper is finished. As she prints her final copy, the printer begins to screech loudly and stops with her last page jammed. Frantic, she rips the page from the printer and shakes the ink cartridge. When she presses "Print," the first three words barely appear on the page before the ink completely disappears.

The only thing she can do is save her paper to a thumb drive and hope that tomorrow provides her with a solution. Exhausted, she shuffles to bed. Before her head reaches the pillow, she remembers a flyer she found for the campus computer lab, which opens at 7 A.M. This may be the solution she was hoping for, if she can get to the campus early.

Because she gets to campus early, she is able to print off the remaining page in the computer lab—thanks to some help from the lab assistant. It may not be her best work, she thinks, but at least it is finished.

"I will return your papers next week," says her professor. He turns to write on the board, and says, "In the meantime, you may want to get started on your next paper on Greek culture."

YOUR GOALS FOR THIS CHAPTER

Your goal in reading this chapter will be to find time and money management strategies that work best for you and that help you keep your life in balance. Specifically, you will be able to:

- Develop a time management plan that helps you achieve your goals and avoid procrastination
- Establish a connection between time management and energy management
- Develop a money management strategy that fits your circumstances and goals

MyStudentSuccessLab (www.mystudentsuccesslab.com) is an online solution designed to help you 'Start strong, Finish stronger' by building skills for ongoing personal and professional development.

The number-one issue that college students say is their biggest challenge is time management. Why?

- College adds new and different responsibilities to an already busy life. Even before you stepped onto campus, you probably felt like your life was busy. Now you are a full-time college student on top of a full-time life.

- The college experience brings high expectations. As a highly motivated, success-oriented person, you are already placing high expectations on yourself. In addition to your own expectations, your professors, advisors, parents, and other people who care about you will also place expectations on you to succeed.

- The college experience includes a wide variety of responsibilities. As a full-time student, you're taking three to five different classes—each with its own requirements and schedules—and you may be involved in clubs or other student organizations, working, and juggling family and social responsibilities as well.

Your Terms for SUCCESS

WHEN YOU SEE . . .	IT MEANS . . .
Academic calendar	The college's calendar, which provides important dates throughout the semester; may include due dates for tuition payments and dropping classes
Add/drop dates	The dates in your academic calendar when you can add or drop a class from your schedule; usually occurs within the first week of classes
Class schedule	Your schedule of classes for the semester
Course calendar/course outline	Your instructor's calendar, which provides important dates throughout the semester; may include due dates for projects and tests
Daily calendar	A calendar that shows one day at a time
Due date	The day that an assignment must be completed and turned in
Energy zapper	An activity or person that lowers your energy levels
Finals week	The week scheduled in the academic calendar in which final exams will be held; your class meeting time may change during this week
Monthly calendar	A calendar that shows one month at a time
Office hours	The hours your intructor is in her office and is avaialble to meet with students; your instructor's office hours can be found in the syllabus
Procrastination	The act of delaying an activity
Re-energizer	An activity or person that increases your energy levels
Student study day	The date in the academic calendar in which no classes or final exams are held; it is intended for students to have a day of studying before the week of finals begin
Weekly calendar	A calendar that shows one week at a time
Withdrawal date	The date in the academic calendar that is the final day that you can withdraw from all of your classes; when you withdraw from classes, a "W" will be added to your transcript next to the classes from which you withdrew

- The college experience puts you in charge. You have far more autonomy to make decisions about how you spend your time in a college setting than you did previously in high school or work. This freedom can be exciting, but it also brings a new level of responsibility for self-managing your time without direct supervision from either your parents or an employer.

Getting organized and staying organized will help you manage your time well.

To face the time management challenge, you need to develop an effective time management strategy. An effective time management strategy will help you complete more tasks in a timely manner, minimize the *stress* that comes from both procrastination and excessive multi-tasking, and give you a satisfying feeling of accomplishment. Darwin B. Nelson and Gary R. Low (2003), in their book *Emotional Intelligence: Achieving Academic and Career Excellence*, state that "[a]n important by-product of good Time Management is a feeling of self-control—we are managing our responsibilities, not being managed by them" (pp. 100–101). In other words, managing your time effectively will help empower you to take control of your life and what happens in it. You will certainly feel more in control of your time after you complete this chapter!

Your time management strategy should include two key components—resources and routines. Resources are the items you need to *have*, and routines are the items you need to *do* in order to manage your time effectively.

Time Management Resources: Calendars, Lists, and Work Space

Many a good student has fallen victim to "assignment amnesia." This occurs when otherwise smart students believe they can remember all of their assignments and appointments without writing them down and without consulting their syllabi or course outlines. Fortunately, there are measures you can take to prevent an attack of assignment amnesia: using a calendar to keep track of important deadlines and events, and maintaining a list of prioritized tasks that you need to complete.

If you use a paper calendar, you have many different types from which to choose. Once you determine the type that works best for you—a monthly, weekly, or daily calendar—make a habit of writing down your tasks, no matter how big or small. Here is an example of a typical list of a day's activities for a student like Laura:

Thursday

Make appointment to have oil changed

Pick up medicine for Mom

Turn in housing deposit for next semester

Study for history quiz on Friday

Write essay for English Composition

Turn in student club membership application

A typical monthly calendar allows you to see several weeks at once so that you can remain aware of upcoming events (Exhibit 4.1), but often there is little space on a monthly calendar to write down detailed lists such as the one above.

EXHIBIT 4.1 Monthly Calendar

Sunday	Monday	Tuesday	Wednesday	Thursday	Friday	Saturday
					1	2
3	4	5	6	7	8	9 Picnic—noon
10	11 Work late	12	13	14	15 Pay bills	16
17	18	19	20	21 Play rehearsal 7:00	22	23
24	25 Nutrition exam 10:00	26	27	28	29	30 Birthday party 2:00

A weekly calendar allows you to glance at one week at a time. A benefit of a weekly calendar is that you have room to write out details of each activity; however, a drawback to a weekly calendar is it is difficult to anticipate what you must do the next week.

EXHIBIT 4.2 Daily Calendar

Friday
March 15, 2013

7:00	Wake up, shower, get ready for school
8:00	Drive to school, arrive early and study in the library
9:00	College Algebra
10:00	English 2
11:00	Study for Biology exam
12:00	Eat lunch and review notes for College Algebra
1:00	Biology—EXAM!!
2:00	Drive to work
3:00	Work
4:00	Work
5:00	Work

Daily calendars (Exhibit 4.2) usually provide the most space to write your day-to-day tasks and appointments, but this kind of calendar may be the most difficult to work with if you need to plan ahead. Since you cannot visually see the rest of the week or month, you may overlook important events or be surprised by them. Use a daily calendar if you are extremely organized and can plan ahead effectively, or use it in addition to a monthly calendar. Exhibit 4.3 shows a typical student's work and school schedule.

If you have reliable Internet access in your home, apartment, or dorm, and access to computers while on campus in computer labs, you may want to consider using a web-based, electronic calendar system and to-do list; also, consider using your phone's calendar to help you stay in track. In many cases, those phone calendars can sync to your computer, which will allow you to stay updated no matter what device you use. Electronic calendars allow you to set up events to automatically repeat themselves (e.g., calculus quiz every Thursday; Dad's birthday on March 18), rearrange priority lists without having to rewrite them, set up reminders and alerts to prompt you about upcoming deadlines and events,

EXHIBIT **4.3** Student's College and Work Schedule

Responsibility	Contact Hours Per Week	Outside Hours Per Week	Total Hours Per Week
College Algebra	3	6–9	9–12
Composition 101	3	6–9	9–12
U.S. History	3	6–9	9–12
Reading	3	6–9	9–12
Work	25		25

TOTAL HOURS EACH WEEK: 61–73 HOURS

and share your calendar with others so that you can coordinate team projects and family responsibilities. The added benefit of a web-based system is that you can access it anytime and anywhere you have Internet access. Google's calendar service is a popular choice among college students, and Toodledo (http://www.toodledo.com) is one option for managing all of your to-do lists and priorities. Even with these electronic systems, you can always print a copy of your calendar and to-do lists to have readily available during class or other times when you don't have Internet access. Whatever system you choose—electronic, paper-based, weekly, monthly, or daily—pick a system that works best for you and can keep you on track.

Once you've chosen a calendar system that works best for you, find your college's academic calendar on the campus website or in the catalog, and add the following deadlines to your schedule:

- Deadlines for registering and filing financial aid forms
- Date for the beginning of classes (or instruction)
- Drop/add dates for changing your schedule
- Due dates for tuition payment
- Withdrawal dates for leaving college before the semester is over
- Registration dates for the next semester
- Holidays or breaks within the semester and between semesters

The ideal calendar and to-do list are first steps to managing your time well, but there is more you can do. Creating a quiet, clutter-free space where you can study and complete assignments will also help you manage your time effectively and efficiently. If you don't have a place in your house or apartment that you can call your own, and a comfortable chair or seat at the kitchen table may

©FUSE / GETTY IMAGES

Schedule time to work with your classmates and talk with faculty and advisors outside of class.

EXHIBIT **4.4** Laura's Monthly Calendar

Monday	Tuesday	Wednesday	Thursday	Friday	Saturday	Sunday
6:30–7:30 Get ready for school	6:30–7:30 Get ready for school	6:30–7:30 Get ready for school	6:30–7:30 Get ready for school	6:30–7:30 Get ready for school	7:00–10:00 Clean house, shop	7:00–10:00 Study
7:30–7:45 Travel to work	7:30–7:45 Travel to work	7:30–7:45 Travel to work	7:30–7:45 Travel to work	7:30–7:45 Travel to work	10:00–11:30 Soccer	10:00–11:00 Go to church
8:00–12:30 Work	8:00–12:30 Work	8:00–12:30 Work	8:00–12:30 Work	8:00–12:30 Work	11:30–12:15 Lunch with team	11:15–12:30 Lunch with parents
12:30–1:15 Eat lunch and run errands	12:30–1:15 Go to doctor's appt.	12:30–1:15 Eat lunch with friend	12:30–1:15 Eat lunch and walk 1 mile	12:30–1:15 Eat lunch and study	12:15–2:00 Run errands	12:45–3:45 Study
1:15–4:45 Work	1:15–4:45 Work	1:15–4:45 Work	1:15–4:45 Work	1:15–4:45 Work	2:00–6:00 Go to library and do research	3:45–5:45 Do yard work
4:45–5:00 Travel	4:45–5:00 Travel	4:45–5:00 Travel	4:45–5:00 Travel	4:45–5:00 Travel	6:00–7:00 Fix and eat dinner	6:00–7:00 Eat dinner
5:00–5:45 Eat dinner and study	5:00–5:45 Eat dinner and study	5:00–5:45 Eat dinner and study	5:00–5:45 Eat dinner and study	5:00–7:00 Eat dinner with friends	7:00–9:00 Study	7:00–8:00 Walk 3 miles
6:00–9:30 Classes	6:00–9:30 Classes	6:00–9:30 Classes	6:00–9:30 Classes	7:00–9:30 See movie	9:00–10:00 Answer email and watch TV	8:00–10:00 Do laundry, get ready for next week
10:00 Go to bed	10:00 Go to bed	10:00 Go to bed	10:00 Go to bed	10:00 Go to bed	10:00 Go to bed	10:00 Go to bed

be all that you can spare, make sure it is comfortable and quiet and has adequate space for books, notebooks, and other supplies. It has to be a place where you *want* to be, or it will be difficult to go there to stay on task. See Exhibit 4.4, a calendar for a typical busy student who must juggle her college work and her life.

Time Management Routines: Daily Reviews and Back Planning

With an effective calendar and to-do list in place, you can now start to establish a time management routine that helps you stay on track and maintain control over your life. For your calendar and task list to be effective, you need to establish a daily routine of reviewing and updating this information. Take a few minutes every evening to review what you've accomplished and check those items off your to-do list (this will be a very satisfying experience!), add new tasks that came up that day, and then review tomorrow's calendar and to-do list so you can anticipate tomorrow's goals. Knowing what to expect for the day will make surprises less likely. Also, if you know that you have an early start tomorrow, you can make special preparations, such as preparing a lunch the night before, getting your backpack organized, making sure you know where you have to go by reviewing a map, and setting your alarm (and backups, if you tend to hit the snooze button a lot!). Stressful mornings tend to get you on the wrong track for the day, and they can typically be avoided with some thoughtful planning the night before. See Exhibit 4.5 for an example of how you can plan your day.

The second element of your time management routine that can help you manage your stress and put you in control of your schedule is a strategy called "back planning." The basic premise of back planning is to look ahead at a deadline for a task, estimate the amount of time it will take to complete the task, and establish a starting point for the task. For example, if you know that you need to write a 20-page paper for English composition, and you expect that all of the research, writing, editing, formatting, and printing will take two weeks, you can schedule time to start the project at least two weeks before its deadline. Back planning works for short-term planning, also—if you know that your morning class starts at 8:30, and it typically takes 45 minutes for you to complete your entire morning routine and find parking, then you know that you need to be walking out the door of your dorm or apartment no later than 7:45 to be on time for class. Establishing these short-term and long-term milestones will help you stay on track to meet deadlines and reduce the stress that's often associated with running behind in your schedule.

Perhaps the most important benefit of back planning is that it attacks one of the biggest threats to student success—procrastination. Procrastination is the tendency to delay starting a task until the deadline is very near. Activities such as cramming for quizzes and exams, pulling all-nighters to finish a paper or project, and missing work or other classes to finish an assignment on the due date are all evidence of procrastination. These types of last-minute, hurried efforts to meet a deadline tend to yield relatively poor academic performance and generate a

EXHIBIT 4.5 Time Log Example

Time	Wednesday's Activities
7:00 A.M.	Get ready for classes; eat breakfast
7:30 A.M.	Review notes for business class
8:00 A.M.	En route to school
8:30 A.M.	Business Communications
9:00 A.M.	Class, continued
9:30 A.M.	Class, continued
10:00 A.M.	See advisor to plan next semester's classes

BUZZ

Q I don't normally keep a calendar or even write down what I need to do. This has served me well in high school. Why do professors make such a big deal about keeping track of my assignments?

A You may have been able to keep track of your work in high school because you had other people helping you keep track of assignments and due dates. To stay on track to complete your work on time and remember all your appointments, here are a few tips:

- Record what you have to do each week and each day. Use either technology or pen and paper to make your list.

- Record your goals or tasks in multiple locations so that you are reminded frequently of what you need to do.

- Revise your list each day. As priorities and tasks change, make sure your list reflects these changes.

- Using a computer or cell phone, set an alarm before the task is due to remind you to complete it.

tremendous amount of emotional, physical, and social stress. However, these desperate strategies are avoidable! With effective back planning, you can alleviate the need to stay up all night before an exam or miss other classes to finish an assignment. An example of back planning for an important assignment can be seen in Exhibit 4.6.

The single biggest obstacle you need to overcome to avoid procrastination is *starting* the project. Procrastination typically occurs when we (yes, professors sometimes procrastinate, too) are confused, intimidated, or overwhelmed by an assignment or task. Our fears get the best of us, and we choose to forget about the assignment for a while, instead of trying to get started. Once we do get started on a project, the fears tend to dissipate, and we discover that we're making more progress than we expected. The problem with procrastination is that if we wait a long time before starting the project, the fear of missing the deadline and being late begins to creep in and we lose our ability to be creative problem solvers. If you've ever tried to remember a phone number, locker combination, or some other mental note, you've probably discovered that it's more difficult to think clearly and solve problems when you're in a hurry. In the same way,

EXHIBIT 4.6 Back Planning Time Management

Sunday	Monday	Tuesday	Wednesday	Thursday	Friday	Saturday
		1	2	3	4	5
6	7	8 1:00 P.M. Receive paper assignment	9 6–7:30 P.M. Choose paper topic; brainstorm or freewrite on topic	10 9–10:30 P.M. Reread brainstorming list; create a draft outline	11	12
13 3–5:00 P.M. Write first draft of paper	14	15 11–12:00 noon Visit writing lab for assistance with paper	16	17	18 8:30–10:30 P.M Write second draft of paper, incorporating tutor's advice	19
20 3–4:30 P.M. Write final draft of paper	21	22	23 8–9:00 P.M. Edit paper; print out on quality paper; place in backpack	24 2:00 P.M. Turn in paper	25	26
27	28	29	30			

it's difficult to be thoughtful and creative when you're trying to study for an exam or write a paper under time pressure.

We've spent a lot of time on procrastination, because it's such a common phenomenon in college, and we see our students suffering unnecessary consequences from it. When you are assigned homework, projects, or papers, take time to use back planning, and clearly establish your start date for the project, as well as important milestones along the way (e.g., first two chapters by September 15). Build those milestones into your calendar system, set time aside for the work, and get started. If you can establish a solid routine of regularly reviewing your calendar and to-do list and using back planning, you'll be taking control of your time and developing skills that will serve you well in college and throughout your life.

What are two or three action items you can complete this week to establish your time management resources and routines?

MANAGE YOUR ENERGY

Just as important as managing your time is managing your energy. Think about this scenario: You have all weekend off from work and your spouse has taken the kids to visit the grandparents. Therefore, you have 48 hours of complete solitude to write a research paper that is due on Monday. Sounds ideal, doesn't it? But what if you have the flu for those two days? Does the time mean anything when you don't have the energy to do any work? What if, instead of having the flu, you've pulled two double shifts and haven't slept more than five hours in two days? Will you be able to use your free 48 hours productively, or will you need to take care of yourself?

Time, in other words, is only valuable if you have the energy to use it well. Energy includes both physical and mental sharpness and focus. Everyone experiences variations in how "sharp" they feel throughout the day. Researchers sometimes refer to this as our circadian rhythm. The key point is to understand yourself well enough to know when you are at the peak of your mental and physical alertness, and when you're not. To determine which times of the day you feel most sharp, place an "X" in the appropriate column for each time of day in Exhibit 4.7. If you work nights and sleep during most of the day, create your own chart with the times that you are awake.

In addition to the time of day, your energy levels rise and fall during the week. Do you find yourself tired on Monday mornings, but full of energy on Fridays? Or do you feel worn out by Thursday evenings, but rejuvenated on Sundays? Depending on your work, school, and personal schedules, you will find that you have regular bursts of energy at certain times of the week. To determine which days of the week you feel most energetic, write an "X" in the appropriate columns in the box in Exhibit 4.8.

Once you've identified the hours in the day and the days in the week when you tend to be at your best, you can build your schedule to maximize your productivity during

4.7 **Time-of-Day Energy Levels**

Time of Day	High Energy	Neutral	Low Energy
6:00 A.M.			
8:00 A.M.			
10:00 A.M.			
12 noon			
2:00 P.M.			
4:00 P.M.			
6:00 P.M.			
8:00 P.M.			
10:00 P.M.			
12 midnight			

EXHIBIT **4.8** **Day-of-Week Energy Levels**

Weekday	High Energy	Neutral	Low Energy
Sunday			
Monday			
Tuesday			
Wednesday			
Thursday			
Friday			
Saturday			

those times, and schedule activities that don't require as much effort or concentration during times when you aren't at your peak. Activities such as writing papers, solving complex math problems, and reading articles and books for class assignments should be reserved for those "peak" times. It's during these times that you will most need your quiet, uncluttered work space, also. This will require some discipline and advanced planning, because you'll be tempted by other tasks and distractions. Take advantage of your mental and physical sharpness during these peak periods to perform activities that are the most important to your college success. Most students are at or near the peak of their mental alertness shortly after waking up in the morning. If that's also the case for you, commit yourself to productivity expert Tony Schwartz's strategy: "Another ritual I have . . . is to always do the most important task of the day first thing in the morning when I'm most rested and least distracted" (Allen, Schwartz, & McGinn, 2011, p. 85).

What should you do during those times when you aren't at your peak? First of all, recognize that it's OK to have some periods of time when you take a break from working hard. In fact, it's actually more productive to take breaks than to try to work hard all day. Again, productivity expert Tony Schwartz offers good advice: "If a person works continuously all through the day, she'll produce less than a person of equal talent who works very intensely for short periods and then recovers before working intensely again" (Allen, Schwartz, and McGinn, 2011, p. 84). The good news is that you can still get

Scheduling time to relax and recharge is just as important as scheduling your class work.

©THINKSTOCK

a lot accomplished, even during times when you don't feel mentally or physically sharp. During those times, you can accommodate the common "time zappers" that can rob college students of their time:

- Reviewing and sending emails
- Making phone calls
- Running errands
- Preparing meals
- Talking with roommates
- Taking a walk, swimming, or doing some other form of meditative exercise

One way to help yourself manage your energy is by becoming aware of what activities relax you when you are stressed and what activities allow you to refill your energy reserves. In Exhibit 4.9, place an "X" in the appropriate column next to each activity. If the activity does both, place an "X" in each column. If the activity neither relaxes nor energizes, then leave both columns blank. Use this chart when planning your time. If an activity rejuvenates you and helps you recharge, you may want to schedule the activity for times when you need more energy. If an activity helps you wind down, you may want to schedule it for after you have completed major tasks.

Avoid the "Black Holes" of Television, Video Games, and Social Media

Often portrayed in science fiction movies or scientific documentaries, black holes in space absorb everything around them, including light. From the perspective of time and energy management, television, video games, and social media like Facebook have the potential to be virtual black holes in your life that can consume far too much of your time and energy. If you plan on watching TV for only 10 minutes, it's really easy to discover that you're still sitting in front of the screen two hours later, and you've accomplished nothing during that time. Video games have the capacity to be even more time consuming because of their interactive nature. Social media, like Facebook and Twitter, have emerged as another potential black hole of your time, consuming both your time

EXHIBIT 4.9 Time and Energy Zappers and Re-energizers

Activity	Zapper	Re-energizer
Watching television		
Spending time with family/ friends		
Pleasure reading		
Doing housework		
Exercising (light to moderate)		
Gardening		
Talking on the phone		
Writing		
Cooking		
Shopping		
Napping		
Participating in a hobby		
Surfing the Internet		
Organizing closets, drawers, files		
Enjoying a nice meal		

INTEGRITY *Matters*

Sometimes doing what is easiest, even if it not the right thing to do, seems like the best way to manage time effectively. For example, a student who does not have enough time to finish a paper may be tempted to download one from the Internet, use someone else's previous work, or ask someone else to write it. Such a shortcut actually shortchanges the educational process. A student who "saves time" by not doing her own work for a class risks more than not learning from the assignment; she may find herself in serious academic jeopardy when the professor confronts her with the evidence that she did not do her own work.

YOUR TURN

In approximately 250 words, describe what ways you have saved time by not doing something or not doing it right. Discuss how you felt about not completing the task or by not completing it to the best of your ability. Describe what you have learned about acting with integrity and managing your time.

and attention by feeding continual distractions to you throughout the day. As you establish your time and energy management strategies, we urge extreme caution in your use of any of these three items. They are popular activities among college students, certainly, but if they aren't consumed in careful moderation, they can absorb your time and energy, and leave you with little in return for your academic pursuits.

Multi-Tasking Should Be Used in Moderation

The process of multi-tasking—simultaneously managing several tasks or devoting your attention to more than one activity at a time—is often lauded as an admirable and even necessary skill. In fact, many people believe that you can get more done and be more productive while multi-tasking; however, the scientific evidence doesn't support this premise. In his article "Manage Your Energy, Not Your Time" (2007), Tony Schwartz explains: "Many executives view multitasking as a necessity in the face of all the demands they juggle, but it actually undermines productivity. Distractions are costly: A temporary shift in attention from one task to another—stopping to answer an e-mail or take a phone call, for instance—increases the amount of time necessary to finish the primary task by as much as 25%, a phenomenon known as 'switching time.' It's far more efficient to fully focus for 90 to 120 minutes, take a true break, and then fully focus on the next activity" (p. 67). If you have a tendency to check your emails, respond to text messages, monitor your Facebook status, and listen to your iPod while attempting to write, study, or organize your calendar, you are undermining your ability to perform well because these simultaneous tasks are sapping both your time and energy. Take the time to shut down the peripheral activities and stimuli and focus on the primary task at hand, and you'll find yourself accomplishing far more than you expected.

USING TECHNOLOGY TO GET AHEAD

Instead of limiting cell phones, video games, and the Internet, use them to help you manage your time. There are many sources to help you!

RECOMMENDED SITES

- http://www.studygs.net/timman.htm: This site provides study guides and strategies that have excellent tips for students to improve their time management strategies.
- http://www.psychologytoday.com/articles/200308/procrastination-ten-things-know: This site provides a list of reasons people procrastinate and what you can do to minimize the negative effects of procrastination.
- http://www.dartmouth.edu/~acskills/success/time.html: This site provides links to additional time management resources for college students.

Now that you've considered when your physical and mental sharpness are at their peak, what are some of the changes you plan to make in your daily and weekly routine to capitalize on this insight?

MONEY MATTERS

One of the greatest challenges for students isn't meeting the academic expectations of college; it is handling the financial issues that come into play when you get there. Some students choose to go to school full-time and not work, while others juggle a job—either part-time or full-time—while going to school. No matter what their financial situation, many are adding the expense of going to college to their other obligations, or they are using grants, loans, or scholarships to cover costs.

As you know by now because you successfully enrolled in college, investing in your future takes more than courage; it also takes some cash, or at least access to funds to cover the costs. Unfortunately, as Catherine Rampell (2009) recently reported for *The New York Times*, the costs of college continue to rise and will likely increase with each passing year. So what can you do? The first step is to become financially literate. There are many resources available that can help you learn more about how to become financially fit. The next step is to create a plan for staying on a budget and for anticipating expenses in the future. The following section provides you with a brief overview of both steps.

Estimate Your College Costs

Estimating what you are going to spend in college for your education is a great first step to understanding your financial situation, and it will help you with budgeting. Since this is your first time in college, it will be helpful to see what you can expect to spend as you work on and complete your degree. Unfortunately, college tuition and fees are only part of the costs involved in earning a degree. No matter what you pay for tuition and fees, it is only a fraction of the actual costs of your education; colleges make up the difference through taxes, state and federal money, and gifts and donations.

To determine your estimated costs, you will need to get very specific about what you will need during the semesters you plan to attend. The following list is only a suggestion of possible supplies: textbooks, notebooks/binders, computer/laptop, backpack, paper (for notes and for printing), pens/pencils, calculator, computer software, jump drive, stapler, hole punch, ruler, and other specialized supplies for labs or certain classes such as photography or drawing. For specialized programs, you may have other materials that you will need to purchase. Create a list of what you know you will need, and then write down how much you think each item will cost. You will use this estimate when you create your budget.

In addition to supplies and tuition, you may also find other costs associated with going to college. For example, your transportation costs may increase as you go from home or work to campus and back. You may also discover that you need regular, reliable Internet access, which will create an additional monthly cost. Unexpected costs such as these can be an awakening to the investment of money and time that wasn't covered during new-student orientation. The following is just a suggested list of possible additional expenses that you may encounter: daycare or babysitting services, transportation (gas, car maintenance, tolls, bus pass), parking, and Internet services. You will want to talk with students who have been at your college for a few semesters or recent graduates to determine what else may be needed. These same students may also provide you with some cost-saving ideas.

Create a Budget

Creating a budget will help you manage your college costs while balancing your other financial obligations and help you stay on track. A budget doesn't have to be a headache. In fact, it is relatively easy to create a budget. The hard part is following it. First, you need to create a customized budget sheet. Exhibit 4.10 shows a sample budget form that you can start with. In the first column, you will estimate your income and your expenses. The middle column will be used to record your actual amounts of income and

EXHIBIT 4.10 Sample Budget Form

Category	Estimated Amount Per Month	Actual Amount Per Month	Difference
Income			
Source 1 (wages/salary)			
Source 2 (scholarship, financial aid, etc.)			
Source 3 (alimony, employee tuition reimbursement, child support)			
Total Income			
Expenses			
Mortgage/rent			
Utilities			
Car payment/transportation			
Insurance			
Groceries			
Household items			
Clothing			
Gas			
Car maintenance			
Cellular phone			
Eating out			
Entertainment			
Health care (medications, doctor's visits, etc.)			
Credit cards or loans			
Total Expenses			
Net Income (Total Income minus Total Expenses)			

expenses. Record any differences in the final column by subtracting the actual amount from the estimated amount. For example, if you estimate that you earn about $1,000 a month, but this month, you earn $1,092, your difference is +$92. If you earn $997, then the difference is –$3. The budget in Exhibit 4.10 provides a sample of what you need to write down each month.

Once you determine the categories that fit your lifestyle, you will need to gather all the bills and paystubs that you have and add up your expenses and income. It is a good idea to review at least three months' worth of bills to get an accurate picture of your expenditures. If you have any bills that are paid less frequently than once a month, then you will need to convert them to a monthly expense. For example, if you pay $240 for car insurance every six months, your monthly expense is $40 ($240 divided by 6 months).

One key to an accurate budget that helps you track your spending is to be honest about your expenses. That means you must write down everything you spend, even the money you spend on snacks or supplies. You may find that you spend $25 a week ($100 a month) on items that are unnecessary. The more you can track unnecessary items, the better you can control your spending.

Set Goals

After you get an accurate picture of your income and expenses, you can start setting short-term and long-term financial goals. Because you are in college and probably trying to keep expenses to a minimum, you may think that creating and working toward financial goals will be a difficult undertaking until you have a job with a steady income and secure future. However, you can start setting small, short-term goals now. For example, your first short-term goal could be tracking your monthly budget and consistently spending 5% less than you earn. Another short-term goal could be to save enough money to pay for your study-abroad experience next year. Meeting these two goals will help you reach larger goals down the road.

You should also write down your long-term financial goals. One of these goals could be to start your own business. However, in order to reach that long-term goal, you will need to make a list of other, short-term goals that will help you reach your long-term goal, and start working toward them.

Budgeting your money for college expenses will be crucial to your staying in college and being less stressed.

©SHUTTERSTOCK

Don't Take Credit

Credit cards can be very tempting when you are in college, because they are so easy to use and the offers pour in just about every day. The reality of credit cards, however, is that they can cause big financial problems, ones that are sometimes difficult to pay off. Think about this: You don't want to start a new career after college that pays a good salary only to send a substantial portion of it to a credit card company.

In case you are still enticed to use a credit card, think about this sobering information. If you were to charge $1,000 on a credit card that charges 17% interest, and you make payments of $100 each month, you will be accruing more in interest than you will be paying each month. And that is only if you do not charge anything else!

Exhibit 4.11 shows that paying twice as much—$200—each month for six months only reduces the balance by $276.21—after paying $1,200. Unfortunately, some students have many more thousands of dollars of credit card debt, and with the current interest rates, it is no wonder that students can find themselves in an endless cycle of charging and paying minimums. If it is at all possible, put the cards away until you are out of college, and then use them wisely.

EXHIBIT **4.11** Credit Card Payments

Month	Previous Balance	Interest (17%)	Balance + Interest	Payment	Remaining Balance
Month 1	$1,000	$170	$1,170	$200	$970
Month 2	$970	$164.90	$1,134.90	$200	$934.90
Month 3	$934.90	$158.93	$1,093.83	$200	$893.83
Month 4	$893.83	$151.95	$1,045.78	$200	$845.78
Month 5	$845.78	$143.78	$989.56	$200	$789.56
Month 6	$789.56	$134.23	$923.79	$200	$723.79

Practice Good Financial Habits

A good financial plan is only good if you stick to it. The following tips can help you increase your financial literacy muscles, especially if you exercise them regularly.

- Balance your checkbook and other accounts every month. Online tools like Quicken and Moneydance can be helpful, if you're comfortable managing your finances using a computer.
- Compare your financial statements with your own recording of expenses and income. This will help you catch any unauthorized charges on your accounts or bank fees that were inappropriately posted to your account.
- Separate your bills from other mail, and create a schedule for paying them. Your paper-based or electronic calendar system is ideal for this purpose. Most bills are due on the same day each month, so you can set up a recurring reminder.
- Sign up for online payment plans if available and if it is easier to pay this way. Just be sure that you have reliable Internet access and use a consistent email addresses so you don't lose track of these transactions.
- If you have a credit card, use it for emergencies only.
- Put a small percentage of your income each month in a separate savings account for unexpected expenses. For example, for every $100 you earn, put $5 (5%) in an emergency savings account. Create a goal to increase your savings percentage.
- Check your college website every semester for updates about changes in tuition and fees.

BUZZ

Q You suggested that we try to avoid using credit cards, but they're so convenient. Cash transactions take longer, and then I have to hassle with the change.

A If you like the simplicity and convenience of a credit card, here are some tips for making it better for you financially:

- Obtain a debit card from your bank.
- Make sure that the debit card doesn't allow you to overdraw your checking account, which can lead to expensive fees and penalties.
- Keep track of your purchases each day by writing them in a transaction record or by downloading them into a spreadsheet or budgeting program from your online account access.

Look at your syllabus to help determine what you need for class that will help you manage your time and money.

- What are the supply requirements listed in your syllabus for each class (e.g., textbook, notebook, graphing calculator)?

- What are the supply requirements that are needed but not listed in your syllabus for each class (e.g., printer ink, copy paper, thumb drive)?

- How much time will you need to spend a week for each class?

Protect Yourself

Budgeting and creating a plan are not quite enough to make sure that you are on firm financial foundation—you will also need to protect yourself from various scams, which can do more harm than just draining your bank account. If anyone you do not know contacts you through email or by phone to ask you to send money or provide a bank account number, delete the email or hang up the phone. Thousands of well-meaning people get scammed this way by providing access to their bank accounts, only to find out that their money is gone and their credit is ruined. If the information sounds too good to be true or doesn't seem "right," it is quite possibly a scam.

Another risk that you have to manage is identity theft. Keep your bank cards in a safe, secure place at all times, and never, ever write down your ATM PIN on a piece of paper. Also, be very cautious any time someone asks you to provide your Social Security number. Never provide it in an email, and make sure that any form requesting this number is from an official authority, like your college's financial aid office or the registrar.

Learn More

There are numerous resources available for you to explore financial matters further. There are many local, state, and federal government programs that can provide free information and counseling if you are interested in getting your finances on track. The best defense is good information about your situation and your possibilities. For starters, you can—and should—request a free credit report. A request form from the Federal Trade Commission is available at www.ftc.gov/credit. You can also find a local (and usually free) financial help center that provides workshops and counseling for people who want to know more about their financial situation. You can find these agencies online or in the phone book. Don't forget that your local library and bookstore offer many good resources on money management and financial matters. Start with a good book, such as *Personal Finance for Dummies* (Tyson, 2009), that defines common terms and provides basic information. Remember that the best way to protect your financial future—and to secure the hard work that you are doing in college to get a better job—is to empower yourself with the knowledge of what you have and what you want to do with it in the future.

60-second PAUSE

What are some of your spending or financial habits that you want to avoid while in college? How can a monthly budget system help you avoid these habits?

from COLLEGE

to UNIVERSITY

How to Handle the New Pressures on Your Time

A good time management strategy that works for you will serve you well when you transfer to a university. Yes, there will be more work and more expected of you when you get closer to completing a bachelor's degree, but there may also be less direction from professors. They will assume you have solid time management skills. The more you practice now, the better you will be able to handle even more restrictions on your time. Additionally, there will be more for you to do as you work toward completing a four-year degree. You may find yourself participating in a career-related club, interning to get experience for your resume, talking to professors about graduating, and putting together applications for jobs. Try out a few strategies and find what works, but also talk to students who have already transferred to find out what new expectations you will encounter.

©ISTOCKPHOTO

from COLLEGE

TO CAREER

©ISTOCKPHOTO

Improving Time Management on the Job

If you decide to go directly from college to work, or back to work, your time and stress management skills can be the difference between a dreaded job and a life-fulfilling career. Time management will be even more important on the job because your actions will affect more people. Just like a move from college to university, the more you practice good time management skills, the more likely you will be able to complete assignments on time. Beware, though, that on the job, the stakes will be much higher than they were in college. Using a calendar and writing down daily tasks will help you keep on top of your to-do list. There may be times when you won't be able to manage your time as effectively as you wish, but if you can be honest and speak up quickly, you may be able to save others time as well.

UNDERSTAND & REMEMBER

Review Questions

Create

Evaluate

Analyze

Apply

Understand

Remember

1. What activities and responsibilities will you have to manage while you are in college? How will managing your time help you stay on top of these tasks?

2. Name and describe two time management strategies. List the advantages and disadvantages of each.

3. What are the different reasons for procrastinating? What strategies are available to eliminate procrastination?

4. What money issues do you need to consider as a college student? Which will you work on while you are a student? Why?

APPLY & ANALYZE

Critical Thinking

1. What will be your greatest challenges to managing your time effectively? What have you learned so far, either from this chapter or from being in college, about what will be expected of you in terms of managing your time?

2. What do you see as your greatest time management strengths? What are your time management weaknesses? What will you do to build upon your strengths while also addressing your weaknesses?

3. Working within a group or with another classmate, describe the types of activities that can zap students' time and energy; then create solutions for managing them. Present your ideas to the class.

EVALUATE

Case Scenarios

1. Janice has been doing very well in her classes. She has been able to manage her time wisely and adjust her schedule anytime something unexpected has come up. However, Janice has had a hectic week. Her boss expects her to stay late for the week to finish a special project; she has an important exam on Thursday evening; her daughter has been sick with a stomach virus; and her husband has been out of town for the last two weeks. Her goal is to take care of each problem without jeopardizing her job, her grade, or her daughter's welfare, but she cannot always balance all of these at all times. She decides to ask her professor if she can take her exam the following week after her boss's special project is finished, and she asks a good friend to take care of her daughter so that she can work late until she finishes the project. For Janice, at this point, her top priority is her job.

   Use the following scale to rate the decision that has been made (1 = Poor Decision, 5 = Excellent Decision). Be prepared to explain your answer.

   Poor Decision ← ——①——— ②——— ③——— ④——— ⑤——→ Excellent Decision

2. Glenn is a constant procrastinator. He feeds on the adrenaline that runs through his veins when he waits until the last minute to complete an assignment. The last time he did this, for a computer programming class, he ended up failing the assignment because he ran out of time and was exhausted for three days because he had stayed up for 36 hours straight. Glenn really wants to break his bad habits, so he creates a study group in which they work on assignments together to get them finished. For example, in his accounting class, each group member completes one of the homework questions and the group then compiles the answers to turn in individually. He also borrowed a friend's paper from a history class and is using it as the foundation for his so that he doesn't have to spend so much time starting his paper from scratch.

Use the following scale to rate the decision that has been made (1 = Poor Decision, 5 = Excellent Decision). Be prepared to explain your answer.

Poor Decision ← ①————②————③————④————⑤ → **Excellent Decision**

3. Korto has started a new job while she is in college so that she can pay for minor living expenses now that she has moved into an apartment by herself. Because her financial aid has been delayed, she cannot pay for both her apartment and her tuition and books at the beginning of the semester. Her college has offered to provide a monthly payment plan, but she has to complete her payments in three months, which she is not sure is enough time if her financial aid does not arrive before then. Thus, she has decided to use her credit card to pay for college expenses because she knows she can at least afford the monthly minimum until her financial aid comes in.

Use the following scale to rate the decision that has been made (1 = Poor Decision, 5 = Excellent Decision). Be prepared to explain your answer.

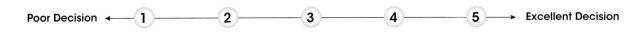

Poor Decision ← ①————②————③————④————⑤ → **Excellent Decision**

CREATE

Research It Further

1. Search the Internet to find three videos of unique ways to manage time. Share those videos with your classmates, and ask them to rank the strategies from most effective to least effective.

2. Create a survey that asks your classmates how they manage their time in college. Once you collect your data, determine which time management strategies are the most used and suggest why you think they are popular. Report your results to the class.

3. What resources are available on your campus to help students manage their money effectively? Investigate resources in the library as well as any offices or departments that provide workshops or financial counseling for students. Compile a one-page list of these resources for your classmates.

TAKE THIS WITH YOU

Based on the goals we set at the beginning of this chapter, here's how you can take this learning with you toward college success:

■ Get a calendar (electronic or printed) and start using it on a daily basis.

■ Start practicing a work and activity routine based on your personal energy patterns.

■ Establish a monthly budget, set goals, and start tracking your progress.

■ Continue learning about financial matters so that you can make smart decisions about your money.

REFERENCES AND RECOMMENDED READINGS

Allen, D., Schwartz, T., & McGinn, D. (2011). Being more productive. *Harvard Business Review*, 89(5), 82–88.

Dodd, P., & Sundheim, D. (2005). *The 25 best time management tools and techniques: How to get more done without driving yourself crazy.* Chelsea, MI: Peak Performance Press.

Hindle, T. (1998). *Manage your time.* New York, NY: DK.

Leland, K., & Bailey, K. (2008). *Time management in an instant: 60 ways to make the most of your day.* Franklin Lakes, NJ: Career Press.

Nelson, D. B., & Low, G. R. (2003). *Emotional intelligence: Achieving academic and career excellence.* Upper Saddle River, NJ: Pearson.

Rampell, C. (2009, October 20). The skyrocketing costs of attending college. *The New York Times.* Retrieved from http://economix.blogs.nytimes.com/2009/10/20/the-skyrocketing-costs-of-attending-college

Schwartz, T. (2007). Manage your energy, not your time. *Harvard Business Review*, 85(10), 63–70.

Sibler, L. (1998). *Time management for the creative person: Right-brain strategies for stopping procrastination, getting control of the clock and calendar, and freeing up your time and your life.* New York: Three Rivers Press.

Tyson, D. (2009). *Personal finance for dummies* (6th ed.). New York, NY: Wiley.

MyStudentSuccessLab

MyStudentSuccessLab (www.mystudentsuccesslab.com) is an online solution designed to help you 'Start strong, Finish stronger' by building skills for ongoing personal and professional development.

5 Stress and Health Choices

EVAN'S STORY

Evan is a student by day and a kickboxer by night, usually competing several times a semester.

Sometimes he wonders if he can do both and be successful in and out of the ring. A few years ago, he saw a doctor because of depression, and he feels the symptoms creeping up on him again.

"Evan, man, you're a little late today," his coach says. "What gives? You are usually early to practice."

"Hey, Coach. Had too much homework to do," Evan replies.

"Evan, I know you are committed to college. That's great, but you have to do your time at the gym."

The words sting Evan. He is highly competitive—you have to be, in this sport—and he prides himself on his athletic ability, even though he has started to pack on the pounds from too much studying and eating poorly.

Then, there is college—another goal that he wants to achieve. When he registered for college, he really thought he could do both kickboxing and college and succeed at both. Evan packs his sweatshirt into his gym bag, stretches, and thinks about the homework he still has to complete before going to bed tonight, which will be around 2 A.M. if he gets home by 11:00. A few energy drinks and a protein bar will be needed to keep him awake to get his work done.

"I've got some extra drills we need to work on tonight," his coach says. "Can you stay another hour after you get your workout in?"

Evan hesitates. He has to finish a paper, and now he will need to stay up all night to get it done, even though that will mean "sleepwalking" through his classes and maybe even his workout tomorrow.

"Sure, Coach," Evan says, and reassures himself that worrying about what he has to do won't make it any better.

 YOUR GOALS FOR THIS CHAPTER

The purpose of this chapter is to provide you with information so that you can make better choices for your physical, mental, and sexual health, which will in turn help you handle stress more effectively. Specifically, you will be able to do the following:

- Define stress and where it can appear in your life
- Describe methods for reducing stress and minimizing stress-related illnesses
- Determine which health issues are important to consider while you are in college
- Develop a personal approach to maintain balance in your overall health

Stress is a physical and psychological response to outside stimuli. In other words, just about anything that stimulates you can cause stress. Not all stress, however, is bad for you. For example, the stress you feel when you see someone get seriously hurt enables you to spring into action to help. For some students, the stress of an upcoming exam gives them the energy and focus to study. Without feeling a little stressed, these students might not feel the need to study at all.

How You Handle Stress Is What Matters

Not everyone, however, handles stress the same way, and what is a stressful situation for you may not be for someone else. How we handle stress depends on our genetic makeup, past experiences, and the stress-reducing techniques that we know and practice. There are ways to reduce stress or change our reaction to it, both physically and psychologically. First, though, it is important to be able to identify causes of stress.

Your Terms for SUCCESS

WHEN YOU SEE . . .	IT MEANS . . .
Acquaintance rape	See *date rape*
Active lifestyle	Maintaining regular exercise
Alcohol abuse	Using alcohol excessively or using it to the impairment of one's senses
Balanced living	Finding balance in one's personal, academic, and professional life that provides a sense of well-being
Date rape	Rape, or forced sexual contact, between two people who know each other or who are dating
Mental abuse	Harmful treatment of the mind or intellect
Mental health	The condition of one's mind or mental processes
Physical health	The condition of one's body
Sedentary	Sitting in one place, not active
Sleep deprivation	The act of not getting enough sleep
Spiritual health	The condition of one's religious or spiritual outlook on life
STDs	Sexually transmitted diseases
Stress	A physical and psychological response to outside stimuli
Stress-related illness	An illness that is caused by the body's reaction to stress
Verbal abuse	Harmful treatment of someone through yelling, name-calling, or insults

EXHIBIT 5.1 Possible Causes of Stress

Self-Doubt	Pressure to succeed (from yourself or others)
Fear of failure or the unknown	Speaking in public
Congested traffic	Lack of support—financial, physical, or psychological
Uncomfortable situations	The demands of a job, such as a promotion/demotion, deadlines, and evaluations
Life experiences, such as the death of a loved one, having a child, getting married, and moving	Too many activities and not enough time to complete them
Waiting in lines	Computer problems

The list in Exhibit 5.1 is not exhaustive, but it can start you thinking about different ways that you experience stress.

Each of us has certain triggers, such as the ones listed in Exhibit 5.1, that stress us out. Usually, however, the same situation doesn't stress us out the same way each time we are in it. Take waiting in line at the bank. One day, you might be extremely angry to be waiting 15 minutes in a line to cash a check because you are late for a job interview. The next time that you are in the same line waiting the same amount of time, you may be calm and relaxed because you are enjoying a little quiet time to think while your mother waits in the car. Thus, it is not necessarily the situation or action that causes negative stress, but more likely other factors that are involved.

When you are suffering from lack of sleep, you may be more likely to react negatively to people and situations that usually would not bother you. When you are feeling unsure of your abilities to be successful in college, you may take constructive criticism as a personal attack. Being aware of times and situations that cause you the most stress is one step to helping manage stress better. If you realize that you are sensitive to others' feedback because you are feeling insecure, then you may be less likely to react negatively.

In Exhibit 5.2, indicate what does and doesn't cause you negative stress by placing an "X" in the appropriate column. Consider other situations or people that cause you to react negatively. The goal is to recognize a pattern of stress and then work to overcome it.

College Has Stressors of Its Own

Because you will find stress in college, at work, and at home, it is important to be able to identify the different stressors in each environment and work toward minimizing the negative stress in each area. Some weeks, you will have to contend with negative stress in only one area, but there will be times when it seems as though each part of your life is making you miserable. The more you understand what you can and cannot control, the more likely you will be able to work through stressful times and stay on track with your goals.

Stress in college is inevitable, but it doesn't have to be overwhelming if you know what you can do to minimize negative stress in the first place. There are several

EXHIBIT **5.2** **What Stresses You Out?**

Situation	Stresses Me	Does Not Stress Me
Starting a big project		
Paying bills		
Being in a messy environment		
Receiving graded papers and exams		
Not getting enough sleep		
Taking a personal or professional risk		
Getting out of bed		
Not getting feedback on my work		
Being distracted by other people		
Thinking about the future		
Taking tests		

ways that students unknowingly cause themselves stress: failing to read the catalog and student handbook about course prerequisites and descriptions, as well as degree program requirements; registering for more hours than they can handle; trying to do too much at work and home; missing deadlines; arriving late for class or appointments; and keeping the same social schedule despite more academic demands.

The information in this chapter should help you minimize your stress in college by providing you with information and strategies for accomplishing your goals. Even if you avoid the above behaviors, you may still find that things don't go your way in college. If you realize that there will be times that you or others will make mistakes, then you will be more likely to bounce back from problems. Minimizing the negative effects of stress can include activities such as reading all information that you receive from the college; paying attention to flyers on doors, bulletin boards, and tables; and talking to your advisor, instructor(s), and counselor on a regular basis.

You will also want to regularly check the college's website for announcements and updates. Be sure, too, to read publications such as newspapers and newsletters that the college sends to the community. As always, ask questions when you are not sure of something, and make an effort to get involved with campus organizations and clubs, because people in these groups often know what is going on around campus.

We all sometimes feel overwhelmed by what we have to accomplish.

©SHUTTERSTOCK

Your Home May Be a Source of Stress

Reducing stress at home will, no doubt, be the first step for minimizing your overall stress. Because your family and friends are likely to be your most important supporters, what they think of you and the demands they place on you will need to be discussed. Some family members may be unsure of what you are doing or worried that your schoolwork will leave little time for them. Your friends may feel the same way, especially if they are used to hanging out with you after work and on the weekends. The key to minimizing stress at home is to communicate your needs. Talk to your loved ones about what you and they can expect when you are taking classes. Sometimes, you'll need to have an honest conversation with your loved ones to explain that because of the demands of college, you won't be able to spend as much time with them as you used to. Or, you may have to revisit your commitments and priorities and step away from some responsibilities that you can no longer manage. Most likely, the amount of free time that you enjoyed in high school will be far less in college.

Work May Also Be a Stressor

For some, stress on the job can be the most difficult to deal with because of the fear of performing poorly and being fired. Stress on the job can also be particularly tough to manage because you may feel uncomfortable confronting coworkers and being honest about your feelings. Additionally, coworkers may be jealous of your success or they may misunderstand the arrangements you have made to work and go to school. You may also be concerned with completing your work tasks as well as your college assignments. The stress you feel on the job may make it seem overwhelming to balance both work and school effectively.

Stress Can Lead to Illness

Stress can cause a variety of health-related problems, and as you read earlier, sleep deprivation is one of those issues. Stress-related illnesses can vary from person to person, but there is one common denominator: by becoming knowledgeable about your stressors and practicing techniques for reducing stress, you can decrease negative health effects. Although some of the following illnesses can be caused by other factors, such as heredity and environment, they can be signs that stress is making you ill:

- Digestive problems, including upset stomach, heartburn, constipation, diarrhea, and ulcers
- Severe headaches and migraines
- High blood pressure, heart attack, and stroke
- Muscle and joint pain
- Cold, flu, and respiratory and sinus infections

It's in the SYLLABUS

Use your syllabus to determine what you will need to be aware of during the semester so that you can better manage your stress.

- What parts of your professors' syllabi will cause you the most stress in terms of meeting expectations?

- What will be easiest for you to meet?

- If you find yourself overwhelmed or confused by the expectations in your courses, what can you do to help eliminate your stress?

Staying healthy by eating well, exercising, and getting adequate sleep are all ways to help prevent stress-related illnesses. Be careful that you do not neglect both your physical and mental health, especially at particularly stressful times, such as the beginning and end of the semester, for you will be more susceptible to stress-related illnesses that could keep you from doing well in college. It's common among college students to disrupt their daily sleep and exercise routine during finals week and other intense periods of academic activities, but the reality is that it's even more important to maintain healthy exercise and nutritional habits during these times because they will help you perform better.

60-second PAUSE

List the top five stressors that are influencing your life right now. What are some specific actions you could take, today, to start managing these stressors?

YOU CAN MANAGE YOUR STRESS

No doubt you have felt stress since enrolling in college. You wouldn't be human if you didn't at least worry at the beginning of the semester how you will manage it all—family, work, college, and a personal life. Stress is normal, but for college students it can seriously derail them from achieving their goals if they cannot manage it successfully. Looking for ways to minimize—not eliminate, because you can't—stress and to maximize balance in your life will make your college experience more enjoyable and successful.

Disarm the Negative Effects of Stress

Because you cannot eliminate all stress, you will need to develop methods for reducing the negative effects that your body and mind experience when they are stressed out. One of the quickest, easiest ways to reduce the negative effects of stress is to take a deep breath. You may have even told someone who was upset to breathe deeply in order to calm down. The breath is, as many cultures have known for thousands of years, an important part of life; for example, in yoga, the ability to control the breath is essential to controlling the mind and body and to bringing fresh air to the lungs and other organs.

Visualization is another method for reducing the effect that stress has on the mind and body. In order to visualize a more relaxed time and place, all you need to do is to find a quiet, comfortable spot, sit down, and close your eyes. Relaxation experts suggest that you visualize a place that makes you feel warm and relaxed. Many people think about a beach, because the mood there is often relaxed and the sound of the ocean is comforting. You will need to find your own special place.

Once you decide where you want to go mentally, you should start noticing the details in your place. If you are at the beach, then you should feel the sunshine's heat. Next, listen to the waves crashing on the surf and smell the salty air. Depending on how long you need to visualize this special place, you may want to stick your toe in the water or lie down on the beach and soak up the rays—leave your stress in those designated beach trash cans. The goal in this method of relaxation is to stay there as long as you need to; when you mentally return to your present location, you should feel refreshed and renewed.

Sometimes physical activity can be a better stress reliever than mental exercises. Getting outside or to the gym to work out your frustrations and stress is an excellent way of maintaining your health. By exercising, you can eliminate the physical side effects of stress while you take your mind off your troubles. If you do not usually exercise, take it slowly. Start with a 15-minute walk around the block, or do some simple stretching exercises on the floor. Overdoing exercise can lead to more stress, so start small and increase the time you spend getting your blood circulating as you get stronger.

If you happen to exercise too much, you can look toward massage therapy to reduce your stress. Although it is a little less conventional than other methods of reducing stress, a massage can improve circulation and alleviate muscle soreness. You can seek professional massage therapy or ask a family member to rub your neck, shoulders, or feet. Massage therapy can give you the rejuvenation you need to tackle the rest of the week.

You have heard the cliché that "Laughter is the best medicine," and it is also an ideal way to eliminate stress. Have you ever been in a very stressful situation when someone made you laugh and you thought, "Boy, I needed that"? You probably felt all the tension melt away as you doubled over giggling. Surrounding yourself with people who make you laugh is one way to keep stress at a minimum. Other ways include renting comedies or reading funny books. Of course, good, old-fashioned acting silly can relieve stress and anxiety as well.

Last, you can comfort yourself with familiar favorites to eliminate the negative effects of stress. A special meal or a visit with your best friend can put you at ease. Looking at old photographs, reminiscing about family trips, and watching your favorite movies can be great stress relievers. If you have enrolled in college in a new town or you have moved out on your own for the first time, you may find comfort in the familiar, whether it is an old pillow or a favorite movie. Make sure, though, that your methods of reducing negative stress

©RICHARD GREEN/ALAMY

Find time to incorporate fun activities to help you manage your stress.

are healthy. Drugs and alcohol may temporarily relieve stress, but they cause more problems in the long run.

Reducing negative stress that you experience on the job, at home, and in college will be easier if the lines of communication are open and you are committed to explaining what is stressing you out. On the job, you may want to talk to your supervisor (rather than coworkers, unless they can truly help) about what is causing you stress and how you can manage it. You may find that your boss can reassure you that you are supported as you juggle both work and college. At home, you may want to talk with your family members about what stresses you out and why. Explain that your college career is temporary and that adjustments that need to be made at home will most likely be temporary until you complete your degree. If you are experiencing stress in college, speaking with a professor or a counselor can help you reduce the negative effects of stress. Remember that the people who work at a college were students, too, and may have some good tips that helped them minimize stress when they were in college.

Flexibility Can Help Minimize Stress

An important method of managing stress is to remain flexible. If you try to control too many aspects of your life, you will quickly discover you can't do it all. Although it is important to manage your time and mark your progress toward your goals, you still need to plan for the unexpected and be willing to make adjustments. Good time managers plan for problems by keeping their schedules loose enough to make room for adjustments. For example, if you have a doctor's appointment at 2:00, you shouldn't schedule a job interview at 3:00. Delays in the doctor's office or traffic problems could keep you from your 3:00 appointment and cause more stress, just like with Evan. Instead, you should give yourself plenty of time between scheduled tasks, especially if you will have to rely on others' time management skills. The idea is to build some margin in your life so you have a buffer to absorb the so-called "unexpected" events in our lives that we can actually expect. This margin can be in the form of time—giving yourself time to

INTEGRITY *Matters*

Have you ever promised someone that you would do something, only to break your promise? No matter why we break promises, the end result always causes us some stress in our lives because such actions, or inactions, can damage our relationships with others.

One way to eliminate stress and anxiety is to make integrity a top priority in your life. Only promise what you know you can deliver, and your negative stress will be less when you maintain your integrity.

YOUR TURN

In approximately 250 words, describe a time when you have let someone down by not delivering on a promise. Discuss how you felt about not honoring your word and how your relationship changed afterward.

handle a traffic jam or a full parking lot to make it to class—or money—setting aside some money each month for an emergency fund to cover the flat tires, lost books, and parking tickets that always seem to come out of nowhere. You can also build margins in your relationships by having some candid conversations with your friends, roommates, and loved ones about how you'll need their help and understanding when you're facing a lot of stress in your life. Simply forewarning your roommates or family that you have a challenging comprehensive exam next week can help them anticipate and effectively manage the situation if you seem more irritable or impatient than usual.

Seek Help for Your Stress If It Becomes Overwhelming

If you ever feel as though you cannot cope with the amount of work and responsibility that you have—despite attempts to reduce your stress—seek professional help. Excessive crying, difficulty breathing, inability to get out of bed, and suicidal thoughts are severe reactions to stress. Knowing when to reach out to other people will be crucial in your recovery.

When asking for help, find someone you trust and who will be objective about your experiences. Sometimes, close friends and family members can be your best allies to combat stress, but other times, an outside party, who will listen to what you have to say without judging, can be extremely helpful. When you talk to someone, be honest about what you are feeling. Don't try to minimize any fear or anxiety. The more the person knows about what you are experiencing, the better able he or she will be to help. Most universities have professional counselors with whom you can meet to share your experiences. Check with your health center or student affairs office if you can't locate contact information on the college website.

Choose something that is causing you negative stress, and create a list of three action items that will help you reduce it.

YOUR PHYSICAL HEALTH MATTERS A LOT IN COLLEGE

Think about this scenario: You have just bought a brand-new car and you are about to drive it off the lot. Before you do, the salesperson provides you with an owner's manual and begins to tell you how often you will need to fill the tank, replace the oil, check the brakes, and rotate the tires. You tell the salesperson you don't need to know any of that stuff, and you drive the car off the lot. Besides, you know that the car needs to be filled up whenever the light on the dashboard comes on. What else is there to know?

For those who own and drive cars, you can imagine what will happen next. One day, maybe in a few months or a few years, you will find the car stops working regularly or stops working at all. In some cases, the repairs are minimal; in other cases, major repairs must be made to get the car into shape. The costs could be astronomical, so much so that you find yourself without a car and without hope for getting another one any time soon.

Now, consider that the car is your body. You know when you are hungry and when you are tired, when you feel happy and when you are stressed, but do you know how to take care of yourself? Maybe you do know that exercising will improve your health and help you manage your stress, but you won't make the time to include fitness as a part of your weekly routine. Just as a car may drive well for a while without regularly scheduled maintenance, there will come a day that the neglect will keep it from running properly or at all.

Learning to take care of your physical and mental health is crucial to getting where you want to go. To continue the car analogy, you won't be arriving at your destination if the vehicle is not in proper working order. One of the benefits of higher education, as stated earlier, is that you learn to make better choices, and that includes making better choices about your health. You can do that by understanding what you can control and how to get information to stay physically and mentally healthy.

Nutrition Gives You Fuel

One key to living a healthy life is making it a priority to eat nutritious food. Getting the recommended daily allowances of fruits, vegetables, whole grains, proteins, and fats is a commonsense approach to healthy eating, but as a society, we are choosing less healthy foods that are quick and easy—and loaded with calories, fat, salt, and sugar. Some of the reasons for poor nutritional choices include lack of time, too little information, and limited access to healthy alternatives. Increased stress is another reason that students make poor food choices; they may choose comfort food over nutritious alternatives.

To make healthier choices, arm yourself with information. As with any aspect of your health, the more you know, the better choices you can make. Learn what healthy foods are and seek them out. Read about and pay attention to serving sizes; too much of even a healthy food can add unneeded calories and contribute to weight gain. Read and learn to interpret food labels and ingredient lists that provide information about what is in the food and how much of it represents recommended daily values. The U.S. Food and Drug Administration (2011) provides detailed information on its Web page "How to Understand and Use the Nutrition Facts Label," which can be accessed at http://www.fda.gov/food/labelingnutrition/consumerinformation/ucm078889.htm. It provides helpful information about what percentages of fat, sodium, and sugars you should limit.

Another way of getting nutritional information is to talk with a physician or a nutritionist to get a better idea of what kinds of food will be best for you to consume. Regular doctor visits will determine if you have any potential health risks, such as high blood pressure or diabetes, which will make your food decisions even more crucial to good health. Keeping chronic illnesses in check with monitoring and medication will not only help you feel better, but it will also keep you healthy for the long term.

Making good food choices is the foundation for overall good health.

©JUSTIN SULLIVAN/GETTY IMAGES

Eating healthy means eating regularly. Most experts recommend eating smaller meals more frequently, rather than heavy meals five to seven hours apart. At the very least, start the day with a healthy breakfast, even if you don't have enough time to sit down and eat a full meal (Zellman, 2011). You will feel more alert and energized throughout the early morning. However, what you eat for breakfast is just as important as eating something. Powdered doughnuts and a sugary, caffeinated soda will not provide you with the nutrients you need to be at your best. A piece of fruit and a cup of yogurt, for example, would be a better choice if you have to eat on the run. In addition to smaller, frequent, nutritious meals, drinking plenty of water throughout the day has numerous health benefits, including regulating body temperature and assisting digestion, but you should also consider drinking juices to get more nutrients (Zellman, 2011).

Avoiding fad diets is another strategy for staying healthy. Although they may promise increased energy and weight loss, the results may be short lived and potentially harmful. A better approach to eating healthy is to stick to the recommended guidelines from the Food and Drug Administration or a health expert. Be aware, too, of the potential for eating disorders, such as anorexia and bulimia. Anorexia, a condition in which people strictly control how much food they eat, and bulimia, a condition in which people cycle between overeating (binge-eating) in a short amount of time and then purging (through vomiting or abusing laxatives), are two eating disorders that can cause serious physical and psychological harm. Students who suffer from anorexia or bulimia, or believe they do, should see a health professional as soon as possible. The website nationaleatingdisorders.org provides definitions of eating disorders as well as a helpline for those who need to talk to an expert.

Why should you be concerned about what you eat and how much you eat? One benefit of eating healthy is that it improves your body's functions. You may find that eating better improves your ability to sleep or reduces the fatigue you feel by the end of the day. Eating well also improves your mental abilities. Studies have shown that eating certain foods, such as fish, can improve your test-taking abilities. Finally, eating healthy and avoiding overeating helps keep stress under control, which in turn keeps stress-related illnesses at a minimum. See Exhibit 5.3 for tips.

EXHIBIT 5.3 Tips for Healthy Eating in College

Find and read reliable information about health issues.

Eat consciously and take time to appreciate the nourishment you are receiving from healthy foods.

Plan your meals and snacks ahead of time so that you are not susceptible to last-minute, poor choices.

Take bottled water in your backpack, and drink it throughout the day.

Take healthy snacks with you to eat between classes to avoid making unhealthy choices at the vending machines or at the student union.

Pay attention to serving sizes, and eat what you need to stay healthy, not the amount that you want to eat.

Make wise choices at vending machines by avoiding food that is high in fat, caffeine, sugar, and salt content.

Make any changes gradually; think long-term health, not short-term results.

Exercise Gives You Energy and Relieves Stress

We all know that making good choices about nutrition and exercise is part of a healthy lifestyle, but busy students often find it difficult to squeeze in time to work out. Take into consideration that as a student, you will spend many hours sitting down studying or working on the computer. Even if you have had a regular exercise routine, you may find that you have to make studying a higher priority.

Because you may have less time for exercise, it will be even more important that you find time to include some exercise in your busy schedule because of the numerous health benefits. At the very least, getting regular exercise will help you relieve stress.

Regular exercise can lower blood pressure, increase your metabolism, improve muscle tone, and lessen your chances of suffering diseases that are directly related to a sedentary lifestyle. It can also improve your mood and your self-confidence. Experts vary on how much exercise is ideal, but most agree 30 minutes of sustained activity three or four times a week will provide you with health benefits.

If you have trouble getting started or staying in an exercise routine, consider setting fitness goals that are reasonable and achievable. Reward yourself whenever you meet your goals, and don't get discouraged if you fall short now and then. Exercising regularly should be a lifestyle, not a short-term activity, so think of your progress as part of a long-term plan to live better. As with any exercise program, see a doctor before you begin and start gradually if you are not usually physically active.

Some students feel like it's not worth the time to work out if they can't be in the gym for an hour or more. Once their schedules get busy, especially during midterms and finals, those one- and two-hour time slots quickly disappear. The truth is that even if you only have 20 minutes, you can engage in a worthwhile physical activity that can improve your health and relieve stress. You can also do interval training, or "alternating bursts of intense activity with intervals of lighter activity," such as incorporating short bursts of running into your walking (Mayo Clinic, 2011). Varying the activities, length, and intensity of your workout will keep boredom at bay and help you keep it up. See Exhibit 5.4 for tips for exercising while balancing your college work.

USING TECHNOLOGY TO GET AHEAD

The Internet provides many quality resources for maintaining your health and wellness. Seek sound face-to-face medical advice from your physician if you have a serious health issue.

RECOMMENDED SITES

- http://www.choosemyplate.gov: This website provides important nutritional information and allows you to analyze your diet and make a personalized plan for eating healthy.
- http://www.mayoclinic.com/health/stress-management/MY00435: The Mayo Clinic provides resources for minimizing the negative effects of stress.
- http://www.webmd.com/fitness-exercise/guide/default.htm: WebMD offers exercising information for everyone, including the beginner.

Sleep Recharges Your Batteries

Getting an adequate amount of sleep each night is as important to maintaining good health as what you eat and how often you exercise, but most people in the United States, especially college students, do not get enough sleep to maintain their health. Experts say that adults should get seven to nine hours of sleep a night to function normally throughout the day, but millions regularly get six hours or less. While you are in college, you may believe that six hours a night sounds like a luxury as you juggle your multiple responsibilities. For sure, there will be times that, because of circumstances, you will not be able to get enough sleep, but those times should be

EXHIBIT 5.4 Tips for Exercising in College

Take a physical education class at your college.

Use the exercise facilities and equipment on your campus.

Take advantage of walking trails or paved walkways on your campus.

Park farther away from the buildings and get extra steps in.

Join a gym and go regularly.

Ask a friend to exercise with you.

Incorporate short sessions of exercise into your studying routine by taking walking or stretching breaks in between reading or writing papers.

Learn how to play a new sport, or investigate a new form of exercise.

few and far between. Maintaining a regular schedule of going to bed and getting up will help you get the amount of sleep you need. Despite the myth of what college life is like, pulling all-nighters to study for tests and complete assignments is strongly discouraged, because it will make you less likely to perform well the next day.

For some students, the idea of keeping a regular sleeping and waking schedule seems impossible because of other factors that limit their ability to sleep. The reasons for many students' sleep deprivation are varied, but may include health problems, such as breathing obstructions and stress. If you believe your lack of sleep is the result of a medical problem, consider seeing a health care professional. For stress-related sleep problems, practicing the stress-relieving strategies discussed earlier in this chapter will help alleviate the symptoms; however, if you find that relaxation techniques do not improve your ability to sleep well, then consider seeing a general practitioner or mental health professional for issues regarding stress.

What you put into your body can affect your sleeping habits. Eating high-fat and high-sugar foods near bedtime can slow you down, even if they seem to speed you up at first. Good sleep can also elude you if you consume alcohol and caffeine—even in small amounts—close to the time that you go to bed. Drugs, including medications for common illnesses, can deprive you of sleep or make you feel sluggish after you take them. Avoid consuming food, drink, or medications that overstimulate or make you drowsy right before bedtime. Never abuse prescription or over-the-counter medications or illegal drugs to stay awake.

In addition to what you put into your body, what you do to it will affect your ability to get a good night's rest. Exercising too close to bedtime will make it harder to fall asleep. However, too little physical exertion during the day can also contribute to difficulty falling and staying asleep. Experts suggest exercising early in the day—an activity as easy as walking for 30 minutes will suffice—in order to sleep more productively at night. Regular exercise will also help you alleviate the negative effects of stress. If you find, though, that you cannot "shut off" your mind because thoughts overwhelm you, consider writing down your worries—anything you may stay up thinking about after the light is off—in a journal, which will help you unwind and put away your day's thoughts.

BUZZ

Q I have heard about the "Freshman 15," and I have noticed I have put on some weight since I have been in college. What can I do to avoid gaining more weight and maybe even lose some?

A Gaining weight in college doesn't have to happen if you plan ahead and make your health a top priority. Here are some tips for avoiding packing on the pounds:

- Talk to your physician or a health provider at your college before doing anything.

- Plan your meals before you are hungry. Find out what healthy choices are available to you, and commit to eating them most of the time.

- Pack healthy snacks and avoid vending machine junk food.

- Park farther away and walk more. Find ways to incorporate exercise throughout the day.

- Check out the college health center or physical activity opportunities.

Because sleep deprivation can contribute to irritability, depression, and physical health problems, it is important to make getting enough sleep a priority throughout the semester. If you have difficulty sticking to a regular sleep schedule, treat it like any other goal and write down what you want to do. Make it easier to achieve your goal by keeping your bed and bedroom free of clutter and by avoiding using your bed as a place to do homework or watch television. In other words, creating a sanctuary in your bedroom, a place where you can truly relax, may alleviate stress and anxiety that contribute to sleeplessness. Finally, avoid taking naps during the day, even on weekends, because they can throw off your sleep schedule. If you have an irregular schedule because of working different hours each day of the week, find a system that is relatively regular and that works for you. You may have to be creative about how you get enough sleep each evening or day.

The bottom line is that sleep deprivation can be dangerous and deadly. How little sleep you get should not be a medal of honor that demonstrates how much you work or how dedicated you are to meeting your goals. Getting enough sleep is a necessary part of living well, enjoying what you do accomplish, and being enjoyable to be around when you are awake.

Drugs and Alcohol Can Quickly Derail Your Health and Life

There are some habits that we know are potentially hazardous to our health, yet some people still do them. Smoking and using tobacco products, taking drugs, and consuming too much alcohol are known risks, but college students sometimes pick up these poor health habits because of peer pressure, a desire to fit in, and a need to find a way to relax or escape.

According to the American Heart Association (2008), about a quarter of Americans smoke, and people with the least education (9–11 years in school) are more likely to smoke than people with more education (more than 16 years in school). Smoking or chewing tobacco carries with it increased risks of heart disease, stroke, high blood pressure, cancer, and emphysema. The more educated you become about the health risks that are associated with smoking and using smokeless tobacco, the more it will be obvious that using tobacco products can cause serious health consequences. There are a variety of methods for quitting; it is worth investigating what your college and community offers if you are a smoker or a user of smokeless tobacco. Your college may provide information, support groups, or physician referrals for students who want to quit.

Alcohol and drugs are two other health issues that affect college students—sometimes even before they get to college. Having parents, partners, or friends who have abused drugs or alcohol is one way students can be affected. They may feel that they have to take care of others who drink too much or take drugs, which can take a toll on their time and emotional well-being. Students may also suffer from abusing drugs and alcohol while in college—and the effects can be far reaching. According to Facts on Tap (2008), a website that offers drug and alcohol education and prevention information, 159,000 first-year college students will drop out of college because of issues related to drug and alcohol abuse.

Being drunk or high can have grave consequences, the least of which is that you will do something you later regret. You increase your risk of having an unwanted sexual experience and causing physical harm to yourself and others. Death from overdosing on drugs and alcohol can happen, even for those who are first-time users. Whether they are consumed for recreational purposes or because of other more serious health reasons, abusing drugs and alcohol should not be a part of your college career because you will find it more difficult to reach your educational and personal goals. See Exhibit 5.5 for guidance on avoiding drugs and alcohol.

In addition to abusing alcohol and illegal substances, using medications for purposes other than for what they were prescribed can have grave consequences, including death. Excessive use of medications that contain amphetamines and narcotics may seem like a good idea at first if you have trouble staying awake or going to sleep, but using them for a longer period than they have been prescribed can lead to dependency.

Yes, We Do Need to Talk about Sex

A discussion of health issues would not be complete without talking about sexual health. Most colleges and universities strive to educate their students, especially those who are recently out of high school, about sexual responsibility, sexual assault, and common sexually transmitted diseases (STDs). Many experts and college officials have been alarmed at the recent statistics that show 73% of students report having unprotected sex while they are in college. More disturbing is that 68% of those having unprotected sex do not consider themselves at risk (Gately, 2003). This last statistic points to a major reason that

---

EXHIBIT 5.5 **Tips for Avoiding Drugs and Alcohol in College**

Educate yourself about the effects of abusing drugs and alcohol.

Cultivate relationships with people who have healthy habits.

Avoid situations in which you know drugs and alcohol will be present.

Take walking breaks instead of smoking breaks.

Find other ways to relax that are healthy, free, and legal.

Talk with a counselor or health care professional if you feel you are about to make a poor decision regarding the use of drugs and alcohol.

Appeal to your vanity, if all else fails: Drugs, alcohol, and tobacco make you look and smell bad.

students, despite sex education in high school or elsewhere, continue to engage in risky sexual behavior. Because most STDs lack immediate visible or physiological symptoms, students who are at risk for contracting a sexually transmitted disease rarely ask to be screened for signs of infection.

Risky behavior, which includes having sex with multiple partners and having unprotected sex, opens the door to possible infections and illnesses such as chlamydia, gonorrhea, genital herpes, HIV, and AIDS (see Exhibit 5.6). Some diseases can be transmitted in ways other than sexual intercourse. Hepatitis B and C are both diseases that can be contracted through shared razors, toothbrushes, body piercings, and tattooing.

If you are sexually active, it is important to be screened regularly for STDs even if you do not have symptoms. Your long-term health and the health of those you come in contact with are at risk if you do not. As with any health issue, educate yourself with the facts about risk factors and symptoms. Then, monitor your behavior, practice safe sex, and see a doctor regularly to maintain good health.

Sexual assaults in the college environment are a troubling phenomenon that you shouldn't ignore. Some of the most common incidents of sexual assault are related to excessive consumption of alcohol and date rapes, which involve two people who actually know each other. The Rape, Abuse, and Incest National Network (RAINN) provides

EXHIBIT 5.6 Common Sexually Transmitted Diseases

STD	Symptoms	Treatment
HIV and AIDS	May have no symptoms; extreme fatigue, rapid weight loss	No cure, but prescribed medication can keep the virus from replicating
Chlamydia	May have no symptoms; abnormal discharge, burning during urination	Antibiotics
Genital herpes	May have no symptoms; itching, burning, bumps in the genital area	No cure, but prescribed medication can help treat outbreaks
Gonorrhea	Pain or burning during urination; yellowish or bloody discharge; men may have no symptoms	Antibiotics
Hepatitis B	Headache, muscle ache, fatigue, low-grade fever, skin and whites of eyes with yellowish tint	No cure, but prescribed medication can help guard against liver damage

numerous resources that students can use to educate themselves about the risks, consequences, and preventive actions. Some important tips for reducing your chances of being involved in such a tragedy, and for helping others avoid risky situations, include the following:

- Be aware of your surroundings at all times. This means take out earphones and avoid talking on your phone when walking, and pay attention to where you are hanging out and who is there.
- Walk tall. Act confident and self-assured when you are moving from one place to another. RAINN calls it "walk[ing] with a purpose."
- Listen to your "little voice." If you feel uncomfortable in a situation or environment, remove yourself. You often know best when something is not right.

One particular type of unhealthy relationship that occurs most frequently among traditional college students is date or acquaintance rape. Simply defined, date rape is a forced sexual act in which one party does not actively consent; often, the two people involved are not complete strangers—hence the terms "date rape" and "acquaintance rape." Both men and women can be victims of date rape, although women are more often victims. Alcohol or a date rape drug such as Rohypnol may be involved in the incident. Many experts warn college-age women and men about the risk factors for date rape and encourage them to get to know who they are going out with, to not get intoxicated, to make sure their food or drinks are not handled by others, and to communicate loud and clear if they find themselves in an uncomfortable situation.

Depression and Suicide Are Sad but Real Occurrences in College

The pressures to succeed and juggle multiple priorities can lead to negative stress and feelings of being overwhelmed. Many times, feeling a little stressed during the semester is normal, but there are times that students can feel as though they are in over their heads, with no hope of getting out. It is no wonder that one of the most common mental health issues on any college campus is depression.

Problems with depression often start before students enroll in college: "Students arrive already having started various medications for depression, anxiety and attention deficit disorders" (Schoenherr, 2004). Signs of depression include loss of pleasure in activities, feelings of hopelessness, inability to get out of bed, increased use of alcohol or drugs, changes in appetite or weight gain or loss, changes in sleep patterns (sleeping too little or too much), extreme sensitivity, excessive crying, lack of energy or interest in participating in activities, and lack of interest in taking care of oneself.

Suicide is another mental health issue that is associated with depression. With the startling statistic that 25% of college students have contemplated suicide, it is no wonder that college health and counseling centers strive to educate students about the signs of severe depression and potential suicide attempts. Thoughts of ending your life should always be taken seriously, and you should seek help immediately. Call a college counselor, an advisor, a hospital emergency room, or 911 if you are thinking about committing suicide. If one of your friends or roommates exhibits any behaviors or says anything that implies suicidal thoughts, do everything you can to put them in contact with professionals on campus or at the local hospital who can help.

HEALTHY LIVING IS A CHOICE YOU MAKE FOR LIFE

There is more to life than just eating well and exercising. Healthy living is a practice that involves all parts of your well being: physical, mental, and spiritual.

A Balanced Life Is a Healthy Life

Living a balanced life means paying attention to and improving all areas of your life—from relationships to cardiovascular health to your inner peace. If one area is overdeveloped, then the other areas will suffer from the lack of balance. There will be times that you will need to put in more hours at work and school, throwing the balance off slightly, but be careful that you make some time for the other areas that have been neglected.

A great way to stay balanced is to strive to create relationships with people on campus. Having healthy relationships with professors, advisors, and classmates will not only enable you to stay connected with your college work, but it will also provide you a personal support network in case you feel as though you need help with the stresses of being in college.

Balancing your life to eliminate stress also entails evaluating your values and priorities whenever you begin to feel stressed. You can then identify areas in your life that are getting out of balance and put those areas higher up on your list of priorities. For example, if you value exercise and are stressed because you realize that you have been spending most of your time at work or at school, you can make working out a higher priority, creating better balance in your life.

Relationships Impact Your Health

Maintaining healthy relationships is as much a part of your good health as eating nutritious foods and exercising, but there are some issues that are signs of unhealthy, even dangerous, relationships. One type of unhealthy relationship issue is abuse: physical, mental, verbal, and sexual. Being in a relationship with someone who is abusive is not healthy. Although the previous statement sounds like common sense, take time to think about it. No one deserves to be hit, controlled, or humiliated, ever.

Although we know that someone who makes us feel bad physically or emotionally can prevent us from being our best, studies find that abused men and women find it difficult to get out of abusive relationships. One reason people stay with abusive partners

Incorporating regular exercise into your routine will help you alleviate some of the negative effects of stress.

is that the abusers are—at first—charming, attentive, and loving. Usually, abusers begin to show subtle signs that something is not right; they may be extremely jealous, verbally insulting, and focused on your every move. Victims may also be dependent financially or emotionally on their abusers, which makes eliminating their influence difficult.

Maintaining a healthy relationship takes time and energy, but there are many ways to make sure your relationships are positive experiences. For example, get to know people well before spending time alone with them. Learn to communicate your wants and needs effectively. Say "no" loud and clear when you do not want something to happen. Watch for signs of abusive and controlling people; sometimes, people show you signs of their true selves in smaller, subtler ways early in a relationship. If a situation makes you uncomfortable, get out of it immediately. Last but not least, do not abuse alcohol and drugs, which can impair your ability to judge situations. If you feel as though you have no options in removing yourself from an abusive relationship, seek professional help.

For most of your relationships, communication will be key to balance and satisfaction. Whether it is your family, friends, roommates, or significant others, you will want to be an advocate for your own feelings and needs and to express them in a respectful manner. Learning to listen actively and critically will also help you strengthen relationships. Good, solid relationships are built on honesty, communication, and a healthy respect for others' physical and emotional well-being.

Getting Help When You Need It

An important part of making good choices and staying healthy is to get regular check-ups and to see a health professional whenever you experience pain, difficulty, or even uncertainty about a health issue. Your college may provide access to a health clinic or health fairs. Free screenings, health seminars, and dispensing of over-the-counter medications are possible services that your college clinic may offer. Take advantage of these types of services, such as blood pressure checks or information about handling diabetes, because they may provide you with life-improving or life-saving information. If your college provides only limited access to health services, then you will need to find other ways to monitor your health. Regular checkups are part of taking care of yourself, both in the short term and the long term.

60-second PAUSE

How do you rate the health of your relationships? Is there a relationship that you can improve? What tips from above will you use to strengthen that relationship?

from COLLEGE

to UNIVERSITY

How Your Stress Will Change and How to Handle the New Pressures

There are many possible stressors awaiting you when you make that move from your community college to university. For example, your professors will be asking more from you academically. To meet the challenges that await you, be honest about them. In addition, recognize the fact that you will be graduating in just a few semesters and that you should plan for life after school. With some work—and the good habits you form at your community college—you can overcome stress with the same success.

Regardless of the new challenges, once you transfer, you will be making connections with people whom you hope will help you get a job after college. Along with your family, these relationships can provide you with a system for handling the demands of a four-year university. Practice stress-reducing activities regularly; you will then be more relaxed and more confident in your abilities.

©SHUTTERSTOCK

from COLLEGE

to CAREER

Making Healthy Lifestyle Changes Is a Good Long-Term Strategy

The purpose of making better choices should be a long-term strategy to create a better life for you and your family. After graduation, you may have to change the time or place that you work out. Maintaining healthy relationships with those who have positive influences on your life is one way to keep stress levels at a minimum and to create a safety net of friends and family when you may need them. Avoiding drugs, alcohol, and other poor health choices will be crucial to performing your best on the job.

Because of the importance of good health, some employers have made healthy choices a top priority. Talk with the human resources department about what your company offers its employees to support healthy habits. They may offer free screening, free or reduced-cost vaccinations, time off for doctors' appointments, health insurance, discounted gym memberships, and planned physical activities.

©ISTOCKPHOTO

UNDERSTAND & REMEMBER

Review Questions

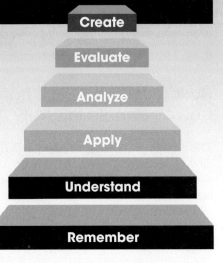

1. What are the different ways students can incorporate exercise into their busy schedules?

2. What are the major health issues that college students face?

3. What can students do if they find themselves in an unhealthy relationship?

4. What are some of the effects for a student who makes poor health choices during a semester?

APPLY & ANALYZE

Critical Thinking

1. What stress-relieving techniques are most helpful to you and why? How will you be sure to find time to relieve stress while you are in college? What possible effects will not managing your stress have on you?

2. When you have a conflict with a person, what can you do to make sure the relationship remains healthy and open?

3. What health issues would you like to work on this semester? How do you intend to make time for working on them? What changes in your lifestyle and time management do you intend to make and why?

EVALUATE

Case Scenarios

1. Vin-Singh has been having trouble sleeping since he started college. He shares an apartment with another student who likes to stay up late and play loud music. Vin-Singh eats well and avoids caffeinated drinks, but he does not exercise regularly and often feels anxious when he tries to sleep. He has a research paper due in one week and a final exam that is worth 50% of his overall grade that he must take in three days. Because he has not been able to sleep well, he has been feeling overwhelmed by what he has left to do before the semester is over. A friend suggested that he get some power energy drinks and caplets to get him through the last week and promised him that once he finishes his final assignment, he will be back to feeling better. Vin-Singh gets the energy boosters and starts taking them.

   Use the following scale to rate the decision that has been made (1 = Poor Decision, 5 = Excellent Decision). Be prepared to explain your answer.

   Poor Decision ←——(1)——————(2)——————(3)——————(4)——————(5)——→ Excellent Decision

2. Wanda has not exercised since she was in high school, and now, 20 years later, she sees the importance of improving her health. In fact, she wonders if the 30 pounds she has gained since high school are keeping her from feeling her best as she juggles the demands of college. She is about to start her last year in college, one that will be stressful for her as she takes classes that will help her pass a nursing licensing exam and get a good job. She also wants to lose the weight and start an aggressive exercise program. Wanda has decided to start lifting weights three times a week, running four times a week, and restricting her calories to 1,200 a day.

Use the following scale to rate the decision that has been made (1 = Poor Decision, 5 = Excellent Decision). Be prepared to explain your answer.

Poor Decision ← ① — ② — ③ — ④ — ⑤ → Excellent Decision

3. Ever since D.J. started college, he has focused on his studies and has cut out all activities that do not help him achieve his educational goals. He has told his friends that he won't be able to hang out with them; he has cut back on his hours at work; he has stopped playing basketball and running; he has even stopped attending religious services so that he can have time to take as many class hours as possible each semester. He wants to graduate with a degree as fast as he can and start working, and his grades are good. Although he has been feeling depressed and tired most days, he knows that these feelings are short-term and that he will return to his routine after he completes his degree. He has 10 months left before he reaches his goal of graduating.

Use the following scale to rate the decision that has been made (1 = Poor Decision, 5 = Excellent Decision). Be prepared to explain your answer.

Poor Decision ← ① — ② — ③ — ④ — ⑤ → Excellent Decision

CREATE

Research It Further

1. Studies have shown that community college students have higher rates of depression and suicide than students at four-year universities. Do you think this is true? After interviewing your classmates or surveying a number of students, record the various reasons that this may be true; then create a list of local resources that could help such students at your institution.

2. Search the Internet for national statistics regarding violence against college students. Determine what groups are more likely to experience physical and sexual abuse. Inform your class of your findings.

3. What does your college offer in terms of health care for its students? Create a list of services and events, along with contact numbers for community services that students may need. Present your list to your classmates.

TAKE THIS WITH YOU

Based on the goals we set at the beginning of this chapter, here's how you can take this learning with you toward college success:

- Identify which stressors you presently experience and which you can reasonably anticipate this semester.

- Create a plan to reduce stress in your life.

- Start working on health issues that are important to you.

- Develop a personal approach to maintain balance in your overall health.

REFERENCES AND RECOMMENDED READINGS

American Heart Association. (2009). Cigarette smoking statistics. Retrieved from www.americanheart.org/presenter.jhtml?identifier=4559

Facts on Tap. (2009). Alcohol and student life. Retrieved from www.factsontap.org/factsontap/alcohol_and_student_life/index.htm

Gately, G. (2003, August 23). College students ignoring risks of unprotected sex. *Health Day News*. Retrieved from www.hon.ch/News/HSN/514968.html

Mayo Clinic. Interval training: Can it boost your calorie-burning power? Retrieved from http://www.mayoclinic.com/health/interval-training/SM00110

RAINN. (2011). Reducing your risk of sexual assault. Retrieved from http://www.rainn.org/get-information/sexual-assault-prevention

Schoenherr, N. (2004). Depression, suicide are the major health issues facing college students, says student health director. *News & Information, Washington University–St. Louis*. Retrieved from news-info.wustl.edu/tips/page/normal/4198.html

U.S. Food and Drug Administration. (2011). How to understand and use the nutrition facts label. Retrieved from http://www.fda.gov/food/labelingnutrition/consumerinformation/ucm078889.html

Zellman, K. M. (2011). 10 ways to lose weight without dieting: Simple changes to your lifestyle can help you lose weight and keep it off. *WebMD*. Retrieved from http://www.webmd.com/diet/features/10-ways-to-lose-weight-without-dieting

MyStudentSuccessLab

MyStudentSuccessLab (www.mystudentsuccesslab.com) is an online solution designed to help you 'Start strong, Finish stronger' by building skills for ongoing personal and professional development.

6 Learning, Memory, and Thinking

Michael can hike 12 miles in a hot sandstorm with 30 pounds of equipment on his back. What Michael can't do, he believes, is understand algebra. He is in the right place—the tutoring center—but he doesn't know if he really belongs here.

Inside the student center, Michael sits back down on a chair and opens his math notebook, where he has scrawled a few notes from the last class.

"The order of operations is F-O-I-L: first, outer, inner, last. But after that, I don't know what to do," he thinks to himself.

If his professor would just slow down and allow students to "get it" before moving on to the next unit, he wouldn't feel so stressed.

"Isn't teaching me algebra his job, not a tutor's?" Michael asks himself.

Michael's teenage difficulty in learning, coupled with his military background, makes it difficult for him to seek help on his own. By the time he got to high school, he was able to slide by, and in the military, his superiors ordered everything he did.

Before he decides to leave, his girlfriend Michelle calls him.

"Michael, do you remember when I struggled through biology? I wanted to be a nurse so much, but I didn't think I had what it took if I couldn't pass one of the first classes," she says.

"Yeah, I do. I remember helping you study before tests."

"Do you remember how much better I did after I went to the tutoring center? I found someone who helped me take better notes and organize my studying time."

Michael doesn't say anything in response, but remembers how she struggled. "This may be the only time I will say this," he jokes, "but you are right. I need to see what kind of help I can get."

Michael walks into the tutoring center.

YOUR GOALS FOR THIS CHAPTER

As Michael will find out from his visit to the tutoring center, there are many activities he can do to improve his memory, sharpen his thinking skills, and improve his learning. By the time you finish reading this chapter, you will be able to:

- Progress through the stages of learning to achieve mastery of a skill
- Develop strategies that support active learning
- Use mnemonic devices to improve your memory

- Identify different types of thinking
- Describe techniques for creative thinking
- Describe a process for analytical thinking
- Engage in an effective process for problem solving

MyStudentSuccessLab (www.mystudentsuccesslab.com) is an online solution designed to help you 'Start strong, Finish stronger' by building skills for ongoing personal and professional development.

It seems like there are dozens of bumper stickers and T-shirts that broadcast what people are born to do. "Born to Run," "Born to Shop," and "Born to Boogie" are just a few that you may see. But could you add "Born to Learn" to the list? All of us, researchers say, are indeed born to learn. Babies do it without giving the process any thought. The process is simple: The more you do something, the more you create connections in the brain that not only help you remember how to do something, but also help you get better at whatever it is you are learning to do. This process is called *growing dendrites*. Dendrites are the treelike structures on the ends of neurons, the nerve cells in the brain. The more you practice something, the more those dendrites grow, improving the connections between the neurons in your brain (Exhibit 6.1).

Your Terms for SUCCESS

WHEN YOU SEE . . .	IT MEANS . . .
Acronym	An abbreviation in which the first letters of each word create a short, easy-to-remember word; AIDS is an acronym for acquired immune deficiency syndrome
Acrostic	A mnemonic device in which the first letter of each word in a sentence stands for information or a process; "Please Excuse My Dear Aunt Sally" is an acrostic for the order of operations in solving math equations: Parentheses, Exponents, Multiplication, Division, Addition, Subtraction
Analytical thinking	Breaking apart information and examining its parts
Cerebellum	The region of the brain that controls sensory perception and motor skills
Chunking	A method for remembering information by grouping it together in small chunks
Creative thinking	Thinking that involves generating ideas
Critical thinking	Thinking that involves reviewing information for accuracy, authority, and logic before considering it useable
Dendrite	The branches at the ends of neurons
Long-term memory	Memory that retains information for longer than a few days
Metacognition	Thinking about thinking
Mnemonic device	A method of remembering information
Neuron	A cell in the nervous system
Prefrontal cortex	A region at the front of the brain where complex thinking is believed to occur
Roman Room	Another term for the loci method of memorization
Short-term memory	Memory that retains information for a few hours or a few days

EXHIBIT **6.1** Dendrite Growth

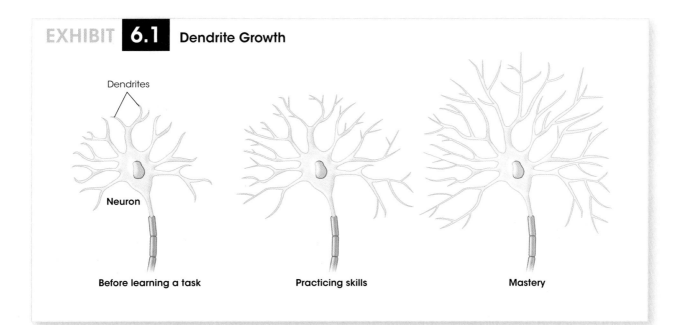

Before learning a task   **Practicing skills**   **Mastery**

If you think about anything that you are good at, you should recognize the same process that you went through to get better and better at it. We often recognize the need to practice sports and musical instruments, but sometimes we don't make the same connections with other skills, such as writing, reading, and math. Michael would feel more confident about seeing a tutor if he realized that learning algebra is a process that requires time for practice, just as he did when he was in the military, practicing and refining his skills at shooting. How much time is needed will be different for different people, but your skills will increase, just as your dendrites will grow.

Learning is a six-stage process, according to Gunn, Richburg, and Smilkstein (2007). The first stage is one that begins with being curious and motivated to learn something new. This could be because you are interested and self-motivated to solve a problem yourself or it could be because you have been assigned a project or task in college or at work and you want to learn more about it. The second stages moves to practicing the skill and learning from mistakes that you make. Feedback--either from yourself or others--will be important at this stage to allow you to see what improvements you need to make. Stages 3 and 4 involve getting more comfortable with the new skill and even taking risks when practicing. For example, if you are learning to play the guitar, by Stages 3 and 4, you will be experimenting with new rhythms and chords. Finally, the Stages 5 and 6 refining the new skill and demonstrating mastery of it. In other words, you will feel that the skill is second nature to you and that you feel comfortable enough with your mastery to teach others the skill (Gunn, Richburg, & Smilkstein, 2007).

It's in the SYLLABUS

By rereading your professors' syllabi and by considering your experiences so far, determine how much time you will need to spend outside of class to meet the goals of each course you are taking.

- Which classes will require the most amount of time? How will you be spending that time?

- What other kinds of learning expectations are there?

- Considering the six stages of learning a new skill, what stages will you need to go through?

Your Mindset Matters!

What happens when you can't get motivated to learn a new skill and make it past the first stage in learning? People who lose interest when learning gets too challenging are described as having a "fixed mindset," while people who thrive when they are being stretched have a "growth mindset." People with a fixed mindset believe that they are either born smart or not, that there is no changing their fixed state of intelligence. People with a growth mindset, on the other hand, believe they can develop talents and skills; even if they fail at a task, they see it as an opportunity to learn more and improve on what they know about the task.

In the story at the beginning of the chapter, you learn that Michael knows how to do many things, which no doubt came from a belief that he could improve on his skills; however, he seems to have a fixed mindset about algebra. Sometimes one bad experience or several in a row can influence how we see ourselves as learners and masters of a skill. Believing in our ability to learn will result in learning and mastery of whatever task we set our "growth" minds to.

We Learn Best When We're Active

How does the information about brain research and learning translate to what you are doing in college? It may be helpful first to identify where, how, and with whom learning can take place. Think about a clock face on which the big hand is pointing to the 12 and the little hand is pointing to the 3—for a 3-credit-hour class, you will be spending three hours learning *inside* the classroom, and the remaining nine hours learning *outside* the classroom (Exhibit 6.2). This means that for every hour you're in class, you need to spend another three hours learning outside class.

©PURESTOCK/ALAMY (RF)

Learning is often more engaging when it is active rather than passive.

You could spend those nine hours a week per class reading the textbook and studying your notes. However, it's helpful to engage in other activities that contribute to learning. Researching and writing papers, completing homework, visiting with your professor during office hours, studying with a classmate or in a group, memorizing terms with flash cards, practicing homework problems, working with a tutor, or tutoring someone else are activities from which you will benefit. Why do you need to do all of that to learn when listening in class, taking notes, and reviewing them before the test worked in high school? The answer is that in college, you will be responsible for more than just memorizing material and restating it on a test or in a paper. Instead, you will be asked to apply (use information in a new situation), analyze (break information down into its parts and examine it), synthesize (create new information based on what you have learned), and evaluate (judge the information), and you will be graded on your ability to do all of those activities well. See Exhibit 6.3 for examples of the types of active learning you will be doing in your college classes.

EXHIBIT 6.2 Learning Inside and Outside of the Classroom

in class

out of class

EXHIBIT 6.3 Active Learning Strategies

Action	Definition	Example
Apply	Use information in a new way or to create a product	Demonstrate by writing and acting out a sketch about how a student may successfully transition into college culture.
Analyze	Break information down into parts and examine each part	Compare and contrast the different ways a student can finance a college education.
Synthesize	Create new information or examine two or more pieces of information	Examine two different views on how to choose a career by discussing each view.
Evaluate	Judge the information	Assess the effectiveness of each of three welding techniques.
Create	Produce, build, or craft a project or object	Design and execute a newsletter for incoming first-year students.

EXHIBIT 6.4 Learning Pyramid

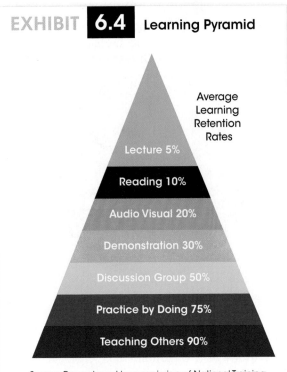

Average Learning Retention Rates

- Lecture 5%
- Reading 10%
- Audio Visual 20%
- Demonstration 30%
- Discussion Group 50%
- Practice by Doing 75%
- Teaching Others 90%

Source: Reproduced by permission of National Training Laboratories, Arlington, VA.

To see an illustration, look at the Learning Pyramid in Exhibit 6.4. Notice that if you listen to a lecture, you will remember only about 5% of the material. In other words, what you hear will be forgotten over time at an enormous rate! What does that mean for students whose instructors rely on lecture to convey information in class? It means that you will need to do more than just listen passively. You may need to record the lecture and listen to it again later, discuss the lecture with classmates, and help others understand it once you have mastered the material. Of course, you may need to read, take notes, and rewrite them as well. The goal for you, regardless of your learning style preference, is to move from learning passively—merely taking in the information through listening or reading—to learning actively—applying, discussing, evaluating, and creating new ideas from the information you hear and read.

60-second PAUSE

You've now learned about growing dendrites, the six stages of the learning process, the importance of having a growth mindset, and the benefits of active learning. What class are you taking this semester that you expect to be really challenging? With this class in mind, how can you apply these concepts to be successful? List at least five ideas. For example, what materials should you bring to class so that you can be an active learner?

ACTIVE LEARNING = DEEP LEARNING

The good news that we've learned from brain research is that spending more time actively learning a subject can translate into deeper learning, and a positive attitude toward challenging learning environments will enable you to learn more. Why? Because as you spend more time studying and engaged in active learning with a positive attitude, you will remember more of what you have learned because you have moved it from your short-term memory to your long-term memory. Memory is divided into two types—short-term memory and long-term memory. When you meet someone for the first time, you will keep that person's name and face in your short-term memory. In general, you can only store five to nine items in your short-term memory. If you try to put too many items in there, you will find that some of them slip away (Miller, 1956). Try this by glancing at the following list for 30 seconds. Then, cover up the list and write down the words you remember in the space provided; the words do not have to be in the order that you see them.

cup	paper	pencil	magnet	ruler	scissors
spoon	towel	tape	apple	knife	straw

_____

_____

_____

How well did you do? If you remembered five to nine items, then you can consider your memory average. It takes some work, though, to transfer information from your short-term memory to your long-term memory.

Your long-term memory is responsible for storing things like names and dates, as well as skills, such as tying your shoe. People can have well-developed memory storage for images (visual), sounds (aural), words (read/write), and processes (kinesthetic).

Modern technologies like computers, smart phones, and ebook readers make it easy for us to have a lot of information at our fingertips. With information so accessible, we might think that it's no longer necessary to memorize anything anymore. The truth is, however, that effective memorization skills are very important to be a successful college student. Quizzes, tests, and other types of examinations are often "closed book," meaning that you can't have your textbook or other materials available during the test. And, because most exams and tests are timed, you wouldn't have enough time to search for information in a book to answer a question, anyway—you either remember the information or you don't. For these reasons, it's very important to develop effective memorization skills.

Memory can be strengthened by participating in mental activities.

©iSTOCKPHOTO

Mnemonic Devices Can Help You Remember

Mnemonic devices are memory aids or strategies that help you remember items, concepts, or series of events. Usually, mnemonic devices are *not* used for deep learning, but there will be times during college when, for example, remembering the names of all the bones in the body or all the constitutional amendments must be conquered before deeper learning can happen. Thus, you may find yourself using mnemonic devices as part of your learning process.

Device 1: The Roman Room

Let's go back to the list of words and figure out how you could remember all of the items. Ancient Romans are credited with being able to remember significant amounts of information by using the Roman Room, or loci method. This visualization technique can be useful when trying to remember a string of seemingly unrelated items or complex material that needs to be pulled together.

To create a Roman Room, visualize a familiar place, such as a room in your house. If your room is connected to other rooms, then you will have more "places" to put ideas. When you visualize your room, pay particular attention to the items that are already in the room, such as furniture or favorite pictures, and unique details, such as peeling paint. The more vivid the visualization, the better able you will be to remember the items you place there.

To see the Roman Room or loci method in action, take another look at the list.

cup	paper	pencil	magnet	ruler	scissors
spoon	towel	tape	apple	knife	straw

Can you place these items in your kitchen? Put the straw in the cup and place it in the cabinet. Tape the paper on the front of the cabinet. Place the towel on the counter next to the apple, spoon, and knife. Then, put the pencil, ruler, magnet, and scissors in the drawer.

Take 30 seconds to review the room above or visualize your own Roman Room with the items listed. Then, cover up both the list and the description of the room and see how many items you can remember. Write the words in the space provided here.

_____

_____

_____

Did you remember more words this time? If not, then visualization strategies may not be the only type of mnemonic device you need to help you remember lots of information. There are other mnemonic strategies that may benefit different learning style preferences. Acrostic sentences and acronyms are two methods that may help students with a read/write learning style preference.

Device 2: Acronyms and Acrostic Sentences

Take the first letters of items in a series to form sentences that help you remember the items and their order, forming acrostic sentences. For example, music students remember the order of the treble clef staff, E, G, B, D, F, with the sentence "Every Good Boy

Does Fine." To recall the order of biological groupings used in taxonomy, just remember "Kids Prefer Cheese Over Fried Green Spinach" (Kingdom, Phylum, Class, Order, Family, Genus, Species).

Take the first letter of items in a series and spell another word to create an acronym. Here are a few examples of acronyms that we use every day: AIDS (acquired immune deficiency syndrome), SADD (Students Against Drunk Driving), REM (rapid eye movement), and SCUBA (self-contained underwater breathing apparatus). Acronyms that have been used to help many students remember terms and the order of items include the following: ROY G BIV (to remember the order of the colors in the rainbow—red, orange, yellow, green, blue, indigo, and violet) and FACE to remember the order of notes in the spaces of the treble staff.

Although there are too many words in the list discussed earlier to create an acronym, you can create an acrostic sentence (or two) with the initial letter of each word. Because the order of the items is not important, feel free to rearrange the letters to make your sentence(s).

| C | P | P | M | R | S | Example: Creative people produce many real skits. |
| S | T | T | A | K | S | |

Device 3: Rhymes and Songs

While a little more difficult to compose than acronyms and acrostics, rhymes and songs, which often appeal to aural learners, are another type of mnemonic device. Who doesn't remember "Thirty days hath September . . . " and "In 1492, Columbus sailed the ocean blue"? Again, simple information works best for these memory strategies. It will take more work to remember the economic effects of Columbus's discovery of the New World, for example.

When you have the time to explore the variety of memory strategies, try them out until you find the one that works best for the subject matter and your learning style. However, many students who need a memory strategy need it to work quickly as they are cramming before a test. Those students may be successful in remembering it when they get to the test the next day, but the possibility of their remembering it weeks, months, or even a year later is slim. That is why professors and tutors discourage students from cramming—it may work some of the time, and it is better than not studying at all for a test, but it often produces more anxiety and stress, and the material is less likely to be in your long-term memory when you need it later.

Device 4: Chunking

With that warning, there will be times, nonetheless, when despite your best intentions, you will need a fail-safe memory technique to help you remember key concepts in a short period of time. One method,

BUZZ

Q If the mnemonic devices you mention only help me to remember stuff for the exam, what good are they?

A These devices can help you get good grades on your exams. If you first memorize concepts and then engage in active learning to really practice and apply them, then they'll move from your short-term to long-term memory. Mnemonic devices also

- Help you look for patterns in material that can be used for later recall.
- Build your confidence in remembering information.
- Serve as the foundation for finding deeper meaning.

TECHNOLOGY *Tips*

called *chunking,* is similar to the Roman Room, or loci method, in that items are grouped together to allow the brain to make connections with the items, making it easier to recall the information later.

To see chunking in action, consider the following 10-digit number:

5114796210

It may be easier to chunk the numbers the way a phone number is divided:

511–479–6210

You probably don't realize that you chunk any time you memorize a phone number or Social Security number. In other words, you are taking the seemingly random numbers and putting them together in groups. The goal in chunking is to reduce a large number of items into only five to nine items. To practice this mnemonic technique, use the following list of key terms: acrostic, acronym, chunking, cramming, loci method, long-term memory, mnemonic device, rhyme, Roman Room, short-term memory, teaching others.

First, make sure that you know the definitions of each term. Record your definition next to each term below:

Acrostic _____

Acronym _____

Chunking _____

Cramming _____

Loci method _____

Long-term memory _____

Mnemonic device _____

Rhyme _____

Roman Room _____

Short-term memory _____

Teaching others _____

Next, group the items together logically. Then, complete the chunking with the remaining terms.

For example, one way to group some of the terms could be:

Mnemonic devices are strategies for remembering items and they include acrostics, acronyms, rhymes, and Roman Rooms.

How else could the terms be grouped together? Use the spaces below to group them.

_____

_____

_____

Look inside one of your textbooks from another class, and locate content (like a list) that you will likely need to memorize for a quiz or test. Then, apply one of the mnemonic devices you've learned from this section to memorize that list.

THINKING IS A SKILL YOU CAN DEVELOP

Think about it. Those are three simple words that you have been asked to do before, but have you ever thought about how you are thinking? The term for thinking about thinking is *metacognition,* or the act of being aware of your own thought processes. So far in this book, you have thought about what you value, how you spend your time, what college culture is, and how you relate to others. You have also been asked to think about what you are reading and learning, whether it has been through the reflection and critical thinking exercises or the end-of-chapter questions and ideas for further research. In fact, this book has been designed so that instead of passively taking in the information, you are actively engaged in thinking it through and creating knowledge.

The same activities that have brought you to this point are the ones you are currently practicing in your classes as well. You are moving beyond just taking information in to send it back out in the same form for a test or paper. Instead, you are building creative, analytical, and critical thinking skills with each course. Strong critical thinking skills will set you apart in the classroom and the workplace: You will be better informed, because you will know to seek out the information you need; you will make better choices, because you will have thought through all the possibilities; and you will continue to improve on your chosen solutions, because you will understand that evaluating your solution is the key to making better future choices.

Creative Thinking Helps You Build Ideas

Creative thinking, or the act of creating ideas for solving problems, is an integral part of education. Without creative thinking, there would be no inventions, new formulas, breakthroughs in technology and science, new art movements, advances in design and architecture—the list is endless. Without creative thinking, there would be no electricity, no indoor plumbing, no automobiles, and no zippers in our clothes. Just getting to your classes would be a totally different experience.

Analytical thinking can help you in classes that require you to learn processes.

©SHUTTERSTOCK

Creative thinking is a skill, a process, and an attitude (Harris, 2002, pp. 1–2). In other words, creative thinkers are not born with special powers of the imagination; they just use their imaginations more regularly than others. The good news is that you can learn to think creatively by following some of the basic ideas shown in Exhibit 6.5.

Robert Harris (2002) states, "Creative thinking creates the ideas with which critical thinking works" (p. 5). To improve your critical thinking and problem-solving abilities, you will need to consider the guidelines in Exhibit 6.5, find ways to practice them, and maintain your curiosity and a positive attitude.

Analytical Thinking Helps You Break Down Ideas

Analytical thinking involves breaking down a subject and examining its parts. Students who learn about computer processing or automotive technology use analytical thinking so that they can understand how a machine works. When they master how the parts work together, they are able to diagnose problems that may occur within the processes. The same is true for students learning about the processes in the body: They use analytical thinking to determine how muscles work or how the lungs are supposed to function. Students of literature will use analytical thinking to break apart short stories or poems to determine what effect the setting has on the characters or what effect language has on the tone of the text.

EXHIBIT 6.5 Creative Thinking Strategies, Definitions, and Activities

Strategy	Explanation	Activity
Improve your imagination each day	Find ways to keep your mind sharp and your imagination flourishing. Turning off the TV and picking up a book is an easy way to stimulate your imagination. If you enjoy kinesthetic activities, create something to get your mind active.	Participate in one thinking or imaginative exercise each day, whether it is doing a crossword puzzle or Sudoku puzzle, constructing an object, or listing the plusses and minuses of the healthiness of what you ate for breakfast.
Ask what someone else would do	Looking at a problem from a different perspective can provide more creative ideas.	Determine what issue you want to generate more ideas for. Then, choose two people—such as Oprah Winfrey or Walt Disney or your mother—and write down the different ways they would approach the issue.
Suspend judgment	For creative thinking, evaluation is not necessary—save it for critical thinking and problem solving.	Make a list of 50 ways to use a paper clip, and do not delete or edit the list in any way. Share your list with others.

Anyone who has tried to figure out why an event has happened (e.g., How did I run out of money before payday?) has used analytical thinking. Just as any skill, however, it takes practice to become better at seeing the parts of a process or a whole unit and determining how the parts work together to create a unified result. To develop your analytical skills, you can follow these guidelines:

- *Break down a whole into its parts.* Ask yourself, "What are the pieces that create the entirety?" For example, if you work at a sandwich shop, you can break the sandwich-making process into its distinct parts, such as taking the order, cutting the bread, and so on.
- *Examine each part for a unique function.* After you identify every step in the sandwich-making process, examine each one to determine its function, such as fulfilling the purchase transaction or putting condiments on the sandwich.
- *Organize parts by function.* What elements can be grouped together? How did you determine what groups to create? You could group all the steps in the sandwich-making process that have something to do with the purchase transaction together in one group, and all the steps in gathering the ingredients in another.
- *Explore the meaning behind the parts.* If possible, find out more information about how each part functions or its meaning. You might discover that keeping track of how many sandwiches you make is an important piece of information for the restaurant owner to manage inventory.
- *Re-examine the whole in light of its parts.* Look back at the whole and determine what you have learned from examining the parts. Do you have a better understanding of how all the parts work together? You can now understand how each step in the sandwich-making process contributes to the success of the restaurant as a whole. You can also appreciate how your individual contributions make a big difference for your employer.

Critical Thinking Helps You Evaluate Ideas

The term *critical thinking* is difficult to define, but it has a long tradition. Critical thinkers such as Socrates and Thomas Aquinas, to name only two, have had a tremendous effect on the way we think about the world. But what makes them critical thinkers? What is a critical thinker? A critical thinker is "someone who uses specific criteria to evaluate reasoning and make decisions" (Diestler, 1998, p. 2). Someone who thinks critically does not take information at its face value; instead, they carefully examine information for accuracy, authority, and logic before using it.

To illustrate the importance of using critical thinking skills, consider this first scenario: Michael receives an email message from a friend who claims that she has sent him a virus unknowingly. Her email message instructs him to search for the offending file and delete it immediately. Unaware of any problems that are usually associated with viruses, he searches for the file and finds it, exactly where his friend said it would be on his computer. Michael's friend is a

BUZZ

Q You say that for every hour in class, we need to study three hours outside class. Is that really true? How will I have enough time to do that if I'm taking four classes this semester?

A There's a reason a student who's enrolled in four classes is called a "full-time" student! Here are some tips for meeting the study demands:

- Schedule five hours each day to study.
- Work in a study group at least once a week.
- Read through your notes each day after your classes.
- Make flash cards and review them.

You use problem-solving and critical thinking skills every day to make decisions.

©SHUTTERSTOCK

trustworthy person and he values her advice, so he deletes the file. He gets an email message the next day from her that says she is sorry that the email she sent him was actually a hoax. Thus, he has deleted a perfectly normal file on his computer.

Now, consider this second scenario: Juanita sends Evan a link to a pop-up blocker because she knows that he hates those annoying intrusions while surfing the Internet. Because Evan has been deceived by free software before, he decides to search several reputable sites that are devoted to reviewing new software. Evan finds that the pop-up blocker is a fraud; instead, if he were to click on the link that Juanita has sent, his computer would have been overrun with pop-up advertisements of questionable origins.

In the first scenario, two people, at least, have been deceived by what appears to be legitimate and helpful information. Who doesn't want to rid her computer of a potentially dangerous virus? Unfortunately, Michael and his friend did not question the information. In the second scenario, however, Evan has encountered false claims before and realizes that he must check out every piece of information that comes to him, regardless of the friendly source. Evan applied critical thinking to the situation. Thinking critically allowed him to review the information he was sent and to search for authoritative sources that provided reliable information so that he could make a decision about what action to take.

As the Information Age evolves, critical thinking skills are not just advantageous; they are essential. Not only do you need to practice these skills, but you also need others to practice them so that you will not constantly have to evaluate every piece of information that you receive. Can you imagine a world in which everything that you read is suspect and there is no sure way of finding out what is true and accurate and what is not? For people who do not think critically, that imagined world is a reality.

Problem Solving Brings It All Together

Although not all critical thinking leads to solving a problem, problem solving relies on critical thinking, as well as creative and analytical thinking. In order to think critically to solve a problem, you will need to go through a process within a group or as an individual. Remember that the more minds working on a problem, the more likely that all sides of the problem can be addressed, which may make the solution better. You may not always have an opportunity to work in a group on a problem, but you may be able to ask others for their advice during the process.

Here are the basic steps of using critical thinking to solve a problem:

- Clearly identify the problem or goal.
- Generate several possible solutions to the problem or goal.
- Critically evaluate each possible solution.
- Choose one of the solutions and develop a plan for putting it in action.
- Evaluate the solution after it is in place.

Step 1: Identify the Problem or Goal

Sometimes a problem is obvious, and other times we may make an incorrect assumption about the real problem. Either way, it's important to take some time to clearly identify the problem before moving on to possible solutions. For example, if you're constantly late for your first class every morning, you might assume it's because you're not getting up early enough. After examining the situation more closely, however, you discover that you're spending too much time trying to find a parking spot before class. The problem may actually be a transportation problem and not a problem with your sleeping habits. Or, instead of a problem, we may be trying to accomplish a particular goal. For example, you might set a goal to save an extra $200 over the next six months so you can buy an ebook reader.

Identifying the problem's cause is the first logical step before you can begin to solve it. If you do not identify the cause—or at least eliminate possible causes—before starting the next step, either you won't solve the problem or you might create a whole new problem to solve.

Step 2: Generate Possible Solutions

This is the step where creative thinking will kick in. When you generate ideas, there are no rules except not to eliminate any ideas because they are too far-fetched or too odd. The goal for this step is to get a lot of ideas on paper, and the more ideas you can think of, the more likely you'll come up with a really creative solution that comes from "outside the box"—a phrase that describes ideas that aren't readily obvious.

When generating ideas, consider creating a list of your possible ideas and role playing (if you are able to work with another person) to get ideas flowing. This is a good time to take advantage of your learning style strength to stretch your imagination. For the "late for class" problem, you might identify some obvious solutions (e.g., riding your bike to class instead of driving), but by giving yourself room to be really creative and open, you might come up with some less-than-obvious ideas, like packing your breakfast in a cooler and eating it *after* you find a parking spot, which doesn't fix the parking problem, but helps resolve the overall problem of arriving late to class by saving you time each morning.

Step 3: Critically Evaluate Each Possible Solution

To "critically evaluate" means that you consider the advantages and disadvantages, strengths and weaknesses, plusses and minuses of every option. Sometimes it's helpful to construct a chart or table that describes each solution in one column and then lists the advantages, strengths, and plusses in the second column and the disadvantages, weaknesses, and minuses in the third column. It's helpful to force yourself to fill in every square in the grid so that you are thorough in considering both sides of a solution, especially if you find yourself preferring one particular solution from the very beginning. This is also a time when the opinions of others can be very helpful. Your friends, parents, professors, and roommates can provide critical perspectives that can help you understand your options better than you could have done yourself. For example, if you're considering the possibility of getting a part-time job to make the money you want to save for your ebook reader, your trusted advisors might help you discover some of the drawbacks of adding work to your weekly schedule because of their own personal experiences with similar circumstances.

Step 4: Select and Implement Your Solution

Some people have a tendency of making decisions too quickly before giving careful consideration to all the possible alternatives and potential outcomes. Other people, however, spend too much time considering all the alternatives and agonizing over the possible outcomes, and they have trouble making a final decision. The best course of action, of course, is to be somewhere in the middle—giving careful thought to each potential solution and then making a final decision in a timely manner. Once you've completed step three and you've carefully evaluated all of your possible solutions,

INTEGRITY *Matters*

You can't be a true critical thinker without maintaining integrity in the process. To think critically with integrity, you will need to be fair in your judgments and represent others' views as accurately as possible. Critical thinkers know that every viewpoint has a counterargument that is equally valid, and critical thinkers with integrity acknowledge those other viewpoints without misrepresenting them.

Critical thinkers who have integrity also do not short-circuit the process of examining and judging an idea. The reward is the assurance that their final conclusions are fair.

YOUR TURN

In approximately 250 words, explain how you would handle the following situation: Your professor asked you to write a paper on affirmative action in which you defend the practice, although you do not agree with that position.

you eventually need to make a decision. Evaluate each possible solution based on its plusses and minuses, pick the one that has the most plusses compared to minuses, and then move on to put the solution into action. It's one thing to decide to do something, but it's a far different step to put that decision into action. If you chose "riding your bike to class" as your solution to getting to class on time in the morning, you need to have a bike with a lock and know where you can park it near your classroom. You might also need to make a test run on a day when you don't have class to figure out how long it will take to get from your dorm or apartment to your class using a different mode of transportation.

Step 5: Evaluate the Solution

This is one of the easiest steps to overlook, yet it's one of the most important. You can become a more effective problem solver and decision maker by revisiting the decisions you've made in the past and evaluating how they turned out in the long run. By examining several decisions over a six-month or one-year period, you'll see patterns, and, if you practice the problem-solving process described here, you'll see a gradual, steady improvement in your decision making and problem solving over time. By practicing this five-step process on a regular basis with relatively simple problems, you'll develop effective skills to tackle the really big problems when they arise. You'll have a lifelong habit that will serve you well.

Identify a decision that you need to make in the near future, or a decision that you had to make in the recent past. Write out the five-step decision-making process, and explain how you could (or did) follow each step in the process, for your specific situation.

from COLLEGE
to UNIVERSITY

Different Types of Thinking Will Be Needed to Continue Your Learning

When you transfer to a university, you will continue to use creative, analytical, and critical thinking skills in upper-level classes. In upper-level classes, your professors will move away from knowledge and comprehension to synthesis and evaluation. You will spend more time doing research and determining if the sources you find are reliable and accurate. You will also use those sources to support your own new ideas, developed through creative thinking, about current issues in your major. All in all, you will be more responsible for the depth and breadth of your education, and strong thinking skills will help you deepen your learning.

©SHUTTERSTOCK

from COLLEGE
to CAREER

How Critical Thinking Will Be Used on the Job

©SHUTTERSTOCK

Critical thinking on the job is essential to a rewarding and successful career. Your employer, no matter what your position, will value your ability to think critically and solve problems, and you will value the work you do if you are allowed to use those skills to improve yourself and your environment.

How will you use critical thinking on the job? There will be, no doubt, countless opportunities to think critically at work. For example, you may realize that the office does not run efficiently and you have evaluated ways to improve the flow of work. You may be asked to think critically about a problem in order to solve it. No matter how you arrive at thinking critically on the job, keep the steps to problem solving handy.

As you have read in this chapter, critical thinking is a process, not an end. Once you have solved a problem, new ones will arise that will require critical thinking. To improve yourself and your progress on the job, you will have to be committed to thinking critically.

UNDERSTAND & REMEMBER

Review Questions

1. What has recent brain research told us about learning?

2. In what ways will you be expected to learn in college?

3. Define creative thinking and analytical thinking. Compare and contrast these ways of thinking.

4. Identify and describe the five steps of critical thinking/problem solving.

Create

Evaluate

Analyze

Apply

Understand

Remember

APPLY & ANALYZE

Critical Thinking

1. This chapter uses figures to illustrate key concepts: three neurons with dendrites developing at each stage of the learning process (Exhibit 6.1) and a Learning Pyramid (Exhibit 6.6). Review both and determine which one is most helpful in conveying the information from the chapter and which one is least helpful. Explain why.

2. After reviewing the mnemonic devices, determine which ones would work best for you and use them to create a memory strategy study sheet. Explain how you are using them to remember key concepts, such as the major ideas in this chapter.

3. Which of the three types of thinking—creative, critical, or analytical—will you most likely use in your future career and why? What steps will you take to hone your thinking skills as you complete your degree?

EVALUATE

Case Scenarios

1. Joan has been named a student ambassador for her college. One of her duties as an ambassador is to help prepare for fall orientation for new students. The advisors have told the student ambassadors that last year, students rated orientation low because they had to wait in long lines to get registered and the information they received was too detailed and difficult to understand. Joan and her fellow ambassadors have been asked to create a new way of providing orientation to students. Joan has decided to use the feedback from last year's orientation to make improvements to the fall orientation by addressing only what the previous students said needed to be changed.

   Use the following scale to rate the decision that has been made (1 = Poor Decision, 5 = Excellent Decision). Be prepared to explain your answer.

Poor Decision ← (1)——————(2)——————(3)——————(4)——————(5) → Excellent Decision

2. Sidra wants to earn money for college tuition next year, but she doesn't have the time to work 40 hours a week. Sidra's creative thinking process results in the following ideas: sell blood, tutor classmates, tattoo herself with a local company's logo and charge them for advertising, sell items on the Internet, work as a telemarketer, house sit for friends and family members. She decides that selling blood once a month and working as a telemarketer for 35 hours a week are her best, most consistent options.

   Use the following scale to rate the decision that has been made (1 = Poor Decision, 5 = Excellent Decision). Be prepared to explain your answer.

   Poor Decision ←———①————②————③————④————⑤——→ Excellent Decision

3. Kenya has decided to apply for a loan forgiveness program that will pay all her tuition as she completes a degree in computer networking. The loan forgiveness program requires that she find a job in networking within three months of graduation, or she will owe back the full amount of her loans. After she completes a year of her degree program, she learns that the job market for networking specialists does not look promising for the next five years, which may mean she will have great difficulty finding a job when she graduates in a year. She decides to change majors and career paths, which means she will be responsible for more than $4,000 from her first year when she graduates. Her new career path, sales, has the potential for her to earn enough to pay back her loan over a few years if she works very hard and is successful in the job.

   Use the following scale to rate the decision that has been made (1 = Poor Decision, 5 = Excellent Decision). Be prepared to explain your answer.

   Poor Decision ←———①————②————③————④————⑤——→ Excellent Decision

CREATE

Research It Further

1. Using the key terms "critical thinking" and "creative thinking," search the Internet for tips for improving critical and creative thinking skills. Make a table of the different tips, and present the information to your classmates.

2. Create a survey to distribute to fellow students that asks them what their top concerns on campus are. Report your results to the class, and choose one to solve using the critical thinking process. Be sure to outline the critical thinking/problem-solving process and report on each step.

3. Interview faculty members in different programs on your campus, and ask them to provide a critical thinking scenario that a graduate in their programs would encounter on the job. Ask them to work through the problem to a feasible solution. Share the different problem-solving scenarios with the class, and ask them to compare and contrast the processes.

TAKE THIS WITH YOU

Based on the goals we set at the beginning of this chapter, here's how you can take this learning with you toward college success:

■ Remember to work your way through the six stages of the learning process when you want to master a skill or concept.

■ Begin to use active learning strategies when you are studying.

■ Employ mnemonic devices when you need to remember broad concepts and terms.

■ Keep your creative thinking skills in shape by keeping your mind sharp with puzzles and games.

■ Start using analytical thinking when you need to examine a situation more closely.

■ Begin every problem-solving process with identifying the problem and then working your way through the remaining four steps.

REFERENCES AND RECOMMENDED READINGS

Diestler, S. (1998). *Becoming a critical thinker: A user friendly manual* (2nd ed.). Upper Saddle River, NJ: Prentice Hall.

Dweck, C. (2006). *Mindset: The new psychology of success*. New York: Random House.

Foer, J. (2007). Remember this. *National Geographic 212(5)*, 32–55.

Gunn, A. M., Richburg, R. W., & Smilkstein, R. (2007). *Igniting student potential: Teaching with the brain's natural learning process*. Thousand Oaks, CA: Corwin Press.

Harris, R. (2002). *Creative problem solving: A step-by-step approach*. Los Angeles: Pyrczak.

Miller, G. (1956). The magical number seven, plus or minus two: Some limits on our capacity for processing information. Retrieved http://www.musanim.com/miller1956

Smilkstein, R. (2003). *We're born to learn: Using the brain's natural learning process to create today's curriculum*. Thousand Oaks, CA: Corwin Press.

MyStudentSuccessLab

MyStudentSuccessLab (www.mystudentsuccesslab.com) is an online solution designed to help you 'Start strong, Finish stronger' by building skills for ongoing personal and professional development.

7 Reading

To Do This Week

- 54 pages of biology textbook.
- 72 pages of aviation textbook.
- 213 pages of an autobiography.

Even though he can bench press hundreds of pounds, Evan feels weak when he thinks about reading. Evan is discovering that college without reading is like kickboxing without sore muscles.

When he ran into Michael in the hall after class earlier this week, he complained about what he has to do and why he doesn't want to do it.

"Evan, I know exactly what you need to do. I just got help with my algebra homework, and the tutor explained it in a way that I could get it," Michael had said.

"It's not that I don't know what to do," Evan said to Michael. "I just don't like to read. It's boring."

Michael laughed. "It does seem boring at first," he said, "but you will get better at reading the more you do it."

"I don't think I want to get *that* good at it," Evan joked.

Despite his joking, Evan goes to the only place he knows can help him: the tutoring center.

"Once you find the article you want, read the article first for meaning. Check out the title, the publication information, the date," the tutor says, "and once you begin reading, stop at every paragraph, at first, and see if you can summarize the author's ideas."

"I think I am getting this, but what am I going to do about the chapters and the book I need to read?" Evan asks.

"Just follow the same process. It works for other types of reading," says the tutor.

Evan knows that like sports, you only get better with practice and by challenging yourself with harder exercises. But he also knows he has a long way to go to get better and better at reading.

YOUR GOALS FOR THIS CHAPTER

Can you imagine getting a degree and *not* reading a page? Technology may have changed the way we read and how we incorporate written information, but it has not changed the importance of reading to become an educated individual. When you complete this chapter, you will be able to:

- Justify the importance of reading effectively in college
- Break down a long reading assignment for better comprehension and understanding
- Identify methods for improving your reading skills
- Use different reading strategies to improve your comprehension

MyStudentSuccessLab (www.mystudentsuccesslab.com) is an online solution designed to help you 'Start strong, Finish stronger' by building skills for ongoing personal and professional development.

If death and taxes are unavoidable parts of life, then reading is an inevitable part of college and lifelong learning; fortunately, reading is more enjoyable and more profitable than death and taxes. The bottom line is that you will not be a successful student if you do not read assigned and supplemental material regularly. Likewise, it will be difficult to practice lifelong learning after college without reading on a regular basis. As previous chapters have mentioned, reading class handouts and college publications, as well as your textbooks, is essential to success in college. The reasons that reading is important to your college education and lifelong learning are many, but here are just a few incentives for making reading an integral part of your daily college work:

- Reading provides you with basic information that you can use to create knowledge of a subject.
- Reading improves your understanding of others and the world around you by exposing you to new viewpoints, ideas, and cultures.
- Reading helps you understand yourself, which will assist you in making better life choices.

With this said, it must be acknowledged that some students just do not enjoy reading because of bad experiences in school or because of learning difficulties. Thus, for some college students, reading can be a challenge to academic fulfillment. Professors

Your Terms for SUCCESS

WHEN YOU SEE . . .	IT MEANS . . .
Active reading	Reading to remember and understand; reading with a purpose
Bibliography	A list of books or other sources
Comprehension	The ability to remember and understand
Context clues	Hints of a word's meaning by how it is used in a sentence
Critical reading	Reading to evaluate and to question
Dyslexia	A learning disability that makes it difficult for a person to read, spell, or listen effectively
Headnote	The summary information that appears at the beginning of a work; often contains background information on the material or the author
Index	An alphabetical list of subjects or terms that appears in a book; appears at the end of a book
Information literacy	The ability to determine if information is needed; to access the information; to assess the usefulness of the information; and to incorporate the information ethically and responsibly
Introduction	The beginning paragraph or pages of a text
Section titles	The titles that appear within the sections of a chapter
SQ3R	A reading strategy that stands for Survey, Question, Read, Recite, and Review
Subvocalization	Sounding out individual words while reading

Reading in college is not optional; rather, it is *crucial* to success. When you make the commitment to enroll in college, you must also follow through with that commitment by tackling the reading that is part of the experience. You will also need to demonstrate integrity when you do not read—be honest with your instructor, if asked, and be honest with yourself that your progress (or lack of) is related to how well you are preparing, through active and critical reading, before class.

YOUR TURN

In approximately 250 words, describe a time in which you have you experienced the feeling of being confused in class because you did not prepare by reading the assignment beforehand. Describe what the experience was like. Discuss what you learned from the experience.

would be ecstatic if all their students read well and enjoyed all the assigned reading material. More realistically, students find some reading dull and difficult to comprehend, and they long to read something "exciting." The not-so-good news is that until you get into classes that pertain to your major or career choice, you may feel that the assigned reading is uninteresting, but the good news is that there are ways to improve your comprehension *and* enjoyment of the reading assignments.

In addition to the change in subject matter that you will encounter in college reading, you will also find the reading load to be more than it was in high school or more than it is for your job. If you are taking four 3-credit-hour classes, you can expect to read more than 100 pages a week if each professor assigns one chapter from the textbook each week. This number does not reflect full-length novels, supplementary articles, required periodical subscriptions, reserved library materials, online resources, and your own notes from class—all of which may be part of your weekly reading load. The truth about college reading is that there will be plenty for you to read and that you will also be held accountable for reading, comprehending, and thinking critically about the material.

Information Literacy

Along with the increased reading load, your professors will also expect that you are an information literate student. That means that you not only know how to read well, but you also know how to find information and use it effectively and ethically. You will learn more about how to research a topic in another chapter, but we'll introduce the concept of information literacy in this chapter as well. The American Library Association (ALA, 2009) defines information literacy as the ability to:

- Decide what information is warranted
- Retrieve the information
- Assess information for its usefulness and credibility
- Use the information for an explicit reason and integrate it with one's own knowledge
- Use the information ethically

The ALA website, www.ala.org, provides even more information about how information literacy is used on college campuses. To become truly information literate, you will need to be proficient at finding information, reading that information thoroughly, assessing the value of the information, and using it effectively in a presentation, paper, or other assignment.

How to Successfully Complete a Reading Assignment

The majority of your reading assignments in college will most likely be assigned by your instructors. When you first get a reading assignment, you will need to spend a little time preparing to read, which will help you maximize the time that you have to complete your assignment. No doubt, in the first week of classes, you will be given handouts, syllabi, and chapters to read in your textbook. How can you manage it all without getting behind and overwhelmed at the start of the semester? These following steps will help you successfully complete your assignment.

Assume All Assigned Material Is Important

Before you begin any reading assignment, remember that all written material that your professors give you needs to be read. You will be held responsible for it immediately or at a later date; therefore, you will need to create a process for reading and remembering what you have read.

Treat the Reading Assignment Seriously

No matter how big or small the assignment, make a conscious effort to read and remember important information. A positive attitude about the reading assignment will help make the other steps easier to complete.

Organize Assignments According to Size, Importance, and Date of Completion

You will want to begin reading with the most important or urgent assignments first, and then work your way down the stack. A shorter assignment can be completed first unless its due date is far off.

Schedule Reading Time as You Would Any Important Appointment

To increase your chances of reading effectively, schedule a definite time and place to read, preferably at the same time each day. Finding a comfortable, quiet area to read is also important because it will put you in the mood to focus on what you are reading. Equally important is to establish routine breaks from reading. Get up, walk around the room, get a drink of water, and get the circulation going in your legs again. Taking breaks in which you physically move around the room will help your concentration and keep you from falling asleep.

Establish a Clear Purpose for Reading

Setting a purpose for reading will make the assignment easier to comprehend and complete. For example, if your reading purpose is to improve your understanding of networking, then when you sit down with the textbook for your computer networking administration class, you are in the right frame of mind. Conversely, if your reading purpose is to be entertained when you read a chapter in economics, you may be disappointed and less receptive to remembering what you have read. One method for helping you set a purpose is to start a reading log (Exhibit 7.1), which will provide a method for reading effectively as well as critically. The first two questions at the bottom of the log support active reading, while the last two questions ask you to think critically about what you have read.

Title of text or chapter _____

Number of pages _____

Author _____

Class _____

Instructor _____

Date reading should be completed _____

Estimated time to complete _____

Reading goals _____

Actual time to complete _____

Reading goals achieved   YES   NO

Skimmed   YES   NO   PARTIALLY

1. What is the reading about?

2. What did I learn from the reading?

3. What questions do I still have about the reading?

4. What difficulties, if any, did I have while reading?

New vocabulary words and their definitions:

Stay Healthy

Finally, take care of yourself throughout the semester as you do your assigned work. You won't be able to read effectively if you are overtired, hungry, or sick. Don't try to force yourself to read if physical or psychological issues distract you. Too much sugar and caffeine and too little sleep can make reading more difficult, as can certain medications and emotional distractions. If you cannot concentrate, return to the material when you are feeling better, but be sure to use this advice sparingly. Sometimes, you will just need to dig and get it done, regardless of how you feel.

Reading in the Disciplines

The type of content that you'll be reading will vary by what classes you're taking. Science and math classes have different reading requirements compared to English and psychology. The following strategies for reading in the disciplines are just a sample of what you may encounter in college.

Math

Take your time to read both the written information and explanations as well as the visual representations of problems and steps for solving them. Reading assigned chapters *before* you get to class will help you follow what the professor is talking about and allow you to ask questions about content that you didn't understand.

Literature

You may find you have more reading in literature classes—novels, short stories, plays, and poetry. Start early with these long reading assignments and take notes along the way. Depending on the complexity of the literature, you may need to read the work a few times, especially poetry, and sound each word out. Although sounding out individual words, or subvocalization (see "Reading Difficulties and How to Overcome Them"), is often considered a reading difficulty, it may be necessary to slow down and read short pieces of literature aloud. Also, pay attention to details when reading fiction and poetry.

Languages

The first goal in reading in a foreign language is to improve your comprehension. Use a dictionary the first time you encounter new vocabulary, and work on improving your speed.

Sciences

Reading in the sciences will take time and focus as you encounter new concepts and processes. Look for visual representations of the content in your textbook, or sketch your own in your notebook.

Social Sciences

Large amounts of assigned material will be part of any social science class. Start reading the chapters early and look for key ideas. People and their theories or their actions (in history) will be key components of the reading. Learning the who, what, when, and where of the material will make it easier to remember. Remember trading cards from the days when you were young? You could use the same concept and develop summary profiles about the various individuals and events you read about in your assigned materials.

Q One of my friends in college told me that her professor reviews everything from the textbook in class, so there's no reason to read the textbook before coming to class. Is that true?

A Some professors do use a portion of class time to review the textbook materials and expect that you have already read it. Here are some tips for making the most of class:

- Prepare for class by reading ahead of time, no matter what.

- Prepare a few questions ahead of time in case you are asked.

- Participate in the discussion.

- Take notes and mark information your professor points out during class.

Reading Difficulties and How to Overcome Them

For some students, like Evan, no matter how much they want to read well, the activity is difficult. Dealing with reading difficulties can make a short reading assignment seem like climbing Mount Everest and can make it hard to stay motivated. The following list describes some common reading difficulties that students experience. It is not intended as a comprehensive list, nor is it intended as a diagnosis for problems that you may experience. If you think you may have a reading difficulty or a learning disability, you should see your college counselor for a proper diagnosis. Your college's counseling services should also provide you with resources that will help you overcome the challenges you may experience because of a learning difficulty. Some reading difficulties are bad habits rather than disorders. The following list provides an overview of common reading challenges.

- *Subvocalization,* or pronouncing each word in your mind as you read, is one type of bad habit that some readers experience.
- *Regression,* or reading the same words or sentences over and over again, is another bad habit. Improving your reading speed, or the rate at which your eyes move across the page, often eliminates the reading habits that slow you down.
- *Moving a finger, pen, or pencil across the page as you read* can also slow down your reading speed. Unless you are stopping to take notes along the way, eliminate the use of an instrument to keep your eyes moving.
- *Poor concentration* can negatively affect how quickly you read. In some cases, poor concentration is part of a larger issue that may be diagnosed by a health professional. If poor concentration is just a bad habit, then you can work toward improving concentration by eliminating distractions, such as television and music, and following the suggestions outlined in this chapter.
- *Dyslexia* is a neurological disorder that makes it difficult for a person to comprehend and recognize written words; they may also have trouble writing and spelling. Approximately 15–20% of all students have dyslexia, and most people with dyslexia have avege or above-average intelligence (International Dyslexia Association, 2011). The good news about dyslexia is that many students have learned to cope with the disorder and have succeeded in college and careers. For example, Paul Orfalea (2007) struggled with both dyslexia and attention deficit disorder his entire life, yet founded Kinko's and became a millionaire entrepreneur.
- *Attention deficit disorder* (ADD) or *attention deficit hyperactivity disorder* (ADHD) are behavioral disorders in which a person has difficulty paying attention. Reading can become just another obstacle that someone with ADD or ADHD must overcome. In order to work through any difficulties that ADD/ADHD may cause, you will need to contact your counseling center. As with dyslexia, ADD/ADHD can be managed so that your reading skills get sharper.
- *Vision problems* are actually the cause of some reading difficulties. A regular eye exam can determine if your difficulties are caused by the need for corrective glasses or contacts. If you think your eyes are the reason that you have difficulty reading words, get your eyes checked by a doctor. You may want to stop first at your college's health clinic, if one is available, for a screening. Also, take advantage of any health fairs that are offered on your campus, where you can get a free screening that may pinpoint the problem.

©SHUTTERSTOCK

Use your college's resources to help strengthen your reading strategies and overcome any reading difficulties you may have.

60-second PAUSE

Briefly list the various ideas that were mentioned in the previous section for how to successfully complete a reading assignment. Underline the techniques that you practiced regularly when you were in high school or working. Circle the techniques that you need to practice more often.

What do you picture in your mind when someone tells you that they've been reading for three hours? Perhaps you envision them reclining in a comfortable chair with a cup of coffee. Although this may be an enjoyable way to read, the reality is that a lot of us would probably fall asleep if we sat in that kind of position for any length of time! When you read books, articles, and online content to learn and study, you'll have a lot more success if you make it a far more active process.

Active reading, a term that you may hear often in college along with *active listening,* means that you are fully engaged in reading by focusing your mind and body on the activity. Many first-time students read passively rather than actively and do not fully concentrate on the material. Just reading the words is not enough for college classes. Instead, you must be a part of the process by making sure you comprehend what you are reading.

Critical reading is another term that you will hear frequently in college. Some students may think that critical reading means having a negative reaction to what they have read, but it actually involves a series of steps to react and respond to the reading—either positively or negatively, depending on the material. The end goal of critical reading is to question and evaluate the material, not to take it at face value. Critical reading, as well as active reading, are skills that will take practice to develop. The following sections provide specific strategies for improving both skills.

Skimming and Scanning

You may already be familiar with the terms *skimming* and *scanning* as they pertain to reading. Skimming is reading material quickly and superficially, paying particular attention to main ideas; use this method of reading when you first get a reading assignment because it can help you get a feel for what the material is, how long it is, and how difficult it will be to read. In order to skim a text effectively, you should read the first and last paragraphs, the main headings of each section, and the first and last sentences of each paragraph; of course, if time is a factor, you can delete some of the steps, or add more, reading the first and last paragraphs of each section. Ideally, skimming should be done before in-depth reading. However, sometimes skimming may be the only chance you have to read the material. If this is the case, be sure to pay attention to the major headings of each section and the first and last paragraphs of the material. Don't be surprised, though, if you miss major ideas that are sandwiched in the middle.

Scanning is looking quickly for a specific item or topic, as you would scan a website for a particular product or a dictionary for a particular word. Scanning also includes examining the table of contents and index of a book to help you find what you are looking for. Just as with skimming, scanning requires that your eyes move quickly over a page. However, the difference between scanning and skimming is that you know what you want to find and will slow down once you find it. Scanning is particularly useful when reviewing sources to use for a paper. You can determine rather quickly if the source pertains to your topic or not. Once you scan, you can then skim or read the text actively.

Improving your reading skills includes learning to read on a computer or with other forms of technology.

©THINKSTOCK

Breaking Down the Material

As stated earlier, part of scanning a text includes examining its parts. Certain pages of a book or article hold valuable information for deciphering the book or article's purpose. Students who want to "hurry up" and read the meat of the assignment often overlook some of the most important parts: The title, author, table of contents, chapter titles, introduction, section headings, headnotes, bibliography, and index are all informative components of a piece of writing. See Exhibit 7.2 for a complete list.

EXHIBIT 7.2 **Parts of a Reading Assignment**

Title	The title of an article or book will give you a clue as to what it is about. When reading any material, take time to think about the significance of the title of the work you are reading, and go back to the title to look for additional meaning once you have completed the whole text.
Author	The author of a text can be just as important as what he or she has to say. Because of their reputations, some authors lend credibility to their words or they instantly make readers suspicious of their motives. If you recognize the author's name, then you should have a good idea of what the text is about. The more you read, the more you will encounter writings by certain people, and you will be able to expect certain viewpoints from them.
Table of Contents	Most books have a table of contents that shows how the book is organized. A table of contents lists the chapters as well as any subsections that appear in the chapters. Lastly, the table of contents contains the beginning page number for each chapter or section. Familiarizing yourself with the table of contents will make it easier to find information when you need it.
Introduction	Sometimes overlooked, the introduction can provide all the information you may need to determine if a particular book is what you want. When researching a topic, you can decide whether a book will be a good source for you by reading the introduction. The introduction typically tells the reader what the whole book is about, what unique features you will find, and what viewpoint is supported.
Chapter Titles	The titles of chapters are a good indication of what you can expect to read within the book. Chapter titles also help you locate information more quickly. Can you imagine trying to find information from a book about taking notes without any chapter titles? You would have to scan each chapter until you found the information you were looking for.
Section Headings	Section headings work in the same way as chapter titles; they indicate how the material is organized, and they give you a sneak peek of what is to come.
Headnotes	Headnotes are the text that appears at the beginning of a section or before an essay that explains or briefly summarizes what you are about to read. These can provide biographical information about the author or can indicate the essay's main points.
Bibliography	A bibliography, or list of references or works cited, usually appears at the end of an article or a book, right before the index. Literally, a bibliography is a list of books that the author has read or used in preparing the text. This section of a book or article is often overlooked, but it actually contains a wealth of information for the reader. If you want to learn more about a topic that the author briefly mentions, you can look at the bibliography to see what other books are listed about the subject.
Index	One of the last elements of a book is its index, which is an alphabetical list of major ideas or words that are keyed to the pages on which they appear. If you need to find information on note taking, for instance, you can use the index to pinpoint the exact page it is on. Indexes (or indices) are especially helpful in research when you are evaluating sources to see whether they contain material about your subject.

It's in the
SYLLABUS

Review your syllabi and determine how many pages (approximately) you are required to read each week for *all* of your classes.

- Do some classes require more reading than others? Which ones?

- Are some of the reading assignments harder than others? Which ones?

- How do you plan to handle the reading load this semester?

- Do you expect to keep up with the readings? Why or why not?

While the reading process as a whole may seem time consuming and unnecessary, especially if you do not have much time to spend reading, the more you do it, the less time it will take because you will know what to look for. Also, your reading speed and comprehension will improve, which will mean that you can complete your assignments more quickly.

Critical Reading

Once you have actively read assigned or researched material, your next step will be to read it critically. In most cases, this will mean re-reading the material, especially if it is short. Be sure to allow yourself plenty of time for this activity. At this point in the critical reading process, you do not necessarily need to answer the questions you raise—you will just want to look for places within the material where you want to know more, want clarification, or disagree with the author's conclusion.

Questioning who the author is and what purpose he or she has in writing the material is the first place to start. Questions to ask include, Is the author an authority? Is he or she credible? Is there an agenda or bias in the writing? If the material comes from a magazine or newspaper or blog, you will also want to question the purpose of that source. When considering the source, you may ask, What is the purpose of presenting this material? If it comes from a newspaper, does the material aim to inform or persuade, or does it present only one side of a debate? If the material comes from a blog or an anonymous website, does the material intend to serve as reliable information, or is it only someone sharing his or her observations with no intention of providing accurate information? Writing these questions in the margins of the text or using a notebook for your questions is a good start to reading critically.

Another important element of information literacy is evaluating what you have read for its usefulness. Just because a book, article, or other content mentions a particular topic that you're studying doesn't mean that it's a relevant source. You need to review the content to determine if it helps you answer the specific questions you have. For example, if you have to write an essay explaining why the Congress of the United States includes both the Senate and the House of Representatives, a website that lists all the members of Congress won't be helpful. Furthermore, if your assignment requires you to argue in favor of a certain law or legislative act, you need to evaluate the material you read to determine if it provides supporting information.

In the era of Google searches and Wikipedia, it seems easy to find a lot of information about virtually any topic you need to study. The challenge is to evaluate this information, for both its credibility and relevance. These skills are crucial for your information literacy, and they will serve you well both in college and throughout the rest of your life.

60-second
PAUSE

What are some clues you would look for in a book, article, or website to determine whether it is from an authoritative source? If you have trouble answering this question, consider how television news programs establish the authoritative credibility of their sources.

READING IS A SKILL YOU CAN DEVELOP

The great news about reading is that it's a skill you can develop and improve over time. If you struggle with reading, you can practice a number of activities that will improve your reading comprehension and efficiency.

Building Your Vocabulary

Have you ever noticed how some people just seem to know the right words to say in any situation, while others struggle to think of what to say? Increasing your vocabulary is a great benefit of reading regularly. Some students get sidelined when they read because they encounter unfamiliar words; few students take the time to look up words that they don't know, and they subsequently miss out on learning new ideas or understanding the intent of the author. It is well worth your time to look up words when you read, and there are some methods you can use to decrease the time you spend flipping through your dictionary.

The first method of learning new vocabulary words is to look for context clues in the sentence. Many times, you can figure out what the word means by how it is used in a sentence or by the words that surround it. Consider the following sentence:

Students often use context clues to *decipher* the meanings of unfamiliar words.

If you didn't know that *decipher* means "to figure out," you could still understand the meaning of the sentence by the words around it and by considering that students are using something (context clues) in order to do something (decipher) to the meanings of unfamiliar words. You could deduce, then, that students are making the unfamiliar words more familiar by using context clues. Now, try this sentence:

It was not until we traveled to Beijing that we realized how *ubiquitous* American fast food was. On every street corner we saw a McDonald's or a KFC restaurant.

If you are not familiar with modern-day Beijing, you may not know that American restaurants are plentiful; in fact, you may believe that China has very little American food. Thus, to understand the meaning of *ubiquitous*, the second sentence provides the context clues. With the phrase "On every street corner" from the second sentence, you should realize that *ubiquitous* means "everywhere."

While context clues will allow you to make sense of most unfamiliar words, there will be times when you cannot rely on the other words in the sentence to help you. For example, can you tell what the words *amenable* and *obsequious* mean in the following sentence?

Charles was *amenable* to going out to eat with Sheila's *obsequious* mother.

In this case, if you don't know what the words mean, the sentence offers little assistance. Does Charles want to go out to eat or doesn't he? Is Sheila's mother someone who is enjoyable to be around or isn't she? To answer these questions, you may need to look up the words. Here is what you would see if you were to look up *amenable* in a dictionary:

a·me·na·ble (ə me′ nə bəl) *adj.* 1. agreeable 2. open to an activity or idea 3. controllable a·me′na·bil′i·ty *n.*—a·me′na·bly *adv.*

Now, look up *obsequious* for yourself and see if you can decipher the sentence.

Another way to figure out what words mean is to know some common Latin and Greek root words, prefixes, and suffixes. For example, if your professor calls astrology a "pseudoscience" and you know that the Greek root *pseudo* means "false," then you will be able to understand that your professor is claiming that astrology is not a true science. In order to learn the common roots of words that we use every day, you will need to study words' origins. A college reading class or looking up words in the dictionary regularly will help you learn to recognize the roots in other words. More tips for building your vocabulary are listed in Exhibit 7.3.

Increasing Your Reading Speed

Knowing how quickly you read is helpful in planning time for reading and in marking your progress. The goal is to increase your speed *and* your comprehension. In order to calculate your reading speed, time yourself while you read. Go back to the "Critical Reading" section and reread those first two paragraphs. This passage is 250 words in length. To calculate your reading speed, divide the number of minutes that it took you to read the passage into 250 to get your reading speed. For example, if it took you two minutes to complete the passage, then (250/2) you read at a rate of 125 WPM (words per minute).

Number of words   250

Number of minutes   ____

 250/___ (number of minutes) = ____ WPM

Average readers read between 200 and 250 words per minute, but that does not reflect their comprehension of the material. Techniques for improving speed are worth

---

EXHIBIT **7.3** **More Tips for Building Your Vocabulary**

Purchase or borrow discipline-specific dictionaries when you begin a class that contains a large amount of terminology (e.g., medical or scientific dictionaries, foreign language dictionaries, and glossaries for literary terms).

Before asking your professor or classmate what a word means, look it up.

Don't be afraid to look up words, even the same word multiple times. You will eventually be able to recall their meanings.

Use new words in conversation to "try them out." Using them regularly will help you remember what they mean.

Write new words on 3 x 5 index cards, and jot down the books and pages where they appear. Look up the definitions when you have time and write them on the cards. Take the cards with you, and review your new words when waiting in line or stuck in traffic.

Buy and browse a thesaurus, a book that contains synonyms for words. A thesaurus is handy when you are searching for a word that is similar to another.

If you have an e-mail account, subscribe to a word-a-day service that sends you a new vocabulary word each day, or buy a word-a-day calendar.

Subscribe to magazines that challenge your reading skills: *The Atlantic Monthly, The New Yorker,* and *Harper's* are examples of print magazines that provide interesting and challenging material.

learning and practicing. For example, instead of carefully processing every word in a sentence, skim the sentence to capture its meaning. This is similar to what you may have learned in typing class—not focusing on each individual letter, but focusing on the entire word instead. Another effective reading technique is to keep the key elements of a sentence (e.g., the subject and verb) in the foreground, and other elements of the sentence (words like "the," "and," and "to") in the background. Other techniques for improving your reading speed are listed in Exhibit 7.4, and your college may offer a speed reading class, or you may be able to find more methods on websites and in books.

Checking Your Comprehension

The most important aspect of reading is comprehending and remembering what you have read. If your textbook has questions at the end of each chapter to help you reinforce what you have learned, get in the habit of answering them when you finish a reading assignment. Even if you just answer the questions in your head, you'll understand the material better. If your textbook does not have questions, write a short

USING TECHNOLOGY TO GET AHEAD

The Internet offers so many great resources to help you improve your reading skills, including sites that "read" texts aloud for you.

RECOMMENDED SITES

■ http://www.dartmouth.edu/~acskills/success/reading.html: This page includes helpful links to other sources, such as "Six Reading Myths."

■ http://www.readinga-z.com/more/reading_strat.html: This site includes reading and word attack strategies that are simple methods for helping students with comprehension issues, including understanding vocabulary.

■ http://www.providence.edu/academic-services/academic-help/Pages/reading.aspx: Providence College offers good tips for college students who want to improve comprehension and reading speed.

EXHIBIT 7.4 More Tips for Building Your Reading Skills

Get comfortable	Make sure your reading space is comfortable and favorable for concentrating, but avoid tackling reading assignments in bed!
Stay focused	Find a time of the day when you are most focused to read and your energy levels are high.
Skim when you can	When the reading is not as important or complex as other assignments, learn to skim quickly. At the very least, skim before reading more closely.
Learn new words	The more words you know, the easier some reading may be.
Avoid overhighlighting	If you want to emphasize an important section, it may be better to mark it with a summary and a short explanation of why it is important rather than merely highlighting or underlining it.
Use a strategy	Use a comprehensive strategy, such as SQ3R, to help you read both actively and critically. A good strategy will involve skimming, questioning, and reviewing what you have read.
Take a class	If your college offers reading classes, even speed reading classes, take advantage of them.

Check your understanding of what you read before moving on to more reading material.

©SHUTTERSTOCK

summary of the chapter in your own words. To reinforce what you have learned, trade summaries with a classmate.

A high WPM reading speed means very little if you do not remember anything that you have read. Your goal should be to improve your reading speed reasonably to help you keep up with the reading demands of college, and to improve your retention and comprehension of the material you read.

Improving Your Reading Attention Span

Each semester will get more demanding in terms of reading, because you will be advancing in your degree program and will be encountering new, more challenging content. Therefore, the more practice that you have in reading effectively, the easier it will be to complete larger reading assignments. If you find that your "reading attention span" is not long, then you can work on lengthening it.

First, you will need to figure out how many pages you can read comfortably without getting distracted or tired. Write down the number in your reading log, a notebook, or a calendar. Each time that you sit down to read an assignment, notice how many pages it is. See if you can "beat" the number in the previous reading session. The more you read and the more you challenge yourself with reading, the better you will get. Just be patient.

60-second **PAUSE**

Which of these reading skills—vocabulary, speed, or comprehension—is your strength? Which of these skills is your biggest challenge? What's one specific action item you can start practicing now, while reading this chapter, to improve that skill?

READING STRATEGIES CAN HELP

As you have read so far, the act of reading is more than just moving your eyes along a page of words. Instead, reading in college requires that you use a reading strategy that will help you retain the information and think critically about what you have read. The following sections provide different types of proven strategies for both printed and electronic books that can help you read more efficiently and effectively.

Practicing Strategies for Printed Books

Printed textbooks, novels, and nonfiction titles and printed copies of articles and chapters may be becoming a relic of the past, but it is likely that you will still be reading printed materials in your classes. Taking notes as you read, either in your textbook or in a notebook, is an excellent way to remember what you have read and to begin the process of critical reading. Writing down key ideas, terms to look up later, and questions that you have as you read helps you stay focused and improves comprehension. However, avoid highlighting large sections of text. Excessive highlighting defeats the purpose of noting only key or very important information. If you can write in your textbook, create a one- or two-word summary of each paragraph or section. If you need to keep the text clean, then use your reading log, presented earlier. You can also use your reading log in conjunction with in-text notes.

Practicing Strategies for eBooks

Electronic books, or ebooks, have been gaining popularity with students, professors, and libraries, and they certainly can be more convenient that printed sources. For example, you may be able to download an ebook on your computer or other handheld device and read it without having to go to the library to check it out. Also, some ebooks cost less than their traditional, printed counterparts. Nonetheless, there are some drawbacks to using ebooks rather than printed books: ebooks are dependent on a student having access to technology, and students cannot sell ebooks back as they can printed texts. You may want to test one out—either using a friend's ebook reader or using an ebook reader at the library—before committing to purchasing an ebook reader to use for a class.

Strategies for reading an ebook are similar to a printed text in that you can preview the overall reading by examining the table of contents and chapter headings, looking for main ideas, and questioning the authority and accuracy of the text. However, ebooks have additional tools that can make reading actively and critically easier. Some ebooks allow you to search for certain terms and will highlight them. This can be useful if you are trying to find a specific section. Ebook tools may also include highlighters and notes that you can use to mark important information and record your own ideas. Often, these can be saved while you have access to the ebook. A print function may also be included in some ebooks, and although printing the entire book may not be possible, you should be able to print pages that you need.

Practicing the SQ3R Reading Strategy

One of the most popular reading strategies, SQ3R, was originally developed in 1946 and is still used today (Robinson, 1970).

(S) Survey: Before reading your text closely, start by examining the headings, subheadings, graphics, charts, and references if included.

(Q) Question: After you look for these major organizational signposts, you can either think or write questions that you have. One way to generate questions it to turn headings and subheadings into questions. For example, the subheading "SQ3R Reading Strategy" can be turned into the question "What is the SQ3R reading strategy?"

(R1) Read: Read each section at a time, making sure you are concentrating on what you have read.

BUZZ

Q No matter how hard I try, I sometimes reach a point where I haven't read all the assigned work in time for a quiz or exam. What should I do if I haven't read the whole chapter, but have a quiz on it in an hour?

A These kinds of situations happen, but there are some things you can do to maximize your understanding of the material:

- Skim the assigned chapter(s).

- If you've had quizzes before, reflect on the types of questions that your professor typically asks.

- Anticipate some of the questions your professor might ask on this quiz, and look for the answers.

Figure out where you can squeeze in a little time to complete your reading assignments.

©JAKOB HELBIG/DIGITAL VISION/GETTY IMAGES

(R2) Recite: At the end of each section that you have read, say aloud what the section was about and answer the questions that you asked during the Question stage. You may also want to write your answers on note cards to review later.

(R3) Review: Any time after you have completed the first four steps, you will be ready to review what you have read. Some experts suggest reviewing within 24 hours of reading, while others recommend reviewing what you have read in short sessions over a period of time.

Connecting Your Reading to Your Life

One of the most difficult reading obstacles that every college student faces, no matter how well he reads, is generating interest in the material. A common complaint of students is that the books and course content they read are "boring." If the material you're reading seems boring, take a few minutes to consider how the content you're reading might apply to careers or societal issues that are relevant to you. For example, if you're reading a chemistry textbook about chemical reactions, take a few minutes to surf the Web to figure out what chemical reactions occur in hydrogen-powered vehicles, or what it's like to have a career as a chemist. You'll enjoy reading more and you'll better comprehend what you're reading if you can make a connection between the reading material and your own personal interests.

Another way to connect your reading with your life is to seek out pleasurable reading yourself. If you have favorite authors or types of writing, go to the library, pick out a favorite book, and give yourself some time to read for fun. Or, if you're interested in a particular sport or recreational activity, find blogs or online interest groups and read those regularly. Make an effort to find reading (and browsing will help) that is interesting, stimulating, and even fun. Reading or browsing through a magazine or newspaper a week will help your reading skills. The habit of reading will also make it easier to stick to the schedule you have set for reading class material. If you have a good book on your table, it can serve as a reward for completing less exciting reading assignments. Once you create good reading habits, you will find yourself reading—and enjoying—even after classes are over. You will soon discover that you are curious to learn new things, and reading will satisfy your thirst for knowledge.

60-second PAUSE

Take a moment to review the reading strategies that you just read about. Which strategy do you think would help you the most? Why? Try practicing that strategy when you read the next chapter in this book, or a chapter of another textbook that you have to read soon.

from COLLEGE

How the Reading Load and Expectations May Change

You have probably noticed that with each chapter's discussion of moving from college to university, the demands are greater, and the reading expectations are no exception. Most definitely, the reading load will increase significantly—you may find that you have hundreds of pages a week to read and comprehend. You may also find that you are expected to do more than just recall the information. In addition, you will need to think critically about the reading by asking questions of the author (What does she mean? How does she know? What are the implications of her argument?) and of yourself (Do I agree? Does this argument make sense?). Professors in upper-level classes will also require you to discuss the readings in class. Most definitely, the discussion will move beyond the content of the reading to the formulation of new ideas and opinions about the topic of the reading. The more you are able to contribute, the more you will get out of the reading and the class.

©SHUTTERSTOCK

from COLLEGE
to CAREER

How Reading Skills Will Help You Succeed

There are very few, if any, careers that do not require some level of reading. The jobs in computer programming and networking require constant reading to stay on top of new developments and trends in the field, as do industrial careers that require you to stay abreast of the latest regulations and laws. No matter how hard you try, there is just no escaping a career without reading.

The good news is that after completing your certificate or degree, you will be a better reader and you will understand the importance of reading regularly. A better vocabulary, improved reading comprehension, and faster reading speed will help you do your job better. An employee who reads well is an asset to a company, because she is usually more attuned to the latest trends and ideas. An employee who reads effectively also knows what is happening in the company and can more easily handle challenges on the job.

©SHUTTERSTOCK

UNDERSTAND & REMEMBER

Review Questions

1. Which reading skills are essential to success in college?

2. What are the differences between active reading and critical reading?

3. What reading strategies help a student understand the reading?

4. What types of reading difficulties might a student encounter? What are some strategies for overcoming these difficulties?

Create

Evaluate

Analyze

Apply

Understand

Remember

APPLY & ANALYZE

Critical Thinking

1. Review the steps in SQ3R, and determine which steps would be the easiest and which would be the most challenging for you. Explain why you think so. Also, mark which steps will most likely be required of you in the classes you are taking now.

2. What have your experiences been so far in terms of reading? What advice can you give to your classmates regarding conquering the reading load and expectations?

3. When undertaking a challenging reading assignment, what strategies can you use to help you complete, understand, and remember the reading?

EVALUATE

Case Scenarios

1. In high school, Will didn't have to read the textbooks for his classes to pass them. His past experience has been that if he just attends, listens, and takes notes, then he can usually do well on the exams. He believes that it is not necessary, or efficient, to read "boring" books when he can get by otherwise by finding information on the Internet that presents the material in a more interesting way. He is taking math, history, literature, and accounting this semester and is proud of himself that he has not bought any textbooks. While he hasn't had a test yet, he thinks he understands everything and even contributes new ideas to class discussions. He does not plan to purchase his books this semester, because he has friends in each class who have offered to share with him.

   Use the following scale to rate the decision that has been made (1 = Poor Decision, 5 = Excellent Decision). Be prepared to explain your answer.

   Poor Decision ← ―①―――②―――③―――④―――⑤→ Excellent Decision

2. Meghan thinks she may have a reading difficulty, but she has never been diagnosed. Instead, she has worked extra hard to keep up with and understand her reading assignments. She is a single parent who works full-time, which means that she has little time for tutoring. She also feels that because she has accomplished so much on her own—taking care of her child, holding down a well-paying job, and supporting her youngest sibling through his college career—she can handle her problem on her own. She has decided to check out a website on reading disabilities and has purchased a set of CDs for $150 that promises she will become a faster reader. She thinks this will help her.

Use the following scale to rate the decision that has been made (1 = Poor Decision, 5 = Excellent Decision). Be prepared to explain your answer.

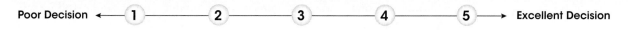

3. Wilson can't remember anything he reads for class, even though he spends hours the night before reading the material. He also has difficulty remembering what words mean. While he is building his vocabulary slowly, he still finds himself looking the same word up several times before he can remember its meaning. He has decided to make flash cards for every new word he encounters and tapes them up all over his apartment. He even keeps a stack of cards with words and definitions in his car, in case he finds himself waiting somewhere. He has also bought crossword puzzle books in the hope of increasing his vocabulary.

Use the following scale to rate the decision that has been made (1 = Poor Decision, 5 = Excellent Decision). Be prepared to explain your answer.

CREATE

Research It Further

1. Using the Internet to supplement what you have learned in this chapter, find several sites that provide information about completing a reading assignment. Choose the most effective strategies for you, and construct a bookmark that you can put inside your textbook that summarizes how to successfully complete a reading assignment.

2. Create a survey that asks members of the campus community what can be done to encourage students to read more. For example, would they be willing to participate in a book club or to host a local author on campus? Use the survey to solicit responses from various people on campus. Report your results to your class.

3. Survey your fellow classmates as to how much reading is assigned to them each week, and then ask them how much they complete each week. Make a chart that illustrates the average amount each week that is assigned and completed. Then, create a list of 10 activities or strategies that can help students complete all of their assigned readings.

TAKE THIS WITH YOU

Now you are ready to relate this to your own life:

■ Identify methods for improving your reading skills.

■ Use different reading strategies to improve your comprehension.

■ Identify reasons your reading will help you in your life or career, such as becoming more knowledgeable; improving your understanding of others' viewpoints, ideas, and cultures; and helping you understand yourself.

■ Break down a long reading assignment by skimming and scanning and identifying its key points.

■ Start building your vocabulary, increasing your reading speed, checking your comprehension, and improving your reading attention span.

■ Begin using a reading strategy, such as SQ3R.

REFERENCES AND RECOMMENDED READINGS

"Information literacy defined." Retrieved from http://www.ala.org/ala/mgrps/divs/acrl/standards/informationliteracycompetency.cfm#ildef

International Dyslexia Association. (2011). Dyslexia basics. Retrieved from http://www.interdys.org

Orfalea, P., & Marsh, A. (2007). *Copy this!: Lessons from a hyperactive dyslexic who turned a bright idea into one of America's best companies*. New York, NY: Workman.

Robinson, F. P. (1970). *Effective study* (4th ed.). New York, NY: Harper & Row.

MyStudentSuccessLab

MyStudentSuccessLab (www.mystudentsuccesslab.com) is an online solution designed to help you 'Start strong, Finish stronger' by building skills for ongoing personal and professional development.

8 Listening and Note Taking

Laura settles in her usual seat in the front row of her world civilization class.

"The clip we are about to watch," her professor says as she pushes the play button, "discusses the ancient library in Timbuktu."

"I love it when she stops lecturing and shows us these videos," her classmate next to her whispers in her ear. Laura misses some of the information.

"Hey? Do you have an extra pen?" her classmate whispers again. She hands him a pen and makes another note to fill in any gaps she has from being distracted.

"You have the material that was assigned for reading, the information I cover in the lecture, and then anything else that I bring in. All of this should be studied for the test," the professor says as the lights come back on.

"And she's not lying," says Laura to herself. Even with help from her mentor and the tutor in the learning assistance center, Laura has her work cut out for her: The information in the book is arranged chronologically, but her professor lectures on causes and effects in history.

Then, there are the tests that cover major themes, such as important reformers or federal policies. Laura has struggled in this class to find the right note-taking method to accommodate all the different types of information.

"Any other questions?" her professor asks and pauses for a few seconds. "Okay, if you realize you do have questions after class, be sure to email me or come by my office early next week. The test will be all essay questions." She smiles, straightens her papers, and heads for the door.

Making sense of her notes may be only part of Laura's challenge, but it is the first one she will have to overcome.

 YOUR GOALS FOR THIS CHAPTER

Laura can attest to the importance of developing a note-taking system, especially for those who have learning difficulties that prevent them from using just one style. When you complete this chapter, you will be able to:

- Practice methods that help you listen more effectively
- Identify barriers to listening
- Apply different note-taking strategies to each of your classes

MyStudentSuccessLab (www.mystudentsuccesslab.com) is an online solution designed to help you 'Start strong, Finish stronger' by building skills for ongoing personal and professional development.

Listening, remembering, and note taking all have something in common: They are necessary in the process of learning. You will not be able to make it successfully through your classes without doing all three. Retaining and recalling information, however, is only part of the process. This chapter helps you with receiving the information, which will in turn help you with the process of turning the information into a knowledge base that you will build on for the rest of your life.

A Prepared Listener Is a Better Listener

Active listening is a term that you may hear in college classes; someone who listens actively is concentrating on what is being said and is taking steps to remember the information. The following tips are intended for those who want to listen actively and effectively. To be an active listener, you must decide that listening is a worthwhile activity and that important information will be shared.

Your Terms for SUCCESS

WHEN YOU SEE . . .	IT MEANS . . .
Active listening	Listening with focus and a purpose
Annotating	Taking notes within a text
Cause/effect	An arrangement of information that connects the cause of an event to its effects
Chronological	An arrangement of information by time
Compare/contrast	An arrangement of information that connects the similarities and differences of two subjects
Cornell /System	A note-taking strategy that involves dividing your paper into an upside-down T, with separate areas for different types of notes
Critical listening	Listening to evaluate the information
Least important/most important	An arrangement of information that lists points based on their importance
Listening barrier	An obstacle, either physical or mental, that keeps you from listening effectively
Outlining	An arrangement of information that is ordered by how the information is presented
Shorthand	A note-taking strategy in which symbols and shortened forms of words are used
T System	Also known as the Cornell System

The first step to effective listening is to *prepare to listen before you get to class*. You will need to read the assigned pages or chapters ahead of time so that you know what the lecture or discussion topic will be. If you have read the chapters ahead of time, you will be familiar with new words and concepts. Preparing to listen also includes reviewing your assigned readings before you get to the classroom. If you have a few minutes between classes or on the bus, pull out your book and skim the major headings, bold-faced terms, and text boxes that appear in the margins. If you have a class that begins at 1 P.M., build time into your schedule to arrive at the classroom or building a few minutes early so that you have time to review the course material before class begins. This will help you keep pace with the professor when he or she starts to discuss various topics in class.

To listen effectively while in class, *avoid in-class distractions*. First, you will need to sit up front, move away from a talkative person, and put away textbooks for other courses, cell phones, pagers, and other distracting items. Your best defense against interruptions is to clear your desk of anything except your textbook, a pen, and paper. Stow other items in your backpack or underneath your desk or table.

If you need to get anything out during class, such as a dictionary, minimize the disruption by being as quiet as possible. If you find yourself next to a chatty classmate or one who likes to write notes to you, simply move. Even if you are politely listening or reading her messages, you will be guilty of disrupting the class by association. Talkative classmates make it difficult for you and others to listen, and they distract you from taking good notes.

Another good way to listen effectively is by *maintaining a positive attitude about the class*. Once you're in college and taking classes, it's easy to start taking your classes for granted and viewing them as a boring waste of time, especially when the content doesn't seem related to anything relevant in your life. Remind yourself that your decision to attend college is important and critical to your long-term success in life. Also, take some time to consider how the topic you're learning about may be relevant to your career or an important economic or social issue that society is facing today. Finally, consider the possibility that at any moment, you could learn something new that you never knew before—this is an exciting perspective that can keep you engaged in the class, no matter what the topic or how it's being discussed.

Minimizing out-of-class distractions is another method of keeping a positive attitude. There will be times that you have to work late, stay up all night with a sick baby, or help a friend who has just had a crisis. If not handled well, these stressful experiences could affect your performance in class. As much as possible, leave your personal life at the door and concentrate on the class that you are sitting in. Even if the lecture for the day is overshadowed by a personal problem, remember that you *can* handle both your academic duties and your personal life.

Finally, *prepare for class psychologically by preparing physically*. Make sure you have eaten something before each class so that you won't be interrupted by a growling stomach. Moreover, dress in layers in case the room is an uncomfortable temperature. Nothing is more distracting than being too hot or too cold. Getting plenty of sleep the night before class will also help you pay attention and listen effectively. Although adequate sleep may be a luxury if you work a late shift or if you get up in the middle of the night to take care of a child, be sure you make an effort to get a good night's sleep often. You won't be able to maintain high concentration and retention or even good health without adequate rest.

Exhibit 8.1 reviews these tips for preparing to listen.

EXHIBIT 8.1 Tips for Preparing to Listen

Tip	Explanation	Example
Prepare ahead of time.	Read all pages from textbooks, handouts, and extra material that your professor assigns or mentions.	Before the lecture on the American Dream in Arthur Miller's *Death of a Salesman*, read the entire play.
Minimize in-class distractions.	Make sure that you have few if any items or people near you that can get your attention.	Turn your phone to silent mode and stow it in your backpack before walking into class.
Maintain a positive attitude.	Stay positive about a class no matter what others have said negatively about it or what you have experienced so far.	On your way to class, think about five positive aspects of the class that will help you achieve your ultimate academic or career goal.
Minimize out-of-class distractions.	Your situation and thoughts can get in the way of concentrating on what is being said. Work to focus on the present, not the past or the future.	If there is something on your mind, write down your concerns before going to class and promise yourself to think about it after class is over.
Prepare physically.	Take care of yourself by getting enough rest and food or drink before you go to class. Wear appropriate clothing so that you will be comfortable.	Grab your jacket, an energy bar, and a bottle of water before you go to your classes.

To Listen Critically Is to Listen Well

As stated previously, active listening, much like active reading, involves focusing on the task at hand and concentrating on what is being conveyed. Another part of listening effectively is listening critically, or the act of processing what you have heard and evaluating it. Listening critically will help you make decisions about what is important and what is not, what is objective and what is biased, and what should be stored for later and what should be discarded.

Listening critically is a skill that should be practiced regularly. Your college professors will invite you to think critically and challenge your assumptions. (This is learning!) As you get more comfortable with listening actively and critically, you will move from merely listening and taking notes that reflect what your instructors have said, to listening to evaluate and ask questions of the notes you have taken. Here are some questions to consider as you work on listening critically:

- *Speaker.* Is the speaker a credible source? How do I know? What possible biases does he or she have? What is his or her experience with the topic?
- *Message.* What is the speaker's purpose? What are the details he or she uses to convey the message?

- *Details.* Is the speaker using facts or opinions? How do I know? Which type of details work best for what the speaker is trying to convey?
- *Self-knowledge.* What do I already know about the topic? How does what the speaker is saying conflict or support my beliefs and opinions? Do I feel I have learned something new?
- *Larger picture.* How does what the speaker is saying fit into the larger picture? How can I relate the message to something I already know about life or the world at large? Are there any connections between what I have heard and what I have experienced?

By looking at your syllabus, determine how the information will be presented in the course.

- Will it be presented by chapters, topics, or units? What are the note-taking expectations for the class?

- Is that information in the syllabus, or did you learn it from your professor or other students?

Answering some of these questions will get you started on the right path to listening critically. Even though you are listening critically and mentally asking questions of what you are hearing, you still need to "tune in" rather than "tune out" when you hear something that you don't agree with or don't understand.

Remember, too, that "critical" does not mean "negative." If you find that what you are hearing is not holding up to what you know about the subject or the speaker is not credible, you can still ask questions that are respectful and curious. Most speakers do not mind being politely challenged or debated.

There Are Barriers to Listening That You Can Overcome

Despite your efforts to prepare for class, you may find barriers to listening effectively, barriers that you cannot avoid no matter how well prepared you are. For example, what should you do if your instructor talks too fast, has an accent that is unfamiliar to you, uses technical jargon or an advanced vocabulary, is disorganized, digresses from the lecture material (tells stories, allows too many irrelevant questions), or does not explain key concepts? Although you cannot coach your instructor in the art of speaking, you can ask him or her to slow down or define terms. Most professors do not mind repeating information or defining specialized language on the board, because they want students to understand the material during lecture or class discussion.

It's neither your responsibility nor your role to tell the professor how to structure his or her discussion or class session. However, there are a few strategies you can use to build better structure around the content. First, ask your professor if he or she would be willing to share a copy of the lecture notes before class so you can review them beforehand. Also, you can take notes, build a structure of your own, and then take time to ask the professor for confirmation that you've captured the main ideas. For example, if the professor is explaining how photosynthesis works, but you're finding the discussion to be disorganized or confusing, take notes and try to describe the process from start to finish. Raise your hand, and ask the professor if you can walk through the steps to make sure you understand them. This process will not only help you, chances are it will help other students in the class who are having a tough time following the discussion as well.

Besides getting enough sleep and sitting comfortably in class, as discussed in the preceding paragraphs, there may be other barriers to listening effectively. If you have an unaccommodated learning disability or a hearing problem, you may not be able to listen productively. Talking to a counselor about learning or hearing difficulties can get you the help you need to listen more effectively. A more common hindrance to listening is students' insecurities about their ability to do well in the course. It is not uncommon for a new student to feel intimidated by the course, the instructor, or other students in the class, at first. The reason for the discomfort could stem from a student's feelings that he or she is not good enough or smart enough to be in college. A student also may feel that everyone else knows what to do, what to say, and how to act, while they do not. This fear is common, and usually it subsides after the first week or two. These feelings are also based on a belief that's rarely true. If you have a question about something the professor said, or if you're confused about something, there's a very good chance that several other students are as well. The question is who will have the courage and leadership qualities to raise their hand and ask the professor to review or clarify something.

Listening Is Just the First Step Toward Remembering

Once you adequately prepare to listen in class and you remove any barriers that inhibit your ability to take in information, you will need to turn your attention to remembering what you hear in class. Taking notes, of course, is one way to retain information. However, there are some other methods that will help you recall information at a later date.

Participating in discussions and activities is an excellent way to remember key concepts. In fact, professors consider student participation as part of active learning. You are more likely to remember a concept if you have incorporated it into your own thinking. There is a reason that students who participate in class discussions are usually the most successful—they have made the material relevant to themselves, which makes remembering it easier for them as well. However, participating in class discussion may be difficult if you are shy or feel out of place in the classroom. Some students refrain from asking questions because they don't want to look ignorant in front of their classmates. These fears are often based on beliefs that are untrue. "Everyone else understands this, and I'm the only one who's confused," "I don't belong in this class," and "If I ask a question, everyone will laugh at me," are some of the thoughts that might run through your head when you're in class. Push past those thoughts and raise your hand. It's a courageous step that will help you gain confidence. You'll quickly discover that other students had the same questions and confusion as you did, that your professor really wants to help you understand the material, and that you remember more about the topics covered in class when there is some class discussion about them.

Then, there is the other end of the spectrum from the silent student—the constant questioner. These students dominate the professor's time by asking questions that sideline the discussion or asking questions about material that has already been covered. Professors value the *quality* of a student's participation and not just its *quantity*. Don't be intimidated by a predominantly quiet classroom or by a student who asks the professor

Prepare for class in advance and get involved in class discussions so that your notes will be more meaningful when you go back to review them.

© THINKSTOCK

excessive questions. If you have a question, ask it. If you don't feel comfortable asking questions during class, visit with your professor after class or during office hours. Some instructors ask students to write questions down and pass them up before class is over. Take advantage of such a practice; you will be able to ask questions without the fear of speaking up in front of classmates.

Recording lectures is another popular method for remembering what you heard in class, if you have the time to listen to the recordings later. Listening to a recording will work best if you have a long commute or if you go over your notes as you listen. Be sure to ask permission before you begin recording, and make sure you have fresh batteries with you in case they run down. Some colleges are using "lecture capture" systems to record the lectures for you to view on the Web later. Ask your professor if such a service is offered at your campus and for his or her class.

Based on everything you've read about listening, how good of a listener do you think you are? On a scale of 1 to 5, with 1 representing that you don't listen well at all and 5 representing that you actively practice almost everything that was suggested in this section, what score would you give yourself? What's one activity you could focus on during your very next class that would help improve your score?

TAKING NOTES IS PART OF THE LISTENING PROCESS

There are numerous methods of taking notes for a class. Your goal should be to find the note-taking strategy that works best for you. Remember that you may have to adapt your note-taking style to each course, each teaching style, and each of your learning style strengths. For example, outlining may work well in a history course in which the instructor writes key terms on the board and organizes the lecture around these key ideas. If your professor prefers unstructured discussion, you will need to adapt your note-taking strategy to make the most of disorganized information.

Whatever you choose for the particular course, your learning style, and the specific situation, remember these tips when taking notes:

- Listen for the main ideas. Instructors will slow down and emphasize information, terms, and definitions. They may even use verbal signposts, such as "The most important thing to remember is . . . ," "This may appear on an exam," or "Two crucial points about . . ." If the instructor writes or hands out an outline, you can be sure that it contains the main points of the lecture.
- Leave plenty of "white space" (blank space on paper) when taking notes. Don't try to fill your page with as much information as possible. You will need the white space to add more notes or to synthesize ideas once you have reviewed.
- Review your notes as soon as possible after class. Waiting for two weeks to review your notes will ensure that you won't remember everything that you have written or how it all fits together. Most experts suggest that you review your notes within two days of the class.

Knowing How Information Is Presented Can Improve Your Note Taking

Learning to listen effectively is the first step to taking good notes, but you will also benefit from understanding how information can be presented during a lecture. As you attend more classes, you will probably notice that professors have a certain way in which they present their material. Some will follow the textbook, presenting information in the same order. Others will lecture only on new material that cannot be found in the textbook or other course materials. Others will present a combination of the two methods. Reading assigned chapters and materials before you attend class will allow you to determine which information in the lecture is new and which has been covered in assigned reading materials.

There are many different ways information can be organized. Recognizing the different ways material can be organized will help you stay organized in your notes and will provide you with strategies for revising and reviewing your notes when you begin studying.

Chronological—details arranged in time (first this happened, then this happened, etc.).

Example of Chronological Lecture Notes

1801: United Kingdom of Great Britain is created

1803: Louisiana Purchase is made by Thomas Jefferson

1815: Battle of Waterloo signals end of Napoleon's career

Cause/effect—details arranged by presenting a cause and then its effects, or an effect and its causes.

Example of Cause/Effect Lecture Notes

Cause: Civil War

Effects: slavery ended, industrialism began, the nation was brought back together, the federal government proved stronger than the states

Compare/contrast—details arranged by similarities and differences.

Example of Compare/Contrast Lecture Notes

Similarities between Robert Frost and Walt Whitman: they were males; they used nature in their poetry; and they were considered "poets of the people."

Differences between Frost and Whitman: Frost's poetry is more structured, while Whitman's is open and loose; Whitman's speakers are more positive and upbeat than Frost's; Whitman lived during the 19th century while Frost lived in both the 19th and 20th centuries.

Most important/least important—details arranged in order of importance.

The most important detail can come first with minor supporting details to follow, or the least important details can start a list that works up to a major detail.

Example of Most Important/Least Important Lecture Notes

Truman Commission (1946)*
Barriers to equal opportunity & toward equalizing opportunity (most important sections of the doc.)

Number who should receive higher education & the role of education (2nd most import.)

The need for general education & a time of crisis (least import. secs.)

*first pres. comm. on hi. ed.

Abbreviations Can Help You Take Notes Faster

As you take more notes in each class, you will find yourself using a few of the same words over and over again. These words are good candidates for abbreviating or denoting in symbols. You can then create your own shorthand. Shortened words such as "ex." for "example," "w/" for "with," and "b/c" for "because" are abbreviations you probably already use in notes and email messages. Symbols that you may already use include % for "percentage," + for "add" or "and," and # for "number." If you use a new abbreviation or symbol for a word, be sure to make a note of what it means; for example, "TR" could mean "Theory of Relativity" in a science course and "Teddy Roosevelt" in a history course. Exhibit 8.2 shows other commonly abbreviated words and symbols.

Developing shorthand abbreviations that are easily understood will allow you more time to concentrate on what is being said. As you get more practice, you will become better at judging what information is worth writing and what is not, and your shorthand will become more efficient. Just remember to read over your notes within a day or two so that your abbreviations are fresh in your mind. It is a good idea, then, to complete the words or concepts so that you won't struggle to remember what all the shortened words mean later in the semester. Plus, this will help reinforce the material in your mind.

EXHIBIT 8.2	Common Abbreviations
At	@
Between	betw, b/w
Decrease	decr
Department	dept
Does not equal	≠
Government	govt
Increase	incr
Equals	=
Example	eg, ex
Important	imp
Information	info
Regarding	re
Significant	sig

Outlining Is an Effective Note-Taking Strategy

Using an outline is a good method for taking notes if the instructor is organized and offers information in a logical pattern. Some instructors encourage outlining by writing key words and concepts on the board or an overhead projecting device. If your instructor organizes lectures or class discussions in this manner, you will be able to write an outline for your notes quite easily. The key to making your outlines effective will be to provide plenty of space between the items so that you can fill in the blank spaces with extra information. An example of an outline for a lecture on effective listening could look like this:

   I. Preparing to Listen Effectively
  II. Listening Critically
 III. Possible Listening Barriers
     A. External
        1. Hunger
        2. Climate discomfort
     B. Internal
        1. Feelings of self-worth
        2. Stress
  IV. How Information Is Presented
     A. Chronological
     B. Cause/Effect
     C. Compare/Contrast
     D. Most Important/Least Important

Your Textbook Provides a Great Note-Taking Resource

Writing in the margins of your textbook can be another effective way to take notes, especially if the reading assignment is lengthy. If you don't mind writing directly in your textbook, you can summarize main points that you have read. Writing brief (two- or three-word) summaries or questions in the margins will help you make sense of and remember what you have read. Brief, marginal summaries will also help you review the material before class, and after class when you start studying for an exam.

Annotating in your textbook and writing down critical questions are two methods of further reinforcing what you have read and will help you prepare for listening and note taking in class. To write critical questions about the reading, ask questions such as "How do I know this to be true?" and "What else should be considered?" Annotating your textbook with your own notes will help you not only reinforce main ideas, but will also help you synthesize the information in new ways that will produce connections between concepts, making the material more memorable and more relevant.

Find a note-taking style that works best for your learning style preference and each class you are taking.

©SHUTTERSTOCK

If you decide to write in the margins of your textbook, be sure that the book you are writing in is not one that you want to sell back to the bookstore. If you do not want to write in your book but still reap the benefits of summarizing the material, you can write your summaries on a separate sheet of paper or even sticky notes that can be removed at the end of the semester. With either strategy, make sure that you label each piece of paper with the chapter title and page number of the book.

Highlighting in your textbook is another method that students use for taking notes on reading material. A highlighter pen can be used to mark important concepts for review, but be careful that you do not highlight too much information. Over-highlighting the text can have the opposite effect—instead of making it easier to understand key terms and information, too much highlighting can make everything seem of equal importance. If you do use a highlighter pen, use it sparingly. For example, don't highlight more than two sentences in a row. A better method would be to use highlighting and written summaries together for the greatest effect. See Chapter 7 to reinforce this idea.

The T System Could Work Well For You

Cornell University professor Dr. Walter Pauk (2004) developed a system for note taking that has been popular with many students. The Cornell System, also known as the T System, is ideal for those who benefit from the visual impact of organized notes, and it can benefit other types of learners, such as Laura, because it is an organized way to take and review notes. The key to the Cornell System is dividing your notebook paper before you begin writing. To do so, you draw a horizontal line across your piece of paper two inches from the bottom of the page. Then, you draw a vertical line from the horizontal line to the top of the page about 2 inches from the left-hand margin. The page should look like Exhibit 8.3.

The largest area, the right-hand column, is used for taking notes during class. The left-hand column is used for writing down questions as you take notes if there is material you don't understand during the lecture or if there are possible exam questions that you think about as you are writing. At the bottom, the final section is reserved for summarizing your notes as you review them. The act of summarizing should help you understand and remember the information.

60-second PAUSE

List the various note-taking strategies that are described in the section you just read. Which of these strategies do you feel would work best for you? Why?

DESIGN YOUR NOTES TO FIT YOU

The following strategies for note taking in the disciplines are just a sample of what you may encounter in college. Another chapter will discuss specific study strategies within each discipline, but here we give some note-taking strategies, grouped by discipline, that will make reviewing your notes and studying easier.

Your Notes Will Vary in Each Discipline

Art

In an art appreciation class, you will need to identify eras (20th century), movements (Cubism), and artists (Picasso), as well as their characteristics, as seen in drawings, paintings, and sculpture. Quickly sketching the works in your notes and listing the characteristic details will help you record the information you are receiving through lectures. You may also notice that in the study of art there are times of intense change (usually coinciding with a world or cultural event), followed by artists who imitate or slightly modify the new style. As you review your notes, look for patterns within groups of artwork and for points of contrast.

Music

In a music appreciation class, the same suggestions for an art appreciation class will work when you take notes. Instead of recreating a painting or sculpture in your notes, you may need to write down descriptions of what you are hearing and what the sounds

TECHNOLOGY *Tips*

remind you of. Are the sounds fast or slow? Do you hear one instrument or many? Does it sound like a stampede or a trip down a lazy river? "Translating" music samples into written notes, as well as reviewing music clips on your own, will strengthen your understanding of the material. As with your art notes, upon review, look for patterns across movements and eras and denote contrasting ideas and elements.

Literature

Taking notes in a literature class will require that you have completed the assigned readings before class and that you have annotated and highlighted your text. Because literature classes, even survey classes, focus more on discussion than on lecture, you will want to be prepared to take notes on the analysis. As with music and art classes, being familiar with basic terminology before you get to class will help you take better notes. As you review your notes, look for ideas that pull the different readings together.

Languages

Foreign language classes center more on speaking and interacting than on listening to a lecture. Taking notes will not necessarily be advantageous, for you will need to focus all your attention on listening actively, processing what is heard, and interacting based on what you have heard. Daily preparation is essential to learning foreign languages; take notes as you encounter new material, and ask questions in class to get clarification on anything you do not understand. Any notes you do take should be reviewed soon after the class. As you review your notes, categorize material, such as "irregular verbs," and include any tips for using or remembering the parts of language.

Science

Concepts and processes are key in science classes, and your notes will reflect that. Prepare for class by reading assigned material, making note of new vocabulary words, and studying diagrams and figures in the text and handouts. As with any class, ask questions if you are having trouble following the steps of a process. As you review your notes, consider the different ways that you can represent these concepts and processes visually and physically to help you remember them better.

History

History class lectures are usually presented in chronological order, so using the tips provided earlier for information that follows a time sequence will help you take notes in this class. However, you will also be required to move beyond specific dates and events by considering overall themes, ideas, and movements. In addition to chronological order, lectures may also use a cause/effect organization, in which you list and elaborate on the effects of a cause or the causes of an effect. An example of a lecture topic in a history class is: "The economic and social effects of the end of the Civil War." As you review your notes, look for major themes and aim to recall actions that have led to important events.

Math

Taking good notes in your math classes will require that you prepare and attend each class meeting. As with foreign languages, studying for math should be an everyday occurrence, because the skills you learn in each class build on the ones you learned in the class before. When reviewing your notes, you may want to recopy them and make sure that you understand, line by line, each problem that you are copying. If you have any questions, you can write them in the margins of your notes and ask questions during the next class meeting.

Match Your Note-Taking Strategies with Your Learning Preferences

Visual learners benefit from seeing the notes on the page, but they may also benefit from creating images out of the material they have written down. Take, for example, a possible lecture on academic integrity. An instructor may talk through or write down a few key ideas on the board or in handouts that look like this:

BUZZ

Q I take a lot of notes in class, but when it's time to review for a quiz or exam, I feel like there's too much material (textbook, assigned readings, notes, etc.) to review. When am I supposed to have time to thoroughly review my notes?

A Remember that reviewing your notes is as important as taking the notes. Here are some tips to make it easier to review:

- Review your notes immediately after class or at the end of the day after a class.

- Edit and add to your notes to clarify certain points.

- Meet with your study group and compare your notes.

**Academic Integrity—doing what is right academically even in the face of adversity

*Two kinds of violations of academic integrity include cheating and plagiarism.

Plagiarism comes in several varieties, but the two most common are no documentation and cut-and-paste. There are also self-plagiarism, following too close to original, word-for-word, and buying papers...

A visual learner may take that same information and create a visual representation of the definitions and types, as shown in Laura's notes in Exhibit 8.4.

Reading notes aloud, recording lectures, or recording yourself talking through material are all strategies for aural learners. Although "taking notes" implies writing down words and then reading through them, there is no reason that aural learners must suppress their learning style strength during the process. An aural learner, like Laura, can pair up with someone who is a read/write learner, like Juanita, and talk through the material that they heard in a recent class. The read/write learner can then record notes or annotate ones she already has and share them with the aural learner.

The act of taking notes by writing them or typing them provides kinesthetic learners with a physical activity that makes remembering what has been written easier. Kinesthetic learners, like Evan, can benefit from using more physical activity or objects when they review their notes shortly after taking them. For example, if you are using formulas to calculate volume in your math class, you may want to review your notes by creating your own volume problems in the kitchen. The act of pouring and measuring water and then calculating your measurements will make it easier to remember the process when you complete homework problems or take a test.

Likewise, a good way for a kinesthetic learner to study for an art class, or any class that uses visual images, is to recreate with paper and colored pencils the artwork you are studying. No need to strive for masterpiece quality when recreating works of art; the physical activity of drawing the wavy lines in the background of Edvard Munch's *The Scream* will help you recall the piece on an exam.

It's Helpful to Discover Your Own Note-Taking Style

Laura has developed a special note-taking system for herself because of a learning disability. After taking an introduction to college course, she discovered that the note-taking systems that were discussed in her textbook did not help her take good notes. Through trial and error, she developed a system that works for her.

To begin with, Laura writes in pencil on her notebook paper. Before class begins, she dates each page and leaves herself plenty of room to write. When taking notes, she writes on only one side of the page; in fact, most of her pages of notes contain fewer than 50 words. While she uses more pieces of paper, her notes are easier to read.

Next, she places stars next to words that the instructor says are important. The most important part of her note-taking system is her use of arrows to make connections between ideas. By giving herself plenty of room, she can add connections that are revealed later in the lecture. If her instructor reviews the material before an exam, Laura highlights what she already has and adds notes in the spaces.

One strategy that Laura has developed to help her with her learning disability is that she doesn't worry about spelling. To make connections between ideas, she draws lines between words that relate to each other. She also makes charts for anything that is compared and contrasted (see Laura's notes in Exhibit 8.4). Finally, she keeps all of her notes in a binder that is divided for each class. Staying organized is an important part of her method. Although she uses only one binder during the semester, she keeps her notes easily organized by removing them after an exam. When she takes out notes she no longer needs, she places them in labeled folders at home. Then she carries with her only the notes she needs at that time.

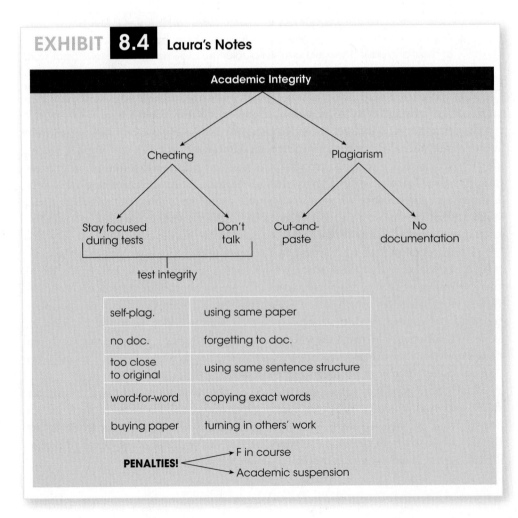

EXHIBIT 8.4 Laura's Notes

Reviewing Your Notes Leads to Deeper Learning

Notes are only as good to the extent that you review them. If you never look at your notes after you take them, they will serve very little purpose. Therefore, to make the most of your notes, you will need to review them. As stated earlier in the chapter, reviewing should be done within two days from the time you took them. With this said, it is easy to be lulled into the sense of "studying" by merely reading over your notes again and again. When reviewing your notes, it is best to reorganize the material, make connections between concepts—even across disciplines—and ask questions about what you are learning.

If you use the Cornell System, then you have a built-in area for adding more information, summarizing, and asking yourself questions. However, if you do not use a particular method, you can still benefit from filling in any blanks or holes in your notes with information you have since learned. As stated earlier, you should also spell out any abbreviations you have that may cause confusion later. After you fill in any gaps, you should also include questions—either on the same page or a new page—that will help you think about the material on a deeper level. For example, asking "Why is it important to know this?" can help you move beyond demonstrating your comprehension of the material to making it relevant and useful for you.

Freewriting about the material that you learned is another way of remembering and learning the information that you have listened to. This technique is often used as a way to generate ideas for writing, but it can also be used to take advantage of all the thoughts you have in your head about the material. For optimum effectiveness, you will need to freewrite within a day or two of the class lecture. With or without your notes, write down (or type into a word processor) all the information that you remember from the class.

The key to freewriting is continuation; in other words, do not stop writing even if you can't spell a certain word or get stuck on a particular idea. Give yourself 5 or 10

INTEGRITY *Matters*

Student or professional note-takers provide an important service for students with disabilities or unique learners so they can receive the same educational opportunities as other students, and there may be a time when you rely on a note-taker.

To maintain integrity, respect your note-taker by not missing class and being prepared for class. The note-taker is a supplement when you are absent or cannot take notes on your own. Act with integrity whether you are borrowing notes from a classmate, relying on a note-taker, or taking notes for someone else.

YOUR TURN

In approximately 250 words, explain how you feel about taking notes for a classmate or relying on others for notes. Discuss the issues you need to consider when relying on a classmate for notes or providing notes for someone else.

EXHIBIT 8.5   Tips for Successful Note Taking

Prepare for class by reading all the assigned material before arriving. If you cannot read all of it, then read as much as you can.

Prepare to listen actively by removing distractions and bringing supplies.

Listen actively; concentrate on what you are hearing, seeing, and experiencing.

Listen critically by asking questions, either on paper or directly in class if your professor encourages questions during class.

Use a note-taking strategy that takes into account both your learning style strength and the subject matter.

Go beyond reviewing your notes by just re-reading them; instead, focus on concepts and main ideas, make connections between the large ideas, and ask critical questions of processes and ideas.

Continue the process regularly throughout the semester.

Save your notes! Your chemistry notes from your freshman year may be useful when you take a polymers class during your senior year. It's also helpful to review your notes as you progress through college, because it can build your confidence in how much you're learning.

Review your notes regularly, or they will have little value.

©ISTOCKPHOTO

minutes to freewrite; then, go through your freewriting material (some of it you will be able to use and some of it you will scratch out) and highlight or rewrite into complete sentences the information that pertains to the lecture. In essence, you will be learning the material in more depth as you write about it.

Finally, reciting notes with a friend can be a useful method for reviewing material. You can do this in person or on the phone. The benefits of reading your notes aloud and discussing them include filling in any gaps of information and reinforcing what you have learned. You can also engage in critical questioning of the material and take turns making connections between major concepts. See Exhibit 8.5 for a review of tips for successful note taking.

60-second PAUSE

What materials and supplies (e.g., notebooks, highlighters) will you need to put your own note-taking style into action? Some students are choosing to use a laptop or tablet computer to take and organize notes. What are some of the benefits or limitations of using these technology tools?

from COLLEGE

Improving Listening and Note-Taking Skills When There Are More Distractions

When you transfer to a four-year university, the good habits that you have practiced at your community college will help you succeed. However, you may find that you have more distractions. There may be more people on campus and in your classes, more organizations and associations to join, more activities to participate in, and more stress in deciding on a major and getting ready to graduate.

In addition to distractions, you may also find that professors at four-year universities lecture less and rely more on student discussions and presentations. Your ability to organize the material will be vitally important to your making sense of the course. If you find yourself at a loss for what to do to take good notes, talk to others at the university. You may also discover that group interaction and work is not only encouraged but is necessary for success.

from COLLEGE

Practicing Critical Listening Skills Will Give You an Edge on the Job

Most of the communication you will do on the job will involve listening: listening to clients' urgent needs, your employer's plans for the next six months, coworkers' explanations of how they would complete a project, and subordinates' questions about how to improve. Being a good listener will involve practicing the critical listening tips we have discussed in this chapter. Critical listening skills will enable you to filter what you are hearing so that you can act appropriately and avoid making errors in action and judgment.

Consider, for example, a coworker who comes to you to complain about a company policy. Without listening actively and critically, you may disregard what the speaker is saying because you don't have time to do anything about it. However, if you take the time to analyze the speaker and the message, as well as what you know about the situation and the larger picture, then you are more likely to act confidently.

UNDERSTAND & REMEMBER

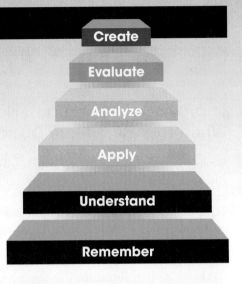

Review Questions

1. What is the difference between active listening and critical listening?

2. What are some potential listening barriers in the classroom?

3. In what ways can information be presented in class?

4. List and describe the different note-taking strategies.

APPLY & ANALYZE

Critical Thinking

1. Think about a time that you listened to someone speak about a topic that you did not agree with. How did you listen? How did you react to what you were hearing? What would you do differently based on what you have learned in this chapter?

2. What are some drawbacks to using the Cornell System, shorthand, and outlines when taking notes? In which classes would the Cornell System be most beneficial, and why?

3. What is your experience with listening effectively and taking notes in college so far? What kinds of issues do you encounter in each class with regard to listening? What kinds of issues do you encounter with note-taking? Which strategies can help you the most with these issues? How?

EVALUATE

Case Scenarios

1. Juan is taking a visual arts class and is having trouble making sense of his notes each week, because they are over information that pertains to specific artwork. The instructor does not hand out reproductions of the art, so the students must sketch the pieces during class, but that takes too long. Juan also has difficulty writing (or sketching quickly), so he decides that it would be better to just listen while the professor lectures and then print off copies of the artwork from the Internet and make notes on the copies at home.

   Use the following scale to rate the decision that has been made (1 = Poor Decision, 5 = Excellent Decision). Be prepared to explain your answer.

Poor Decision ← ①——②——③——④——⑤ → Excellent Decision

2. Theo has borrowed Jon's notes for his College Algebra class and has promised to return them before the next exam. However, Theo has lost them, and with only two days left before the next test, he is not sure what to do. Jon is a good student and probably doesn't need them, but Theo wants to be able to borrow future notes from Jon. He decides to borrow another classmate's notes, copy them, and then give Jon the copies after explaining what happened.

   Use the following scale to rate the decision that has been made (1 = Poor Decision, 5 = Excellent Decision). Be prepared to explain your answer.

   Poor Decision ← 1 —— 2 —— 3 —— 4 —— 5 → Excellent Decision

3. Karla has a learning difficulty, and she struggles with taking notes. The counselor has assigned her a note-taker. Now that Karla is getting help with writing down notes, she has stopped preparing for class and has stopped listening closely. Sometimes, she doesn't get notes from her note-taker until a week later. Instead of complaining to her disability counselor, she decides to ask another classmate if she can borrow his notes each week.

   Use the following scale to rate the decision that has been made (1 = Poor Decision, 5 = Excellent Decision). Be prepared to explain your answer.

   Poor Decision ← 1 —— 2 —— 3 —— 4 —— 5 → Excellent Decision

CREATE

Research It Further

1. Take a survey of the students in one of your other classes as to which of the discussed note-taking strategies they use the most. Create a table of your results, and present it to your classmates.

2. Using the keyword "note-taking strategies," search the Internet for websites that offer note-taking methods. Choose two or three and review the information to determine which site offers the most practical and complete tips. Present your findings to the class.

3. Create your own note-taking or listening strategy and present it to the class, highlighting the benefits of your method over another method.

TAKE THIS WITH YOU

Based on the goals we set at the beginning of this chapter, here's how you can take this learning with you toward college success:

■ Practice active listening by focusing on what the speaker is saying and remembering what he or she has said before responding or forming an opinion.

■ Start listening critically by considering the speaker's authority, credibility, and accuracy.

■ Begin to identify listening barriers that you face in your classes, and practice strategies for eliminating them.

■ Choose the best note-taking strategy for each class you are taking.

■ Review your notes within a day or two of taking them.

REFERENCES AND RECOMMENDED READINGS

Beglar, D., & Murray, N. (2009). *Contemporary topics 3: Academic and note-taking skills* (3rd ed.). Boston, MA: Pearson.

Kline, J. A. (1996). *Effective listening*. Montgomery, AL: Maxwell Air Force Base, Air University Press.

Pauk, W., & Owens, J. R. Q. (2004). *How to study in college*. Boston, MA: Cengage.

Rowson, P. (2007). *Communicating with more confidence*. Easy Step-by-Step Guides (Rev.). Hayling, UK: Summersdale.

Spears, D. (2008). *Developing critical reading skills*. New York, NY: McGraw-Hill.

MyStudentSuccessLab

MyStudentSuccessLab (www.mystudentsuccesslab.com) is an online solution designed to help you 'Start strong, Finish stronger' by building skills for ongoing personal and professional development.

9 Writing, Presenting, and Information Literacy

"A 15-page research paper and 5-minute PowerPoint presentation. Due during the last week of class," Juanita repeats to her mother over the phone.

"What do you have to write it on?" her mother asks.

"We get to pick from a list, but I don't even know what some of the topics are, like 'conflict manage-ment theory,'" Juanita says as she looks over the list again. "I guess that is the point of research."

"You better get started, Juanita. I know how you are about writing papers—even when you end u doing well."

Juanita remembered how many nights she stayed up writing papers at the last minute because she didn't know for sure how to get started. She also felt she did better during the rush and excitemen of the clock ticking.

"I guess this is my chance to break those bad habits," Juanita says. "Michael told me that Dr. Kirsey is tough on grading."

"I thought this was sociology, not English," her mother says.

"It is, Mom, but all of my instructors still expect me to write a good paper. Most of them have Ph.D.s! If it is not written wel or doesn't use the right kind of resources, then you can kiss a good grade goodbye," Juanita says. "And it is not just a paper. have to get up and say something about what I learned. You know how nervous I get doing that."

"You're a good writer, Juanita. You have always loved to write," her mother says. Juanita hears the sound of water in the back ground, a sign her mother is cleaning up the kitchen.

Juanita tells her mother she will call her later, and she heads toward the library to get started on her 15-page paper and presentation on a topic that she knows nothing about right now.

 YOUR GOALS FOR THIS CHAPTER

Regardless of your major or final career destination, you will be asked to write in college and in your job. As Juanita knows from college classes so far, writing well is an important skill, and you will have the chance to improve your writing while you're in college. Specifically, after reading this chapter, you will be able to:

- Anticipate the types of writing assignments you'll be assigned and your professors' expectations for these assignments

- Identify the steps in the writing process
- Recognize all the stages of effective research
- Create and deliver an effective presentation

MyStudentSuccessLab (www.mystudentsuccesslab.com) is an online solution designed to help you 'Start strong, Finish stronger' by building skills for ongoing personal and professional development.

Homework has a whole new meaning in college. These assignments are more than just a basic review of what you learned in class, and they certainly are not the dreaded "busy work" that you experienced in high school. Instead, the assignments you will be given in college will challenge you to think in ways that you may not be used to, and they will demand much more time than you may have taken to complete assignments in high school. While you will encounter familiar assignments, such as extra problem-solving questions in math classes and research papers in English classes, you may also be required to complete a class multimedia project that involves using PowerPoint or even a community-based project that entails working with various agencies to develop a real-world solution to a problem and then presenting it to local community leaders. Other types of writing and presentation assignments include those listed in Exhibit 9.1.

Take the Time to First Understand the Assignment

Before you can bask in the glory of a well-done project or essay, you will have to start with the first, sometimes most crucial step in succeeding—understanding the assignment. Too many students start writing right away without fully understanding the directions, the requirements, and the time, equipment, and skills that are necessary to complete the assignment.

EXHIBIT 9.1 **College Writing and Presentation Assignments**

Journal	Personal reflections on given topics or on your experience during the semester; often considered an informal writing assignment.
Portfolio	A collection of writing that is usually used to showcase development over time.
Project proposal	A written intention of what a project topic, argument, or scope will be; usually a short assignment that is completed early in the process of a larger project.
Essay	Literally defined as an "attempt"; an original composition that presents an argument or viewpoint on a topic.
Research paper	A formal assignment that requires the use of appropriate sources; usually requires an original argument or approach to present the research.
Report	A retelling of a process or experience.
Demonstration	A show of a process or the mastery of a skill.
In-class and out-of-class group assignment	Collaborative work that requires participation by all members.
Formal and informal classroom presentation	A brief expression of an opinion, topic, or experience, or an elaborate, lengthy presentation that includes visual aids.

Your Terms for SUCCESS

WHEN YOU SEE . . .	IT MEANS . . .
Brainstorming	A prewriting technique that involves writing down everything that comes to mind in a list
Clustering	A prewriting technique that involves visually representing how a subject is related to other subjects; also called mind mapping
Concrete details	Details or examples that appeal to a reader's sight, taste, smell, touch, or hearing
Conclusion	The last paragraph of an essay that presents your overall points and final thoughts
Essay	Literally "an attempt"; a type of assignment that has an introduction, a thesis, body paragraphs, and a conclusion, but often does not contain extensive research. Instead, it often focuses on author's experiences, ideas, and logical arguments
Freewriting	A prewriting technique that involves writing freely and without consideration of punctuation, grammar, or spelling
Organization	The order in which information is presented in your essay or paper
Outline	The essential parts of a paper or speech; usually presented in a specific outline format using Roman numerals for each major part
Peer review	A process in which a peer, or classmate, evaluates your paper or project
Physical delivery	The bodily and facial movements that enhance or distract from a speech
Portfolio	A collection of separate assignments or of drafts of an assignment
Research	The act of finding, evaluating, and incorporating sources into an assignment
Rough draft	An unpolished attempt at an assignment
Thesis	The central idea of an essay that is supported throughout the writing
Transitions	Words or phrases that signal changes in thought or additional ideas

Know the Difference Between Due and Do

There are two words you will hear when your professor discusses a writing assignment with you, and although they sound similar, they have two different meanings: "do" and "due." You will "do" your paper, meaning research and write it, well before it is "due" to be turned in. Waiting to write an essay the night before or even the day it is due can be an undertaking much larger than one originally anticipated. Most assignments in college will require hours of researching, taking notes, constructing outlines, writing drafts, and formatting and printing the final document. In some cases, you may need the entire semester to work on a large project. You may also need to allot enough time to use a computer or other technology that is required of you. These tasks add to the

Preparing ahead of time to complete a writing assignment is part of the writing process.

© THINKSTOCK

time it takes to finish an assignment, so say goodbye to quickly jotting down answers or writing an assignment the hour before class. You should begin to D-O the project well before it is D-U-E.

Read and Follow Directions

Giving yourself adequate time to complete an assignment will allow you to carefully read and follow the directions. Too often, students rush through an assignment sheet only to omit a critical requirement. For example, will you need to submit your assignment via email? Will you need to prepare a list of resources you used to complete it? Does it need to be typed? Does it require a cover page? Will you need to make visual aids? All of these are possible requirements, and if you are unsure of what is expected of you, despite the assignment details, be sure to ask for clarification. Consider the assignment given in Exhibit 9.2, and see if you can determine what requirements you will need to fulfill as you complete it. Underline, circle, or highlight the important information.

Every Assignment Will Have a Length, Audience, and Purpose

Length, audience, and purpose are other key factors in understanding writing assignments. For many assignments, you will be assigned a length, such as a 2-page paper or a 1,500-word essay. Instructors often specify the length of an assignment to give you a sense of how detailed and comprehensive your coverage should be. For instance, if

---

EXHIBIT 9.2 **Example of Assignment Directions**

Topic Proposal

Due: Wednesday, April 18

Before you begin work on your research paper, you will submit a proposal to me for approval. This process is much like proposals that scholars submit to determine if they will be accepted for a conference. Your proposal must be typed and must contain the following all on one or two pages:

- Your name
- Working title of your research paper
- Working thesis of your research paper
- A 75-word abstract (summary) of your topic
- A 100-word description of how you plan to research your topic

your instructor assigns you a 1-page review of a website, then a 10-page paper will not be appropriate because too much information will be included. Conversely, if you have a 2,500-word research paper to write, a 750-word paper will not suffice because there will not be enough information and reflection to fulfill the assignment. If you worry that you cannot meet the length requirement of an assignment, talk with your instructor as soon as possible. He or she will be able to help you narrow or expand your topic so that you will have enough material.

The audience for your assignment describes who will be reading the paper. Is your reader an expert in the topic, or a fellow college student who has never heard of the topic before? You would write the assignment differently for these two audiences, so you need to know what audience your instructor wants you to address before beginning the assignment. Do not assume that the audience is just your professor. If the professor doesn't specify the audience, ask for clarification. If an audience is not specified for your assignment, and you don't get clarification from your instructor, imagine that you are writing to college students who have been studying the same subject—for example, your classmates. How you present your ideas and the words you use should be appropriate for other college students.

There may be, however, times when you will be assigned a particular audience as part of the requirements for a writing project. The reason that instructors do this is to help you focus your ideas, language, and argument. Consider, for example, an assignment that may be part of a health class:

Writing Assignment for Concepts of Health and Wellness

Due Date: Friday, March 8, 2013

Format: MLA or APA

Assignment: In a three-page paper, argue whether or not sports and energy drinks are "gateway" drugs. Be sure to provide five references from reputable sources, preferably science or health journals.

This is a straightforward assignment that can be completed by anyone who has access to current information. However, how would the assignment change if your audience were 12-year-old elementary school students? What information would you add or eliminate? What kind of language would you use? Would you include visual aids, such as diagrams or cartoons? How much detail would you provide? These are all details you will have to consider because your audience will have certain limitations. Unfamiliar vocabulary, technical terms, detailed information, and photographs may be inappropriate for this target audience. Simple terms, diagrams, and personal stories about kids their own age may be a better way to convey the more complicated information.

Now, consider the same topic with an audience of college students. Again, you will have the same questions: What information would you add or eliminate? What kind of language would you use? Would you include visual aids, such as diagrams or cartoons? How much detail would you provide? Obviously, this audience will have different needs than the elementary school students. Because your audience is more mature, you will need to think about how to approach a topic that they have definite ideas about. Some may be resistant to hearing about the topic because they believe it is not appropriate to discuss; others may feel they know enough to make their own decisions. Still others will not see the relevance for them. As our two examples show, these challenges are unique to your audience—changing *who* you are writing for changes *how* you present the information.

It's in the SYLLABUS

A final consideration for your assignment is your purpose. Your purpose for writing will be closely connected to your assignment (see the assignment types discussed previously and detailed in Exhibit 9.1), but there are other purposes for writing. For example, in addition to evaluating a website, your purpose could also be to make your audience laugh. As you compare two popular diet plans in a paper, your purpose could be to persuade readers that one of the plans is a healthier choice. The purposes for writing are endless, but it is important to ask yourself why you are writing and what you want to accomplish besides just completing an assignment or getting a good grade! The answers to those questions will be your purpose for writing, and knowing that purpose will help you complete your assignment effectively.

Your Instructor's Prompts Determine the Writing Assignment

No two writing assignments in college will look the same, in part because each professor will have a different kind of *prompt*, or verb to describe what kind of response you should provide. Exhibit 9.3 lists and explains many of the types of prompts you will encounter in college. Each one asks for a different type of writing assignment, so be sure to review your instructor's guidelines carefully so that you can make sure you are fulfilling the assignment correctly.

Exams and Portfolios Provide Additional Writing Opportunities

Research papers and essays will not be the only assignments you will do to show your professors how well you write and think. You may also be asked to demonstrate your writing ability in other formats and for different occasions. Essay exams and portfolios are the two most popular types of assignments that will require an ability to write well, but you may also need to demonstrate your writing skills in group projects and multimedia presentations. The key to success is to learn what additional writing skills are necessary for these different formats and occasions.

Essay Exams

Writing essay exams always causes a little more anxiety than any other writing assignments because of the pressure of recalling information and writing with the clock ticking. Because you don't have the luxury of unlimited time to write an essay on an exam, you will have to prepare. Students who have trouble writing an essay in a timed environment should be comforted that they can improve their performance by practicing for the exam.

If you know the essay topic beforehand, you can practice writing your response to it by allowing yourself the same amount of time that you will have when you take the test. The key to writing well under pressure is to simulate the same circumstances when you practice. If you don't know what the topic is beforehand, you can still prepare for

EXHIBIT  9.3   Writing Prompts, Definitions, and Explanations

Writing Prompt	Definition	Explanation
Summary	A brief retelling of a subject.	In a summary, you will cover the main points of an event or a text, but summaries do not contain your opinion on the subject.
Evaluation	Asks for your opinion.	You will need to consider the subject's strengths and weaknesses, and you will need to provide specific examples to support your ideas.
Discussion or description	Provides specific details about the topic.	The more specific details you can provide, the more likely you will adequately describe or define the subject.
Analysis	Breaks a subject apart and looks at its components carefully.	Once you have investigated the parts, you must put the subject back together again.
Compare and contrast	Examines two subjects more carefully to make a significant point about them.	Before you describe their similarities and then their differences, you will set up the reason for the comparison and contrast.
Synthesis	Combines two or more sources into an essay.	A synthesis uses your perspective or argument as the foundation and provides the reader with ideas and support from other sources.
Persuasive argument	Takes a stand about a topic and encourages readers to agree.	A persuasive argument is most effective when specific, accurate evidence is used. Effective persuasion requires that you treat your readers with respect and that you present your argument fairly.

the essay exam by going back over your notes and checking to see if your professor talked about any major issues that would make a good essay topic. Then practice writing responses to questions you think might be on the exam.

Another helpful strategy is to develop an outline before beginning to write the full answer. List the key points that an essay on a particular topic should include, and organize those points in a fashion that provides a logical structure. For example, if your instructor asks you to describe how photosynthesis works, your outline should include the terminology and processes in the order in which they occur. Depending on the length of the essay you've been asked to write, you could even use the outline as the headings and subheadings for your essay. If your answer describes three reasons why Gothic architecture makes use of arches, you could provide three headings in the essay corresponding to the three reasons.

Portfolios

A writing portfolio is a collection of your writing throughout the semester. This type of project is popular with instructors because it allows students to work on their writing all semester. Instead of getting a grade on the first draft that is turned in, students can revise papers and improve them over time. A benefit of the portfolio method is that students don't have to write perfectly in their first drafts and can polish their writing as the semester progresses.

The best way to handle a writing portfolio is to review the requirements for it, including due dates and policies on completing final drafts, and write and revise your papers early and often. If you have questions about the expectations, especially if you have never completed a portfolio before, ask your instructor and schedule periodic meetings to make sure that you are completing the components successfully. Finally, take advantage of the opportunity to submit multiple drafts and receive feedback on them. Revising essays for a portfolio takes time, but it is rewarding to receive extensive feedback and help with improving your writing.

How Your Professor Grades Your Writing Shouldn't Be a Mystery

Your college professors may vary widely in how they evaluate and grade your written assignments. Some professors look for and reward key words and concepts in an essay exam, whereas others mark and count off for grammatical, mechanical, and organizational problems even if the key concepts are easily identifiable. You will soon learn, if you have not already, that each professor has his or her own criteria for grading written assignments, and the sooner you learn what the criteria are, the better able you will be to complete the assignments satisfactorily.

If your professor does not give you a list of grading criteria, respectfully ask for a sample assignment or a list of what the professor will be looking for. You could also bring in a sample of your own writing—such as your practice effort to write an exam essay—to your professor's office hours and ask for some feedback. Talking with the professor before and after the assignment is graded is the best way to know what to expect. Asking other students who have taken classes with the professor (and who did well!) is another way to get an idea of how you will be evaluated.

More and more professors are using *rubrics* for grading assignments, including written work. If your professor provides a rubric, review it carefully because it will provide the criteria that your professor will use in determining a grade. When you practice writing essays, you could even ask a fellow classmate to use the rubric to score your answer. You can also score your own writing using the rubric to check your work before someone else looks at it. If your professor doesn't mention a rubric or provide one before the assignment, respectfully ask them if they have one available that you could use to prepare for an assignment or exam.

Remember that professors expect you to write at a college level and that your writing assignments should reflect the characteristics that are discussed at the beginning of this chapter. You may find that

BUZZ

Q I hate essay exams. I never do well on them because I run out of time. Is there anything I can do?

A Essay exams are part of the college experience, but there are some tips to doing well on them:

- Create outlines of answers to possible essay topics and memorize the outlines. You can write down the outlines and then write your responses based on the structures you have created once you get the test.

- *Practice* writing in a *timed* environment. Give yourself a limited amount of time to read the topic, think about what you want to say, and write the essay.

EXHIBIT **9.4** Top-Ten Expectations for College Writing

Expectation	What It Means
Fulfillment of the assignment	Your paper faithfully follows the assignment guidelines.
Original thought	Your paper presents your viewpoint of the topic.
Main point or idea	Your paper conveys one major idea.
Organized	Your paragraphs and the details within those paragraphs are presented logically.
Focused paragraphs	Your paragraphs present one minor idea at a time. Each minor idea supports your overall point.
Concrete, specific details	Your concrete details appeal to the reader's senses; your specific details provide a clear picture of your point.
Neat presentation	Your paper is neatly word-processed and printed on clean, quality paper.
Grammatical sentences	Your sentences are complete and error-free.
Correct spelling	All of your words are spelled and capitalized correctly.
Punctual	Your assignment is turned in on time.

although you received good grades on papers in high school, you have to work much harder for those same grades on papers in college. In addition to higher standards, you should be aware that your professors' job is to make you a better thinker and writer, no matter what the subject. They will be correcting errors and making suggestions for improvement. You also need to prepare for the reality that a professor in one class will use very different criteria for evaluating your writing than another professor. Just as you'll have to prepare yourself for different types of managers in your future career, you'll have to adapt to different types of professors each semester. See Exhibit 9.4 for a summary of expectations for college writing.

Having just mentioned future managers and careers, this is a good place to mention that professors and colleges require a lot of writing assignments and work hard to help you become a good writer because writing is an absolutely critical skill for your future life and career. Even as the forms of technology that we use to communicate—smartphones, social media, tweets—change, our reliance on the written word to communicate with one another and manage our personal and professional relationships endures. Effective writers have influence and success in life because they can communicate their ideas to others. The guidance and direction we offer in this chapter will serve you for a lifetime.

60-second PAUSE

Think about all the writing assignments you'll need to complete. For each assignment, identify what type of assignment it is (revisit the list of different assignments in Exhibit 9.1; e.g., journals, essay exams), and state its length, audience, and purpose.

There may be times when a writing assignment is confusing or overwhelming. If at any time you don't understand what you are supposed to do or you feel stressed about the assignment, contact your instructor as soon as you can. Stressing out about the assignment will only make it seem impossible to complete. Instructors know you have other responsibilities and classes and are often willing to work with you if you have planned ahead and asked for help early.

When getting help with an assignment, be sure to ask your instructor first—he or she is the one who will best know what needs to be done. If your college has a writing center, you should make an appointment with a tutor as soon as you realize you need some help. Writing center tutors will be able to explain what you need to do to complete the assignment.

Other students in the class and friends who are not in the class can be other sources of help, but use their help cautiously. Your classmates may not know much more about the expectations than you do. Moreover, your instructor may prohibit any kind of collaboration, even if it is to better understand what you need to do. Getting help from anyone who is not in the class or not taking college courses should be your last resort, because they are farther removed from your instructor's expectations.

No matter who helps you with the assignment, be sure that you are doing the assignment rather than someone else doing it for you. Some students, out of fear or frustration, have had other people complete part or all of their assignments. The most obvious reason that you should not allow someone else to help too much is that your instructor could penalize you for not doing the assignment yourself. More important, if you do not complete the assignment yourself, you are robbing yourself of an opportunity to learn more about the subject that you are studying and about yourself.

Peer Review Is a Great Opportunity for Feedback

Peer review is a process that you may go through in your composition classes or in classes that have an important group project as part of your grade. Peer review is defined as a process in which a classmate evaluates your work. This may occur in a peer review workshop, common in writing classes, where you and a classmate exchange papers and assess how well each of you has met the assignment requirements. You may also be looking for grammatical and spelling errors, which can be corrected before your final draft or project is submitted. Peer review, especially if assigned as part of your work in a class, can be extremely helpful to you. It can show you what others in the class are writing about and how they are completing assignments, which can in turn help you gauge how well you are doing. It can also help you learn how to correct mistakes, for you may find it easier to see errors in others' papers than in yours. Finally, it can help you get your paper in shape before you complete it for submission.

Sometimes your professor will formally arrange a peer review process in your class or a workshop. This is a great opportunity to improve your paper before you turn it in

Reviewing a peer's work may be a required component of a writing assignment.

© THINKSTOCK

for a grade. However, if the professor doesn't initiate a peer review process, ask your instructor if they are supportive of you organizing your own peer review process with an informal study group in the class. As long as students are not plagiarizing from one another or cheating in some other way (topics we'll discuss later), professors may be supportive of this approach, and you'll benefit from it by getting help and support from your peers to develop a finished and polished paper.

Tutoring May Also Be Available

Another form of assistance available to you as you write your papers is tutoring. Most colleges have a learning assistance center or tutoring lab where other students or professional tutors are available to help those who need it. Tutoring is especially valuable if certain skills, such as grammar and spelling, need to be practiced and refined. The tutors at your college are usually trained to help students with the most common problems, and they have the added benefit of having completed the very courses they tutor in, so they know what to expect in terms of assignments and grading. Tutors, just as peer reviewers, however, cannot assure a good grade on an assignment that is reviewed. They can, though, point out areas that need to be improved and provide you with resources to help you become more aware of your strengths and weaknesses as a writer.

Make Sure You Know When You're Receiving Too Much Help

How do you know when you have received too much help on a writing assignment? If someone else writes whole sentences, paragraphs, and pages for you or supplies you with many main ideas and examples that you use in your paper, then you have probably received too much assistance on your writing assignment. Some professors disapprove of editing and proofreading services as well. When in doubt, check with your professor and explain what kind of help you are getting.

Take a moment to search your college's website to find information about the campus writing center, tutoring center, and any other writing support services it has available. Write down the location, email address, URL, and operating hours of each support service.

WRITING IS A PROCESS

Prewriting Techniques Can Help You Get Started

Once you have read and understood the writing assignment, it is time to use one or more prewriting techniques to get your ideas down on paper before you start organizing them and writing your rough draft. You probably have your own way of writing, but it is worth investigating some of these proven methods for generating ideas.

Writing is a process that takes time.

©FOTOLIA

There are three common prewriting techniques that you can use to generate details for your paper. *Freewriting* is a simple way to get ideas down on paper. The only rules in freewriting are to start with an idea and stop only after you have filled a page or after a certain amount of time has passed. When freewriting, you can allow your mind to wander off the subject, but you should write down everything that comes to mind. Later, when you start organizing your details, you can eliminate anything that does not pertain to your subject. If you are a good typist, you can freewrite by typing into a blank document. Don't worry about spelling, grammar, or punctuation when you freewrite—the purpose is to free your mind of that little voice that censors everything you think. (A tip—don't look at the screen when you're freewriting.)

Clustering is another method of prewriting that works well for those who learn better by visualizing concepts. Clusters, or think links, are visual representations of ideas and their relationship to each other. The key to clustering is to start in the middle of a sheet of paper, write down your topic, and circle it. Draw a line from your subject and write down a related topic that is part of the subject. For instance, "types," "prevention," and "treatment" are all parts of the topic "sexually transmitted diseases." In addition, subtopics branch off "prevention": "abstinence" and "condoms." The words and phrases that surround a topic or subtopic must be connected to it, both logically and literally, by drawing a line. If you like using the Web or an iPad, Popplet is a great app that can help you create these visual clusters.

Another effective method for generating ideas is *brainstorming*, a process that involves writing down ideas as they come to you. The goal in brainstorming is to get as many ideas as possible down on paper, no matter how ridiculous or off-topic they are. The more details you generate, the more you have to work with as you begin organizing your paper. To brainstorm, simply write your topic at the top of a sheet of paper, or type it into a new document on your computer, and then start listing any and all ideas that come to mind.

A Topic Sentence or Thesis Will Help You Organize the Details

Once you make a list of details that you would like to use in your paper but before you decide how you would like to organize them, give some thought as to what your main point will be: a topic sentence if it is a paragraph or a thesis if it is an essay. Your main point will be at least one sentence that tells the reader what the entire essay or paper will present or argue.

Mark Twain (2011) once said, "I didn't have time to write a short letter, so I wrote a long one instead." The point he was making in this quote is that it's actually more difficult to narrow your topic down to a concise sentence or thesis than it is to write a long essay that covers every aspect of a topic. Don't be discouraged if it seems difficult to summarize your topic into a single topic sentence or thesis statement. Give yourself time to write a few versions, review them, and then try again. Even though the process will yield only a small amount of writing, a thoughtfully developed summary provides a solid foundation on which you can build the details of your assignment.

Once you have your topic sentence or thesis, you can use a variety of methods to organize them in your paper effectively. You can arrange them from most to least important detail or least to most important detail. Details can also be arranged chronologically, especially if you are writing about an event that needs to follow a specific time line. Moreover, details can be arranged from general ideas to specific details, or specific details to general ideas. It is important to organize your details logically; how you arrange the supporting details will depend on your purpose and audience.

For example, suppose you are writing a paper on the greatest challenges to diversity on your campus, and your details include the lack of cultural appreciation activities, a recent racially motivated incident, the fact that there are few minorities in administrative roles, and the lack of African American literature classes offered. The current order of the details provides no logical connections among them, so your reader will have a difficult time understanding the magnitude of the problem. Instead, you could order them according to importance. When Juanita chooses a topic and completes her research, she will want to consider the order in which to present her findings. Should she start with the most shocking or the most obvious? These will be questions that will start her on the process of organizing her paper for maximum impact.

Which of the aforementioned details do you think is the most important indication of the challenges to diversity on your campus? Certainly, the most striking is the racially motivated incident. You could use it as the first, most important detail in your paper, something that will grab your readers' attention and keep them interested and sympathetic to your thesis. On the other hand, you could start your essay with the least important detail and use the incident detail as your last, most important point. How you arrange your details depends on your purpose for writing, but each detail should build on the next and support your thesis.

A Paragraph Should Cover One—and Only One—Topic

Paragraphs, which are a group of sentences that are considered one complete unit, are the building blocks of an essay. Well-developed paragraphs can be any length. However, if a paragraph is too short, the reader will think that something is missing; if it is too long, the reader may get lost in what you are trying to say. The key to writing a good paragraph—and you will write many in your college career—is to stay focused on one topic at a time and to let the reader know what that main idea is with a sentence called a *topic sentence*. A topic sentence can appear at the beginning of the paragraph, in the middle, or at the end. As a general rule of thumb, paragraphs should not include more than five sentences.

Once you have determined what the paragraph will focus on, you can start putting your details in place. Just as you have considered the overall arrangement of the details in your paper, you will need to give some thought to arranging the details *within* the paragraphs. The same types of organization of details for an entire paper work for paragraphs as well: general to specific, specific to general, order of importance, or chronological. You can use a different method for each paragraph as long as all the paragraphs support your thesis.

Transitions Help You Move from One Thought to Another

To make your sentences flow smoothly and your paragraphs relate clearly to one another, you will need to use transitions. Transitions are words or phrases that signal to the reader that you are moving from one thought to the next. Imagine describing over the phone how to get from the college to your house. If you didn't use transitions, your listener might be confused as to how to get there. Words such as "First," "Next," "Then," and "After" are transitional words that would help the listener see how the sentences of the directions relate to one another.

When you move from paragraph to paragraph in your paper, you will definitely need a strong transitional phrase or sentence to indicate that you are introducing a new idea or that a point is forthcoming. Phrases such as "In addition to," "Even though," and "Contrary to the point above" are strong enough to slow the reader down to pay attention to your next major point. These words serve as signposts to indicate the beginning of each idea and how each idea connects to the others. A paragraph may begin with the words "The first step," which tells you something important: This idea is the first in a series of steps that will follow. The phrase "In other words" indicates that the author is restating her point in case you missed it. The phrase "If you have done your reading" ties into the idea from the previous sentence. The transition "Also" tells you that another point is being made in addition to the one at the beginning of the paragraph. Finally, the phrase "For example" provides an example for achieving the goal in the previous sentence.

In addition to connecting ideas, transitions improve the readability of the paper. If you read your work out loud and it sounds "choppy," or repetitive in rhythm, you may need to add transitions. Adding transitions effectively takes practice. If you need help, see your instructor or someone in the writing center at your college. With a little work, the flow of your writing will improve.

BUZZ

Q I always get help from a good friend who is majoring in writing and communications when I have to write a paper. He helps me brainstorm ideas, and then I have him proofread my paper to find errors that I would have missed. Is this plagiarism?

A Plagiarism is simply defined as taking someone else's words and ideas without acknowledging them. Here are some tips for avoiding sticky situations with friends:

- Ask your friend to help you by bouncing off ideas for your paper, not create outlines or parts of the paper.

- Ask your friend to point out a few typos or grammatical errors, not to correct all errors without you.

- Ask your professor if you are ever unsure about the help you are receiving.

Build Paragraphs Into a Complete Essay

The word *essay* has its origins in French and means "an attempt" or "a trial." For college students, writing essays is an attempt, or a trial, in some sense, to meet the assignment without going crazy! In the context of college, an essay is a written composition on a particular subject that offers the author's view. If, for example, you are asked to write an essay on the death penalty or obesity in children, then you will need to present your viewpoint on the subject. Essays do not usually contain research; instead, they are built on your observations, logic, and opinions. They are, in essence, an attempt by you to convey your viewpoint on a subject and perhaps to learn something more about what you think about that subject.

When you are assigned an essay for a class, you need to include some basic components. Without all of them, your essay is simply a piece of writing—just as a few bones do not make up an entire skeleton. At the least, you will need a title, introduction, thesis, body paragraphs, and a conclusion. You have already reviewed the process by which you create the ideas and details that will be part of the paragraphs. To make it a complete essay, you will need to include a thesis statement—limited to a sentence or two—that provides an overall declaration of what your entire essay is about. Your introductory paragraph provides an overview of the topic, and your conclusion restates or reflects on the main points you make. Your title connects to your essay's topic or thesis so that your reader has an idea, before reading, what the essay is about.

Jasmine Student

Amy Baldwin

ENGL 1312

November 14, 2010

Existential Meaning in "Acquainted with the Night" and "The Road Not Taken" by Robert Frost

Acclaimed poet Robert Frost is known for his elegant yet simplistic poems that contain a veiled but biting reflection of human nature. Frost was heavily traveled both internationally and across the United States, and thus was no stranger to self-exploration, a concept that he conveys through his poetry (Pritchard). By examining the speaker, structure, word choice, and imagery, one can see that both of Frost's poems "Acquainted with the Night" and "The Road Not Taken" are connected by the themes of the human search for and creation of meaning in an inherently meaningless world.

In "Acquainted with the Night," the speaker is creating meanings for himself and his world by moving outside of society's definitions and values. The repetition of "I have" signifies that the speaker is a single, lonely individual, rather than a group (lines 1, 5, 14). This indicates that the search for significance is a lonely one. It also indicates that the speaker is reflecting on himself and his own quest for meaning. That the "I have" repetition gradually fades from the poem expresses a loss of the self when the speaker reflects on himself (lines 1, 5, 14). Then the last line returns the "I have" to the poem, signifying that you will lose your idea of yourself in your reflection, but you can always create yourself once more (lines 1, 5, 14). Taken in a literal sense, the speaker's actions are intriguing. Most people would not "[outwalk] the furthest city light," but the speaker

Your name, course information, and title go at the top

Introduction provides overview and thesis.

The road itself is a sign of motion in a specified direction, which road a speaker takes is consequential to the direction that his life takes, at least that is what the younger and older selves imagine. That the poem takes place in a wood, rather than the cityscape from "Acquainted with the Night," signifies wildness. There is no need for the speaker to escape from ready-made meanings; he simply has to create his own. The recklessness and freedom of the youthful self's choice is expressed by this setting. The choice was made free from convention and only at the discretion of individual nature, which is to take the seldom used road. However, the older self sighs at the choice with regret for what might have been (line 16). Although the younger and older selves fear that they made a mistake in their choice, the middle aged self acknowledges that he takes the path that makes more sense to him. The speaker's choice of one path, rather than the meanings held in each path, is what truly makes all the difference.

Although these poems were written over a decade apart, Frost carries an existential undertone through both of them. "Acquainted with the Night" suggests the process of breaking down meanings and understanding the void meaninglessness beyond them, only to build up your own meanings. "The Road Not Taken" examines the meanings that we apply to our decisions, understanding them to be innate to the choices. Both poems explore the creation of meaning in an inherently meaningless world. We do not search for understanding; we create it.

Conclusion wraps up all major points.

Body paragraphs have one topic that is discussed throughout.

Be Sure to Avoid Plagiarism

Plagiarism is the act of using someone else's words, images, and ideas without properly and accurately acknowledging them. This definition can also cover artwork and computer programming code. Basically, any material that you use within an assignment, excluding information that is considered common knowledge, must be properly and accurately acknowledged. That means you must be familiar with and use the correct documentation format that your professor requires. Common documentation formats include MLA (Modern Language Association), APA (American Psychological Association), and CBE (Council of Biology Editors). Your professors will expect you to learn how to use a documentation format and use it consistently.

Any time that you are creating, writing, or producing an assignment, either as an individual or as part of a group, you will need to document the information and sources you use. If your professor wants the assignment to be completely original—without the use of sources—then you will need to adhere to those guidelines. If you are completing

At no time should you copy the homework answers that another student has written. Just as you would not share answers during a test, it is best not to share your answers on work that is assigned out of class. If you have taken a class in a previous semester, you will also want to keep your assignments from being shared. Instructors may use the same assignments from semester to semester, and you don't want to put a fellow student in an awkward or potentially bad situation.

YOUR TURN

In approximately 250 words, explain how students can compromise academic integrity, perhaps without even knowing it. Then, describe what safeguards students can put in place to ensure academic integrity when working with others, whether fellow students or tutors.

an assignment as part of a group, you may be asked to document which group members completed which parts of the assignment.

The following is a list of specific instances of plagiarism to avoid in all of your assignments:

- Buying or downloading for free a paper off the Internet and turning it in as your own.
- Copying and pasting material from the Internet or print sources without acknowledging or properly documenting the sources.
- Allowing someone else to write all or part of your paper.
- Creating a "patchwork" of unacknowledged material in your paper by copying words, sentences, or paragraphs from someone else and changing only a few words.
- Including fictitious references in your paper.

The simplest rule to remember when it comes to plagiarism is that if you had to look up the information or you used part or the whole of someone else's idea, image, or exact words, you must let your professor or reader know. As in every unclear situation you may encounter, always ask for clarification. Your professor will be able to help you determine what you need to do if you are unsure.

60-second PAUSE

From memory (without looking back in this chapter), write down the steps in the writing process. Then, look back in this chapter and locate one example of a topic sentence and one transition sentence.

RESEARCH AND INFORMATION LITERACY
ARE ALSO PROCESSES

Research papers differ from essays and other written assignments in that they require you to investigate and incorporate sources to support your ideas. They also require that you go through the process of becoming an information-literate consumer. You will need to consider length, audience, and purpose, and you will need to pay close attention to the requirements of the assignment. Instructors may require that you research certain journals or databases, or they may ask for survey results or literature reviews. As with any writing assignment, you should start early and break it up into manageable parts. For a research paper, you will need to invest a considerable amount of time and energy.

Step 1: Choose a Topic

The assignment information you are given may help you determine what your topic will be. In some cases, your professor will be very specific; for example, an assignment may be, "Write a research paper in which you present three methods for teaching preschool children to read." Other professors may be less direct and give you a topic such as: "Write a paper on an important historical event." If you are ever unsure as to what your topic should be, always ask well before the assignment is due. Oftentimes, you can get ideas for narrowing your topic from your professor or your classmates.

Before you settle on a topic to research, consider the assignment's purpose and length. If you are writing a 10-page paper, your topic will need to be broader than if you were writing a 5-page paper. Also, if you are required to argue a point rather than provide basic information, your topic, and your subsequent research, will be focused differently. Determining your topic first, regardless of what it is, will save you time when you begin to find sources for your paper.

Step 2: Find, Evaluate, and Catalog Your Sources

Once you determine your topic, you can then begin to search for sources for your paper. You will definitely want to learn how to use your library's catalog and databases before you start your research. Often, the library will provide an orientation to students or you can get one-on-one assistance from a staff member. Never waste valuable time by being confused—ask someone for help if you are not sure how to find information.

Your assignment and topic will influence what kinds of sources you will use for your paper. If your education class requires that you find websites that provide information on cyberbullying in elementary schools, then you will know what kinds of sources you will use for your paper (only websites). However, if your education class requires that you write a research paper on the latest studies on cyberbullying, you will most likely use multiple sources, such as accessing journals in your library's databases to find scholarly articles on the subject and reviewing school and scholarly websites.

Once you find your sources, you will need to spend time deciding if they are reliable, credible, and useable for your paper. Again, look to your assignment or to your professor for guidance if you are unsure whether the source is acceptable for your paper. Most likely, if it is source that you have found in the library's catalog or databases, it should be a credible source. Chapter 7 provides more information on evaluating sources that can be useful in the research process as well.

When you find a source that you plan to use in your paper, you need to catalog information about that source. How you do this will depend on the *documentation style* that your professor requires. Two of the most common are MLA (Modern Language Association) and APA (American Psychological Association), but there are more that you will need to be familiar with: Chicago Manual of Style (CMS) and Council of Biology Editors (CBE) are just two additional ones. A documentation style simply means the format in which you acknowledge your sources within your paper and at the end in the references or works cited page.

Regardless of which style you use, incorporating sources into your paper requires that you provide essential information, usually the author's name and the title of the source, when you first use it in your paper. This means that whether you are quoting directly or paraphrasing, which is putting the author's ideas into your own words, you will need to let your reader know where the information comes from. Proper acknowledgment and documentation are essential to incorporating your sources correctly. Your professor will certainly want to hear what *your* thoughts on the topic are, but she will also expect that you have found sources to support your ideas and documented them properly.

USING TECHNOLOGY TO GET AHEAD

Your college's website can provide you with links to resources, such as the tutoring center and the library, that can help you with your assignments. Many colleges place their tutoring center hours on their website along with some electronic resources for students who cannot come to campus to access the services. Likewise, more and more college libraries provide accessible information that can help students in the research process. Visit both and see what information and assistance is available at your fingertips.

RECOMMENDED SITES

- http://www.ccc.commnet.edu/mla/index.shtml: Capital Community College provides a thorough resource for college students for following the research process.

- http://owl.english.purdue.edu/owl/resource/658/1/: Purdue's Online Writing Lab (OWL) is a well-established "go-to" site for all things related to writing in college.

- http://www.aresearchguide.com/3tips.html: Making presentations just got a little easier with the strategies provided at this site.

Step 3: Use Your Sources to Support Your Argument or Thesis

Once you've located sources that provide reliable and relevant information for your paper, you can use these sources to organize, strengthen, and support your argument or thesis. A research paper is different from an essay because an essay relies primarily on your own opinion, whereas a research paper draws on outside sources to support your point.

What types of advertisements or news articles do you believe are the most persuasive? Chances are you consider ads or articles that use factual data, expert sources, and logical arguments to support their points to be particularly persuasive. The same approach applies to your research paper. If the purpose of your paper is to argue a point, make a recommendation, or critically evaluate a theory or philosophy, your paper will have a stronger argument if you can support it with verifiable facts and outside sources. Once you've written a draft version of your research paper, carefully review it and use a highlighter to mark every statement you make that someone might argue against, or any claim you make that someone might doubt. Then, consider whether you can find an outside source to support your argument or claim. For example, if you're writing a report about the effects of the BP oil spill on the Gulf Coast economy, you could find economic data and quotes from industry experts to support your claims that the oil spill caused negative effects to the region. Your research paper will be a better paper if you can provide research support for most, if not all, of your claims.

Look back in the previous chapter of this textbook, and locate two examples of using outside sources to support a statement or claim. Did you notice those sources the first time you read the chapter? How do references like these affect your beliefs about the content you are reading?

SPEAKING AND PRESENTING ARE LIFE SKILLS THAT WILL SERVE YOU WELL

Learning to speak and present on a topic effectively in college is a skill that will benefit you not only on the job but also in life. For example, you may need to speak on behalf of the parents at your children's school as president of the Parents and Teachers Association, or you may be asked to make weekly announcements at your church. In your college classes, you will more than likely get a specific assignment (Give a five-minute persuasive speech on a current event) or a specific topic (cloning). However, not all speaking experiences will begin with detailed directions. You may be asked to introduce someone or to "Talk for about 10 minutes about whatever you think will interest the audience." Even the moments when you raise your hand in class to answer a question or make a point are opportunities to speak and present. Regardless of how you are assigned a speech, the process will be the same: You will need to plan, prepare, deliver, and assess.

Your Speaking Plan Includes Your Topic, Purpose, and Audience

Choosing a topic is the first step to preparing to speak, just as it is in the writing process. At times, you will be provided a topic, but in some of your classes—or for some occasions—you will be allowed to create your own. Topics for speeches can come from your personal experience, current events, or in-depth research. If you are not sure which personal experience, current event, or research topic you want to explore, it is a good idea to use brainstorming or another method of generating ideas (previously discussed) to determine which topic interests you the most. It's also valuable to select a topic for which you have a passionate interest or some personal experience. This kind of relevance will help you convey enthusiasm and confidence, even when you're a bit nervous.

Deciding what your purpose is will be your next step. You may need to inform, persuade, or entertain your audience. If you will be informing them about your topic,

Presenting in front of fellow students will be a part of many of your classes.

you will more than likely use details and language that present the information in an unbiased manner. If you will be persuading your audience, you will more than likely use examples and language to change their attitudes or beliefs. Entertaining your audience will also determine how you will present your topic because you will include information, details, and language that will get a laugh or amuse. Your speech can have more than one purpose—and sometimes all three—but one will be the most emphasized.

Just as writers need to decide who their audience is before they begin writing, speakers must also consider whom they will be addressing. Audience analysis is the process by which speakers determine who will be the receivers of the message. Audience analysis questions include the following: How many people will be in the audience? What are the characteristics of the audience (gender, ages, race, culture, educational background, learning style, etc.)? What are their attitudes toward your topic? What do they know about the topic?

Occasion analysis questions include the following: When are you speaking? How long will you have to speak? What is the space like (if you can find out in advance)? What else will you need? Visual aids? Handouts? Will there be time allotted for questions or discussion?

Your Voice Is the Vehicle That Delivers the Speech

What if you crafted a fantastic speech and no one ever heard it because they couldn't understand what you were saying? Sound impossible? It has, unfortunately, happened before: A great speech is lost because the speaker didn't project his voice or mumbled through the words. Vocal delivery, then, is the most important aspect to getting the words out successfully. Consider the following suggestions when practicing and delivering a speech:

- *Volume.* Speak loud enough so that everyone can hear you clearly. You may feel unnatural speaking at this volume, but you need your voice to carry across the entire room, and over the distracting noises that may be occurring.

- *Pace and Pronunciation.* Speak slowly and deliberately, making sure that you are properly pronouncing words (check the dictionary) and using correct grammar (consult a writing handbook). Open your mouth and move your lips to ensure that you are enunciating. Speaker credibility is lost when words are not used properly or are poorly pronounced.
- *Variation.* Use variety when speaking. Vary volume, pitch, and speed to create interest and capture attention. Pause between points for effect. Do you remember the monotone teacher in the movie *Ferris Bueller's Day Off*? He didn't vary his volume, pitch, or speed, and his students were either asleep or not paying attention.

Your Body Speaks, Too

Appropriate nonverbal communication while you are speaking can mean the difference between an effective and an ineffective speech. Paying attention to and practicing your body movements will help you develop good physical habits when speaking. Here are just a few to consider:

- Dress appropriately. If you look professional, you appear more credible and feel more confident. Unless you are making a point by dressing down or in a chicken outfit, dress up. A neat and clean appearance also suggests attention to detail and importance.
- Smile at your audience. It demonstrates a positive attitude and puts your audience at ease.
- Plant your feet. Place them firmly on the floor and stand up straight. Slouching or slumping lessens your effectiveness.
- Act naturally. The more you practice, the more comfortable you will be with your body movements and the less likely you will be to use unnatural, mechanical hand gestures and head movements.
- Move from the waist up only. Shuffling and pacing are distracting.
- Step out in front. Get in front of the podium when speaking to smaller groups of 30 or fewer because it helps create intimacy and connection.
- Use hand gestures appropriately. Keep arms and hands close to the body; avoid pointing your finger to emphasize an idea; instead, use a closed fist with thumb slightly up; open hands work well, but avoid banging on the podium or table.
- Maintain eye contact. Use the "Figure 8" method of scanning the room so that each area gets your attention throughout the presentation. Think of an 8 lying on its side and trace the curves and lines with your eyes, starting either on the right or the left of your audience.

Visual Aids Can Complement Your Speech

In addition to considering your delivery methods, both physical and vocal, you may also want to keep in mind how you will use any visual aids. According to Arthur Bradbury (2006), "For a truly powerful *and memorable* presentation you will need to include some form of visual aid" (p. 84). A visual aid can be anything from an object, such as a doll or book, to a more elaborately created poster or handout that the audience can view while you are speaking and that can emphasize certain points. Slide presentation software can also provide your audience with a visual representation of your topic.

When using visual aids, remember that they are most effective when they help the audience remember your key points, see a point you are making more clearly, and enliven your presentation without distracting the audience from listening to you. Here are a few tips for handling your visual aids:

- Less is always more with visual aids; make sure they are simple and easy to understand. For example, rarely should a single slide contain more than 25 words, and the font should be at least 24 point.
- To be seen and not heard was once a virtue, but you will want both in a presentation with visual aids. Make sure that your aids can be seen clearly by a person at the back of the room. Clear writing and large fonts on a slide presentation will help your audience get your point.
- Be the center of attention even with a visual aid. Your visual aids should not take away attention from your speech or dominate your presentation. A well-considered prop or visual aid should enhance, not become, your speech.

What's the most compelling speech or presentation you remember from the last year? What qualities did the presenter and the presentation have that impacted you? What can you learn from this example that you could apply to your own presentations?

from COLLEGE

How Writing Assignments and Expectations Will Change

When you take upper-level courses at a university, you will write more and the expectations will be higher. Your professors at the university will definitely assume that any writing challenges that you had in your first two years of college have been overcome. Your professors will be concerned with the strength and originality of your argument and with the depth and breadth of your research.

You will also be writing more to discover what you think about a particular topic. You will also find writing and research more enjoyable as you settle into a major course of study. Most students who transfer and take courses in their majors learn that they enjoy writing about subjects that will help them in their careers. This kind of satisfaction comes over time, and with each writing assignment you complete, you will become a better writer and thinker, which will help you make your transition to a four-year university that much easier.

© iSTOCKPHOTO

from COLLEGE

to CAREER

Why Strong Speaking Skills Will Set You Apart at Work

© SHUTTERSTOCK

Your speech communication class is not the last occasion that you will speak in front of people. No matter what career path you take, chances are likely that you will need to use those communication skills to work in groups, relate to your boss, and instruct or present information to your coworkers. Examples include making a presentation to a client, summarizing the company's goals and projects to new employees, and presenting a new idea for efficiency to management. These will all be instances in which you will be able to use your speaking skills for other occasions besides Public Speaking 101. Solid public speaking skills will set you apart from your coworkers as someone who can communicate even the most complicated or mundane aspects of the company. That ability will garner respect and admiration from those who work with you.

UNDERSTAND & REMEMBER

Review Questions

1. What are five of the writing expectations you will encounter in college?

2. What does the writing process include?

3. When conducting research, how should you use the information you find?

4. What should you consider when preparing and delivering a speech or presentation?

Create

Evaluate

Analyze

Apply

Understand

Remember

APPLY & ANALYZE

Critical Thinking

1. Why is writing effectively an important life skill? In what other areas of your life will you use this skill?

2. What parts of the research writing process can be the most difficult? What can students to do to make the process easier?

3. Why do you think most people fear public speaking? What can you do that will help you overcome any fears you have about speaking to an audience?

EVALUATE

Case Scenarios

1. Renée is barely passing her literature class. She has not done well on the tests or the writing assignments, so she has asked someone to help her write her final literary analysis paper. A friend of her mother has offered to help her write her paper, and when she meets with Renée, her mother's friend offers to write down all of Renée's ideas, organize them, and reword her sentences. The result is that Renée's paper is an A paper, something that she has not been able to achieve all semester. She is thrilled that she has finally received a good grade.

   Use the following scale to rate the decision that has been made (1 = Poor Decision, 5 = Excellent Decision). Be prepared to explain your answer.

   Poor Decision ← ①——②——③——④——⑤ → Excellent Decision

2. Paul is having a hard time understanding the research assignment that his government professor handed out to the class. He had two months to work on the paper, but he hasn't done anything yet, and now he has only two weeks. He has decided to make an appointment with his professor before beginning the assignment, but she cannot see him until the end of the week, which will mean he will lose four days of working on the paper before he can begin. Nonetheless, he is determined to start off right, and he is afraid if he starts working on it first, before speaking to her, he will get confused and end up feeling as though he wasted time.

   Use the following scale to rate the decision that has been made (1 = Poor Decision, 5 = Excellent Decision). Be prepared to explain your answer.

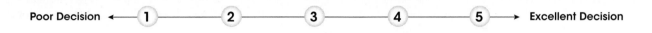

3. Pietra is afraid of public speaking, and she has been postponing taking her speech class until her last semester in college. When she does enroll, she feels that familiar fear that has kept her from taking the course until now and she cannot seem to shake it. The professor has lectured about overcoming speaking anxiety and Pietra has read the material in her textbook, but she doesn't think that she will be able to pass the class. She has her first speech tomorrow and she thinks that if she tells her professor she is sick, she can make up the assignment outside of class where no one can see her mess up. Even if her professor doesn't let her make it up, she thinks, she can just work really hard to make sure she still passes the class.

   Use the following scale to rate the decision that has been made (1 = Poor Decision, 5 = Excellent Decision). Be prepared to explain your answer.

CREATE

Research It Further

1. Using the Internet, create a "hot list" of writing sites that would be beneficial to college students. You may want to focus on a particular aspect of writing, such as grammar, or you can create a list for several topics that concern college writers.

2. Interview two or three people who work on campus, and ask them how they use writing on their jobs. Find out what aspects of writing effectively they pay close attention to and what their writing pet peeves are when reading what others have written. Report your results to your class.

3. Create a survey of students' attitudes toward and concerns about public speaking. Poll your class and other students and compile your results. Then, choose three concerns and find out what resources your college has that can help those students. Present your findings to your class.

TAKE THIS WITH YOU

Based on the goals we set at the beginning of this chapter, here's how you can take this learning with you toward college success:

■ Find out what types of writing assignments you'll be assigned and your professors' expectations for these assignments.

■ Start thinking about the steps in the writing process you will need to spend the most time on and get help at the stages you need it most.

■ Get started on the research writing process as soon as you are assigned a paper.

■ Begin to practice your presentation skills by remembering to use visual aids, vocal delivery, and physical delivery effectively.

REFERENCES AND RECOMMENDED READINGS

Bradbury, A. (2006). *Successful presentation skills* (3rd ed.). London, UK: Kogan Page.

Strunk, W., & White, E. B. (2008). *The elements of style* (50th anniv. ed.). New York, NY: Longman.

Tracy, B. (2008). *Speak to win: How to present with power in any situation.* New York, NY: AMACOM Books.

Twain, M. (2011). Quote retrieved from http://thinkexist.com/quotation/i_didn-t_have_time_to_write_a_short_letter_so_i/338386.html

Wilder, L. (1999). *Seven steps to fearless speaking.* New York, NY: John Wiley & Sons.

Zinsser, W. (2006). *On writing well* (30th anniv. ed.). New York, NY: Harper Paperbacks.

MyStudentSuccessLab

MyStudentSuccessLab (www.mystudentsuccesslab.com) is an online solution designed to help you 'Start strong, Finish stronger' by building skills for ongoing personal and professional development.

10 Studying and Taking Tests

Studying the origins of life in their Biology 101 class is becoming an exercise in their own survival. Juanita, Evan, Michael, and Laura formed a study group early in the semester, and now it has become a precious lifeline.

"So much work for just one class," Michael says. "It's insane."

Juanita replies, "I'm taking world literature and psychology. The reading alone takes me hours each night."

Michael thinks he has studied too much of the wrong things, and Juanita has severe test anxiety any time she takes a test.

"Are you starting without me?" Laura asks as she drops her heavy backpack on the booth seat by Michael.

"Of course not," Juanita says. "Michael was just complaining about how much work this class is."

"My mother finished her degree right before I started school and I remember how much she studied. If she can do it, I think can," Laura says.

"Does anyone know what the test will cover?" Michael says.

"I have to study everything, even if I don't think it will be on the test," says Juanita. "If I'm not over-prepared, I won't do well."

"I suggest we start going over everything that we have done since the first chapter," Juanita suggests. "If we work on this for the next four hours, then we can study four more tomorrow."

Evan says, "If we just review our notes, we should be fine. When was the last time you failed a test? They have to give you something for just taking it."

"If I don't know it now, I won't know it in two days," says Laura.

Michael chews on the end of his pen. "I don't have much time to study tonight. My girlfriend needs a ride to work," he says.

"We need to start somewhere, even if we can't all stay the whole time," says Juanita.

YOUR GOALS FOR THIS CHAPTER

As they discuss in their study group, Juanita, Michael, Evan, and Laura have various levels of preparation for their upcoming biology test and different perspectives on how they should study over the next two days. This chapter's purpose is to help you improve your study skills, which will in turn help you improve your test-taking strategies. Specifically, at the end of this chapter you will be able to:

- Determine the best study strategies
- Anticipate and identify different types of test questions
- Recognize the unique features of different types of tests
- Practice effective test-taking strategies

MyStudentSuccessLab (www.mystudentsuccesslab.com) is an online solution designed to help you 'Start strong, Finish stronger' by building skills for ongoing personal and professional development.

Although the terms are usually used interchangeably, a *test* is defined as a set of questions that are used to evaluate one's skills, aptitudes, and abilities on certain topics. Usually, tests assess your knowledge and abilities on a part of a course. An *exam*, however, by definition, is an assessment of the material of an entire course. Final exams are sometimes called *comprehensive* or *cumulative* exams, which indicate that they will cover what you have studied all semester or term.

Unless your professor tells you directly what will be on the test, assume that anything that was assigned or covered in class may be there. Just about every college student has a story about taking a test that covered reading assignments and not what was discussed in class. These students were surprised to realize that studying the lecture notes was not enough. The following is a list of items that you may be tested on for any class:

- Material from the lecture, discussion, and in-class and out-of-class activities
- Information provided by a guest speaker
- Information from a workshop or field trip
- Multimedia productions, such as video or audio
- Assigned readings, including chapters in the textbook
- Handouts, including PowerPoint slides and outlines

Your Terms for SUCCESS

WHEN YOU SEE . . .	IT MEANS . . .
Academic integrity	Refraining from cheating or using unapproved resources for a test or an assignment; completing a test or an assignment on your own
"Cheat" sheet	A studying method that includes recording information, outlines, or formulas on a small card or sheet of paper; sometimes allowed by instructors to be used while taking a test
Comprehensive exam	An exam that covers an entire semester's worth of material; usually given as a final exam
Course objective	A goal that the instructor has identified for the student to meet once the course is completed
Essay test question	A test question that requires a student to answer in the form of an essay
Final exam	An exam that is given at the end of a semester
Matching test question	A test question that provides one column of descriptors and another column of words that must be matched with the appropriate descriptor
Multiple-choice test question	A type of test question in which an incomplete sentence or a question is given and the correct response must be chosen from a list of possibilities
Objective test question	A question that presents a limited number of possible answers; includes matching, multiple choice, true/false, and short answer
Online test	A test that is taken through the Internet or through a Course Management System, such as Angel or Blackboard
Open-book test	A test one takes in which one can look up answers in a textbook or in one's notes

You can be assured that you will encounter a variety of test types. Take clues from what you do in class to help determine what kind of test questions you may encounter. For example, if your professor spends time applying information from a chapter during class or as an assignment, then you will likely have test questions that will ask you to apply the information as well. Listen for clues that the professor gives you, such as "You should write this down," and "This is a really important point." Other cue phrases include "You may see this again on a test," and "If you saw this on a test, how would you answer it?" When you hear these phrases, write them down and review them when studying over your other notes. A professor who says these things is begging you to take notice!

The best advice is plain and simple: Study for all tests. No exceptions. Sometimes you will find that you do not need to study as much for some classes; however, remember that studying effectively is a habit. To form a long-term habit, you must do it even when you don't think you have to, which is fundamental to making an activity part of a routine.

Set a Place and Time for Studying That Works Best for You

The best time to begin studying is as soon as the semester starts. Be careful of the mindset that because you are not in class every day you don't need to study every day. Some students begin studying the night or day before an exam, which may be too late to review and remember all the material that has been covered over the past several weeks. As stated in Chapter 8, it's best to start reviewing your notes within two days of taking them. If possible, you should start studying for future exams right now, today.

If you are a typical college student, then your time will be limited. You may not have the luxury of large blocks of time, so you will need to be creative about studying. Because it is more effective to study for short periods of time, consider studying in between classes, during breaks at work, and on the way to work and school (provided you are not driving). Another way to ensure that you study during the day is to get in the habit of always carrying your notes or books with you—this way you'll be able to take advantage of any unexpected "free" time. You can also get up earlier or stay up later so you can spend a few minutes studying before starting or ending your day.

If you have the luxury of choosing when to study, rather than sandwiching it in between work and family responsibilities, pay attention to what time of day you are most alert and receptive to learning. The best time of day for you to study is dependent on your schedule, your responsibilities, your age, and your personal preferences. Some people identify themselves as "night owls," whereas others claim to be "morning people." Whatever your peak performance time, be sure to study your most difficult subjects at that time. If you have a predictable schedule all semester, plan to study at the same time each day.

The environment in which you study is just as important as the time of day and the length of time you spend studying. You will need to find the kind of environment that works well for you. Some people need complete silence with no visual distractions, whereas others need a little background noise to stay focused. At the least, create a place that is comfortable, has good lighting, and has space for your supplies and books. It is easier to make time to study when you have a place to do it. If you have nowhere at home that is quiet and roomy, then search for a place on campus or find a local library that offers study space. Some people find that studying away from home is better because they are not distracted by the television, phone, or family members.

Small children can pose a particular difficulty in finding quiet time. If you have small children, make a concerted effort to find a quiet spot. You may need to hire a babysitter or find a classmate who can trade child care services with you when you want to study. For example, you could offer to babysit a classmate's kids when he needs to study in exchange for him watching yours when you have a paper to write. Some college students who are also parents find time to study only when their children are asleep. Therefore, their best studying takes place late at night or early in the morning at home. Do whatever works best for you.

Effective Studying Is Active and Has a Purpose and Goals

Studying effectively will include studying with a purpose, setting goals, and studying actively. This includes focusing on what you are studying, reviewing and rewriting notes, and even teaching concepts to classmates. Keeping up with how much you study and *how* you study will also help you study effectively. If you find that you did not do well on a test, you can review the steps you took to study beforehand and make adjustments the next time.

Set Goals for Your Studying

Once you have determined when, where, and how much you need to study, set study and test-taking goals. Just as you set short-term and long-term goals in Chapter 2, write down goals that you want to achieve when studying and taking tests. Remember the title of Henriette Anne Klauser's book, *Write It Down, Make It Happen* (2001). This also applies to something as short term as studying for and taking a test. Your goals could be as simple as:

- I will use my time wisely so that I am able to study all my notes.
- I will ask the instructor questions about any notes that I do not understand.
- I will remain calm before, during, and after the exam by practicing breathing techniques and by relaxing.

Of course, your goals could also include studying with a group or making a high grade. If you have never written down goals for studying or taking tests, then start small. Once you have achieved your study and test-taking goals, create newer and more challenging ones with each test, such as:

- I will improve my writing skills by practicing the essay questions in a timed environment.
- I will improve my overall retention of the material after the test.

Study Actively

Goal setting is just one of the ways to prepare for exams; equally important is how you approach studying. In order to build a body of knowledge, you will want to study to *learn*, not just to *remember*. In other words, you will want to transfer information from your short-term memory, which holds information for a short period of time, to your long-term memory, which can be retrieved long after it is "deposited" there.

One of the ways to improve your memory of the material you have learned is to actively take it in when you study. The goal of active studying is to make connections between concepts and theories so that you can more easily recall the information and write or speak knowledgeably about it. To achieve this kind of mastery, instead of simply rereading notes or passively reviewing the major headings in your textbook, your studying should include activities such as the following:

- Rewriting or summarizing your notes
- Rearranging the order of the material from most important to least important, from least important to most important, or in chronological order
- Making connections between what you have learned in one chapter, unit, or class, and material you have learned in other places
- Making connections between what you have learned in class and what you have experienced in the real world
- Explaining concepts to someone else who is not familiar with the topic
- Making visual representations of the material

A Study Log Can Help You Track Your Progress

After considering your study goals, you may also want to create a study log that will help you keep track of your tests and preparation steps. The study log in Exhibit 10.1 provides space for you to capture important information about the type of class, type of test, and methods for studying. Notice, too, that the study log describes how much the test is worth, an important consideration, especially if the test is worth a significant portion of your grade. Without taking the time to consider the value of a test, you might make the mistake of spending too much time studying for one test that is worth only a few points, and not studying enough for a test that is worth a significant portion of your grade. A study log will help you prioritize your studying strategy.

EXHIBIT 10.1 Study Log

Class	Chemistry
Date	Tuesday, October 12
Material	Chapters 4–7, extra lecture material
Practice/Previous Tests	In library on reserve; answer key for practice test
Question Types	Multiple choice, problem solving
Study Methods	Review notes, work through extra problems, go through practice test, study with group
Time Needed	8 hours total over 4 days
Approved Materials for Test	Paper, pencil, calculator
Number of Points/Percentage of Grade	150, 15% of overall grade
Notes	Talk to Regina about what to expect. She had this course last semester.

Course Objectives Are Valuable Clues About the Important Concepts

Another step in studying effectively is to understand the objectives of the course. You will find the course objectives in the syllabus or in other material that has been handed out to you in class. If one of your course objectives is to identify the processes of cell replication, then you can be sure that you will be tested on the processes of cell replication in some manner. Making sure that you study the material that appears in course objectives will help you focus your time and energy on the right course content.

Your Time Is Precious—Use It Wisely

How much time you spend and how many study sessions you have will depend on the type of learner you are. You could start with 45 minutes of studying three different times a day over the period of a week to see how well you retain and remember the material, and then adjust your schedule as needed. Just remember to be conscious of how effective your study sessions are. If they are not helping you meet your study goals, then make changes in your schedule. In Evan's case, his biology study group may not be helping him study in the manner that is most effective for him. If this is the case, he may need to find a different group that fits his study goals better or consider if studying alone is his best option.

No matter how much time you spend studying, it won't be effective if you are unable to concentrate on the subject. Many times, you will find yourself distracted by external and internal commotion. Externally, you may have a noisy or messy house, or you may have others who need or want your time and attention. Internally, you may be preoccupied by illness, stress, self-doubt, or fear. Both internal and external distractions make it difficult to study effectively, so you must take care of them or tune them out. If not, you will find that the time you spend studying is not productive.

For some students, planning ahead to study effectively is not an option. Because of poor time management or procrastination, these students often try to study in one long session of cramming. Cramming and marathon sessions should be avoided when studying for an exam because they usually produce more anxiety than learning. If you do find yourself in a situation in which you must cram, try to maximize the effectiveness of the long hours and loads of material. Organize your time into short periods, no more than one hour at a time, and take many breaks. When you return from your break, review the material you had just been studying before you begin on new material. You may want to try a combination of writing down what you know, drawing pictures to represent the material, reciting key concepts aloud, creating songs with the material, or building a model of a key idea. The more learning preferences you use to understand the material, the better your chance of remembering it all for the test.

Other study tips include making flash cards to quiz yourself or others, if you are in a study group. You can also record questions and answers. Instead of playing the recording straight through, stop the

It's in the SYLLABUS

Look at your syllabus to get clues about the tests you will have.

- What types of test questions do you anticipate from your classes?

- What evidence in the syllabus leads you to believe you will have certain types of test questions? (Hint: Look at the course description, if included.)

- How often will you have tests?

- How will the tests be organized—around units, chapters, concepts?

- Will tests be online, on-campus, take-home?

recording after each question so you can answer the question aloud. Then, play the answer and see how well you have done. If you can push yourself to enjoy studying, you will be more likely to do it often.

"Cheat" Sheets Aren't Cheating

Creating "cheat" sheets was once considered an activity only for those who intended to cheat; however, many educators have seen the benefit that creating such sheets can have. You may have a professor who tells you that you can bring a three-by-five-inch index card to the exam with anything you want written on it. Students who may not have studied much beforehand usually jump at the chance to cram as much information as possible on that tiny, white space. The result is that students retain more of the information than they would if they had not created the cheat sheet. Many times, the cheat sheet is not needed because the student has, in effect, studied adequately in making the sheet.

To create an effective cheat sheet, organization is important. One way to organize the card is to divide it into thirds on both sides so that you have six sections (three on one side, three on the other) to work with. Then, use the top of each section to write a specific category such as "Formulas" or "Krebs Cycle." Underneath each heading, write the information that pertains to the category. If you are listing formulas, for example, be sure to write clearly and double check that all elements of the formula are correct.

Even if you are not allowed to bring a cheat sheet—only bring one if you are given permission—you can still reap the benefits of this technique by closing your books and notes and writing down as much information as you can remember about the subject. For example, if you have a test on genetics, take a blank card and write everything you know about DNA on the front and back. In this case, organization is not important; what is important is to see how much you have learned already. Once you have filled up the card, go back through your notes and books to see what you have missed. Another approach is to anticipate some of the questions you might see on the exam, and use the cheat sheet to develop an outline for the answer. For example, if you anticipate a question about the structure of the legislative branch of the federal government, your outline would include the composition and structure of the House of Representatives and the Senate.

Previous Tests and Practice Tests Can Provide Great Study Aids

If allowed by the instructor, study copies of old tests. Your instructor will put them on reserve in the library, post them online in an online learning system, or hand them out in class. Previous exams are an excellent source for what kinds of questions you will be asked. If someone offers to give you his old tests from the previous semester, ask your instructor first if you can study from them before taking them.

Equally beneficial to understanding how your professor will test you is to take advantage of practice exams if they are offered. Some instructors may provide opportunities for you to stop by during office hours to take a practice exam or to take an online practice test where you can get instant feedback. If your course materials are available online through a learning management system (LMS), like Blackboard or Moodle, your professor may provide practice tests and quizzes available from the textbook publisher or from prior semesters.

Don't Face It Alone! A Study Group Can Help You Succeed

Study groups can greatly improve your understanding of material.

© IAN SHAW / ALAMY

Juanita, Michael, Laura, and Evan took the advice of their orientation leaders early in the semester to create a study group for one of their classes, and they have realized that there are several benefits of studying in groups. First, you have access to more notes and may find that you have missed important information. Second, you experience others' perspectives about the subject, and you may find that your classmates explain major concepts better than your professor. Third, you have a built-in support group while you take classes, because in the process of studying, you establish friendships.

A key to a successful study group is to limit the group to four or five participants or fewer. The more participants there are, the harder it will be to remain on track. It is also best to study with people who are not close friends so that you minimize distractions and off-topic conversations. When choosing members of your group, it is a good idea to discuss expectations for the group. If prospective members think that others will be helping them but they won't be contributing themselves, then they may not be right for your group. You will need members who will take on specific responsibilities that will benefit the whole group.

BUZZ

Q I am part of a study group, and while we started off on the right foot at the beginning of the semester, we are now more of a social group rather than a study group. I really need the support of the group for studying, but what can I do to get us back on track?

A When study groups work well, they can be a wonderful way to deepen your learning and strengthen friendships. Here are some tips to get back on track:

- Reserve a room at the library or find a comfortable, neutral place where you can all fit comfortably.

- Consider limiting your group—too many people often equals too many ideas of how to study.

- Give your group a definite structure by assigning roles for each meeting time. Make sure the responsibility rotates throughout the group.

Once you have chosen your group participants, you should exchange contact information (phone numbers and email addresses) and choose a leader. The leader can change from meeting to meeting, but one person should be in charge of contacting everyone to announce the meeting time and place for the first session. The leader should also be responsible for keeping everyone on task if the group gets off topic, and for assigning roles to each person, just as Juanita does for her group when she leads a study session.

When you meet with your group, be sure that each person contributes to the study session and "teaches" his or her assigned part. (Remember from the learning pyramid that teaching someone else about a topic is one of the highest levels of learning.) Periodically, the group should take breaks to keep people focused. To make studying comfortable, try to meet in a quiet location that allows food and drink; this way, there will be fewer breaks and fewer people will be distracted by hunger or thirst. Also consider taking turns bringing snacks and beverages or chipping in for a meal. Better yet, go out for a meal *after* you study so that everyone has a goal to look forward to.

The difficulty of forming study groups in college is that many students lead full lives and have very little time to schedule extra activities. They also may not have consistent free time, since they work different shifts each week or have different family responsibilities from day to day. To make your study group work, you may need to be creative about how you meet and how you organize your time. For example, you may want to join a chat room or use email to create a sample exam and "quiz" each other about the concepts on the exam.

60-second PAUSE

Without looking back at the section you just read, what are three ideas for effective studying that you remember and that you feel could work well for you? What can you do this week to put these ideas in action? Take a moment to write a brief "action plan" for your ideas. Then, scan what you just read to locate some good ideas that you did not recall.

TEST QUESTIONS WILL VARY, AND SO SHOULD YOUR ANSWERS

Learning how to take tests is just as important as learning the material. Knowing how to answer each type of possible test question will make taking an exam that much easier, and you will have less anxiety because you will know what to expect.

There are two categories of question types: objective and subjective. Objective questions, which require lower-level thinking because they ask you to recall facts and concepts, usually in the form of multiple choice, true/false, fill-in-the-blank, and short answer. Subjective questions ask for your opinion about the material or ask you to apply the material in a new way. Essay and problem-solving (critical thinking) questions are subjective because there are a variety of ways the questions can be answered correctly.

Sometimes, objective questions are easier to answer because they provide a correct answer within the choices. However, objective questions can demand significant brainpower, especially when you must recall an answer with very few clues, which is often the case with fill-in-the-blank questions. Because objective questions usually suggest only one correct answer, some students believe that there are no "wrong" answers for subjective questions, and that may be true, but there *are* better ways to answer them. In the following sections, we discuss typical test questions and how to answer them.

Multiple Choice

Multiple-choice questions can test your recall of information, or they can assess your ability to apply information or analyze situations. Despite their reputation for being easier, expect more difficult and time-consuming multiple-choice questions for college exams, and don't be alarmed if the answers are not obvious.

When answering multiple-choice questions, the first step is to read the question or statement carefully. Then, mark any special

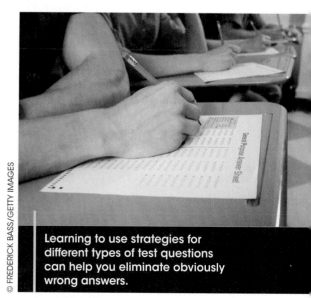

© FREDERICK BASS/GETTY IMAGES

Learning to use strategies for different types of test questions can help you eliminate obviously wrong answers.

words in the question or statement, such as "not," "always," and "only." Before looking at the choices, see if you can answer the question yourself. For example, consider the following multiple-choice question:

Notice the word "NOT" and think in terms of what is not an acceptable answer.

What should you NOT do to alleviate anxiety when taking a test?

Should A. Arrive early for the exam. *This is something you SHOULD do, so it is not the correct answer.*

Should NOT B. Skip over the directions. *This is something you should NOT do, so it may be the right answer. Keep reading the rest of the choices and lightly mark this one.*

Should C. Pay attention to the time limit. *This is something you SHOULD do, so it is not the correct answer.*

Should D. Read all the questions before answering. *This is something you SHOULD do, so it is not the correct answer.*

After you have read through all the choices, the only correct answer is B.

Consider another multiple-choice question and do the same thing you did before by looking for key words and writing your response to each option next to the assigned letter:

When answering an essay question on a test, be sure to *This is a positive statement, so you will be looking for things you should do. Also, notice the choice "All of the Above" before you start reading all the choices.*

Should A. Answer each part of the question thoroughly.

Should B. Organize your essay before writing it by sketching out a quick outline.

Should C. Read the directions carefully.

Yes, all of them D. All of the above.

The correct answer is "D. All of the above."

When you are ready to answer the multiple-choice question, read each choice carefully and eliminate any answer that is obviously wrong. If you have to guess, eliminate any answer that is misspelled (usually a sign that the instructor has hurriedly added false answers) and any answer that is shorter than the others. Also, pay attention to choices labeled "All of the above" and "None of the above." If you can determine that at least two of the choices are correct, then "All of the above" is probably the correct answer. Likewise, if at least two of the choices are not correct, then "None of the above" is probably the correct answer.

When studying for a test that will include multiple-choice questions, be sure you know all the material well and practice answering multiple-choice questions by using those in your text (or on a companion textbook website if one is available) or create your own multiple-choice questions based on the material you are studying. You can work through them yourself as part of your studying or you may share with a classmate who has also created multiple-choice questions and take turns answering them.

Matching

A matching section on an exam presents you with two columns: a list of words or phrases that are to be matched with a list of descriptors. Professors who use matching sections usually require basic recall of information, but you will need to read the directions carefully. There may be more than one match for an item in the list or there may be extra descriptors that are not matched to anything. All of these distracters are there to make sure you know the content well enough to make the right decisions.

To complete matching questions, first read through the entire list and choices to match before beginning. Then, determine if there could be multiple matches to a word in the list. Make sure that you have chosen the correct letter to match with each word in the list. If there are a few terms that you don't know for sure, try to use the process of elimination to narrow the possible choices down by matching the terms you do know for sure. Also, because not all terms will be the same type, you may be able to eliminate some descriptors because they do not logically "go with" them. For example, a matching term may be "Emancipation Proclamation" and a descriptor may be "Person responsible for passing Prohibition legislation." Because the Emancipation Proclamation is not a "person," you can easily eliminate that descriptor as a potential choice.

To study for matching, you will need to know major terms, people, and events from the material. Because professors often use similar definitions and descriptions, rather than those directly from the text or glossary, it may be helpful to rewrite your definitions and descriptions in your own words. If you have a study partner or group, ask them to do the same and share the answers they record.

Match the following descriptions of interests and strengths with the appropriate multiple intelligences category. The categories may be used more than once; some may not be used at all.

Notice that the directions say that some terms may be used more than once and others may not be used. Chances are good that you will do both.

Match the following descriptions of interests and strengths with the appropriate multiple intelligences category. The categories may be used more than once; some may not be used at all.

1. Enjoy outdoor activities

2. Know how and why they act

3. Good at design, architecture

4. Choose careers in science, computer technology, engineering

5. Use voice or instruments to express themselves

6. Enjoy reading and writing

7. Can read others' feelings well

8. Fascinated with pictures

A. Verbal/linguistic

B. Logical/mathematical

C. Visual/spatial

D. Bodily/kinesthetic

E. Musical/rhythmic

F. Interpersonal

G. Intrapersonal

H. Naturalistic

Pictures are visual representations, so this is the best answer.

Music and instruments go together, so this is the best answer.

"Inter" means within (in comparison with "intra," which means between), and "personal" refers to persons, so "within a person" goes with knowing yourself.

Answers: 1. H. 2. F. 3. C. 4. B. 5. E. 6. A. 7. G. 8. C.

True/False

True/false questions can be tough, even though there are only two possible answers: true or false. Guessing or randomly answering true/false questions should be done as a last resort. It is better to read the statement carefully, noting key words that could point to the correct answer, such as "frequently," "sometimes," and "a few." These words usually indicate a true statement. Words such as "never," "only," and "always" usually indicate a false statement. If you're struggling with a particular true/false statement, take a moment to "flip" the statement and see if your answer would switch from true to false or false to true. This can help you work through any double negatives and other somewhat confusing phrases.

Studying for true/false test questions is similar to using the study tips described earlier for multiple choice and matching: know the material or course content well enough that when presented with questions about it, you can recognize major concepts and questions. Also, write out sample true/false questions that you think would make good additions to the test. Share with a study partner or group, and take turns answering each other's sample questions.

Determine if the statements are true or false. Circle the appropriate choice.

1. Howard Gardner's theory of Multiple Intelligences includes the (category) Nutritional/Health.

   A. True

   B. False

   To answer this correctly, you need to know Gardner's categories and not get this made-up category confused with "Naturalistic."

2. OK5R is a (test-taking) strategy.

   A. True

   B. False

   The key word here is "test-taking." OK5R is a reading strategy. One of the five Rs is "reading."

3. Priorities are what are important and they (never) change.

   A. True

   B. False

   The word "never" should be a clue that this is false. A review of the definition will note that priorities change depending on what is going on in your life at any given moment.

The answers for the True/False are as follows: 1. B. 2. B. 3. B.

Fill-in-the-Blank/Short Answer

Fill-in-the-blank and short answer questions require that you recall definitions of key terms or items in a series. To complete these types of questions, first read the sentence or question carefully. Often, points will be lost if you don't answer exactly or misspell the correct term. These can be particularly difficult if you are not familiar enough with material. One way to study for these question types is to create flash cards in which you place terms or major concepts on one side and a definition or description of the term or concept on the other side.

1. The (T System) for taking notes is also known as the _____.

The T System is another name for Cornell Method. There is little other information in this sentence to provide you with hints, so you will need to know alternative names for terms.

2. (Abbreviating) words and phrases is called _____.

If you have studied your definitions with flash cards, then recalling that the abbreviations goes with "shorthand" should be easy.

3. An instructor who is (difficult to understand) because he or she has an unfamiliar accent is an example of a listening _____.

This phrase should clue you into the barriers that one can encounter when trying to listen.

Answers for the fill-in-the-blank/short answer are 1. Cornell Method. 2. Shorthand. 3. Barrier.

Problem Solving

Problem-solving, or critical thinking, questions are used by instructors so that students can demonstrate or apply the concepts or ideas they have learned. When you answer a problem-solving question, read the question carefully, marking multiple steps or parts to the directions. Next, determine what information you will need to solve the problem. Then, break the problem into parts and write down what process or operation you will need to perform. Work through the problem, and once you arrive at an answer, check the question again to make sure you have adequately answered it.

Here is an example of a problem-solving question, with an explanation for solving the problem following:

> Rosa has a scholarship that requires she maintain a 3.2 GPA while she is in college. During her first semester, she had four 3-credit-hour courses and made two A's and two B's. Now, she is taking one 4-credit-hour course and four 3-credit-hour courses. Can she make an A in her 4-credit-hour course and B's in her 3-credit-hour courses and keep her scholarship?

In order to answer this question correctly, you will need to know how to calculate GPA. If we break the steps down further, you will need to know the definition of grade points and quality points and how GPA is calculated when a student has taken classes for more than one semester. Then, you will need to know how to multiply, add, and divide. These sound like commonsense steps, but writing down every operation that you will need to perform will enable you to prepare to answer the question correctly and help you check the process by which you arrived at the answer.

Studying for problem-solving tests, such as math and science tests, most likely will involve practicing similar problems. Look to the additional problems in your textbook, homework assignments, and notes for extra practice. Also, you may find sample problems much like the ones you are studying online, with answers provided so that you can check yourself.

1. Lenise is taking a history class in which her grade is made up of four exams, all of

Total number of points possible.

which are worth 100 points with a total of (400) points that are available to earn during the

semester. So far, she has made a (65% and a 74%.) What are the lowest grades she can

Convert these to 65/100 and 74/100 because you know that each test is worth 100 points. She has a total of 139 points so far.

make to get a ("C") in the course? Is it mathematically possible for her to earn a ("B")?

You will need to know the minimum percentage for a C and a B in this context. Many universities designate a 70% as a C and 80% as a B. If this is the case, then, the student needs to earn 280 points (70% of 400) to earn a C and 320 points (80% of 400) to earn a B.

The answer to the problem-solving question is a 70.5 (or 71%) on the remaining two tests, and, yes, she has the opportunity to earn a B if she makes at least a 90.5 (or 91%) on the last two tests.

Essay Questions

Instructors use essay questions to help them measure students' ability to analyze, synthesize, and evaluate the concepts they have learned. This type of question gauges more than students' recall of facts or terms. You can be assured that you will encounter more essay questions in college because they allow students to demonstrate a deeper understanding of the material. In an earlier chapter, we defined an essay as a statement of one's own opinions on a topic. In an exam context, the term "essay" can also refer to questions that require more detailed, well-developed answers that use material from the course to support a particular thesis or describe a particular concept. Your answers to essay questions in an exam should not be based on your own opinion (unless the professor specifically asks for your opinion). Instead, your answer should demonstrate your understanding and recall of important information from the class (e.g., textbook readings, lecture notes) to address a particular challenge or to explain an idea.

One thing to remember about essay questions is that, although you won't have an enormous amount of time to complete an essay, your professor will still expect that you answer the question thoroughly and clearly. Always read the directions carefully. If the essay question has more than one part, be sure to mark each part and answer it in the body of the essay. If the directions specify a length, be sure to meet or exceed it. Before you begin writing, create a brief outline of what you will cover in the essay. Make a short list of transitions and details so that you can refer to it if you get stuck during the exam.

Finally, because your professor will be reading and grading many essays, a clearly organized essay will stand out and make it easy for her to tell that you have discussed the key points. Just be sure to give yourself plenty of time to write the essay and use any remaining time you have to proofread and edit your work.

Study for essay questions just as you would problem-solving questions by practicing with possible topics. If your professor has provided a list of topics or sample topics, use them to create outlines and memorize those outlines; they will serve as the basis for your essay. If you do not receive any sample topics, create your own by reviewing the course material and your notes to find emphasized topics or material that you spent the most time on. These may be good indications of essay topics.

These words indicate an argument should be written. Think about what kinds of evidence you will use to prove your point. Don't worry about whether or not you agree with the premise. The quality of your argument will be assessed.

These words should appear in your essay to tie back to the prompt. You may want to take some time first to brainstorm a list of ways colleges can be diverse and the costs (financial or otherwise) involved with each idea.

1. Justify this statement: Colleges should strive, at whatever cost, to ensure that their campuses are diverse.

2. Compare the costs versus the benefits of investing time and money in a college degree.

These words indicate that you will be looking at two elements side by side.

These words indicate that you will present the drawbacks and the advantages of both of the subjects.

These words or synonyms will be used in your answer — they are part of the topic you are exploring.

60-second PAUSE

TESTS ALSO COME IN DIFFERENT FORMS

Just as important as what types of questions you will encounter is what kinds of tests you can expect in different classes. For example, a math test will look quite different from a music test, and the strategies for studying for them and taking them will be different. Here we discuss a few different types of tests you may encounter in college. You may be able to apply the same tips to exams in other disciplines.

Math and Science Tests

For taking math and science tests, it is best to work through the problems you know first, then complete the problems that you do not know as well. If you complete your test early, consider reworking the test questions again on another sheet of paper and comparing your answers. If you discover two different answers for the same problem, figure out which answer contains the error. Always show your work and complete as many parts of a multiple-part problem as possible. You may receive partial credit for completing the process correctly even if you have not arrived at the right answer.

When answering questions on science tests that involve processes or major concepts, it may help to draw a picture to create a visual of the process to help you answer questions about the steps. Regardless of what question types you will encounter, you will need to recall terms and definitions.

Fine Arts and Literature Tests

When taking exams in fine arts and literature classes, it is as important to explain the significance of the selected work as it is to identify key passages, creators, terms, and eras. When taking exams in both disciplines, work through the easier questions first, and save plenty of time for the writing portions. Think about the major themes and the historical importance of the works, and look for those themes to be part of the questions on the test. While recall of facts about eras, dates, and creators of works will be part of the exam, there should be a significant emphasis on synthesizing the material.

© SHUTTERSTOCK

Different courses will require different types of tests.

INTEGRITY *Matters*

The Center for Academic Integrity (2011) has reported that nearly 75% of college students admit to cheating at least once. Some don't believe that their professors notice or care about their work; some believe that they can justify their cheating because the test is unfair; others believe that getting the good grade is the most important goal if scholarships and program admissions demand high standards.

No matter what the reason, cheating can ruin your college experience. Colleges do take cheating seriously and often have no tolerance for those who cheat. Penalties can range from an F in the course to expulsion from the college.

YOUR TURN

In approximately 250 words, discuss why you think such a high percentage of college students have reported that they have cheated.
Source: Center for Academic Integrity (2011). Retrieved from www.academicintegrity.org

Open-Book and Take-Home Tests

There will be occasions when you are given an open-book or take-home test. Although they sound as if they are the easiest kind of test to take, professors who hand out open-book tests make sure that you work hard to answer the questions correctly. In other words, these may be harder than in-class, closed-book exams. If you know ahead of time that you will be given an open-book exam, you will still need to study for it. Instead of spending too much time looking through your book and notes for the answers to the questions, you should be able to find the answers quickly. Chances are good that you will have many questions on an open-book exam to test how much you know about the subject. Likewise, take-home exams are often more difficult and time consuming than a regular test. At the least, your instructor will expect more from you if he allows you to take the test home to complete it. Because expectations are higher, you will need to give yourself plenty of time to formulate your answers and to check your work. Even though you will be unsupervised when writing the exam and probably expected to use a variety of resources for help, you will still need to maintain integrity. In other words, unless you receive permission from your instructor, do not accept or give help to other classmates.

Online Tests

Whether you take an online class or not, you may be required to take a quiz or test through an online learning system or through a website, such as a publisher's site that supports your textbook. Online tests are usually timed, which means you will need to keep an eye on how much time you have left after you answer each question. Instructors often place a time limit for online exams to discourage students from reviewing notes, going through the text, or surfing the Internet for answers. If your professor provides a practice test, consider taking it so that you can get a good feel for how much time you will have and what types of questions you will answer. Additional considerations include revisiting questions, if possible, to make sure you have not chosen the wrong answers for multiple-choice questions; ensuring that you have saved your answers before submitting your exam; and not sharing information about the exam with other students who have not taken it yet. If the online test gives you a results page or a completion page, it's generally a good idea to print this page and keep it with your course materials. Occasionally, glitches occur with online tests, and having some form of documentation as evidence of your completion can be a lifesaver, similar to having a receipt of your purchase if you ever need to return some merchandise you bought at a store.

Comprehensive Exams

Comprehensive, or cumulative, exams are usually given during a week dedicated for "finals." Not all final tests are comprehensive—some professors choose to give their students shorter tests instead. However, most of the finals you will take in college will reflect the culmination of what you have learned all semester. Taking comprehensive exams at the end of the semester will seem like a daunting task if you have several classes, but there are some tips that will help you manage the task. First, it is important that you study for all your classes regularly. Reviewing notes daily will help you keep the information fresh. Second, make sure that you keep your notes and course materials organized so that you can easily find what you have covered throughout the semester. When you get closer to the date of your final exam, begin studying more intensely by reviewing the most current material and working backwards toward the material that was covered at the beginning of the semester. You'll discover that if you've been reviewing and rewriting your notes and course materials on a daily or weekly basis throughout the semester, the challenge of studying for a comprehensive exam will be far less daunting, and even somewhat enjoyable. Studying for comprehensive exams can be a rewarding time when you reflect on everything you've learned in the semester, and you can see how various concepts that didn't seem related before now fit together.

60-second PAUSE

Make a list of all the courses you're taking this semester and the exams that are scheduled in each. Take a moment to anticipate the types of exams these may be, consulting the syllabus for each class for clues.

TEST-TAKING STRATEGIES PROVIDE A GAME PLAN FOR SUCCESS

Get Your Body Ready

Before you begin to think about what is on a test and how you should study, you must make sure that you are taking care of yourself. Eating and sleeping are fundamental to doing well on tests. If you are not healthy, then you cannot perform at your highest level. Just as athletes prepare for performance days in advance by eating carbohydrates and resting, you should focus on getting regular sleep and eating well days before the exam. At the very least, get a good night's rest the night before the test and avoid refined sugar (candy, cakes, and cookies) and caffeine. For more specific information on staying healthy, refer to Chapter 5.

Maintaining a good attitude as you prepare for the exam is another successful strategy. Monitor and eliminate any negative self-talk about your ability to do well on exams. Instead, visualize yourself taking the test successfully and earning a good grade.

Set the Stage for a Good Testing Environment

Once you have prepared for the test, both physically and mentally, you should be ready to take it. Before you leave for class, be sure that you have the appropriate supplies: Will you need a watch, paper, pen, pencil, calculator, or dictionary and thesaurus? Are there any approved test-taking aids that you need to bring as well? Will you be able to use your textbook or a "cheat" sheet with formulas on it? Once you arrive in class, take a seat away from distractions and where you feel comfortable to spread out and get to work. If you are not wearing a watch, sit somewhere you will be able to see a clock. Cell phone access, which many students use to keep track of time, may be restricted during tests, so be sure to keep track of time some other way. When taking tests that use a Scantron or bubble form on which you have to pencil in your answers by filling in circles, be sure to bring at least two sharpened pencils.

When the Test Begins, Take Time to Read It All First

When you first get the test, read through all the questions, noting which ones will take longer to answer than the others. Taking that time to read all the questions is actually a time saver, because you will know what to expect and how to pace yourself. Turn the paper over and check out the back. Your instructor may have made two-sided copies of the test, which means you will have questions on the back and front of the paper.

As you read through the test, make note of the types of questions and use the tips in this chapter to answer them. Read the directions for each section carefully and mark any special instructions. For example, in a matching section, there may be more than one match for an item in one of the columns; in an essay writing section, there may be a choice of topics. Also, be aware of how many points each section is worth. If one section is worth half the points for the entire exam, you will need to spend a majority of your time working on that part.

Pacing yourself during the exam is very important. Before you begin the test, you should determine how much time you need to spend on each section based on the types of questions, your comfort level with the questions, and the amount of points each section is worth. As a general rule, you should spend less than a minute per multiple choice and true/false question and 15 minutes or more to answer an essay question. For the other types of questions, you will need to spend some-

Get yourself physically ready for your test, as well as mentally.

©SHUTTERSTOCK

where between one and five minutes per question. If you get off track and spend too much time on one section, don't panic. You will just need to work quickly and carefully on the rest of the exam.

Work the easiest questions first, marking questions that you don't know the answer to or that you find confusing. Don't come back to them until you have completed all the questions that you can easily answer. If you are unsure of an answer, mark that question, as well, and plan to review it before turning in your exam. If a question or problem has multiple parts, work through as many of the parts as you can. Do not leave questions unanswered. Partial answers may receive partial credit unless you have been instructed otherwise.

Finally, leave yourself 5–10 minutes to check your work. If you finish an exam early, always go back through the questions and go over your answers, ensuring that all questions are answered and that all parts are completed. If you have written an essay, read through your response and check for grammatical, spelling, and punctuation errors. Initial each page and number the pages of your essay, if appropriate. Also, make sure that you write your name on every page of the exam (unless instructed otherwise). Turn in your exam and any paper on which you worked problems or drafted an essay.

Exams Will Test Your Integrity

You may have recently read about the new lengths that students go to in order to cheat on exams or to plagiarize. Advances in technology have made cheating easier and have made it seem more widespread. Although there is no clear evidence that more students are cheating now than were 30 years ago, there does seem to be more confusion about what constitutes cheating. For example, some professors require group presentations and collaboration on projects; however, very few offer guidelines on who should do what and how to document the part that each student does. In addition, collaboration on homework assignments, which was encouraged in high school, may now be prohibited in college. When in doubt about how you should complete homework or group projects, ask your instructor for specific guidelines.

The integrity rules are a little clearer when taking a test. Unless otherwise stated, do not use notes, books, or classmates as references for the exam. Most instructors will ask you to clear your desk of any material except paper and a pen or will ask you to move away from the nearest person. All of these actions are to ensure that there are no questions about the originality of the work. Other instructors are more trusting of students and may leave the classroom or give the class a take-home test. An instructor who allows such freedom is sending you a message about integrity: He trusts that his students will act maturely, responsibly, and honestly. Violating that trust can have grave consequences, because not only does the cheating student create problems for herself, but she has also damaged the relationship of trust for the entire class.

To ensure that you act with integrity when taking an exam, whether supervised or not, do your own work and keep your work surface clear of books, papers, folders, cell phones, pagers, and even drink bottles. If possible, distance yourself from other students so that they are less likely to cheat off you. If you are ever in doubt, however, about your actions or the requirements for an exam, be sure to ask your professor.

Keep Your Test Anxiety in Moderation

The test-taking strategies and suggestions for preparing for exams can help reduce some of your anxiety, but it's not unusual to still experience some nervousness. Some degree of nervousness is normal and can actually give you an adrenaline boost. If you find yourself experiencing extreme anxiety accompanied by excessive sweating, nausea, and crying, schedule time to see an academic or health center advisor.

In order to cope with mild anxiety, there are a variety of activities you can do to relieve tension. Basic relaxation techniques, such as deep breathing and visualizations, can take the edge off the tension of taking a test. Taking the time to breathe deeply whenever you feel overwhelmed will help you stay in control. Also, visualizing yourself relaxing or succeeding at a test can help you get beyond self-defeating doubt and stress.

Reflect on your test-taking success to date. In general, have you performed well on tests, or do they tend to be a real challenge? What test-taking strategies described earlier could you use to improve your success in college?

from COLLEGE

How Studying and Testing May Differ after Transfer

As you take upper-level classes, you may find that tests and papers seem to get fewer and farther between, but their importance to the overall course is greater. Your reading load will increase, and the subject matter will get more technical. You may also find yourself reading a variety of material: textbooks, journal articles, lab manuals, dissertations, novels, surveys, charts, graphs, and statistics.

Your critical thinking skills will be essential to making it through these courses. Your professors will also expect that you have strong study skills and solid test-taking strategies. If you have a solid foundation of skills and strategies, then you will be successful. You will just need to monitor your progress and make adjustments as necessary.

©ISTOCKPHOTO

from COLLEGE
to CAREER

Preparation Counts

Just as you will prepare for exams and presentations in college, you will use the same skills on the job. Time management, attention to detail, and careful preparation will be necessary to be successful in your career. Depending on your career choice, you may have to pass proficiency tests or certification exams at least once, or even yearly.

Although the pressure to pass will be greater, chances are good that since you have been to college and passed many tests, your test-taking skills will get you through exams on the job. In addition to reviewing the test-taking strategies that are outlined in this chapter, you should also take advantage of any test preparation seminars that your employer offers. Also, now is the time to demonstrate your ability to study with others. There is no better study group than your coworkers, because they all have the same investment as you.

©ANNIE FULLER/PEARSON

UNDERSTAND & REMEMBER

Review Questions

Create

Evaluate

Analyze

Apply

Understand

Remember

1. What are the differences between objective and subjective test questions? What are the differences in what you should do to answer objective and subjective test questions effectively?

2. What kinds of questions can you expect to be asked on science tests? On literature tests? How will these test questions possibly differ?

3. What are the "rules" for studying in a group?

4. In what ways can a student beat test anxiety?

APPLY & ANALYZE

Critical Thinking

1. When you are short on time, what study strategies would be the most effective for you? Explain why these strategies would work best in a time crunch.

2. What types of questions are most challenging for you? What strategies can you employ to master them?

3. Compare studying in a group with studying on your own. What are the benefits of both? What are the drawbacks?

EVALUATE

Case Scenarios

1. Sylvia's accounting professor has announced to his class that he allows students to study from old tests. In fact, he keeps a folder of previous exams in the library for students to access. One of Sylvia's classmates asks her if she wants to study for the test, and she agrees. When they meet, her classmate pulls out a copy of a test with the current semester's date on it. Sylvia questions her classmate, who says that the professor gave her a rough draft of a test that he decided not to use. When Sylvia gets to class, she recognizes every question because it is the same test that her classmate had, but she decides to take the test without saying anything to her professor.

   Use the following scale to rate the decision that has been made (1 = Poor Decision, 5 = Excellent Decision). Be prepared to explain your answer.

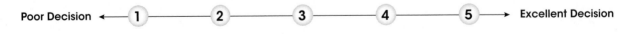

Poor Decision ◄——— 1 ——— 2 ——— 3 ——— 4 ——— 5 ——► Excellent Decision

2. Ryan does not think he knows how to study well. He glided through high school without cracking open a book. Now, he is in college and taking five classes: Intermediate Algebra, Reading Improvement, Introduction to Sociology, Speech Communication, and Concepts of Health and Wellness. He is struggling through his health and math classes and has made low C's and a D on recent tests, so he has asked some classmates to get together over beer and pizza to study for the rest of the semester.

Use the following scale to rate the decision that has been made (1 = Poor Decision, 5 = Excellent Decision). Be prepared to explain your answer.

Poor Decision ← ①———②———③———④———⑤ → Excellent Decision

3. Betty gets sweaty palms and wants to throw up each time she takes a test. She has failed classes before because she couldn't calm herself down enough to take a major test. This semester, though, Betty wants to do better because she cannot keep dropping or failing her classes. She has talked to her classmates about what they do to ease their anxiety. One student told her about some herbal tea drinks that calm your nerves before a test, but they make you very sleepy afterwards. Another friend suggests that she take some energy supplements because they will keep her from worrying about the test. She decides to take the tea before her test.

Use the following scale to rate the decision that has been made (1 = Poor Decision, 5 = Excellent Decision). Be prepared to explain your answer.

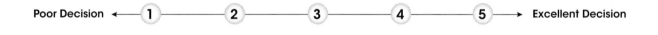

Poor Decision ← ①———②———③———④———⑤ → Excellent Decision

CREATE

Research It Further

1. Using the Internet, investigate methods of cheating that have occurred with "high-stakes" testing, such as licensure and college-entrance exams. Report the information to your class, and provide a list of strategies that test givers can take to discourage cheating.

2. Survey your campus for the most popular study places. Create a map and a list of the "best features" of each study area to share with your classmates.

3. Based on interviewing your classmates, create a list of tips that could help students study and take tests effectively. Divide your tips into categories that would help visual, aural, and kinesthetic learners.

Based on the goals we set at the beginning of this chapter, here's how you can take this learning with you toward college success:

- Find the study strategy that best works for you, whether it is keeping a study log, developing "cheat" sheets, or participating in a study group.

- Start anticipating different types of test questions you may be asked in your classes and practice answering the question types.

- Ask your professors what types of tests you will have, and prepare for them accordingly.

- Start practicing effective test-taking strategies with sample tests.

- Begin reducing your test anxiety by being prepared and practicing with different types of test questions.

REFERENCES AND RECOMMENDED READINGS

Klauser, H. A. (2001). *Write it down, make it happen: Knowing what you want and getting it!* New York, NY: Simon & Schuster.

Paul, M. A., & Paul, K. (2009). *Study smarter, not harder.* Bellingham, WA: Self Counsel Press.

Roubidoux, S. (2008). *101 ways to make studying easier and faster for college students: What every student needs to know explained simply.* Ocala, FL: Atlantic Publishing Group.

MyStudentSuccessLab

MyStudentSuccessLab (www.mystudentsuccesslab.com) is an online solution designed to help you 'Start strong, Finish stronger' by building skills for ongoing personal and professional development.

11 Planning for Your Degree

"Hey, Laura, who are you taking for world history?" asks Juanita. Laura pulls out her schedule for next semester and looks.

"I have Dr. Franks," she says. "I interviewed him and Professor Martinsen last week to see which one would be a good fit for me." Laura takes a moment to take off her jacket while Juanita checks her phone to see if her mother has called her.

"Really? I just checked out that website where you can write about your instructors. I think I am going to get Dr. Bernstein. He makes you do a group project rather than exam." Juanita says.

"It's hard to get a good idea of what they are like just from a website, don't you think?" asks Laura. Because of Laura's dyslexia, she spends lots of time rewriting her notes and working on assignments. Getting professors that she feels comfortable with is important to her.

"Maybe I need to find someone who can also help me with my degree plan. I am still unsure about what I want to major in. I need to get this decided soon," Juanita says.

"Are you still worried that your parents are going to be upset if you choose something other than engineering?" Laura asks.

"Probably, but now that I am 18, I guess I don't have to worry about my mom calling my advisor to tell him what I should major in," she says.

"I tell you what. Pick up your things and come with me. I need to go to counseling anyway to talk about my scholarship," says Laura.

Laura gathers her books and stuffs them in her backpack. Then, Juanita follows Laura to the counseling center, hoping to get some answers to her questions about how she should plan not only her next semester, but also her life.

YOUR GOALS FOR THIS CHAPTER

As both Laura and Juanita remind us, these last weeks will be filled with decisions to make about finances and course work, but once you have successfully completed a certificate or degree program you will be able to say, "I did it!" This chapter provides information that will enable you to:

- Identify the required steps to complete your degree
- Anticipate what to expect at the end of the semester
- Evaluate alternative methods for paying for college
- List the benefits of both staying in college and returning after a break

MyStudentSuccessLab (www.mystudentsuccesslab.com) is an online solution designed to help you 'Start strong, Finish stronger' by building skills for ongoing personal and professional development.

COMPLETING YOUR DEGREE IS A GOAL, AND YOU NEED A PLAN

It is never too early to begin thinking about your educational future, especially if it involves completing a certificate or degree. Understanding what you need to do—in addition to passing your courses—may mean the difference between graduating on time and staying another semester to finish just one class. Visiting your advisor regularly can help you stay on track, as can reviewing the college catalog and reading the college's website and other information sources for updates.

Your Terms for SUCCESS

WHEN YOU SEE . . .	IT MEANS . . .
Accelerated classes	You will take classes at a faster pace than a regular semester; may require more time per week to complete the classes, but may also allow you to complete sequences of classes more quickly than if you took classes during a traditional term
Cooperative learning	You will be required to work in small groups or teams to complete class assignments; goals of the group work will vary, but usually require that all members contribute to the learning process
FASFA	Free Application for Student Federal Aid
Hybrid classes	You will attend classes on campus for part of the semester and will use an online learning system to supplement your learning the days you are not in class; will require access to a computer and the Internet
Intersession classes	You will attend a class in between regular semesters; sometimes offered in January or May before or after a spring semester or term; usually faster-paced and limited to only one or two classes available for you to take
Learning communities	You will take classes with a "cohort" or the same group of students for two or more classes; classes often share similar assignments and course content
Perkins Loan	Low-interest loan that helps students pay for undergraduate education
PLUS loan	Parent Loan for Undergraduate Students
Self-paced class	You will complete the course requirements at your own pace; if you need more time than a traditional semester, you are allowed to continue in the class until you have successfully mastered the course content
Service learning	You will be required to participate in a community project as part of your course, which will reinforce the concepts and content of the course and may also include an opportunity for you to reflect on what you learned
Web-enhanced class	You will use the Internet to supplement your learning in the class; requires access to a computer and the Internet; sometimes used interchangeably with "hybrid"
Work study	A financial aid program that allows students to earn money while working on campus; depending on the position's job duties, you may be able to study when you are not engaged in a task

This Is YOUR Degree

In most cases, your goal for enrolling in a community college is to complete an associate's degree. Even if it's facing tough budget times, your college invests a lot of resources to help you succeed in this goal. Professors, advisors, tutors, classrooms, computer labs, websites, dorms, college unions, and dining halls are just a few of the resources that a college establishes to help you succeed. These are all here for you, and every member of the staff and faculty who work at your college are committed to your success. But, these resources and services will only be helpful if you take personal responsibility for completing your degree. In college, the responsibility shifts to you, and it's up to you to take the initiative to schedule appointments, complete the appropriate forms and applications for scholarships and entry to a major, and make sure that the courses you take fulfill the requirements for the degree you are pursuing.

If all of this sounds a bit intimidating, don't worry. The faculty and staff at your college are very willing to help. You just need to ask for that help. But, before you schedule an appointment with an academic or financial aid advisor or a professor, make sure that you've studied the issue yourself. Although they are supportive and kind, you'll find that faculty and staff at a college have very high expectations for students like yourself, and they will expect you to take the lead

USING TECHNOLOGY TO GET AHEAD

Your college website, as well as other sites devoted to college degrees and majors, can give you information about different types of degrees and their requirements.

RECOMMENDED SITES

- http://www.collegeboard.com/student/csearch/where-to-start/38.html: The College Board provides a wealth of information about planning and paying for college.
- http://www.collegedegree.com: This site offers links to various programs by degree type.
- http://www.payscale.com/best-colleges/popular-majors.asp: This site provides lists of popular majors, as well as links about careers and their average salaries.

©THINKSTOCK

Use the resources and people on your campus to help you choose a major or degree plan.

BUZZ

Q I have no idea what degree to pursue, and I need to declare my major next semester. My parents want me to go to law school, and a few of my friends want me to join Teach for America. I am so confused.

A First, it is normal to be unsure of such an important decision, but there are some tips for making it easier to declare what degree you want.

- Explore your career values and interests through a program such as Kuder or DISCOVER. Your career counseling office may be able to provide these for you.

- Think about what activities have given you joy in the past, and consider what parts of the activities were most enjoyable. The answers can give you a general idea of what you like.

- Get some experience in different fields through internships, shadowing, or volunteer work.

- Realize that you will most likely have three or four careers in different fields throughout your lifetime.

on solving a problem or suggesting an appropriate course of action. They can advise you, but you will be asked to ultimately make the final decision. To help you develop a plan of study for your degree, then, we'll break an associate's degree into individual parts and show you how it all comes together, putting you on the stage to receive your diploma. Exhibit 11.1 provides an overview of different degree plans at both community colleges and universities. Exhibit 11.2 provides definitions of the different parts of the degree plan that you will need to consider when choosing classes.

Your plan of study, or degree plan, is a living document, and you are its primary author. Your advisors and professors can help you develop it, but the final decision about the courses you'll take and when you'll take them is up to you. When you first get started in college, take time to develop your plan of study and review it with others. Then, as your interests take shape and conditions change, you can update your plan of study accordingly. With the help of the faculty and staff at your college, your plan of study is a map that will guide you through the successful completion of your major. See Exhibit 11.3 for an example of a degree plan.

EXHIBIT 11.1 Program Types

Program Type	Length/Requirements	Purpose
Certificate	One semester or two; 15–30 credit hours	To obtain skills necessary for a job-related or personal goal or for direct entry into the workforce; not intended to fit into a higher degree
Associate of Applied Science Degree	Four semesters; about 60 credit hours	To obtain knowledge and skills for direct entry into the workforce; usually not intended to fit into a higher degree
Associate of Arts/ Science Degree	Four semesters; about 60 credit hours	To obtain knowledge and skills for transfer to a higher degree program or for direct entry into the workforce
Bachelor of Arts/ Science Degree	Eight semesters; about 120 credit hours	To obtain knowledge and skills for transfer to a graduate degree program or for direct entry into the workforce
Master's Degree	Number of semesters depends; about 30 credit hours beyond bachelor's degree	To obtain knowledge, skills, and mastery of a field or discipline for further graduate study or entry into the workforce
Doctoral Degree	Number of semesters depends; about 60 credit hours beyond bachelor's degree	To obtain knowledge, skills, and mastery of a field for research in that field and/or entry into the workforce

EXHIBIT  **11.2**   **Three Parts to the Major**

Courses	Definition	What to Do
General education (GE) courses	These are sometimes called the "basics" or "core curriculum." Courses such as psychology, composition, algebra, and speech communication often make up the first two years of a four-year degree.	Check your degree plan to determine what GE courses are required for your degree. Make note of the courses that are prerequisites to other courses. Try to complete these courses in the first four semesters.
Major courses	These courses are required for you to complete a specific degree. Often, some GE courses are prerequisites to major courses.	Check your degree plan to determine which courses must be completed as prerequisites. Keep your advisor informed as to your progress.
Concentration or specialized courses	These courses provide in-depth exposure to material related to your major field. They may have prerequisites that must be completed first.	Check your degree plan to determine if specialized courses are suggested or listed. Talk to your advisor about any special permissions needed to take these classes, and about your progress in them.

60-second PAUSE

If you've already chosen a major, provide three reasons that you selected the degree you did. If you're undecided and haven't chosen a specific degree, describe three criteria you could use to select one.

A SUCCESSFUL SEMESTER REQUIRES A STRONG FINISH

The end of the semester is a good time to start assessing how you have done and where you want to go. Before you can begin planning for next semester, there will be some loose ends to tie up for your current semester. You should now know what to expect at the beginning of next semester, and with that additional information, you should be able to make better choices and prepare yourself for what lies ahead.

EXHIBIT 11.3 Degree Plan

Early Childhood Development [the department]

Associate of Applied Science [type of degree—usually completed in four semesters]

Option: Early Childhood Education [the emphasis within the degree]

This option is for early childhood caregivers and paraprofessionals who wish to improve their skills and credentials. Early childhood curriculum is the focus. This option is also appropriate for supervisors, for curriculum coordinators, and for CDA renewal. [description of how this degree will benefit you]

[Suggested schedule for each semester. It is usually not mandatory that you take the courses in the order that they suggest, unless one is a prerequisite for another.]

First Semester		Credit Hours
ECD 1003	Foundations of Early Childhood Education	3
ECD 1103	Child Development	3
ECD 1203	Healthy, Safe Learning Environment	3
ECD 1303	Practicum I	3
ENGL 1311	English Composition I	3
Total Credit Hours		15
Second Semester		
ECD 2003	Child Behavior	3
ECD 2103	Preschool Curriculum *or*	
ECD 2403	Infant/Toddler Curriculum	3
ECD 2503	Nutrition for the Young Child	3
ECD 2303	Practicum II	3
MATH 1301	College Business Mathematics	3
Total Credit Hours		15
Third Semester		
ECD 2703	Language Arts	3
ECD 2803	Special Needs	3
ENGL 1312	English Composition II	3
PSYC 2300	Psychology and the Human Experience	3
HLSC 1304	Concepts of Lifetime Health and Wellness,	
MUSC 2300	Introduction to Music, *or*	
ARTS 2300	Introduction to Visual Arts	3
Total Credit Hours		15
Fourth Semester		
ECD 2903	Trends in Curriculum	3
BUS 1303	Introduction to Computers *or higher-level computer course*	3
SOCI 2300	Introduction to Sociology	3
SPCH 1300	Speech Communication	3
ANTH 2310	Cultural Anthropology *or*	
PSYC 2300	Developmental Psychology	3
Total Credit Hours		15
Total Hours for A.A.S.		60

Course Evaluations Provide Important Feedback

Course evaluations by students (sometimes called "student" evaluations because students evaluate the course and the instructor) are an integral part of taking a college class. Each semester you may be asked to complete an evaluation form for your instructor. The evaluations are anonymous and are not given to the instructor until grades have been posted; thus, you should feel comfortable being open and honest about the course when answering the form's questions.

The purpose of course evaluations is to provide the instructor and administrators a description of how students feel about the instruction they received in the course. Some colleges look very closely at course evaluations and determine raises and promotions based in part on the scores that instructors receive. Other colleges merely use them as discussion tools to improve the instructors' teaching. No matter how your college uses the information, providing candid and constructive criticism, rather than general comments, is most helpful to the instructor.

Phrases such as "Professor Banks is not a good instructor" and "Dr. Wright is perfect" do not provide specific information that will help your instructor improve or help him or her to continue doing what you think works very well. Instead, you may want to offer suggestions such as "The instructor graded fairly and handed back exams in a timely manner" or "The professor rarely explained the assignments." These statements allow your instructors to pinpoint exactly what worked for you and what didn't.

Most student evaluation forms contain questions that you answer by checking a box or filling in a bubble, as well as questions that you answer by writing a narrative response. Here are examples of the two types of questions that you may see on a course evaluation form:

1. My instructor uses class time effectively.

   A. Strongly Agree   **B.** Agree   **C.** Strongly Disagree

2. My instructor grades fairly.

   A. Strongly Agree   **B.** Agree   **C.** Strongly Disagree

3. What can your instructor do to improve the course?

4. What does your instructor do well?

When answering questions such as these, take time to reflect on the instructor's performance during the semester. Create a list of activities that you did in class during the semester and think about them. Then, consider the overall performance of your instructor. Did he come to class on time? Was she easy to contact when you needed her? Did he act professionally? Did she seem to have a good knowledge of the subject matter? Remember that the objective of student evaluations is to provide feedback that will help instructors improve, so the more information you provide, the better.

You Can Survive Finals!

Another traditional "ending" to the semester is final exams. Surviving "finals week" is often considered a well-earned badge of honor for a college student. The reasons that finals are so stressful for some college students are that they often carry more weight

It's in the SYLLABUS

Look to your syllabus for information regarding the final exam. You should find out if it will be comprehensive, and what percentage of your overall grade account for.

■ Start asking questions about the final exams in your classes.

■ Consider the following questions to ask your instructors: How long do we have to take it? Are there previous exams we can use for studying?

than any other tests during the semester, they contain questions about material from the entire semester, and they are all scheduled around the same time.

To help you survive finals, work on some test-taking skills and become comfortable with the different types of exams you might be expected to take. Go back to the test-taking and studying chapter and review the material about taking tests. There are additional steps you can follow to quickly get ready for your exams in these final weeks of the semester. First, be sure to note the day, place, and time of each final and write it down on your calendar. Double-check this information a week before the exam. Be aware that where and when you take your finals may differ from where and when you took your classes during the semester. Whenever possible, confirm the exam time and location of the exam with your professor.

A few weeks before the final, ask questions about the exam. What will you be allowed to use? What do you need to bring? What should you study? Is photo identification required? Get plenty of rest during the days that lead up to the exam. When you take the exam, use your time wisely. Final exams usually take longer to complete than regular tests, so be sure you use the entire time that you are allotted (usually one to three hours). Be prepared by bringing ample writing supplies and any approved items, such as a calculator or dictionary.

Consider Your Options for Next Semester

Even if you have not completed your classes this semester, you can start planning for next semester. By now, you should be familiar with the college catalog and can identify the courses that you may want to take by reading their descriptions and checking your plan of study. Both the description and your plan will help you determine which classes you need to take, in order. Exhibit 11.4 shows a typical catalog description for a developmental math course.

In addition to reviewing the catalog descriptions for a course, you will also want to determine if the course has a prerequisite you must take beforehand. In the Elementary

---

EXHIBIT **11.4** **Catalog Description**

DEVE 0336. Elementary Algebra

This course includes, but is not limited to, the following concepts: operations on integers and rational numbers; solving linear equations and inequalities in one variable; graphing linear equations and inequalities in two variables; operations on exponents and polynomials; and problem-solving techniques.

Prerequisite: DEVE 0334 with a grade of C or better, or a COMPASS Algebra placement test score from 23 to 32, or a score of 16 or 17 on the mathematic section of the ACT. Final grade will be A, B, C, or NC

(no credit) (3 credit hours)

This information shows that you must complete a course successfully before enrolling in this one.

Algebra example in Exhibit 11.4, a student will need to either provide a test score that meets the minimum requirement, or she will need to successfully complete the *pre-requisite*. Courses that have *corequisites* are other courses that must be taken before or at the same time as the course. For instance, a Chemistry I course may have a corequisite of Intermediate Algebra, which means a student must complete the course before enrolling in Chemistry I or can take the course during the same semester.

Classes Come in Different Formats

In addition to which courses to take, you may also want to research your options for the design of the courses. Many colleges are now offering classes in a variety of formats. You may have the opportunity to take classes in a *learning community,* which means that two or more classes are linked together by a certain topic. The students in the learning community classes stay together for each course. For example, a class of 25 students may take a morning Speech Communication class and then the same students take an afternoon College Writing class together. Even though each class is taught by a different professor, each class may study a similar topic or the students in the learning community may be required to work on a project that links both courses together.

Blended or *hybrid* classes are another format that you may want to consider when registering for next semester. This usually means that some part of the class will be online and that you will be required to complete work online. In these courses, you may only meet once a week, instead of two or three times, in a traditional face-to-face format on campus, and then do the rest of your course work online. Good computer skills, access to a computer, and a reliable Internet connection will be requirements for this type of class.

Some courses may be offered entirely online. There are no face-to-face class meetings, and you have to complete all of the requirements for the course by reading and reviewing content from the course website and uploading your assignments electronically within specified deadlines. In these classes, you communicate with your instructor primarily through email, chat, and live Web video, although you may have an opportunity to meet with him during his office hours, if he offers any.

Another course format is *alternative pacing.* These courses can also be called *accelerated classes,* where you are able to complete your work in a class at a faster pace than a regular 16-week semester. They can also be *self-paced classes,* in which you work at your own pace, whether it is over one or more semesters. Usually, accelerated and self-paced classes require online work and testing to ensure you are mastering the material.

Finally, *intersession* classes are those offered between semesters, and function much like accelerated classes. Intersession classes may give you an opportunity to catch up or get ahead with a particular course, but you need to be prepared to invest all your effort and energy in these classes because they cover a large amount of material in a short period of time.

With all of these different formats—traditional face-to-face, learning communities, hybrid, online, self-paced, intersession—how do you know which option is best for you? As with any decision in college, it's a good idea to consult with your advisors and professors, and any college upperclassmen who have been successful in college so far. Learning communities are great if you want to get to know other students really well and be part of a cohort of students who are all taking the same classes. If you're a freshman just getting acclimated to the college environment, or a transfer student who wants to join others in the transition to a four-year college, the learning community format may work well for you.

Traditional face-to-face classes are a good choice if you learn best in the typical classroom setting. Your classes meet regularly, you see your classmates and professor often, and you complete your homework and reading outside of class. You could consider hybrid or online classes if you have scheduling complications that would make it difficult for you to attend the live face-to-face classes, and if you want more flexibility over when you review the course materials and complete the assignments. If you have work or family responsibilities during the day, hybrid and online courses give you more flexibility to do your classwork early in the morning or at night.

Alternative pacing classes may also be an ideal option if you have certain scheduling preferences or restrictions. For example, if you don't have plans during your semester break and you want to get ahead on some of your core requirements, you could take a core course during the winter intersession. See Exhibit 11.5 for an overview of course formats.

Learning Also Has Different Formats

After considering the format of your classes, you may also want to think about how classes may require you to learn. *Service learning* is gaining popularity at many colleges, and it involves community service as part of the learning process. A course that includes a service learning project may require that students work at a homeless shelter, design a neighborhood playground, or test area drinking water. The project will depend on the course, and the hours needed to complete the project will depend on the instructor's assignments, but such a course offers a unique opportunity for students to apply the concepts they learn in class to help solve a community issue. *Cooperative learning* is another type of format that requires students to work in small teams to learn the material in a course. Cooperative learning groups work all semester to help their teammates learn concepts and complete projects. Different from small group work that you may participate in for other classes, cooperative learning is sustained and deliberate—the teams work together for the entire semester. *Internships* and *co-ops* provide learning experiences in the context of a job. If your college offers credit for either of these types of courses, you could earn college credit while working and earning money. The types of jobs that qualify for internships and co-ops need to be approved by a professor or advisor beforehand, so be sure to meet with them to discuss this opportunity.

Your Choice of Professors Is an Important Decision

Just as important as what classes, and in which formats, you take next semester is with whom you take those classes. By now, you should realize that choosing the right professor could make the difference in how much you enjoy and learn in a class. If you have the option of choosing a professor, then you should start talking with other students about them. Ask specific questions and ask a variety of people. Remember that each student has his or her own view of what makes a good professor, a view that might not match your own. Questions you should ask need to move beyond "Is she a good teacher?" Instead, you should ask about her teaching style, the types of assignments she gives, and how available she is during office hours. Be wary of Internet sites that rate professors. They are not reliable because anyone can post just about anything they want without regard to accuracy, or sometimes decency. There is no mechanism to keep the same people from posting multiple positive or negative comments, which can pre-

EXHIBIT 11.5 Course Formats

Format	Definition	What to Do
Traditional/ face-to-face	This format requires you to attend class on campus.	Determine which courses would be better for you to attend in a traditional format, and make sure the courses fit in your weekly schedule.
Learning community	This format requires you to take more than one course with the same group of students, sometimes called a "cohort."	Make sure that the learning community classes are part of your degree plan. Check the schedule to determine if the courses are back to back or close together and that you have time to take both.
Blended/hybrid	This format requires some face-to-face interaction, as well as online work.	Be sure you have reliable access to a computer and the Internet. Pay attention to how the course is scheduled. You may be required to meet all semester or only for a portion of the semester.
Online	This format requires online work and may have required on-campus components, such as tests.	Be sure you have reliable access to a computer and the Internet. Note any on-campus requirements, and be sure to log in regularly to complete your work.
Intersession	This format is provided in between regular terms.	Make note of the length of time and how many days each class will be held. Be prepared for an intense, fast-paced learning experience.
Self-paced	This format allows you to complete work at your own pace.	Be sure you have the self-discipline to complete this type of course, and make note of any specific requirements of final completion.
Study abroad	This format allows you to experience another country and culture while studying courses.	Be sure to review the requirements and costs before embarking on a study-abroad course or program. Determine what the expectations are and how you will meet them.

When planning for next semester, consider the obligations that you have and how you will balance college with them.

© THINKSTOCK

sent only part of the picture. Online rating sites also tend to capture only the most extreme student opinions—both positive and negative—so you may not be getting information from the majority of the students who were somewhere in between.

An even better way to determine which instructors are the best for you is to talk with them before you enroll in their classes and review their course syllabi. Make an appointment with a potential instructor and ask pertinent questions: How much reading is involved? How do you teach the course? What led you to become a professor? Do you require a research paper? What do you expect students to know when they complete the course? The benefits of interviewing your instructor before you sign up for the class are that you get to determine whether the instructor is a good fit with your learning style and that you get to make a good impression by demonstrating your maturity and interest in your education.

Build Your Schedule to Fit You

What worked this semester and what didn't? Why? What will change for you next semester? Did you have enough time in between classes? Did you waste time that could have been spent more productively? All of these questions will need to be answered before you set your schedule for next semester.

When planning your next semester (and beyond), consider four factors: how many hours you need to take, how many hours you need to work, what other obligations (planned trips for work or with family, for example) you have, and how much stress these three factors will cause.

- *Number of credit hours.* To determine how many credit hours you need to take, be sure to review your financial aid, scholarship, and plan of study. If you are receiving financial aid, you may be required to take a full load, which often means at least 12 hours. As you can see in Exhibit 11.3, this plan of study requires 15 hours each semester in order to finish the degree in four semesters.
- *Number of study hours.* As a general rule, for every hour that you are in a face-to-face class, you will need a minimum of two and most likely three hours outside of class to study and learn the material and complete homework assignments and projects. For example, if your class meets four hours every week, you should set aside another eight hours during the week to study for that class. When you apply this guideline to your schedule, you'll quickly realize why 12 semester units typically makes you a "full-time" student. Classes alone are a full-time job, which is why the responsibility of having work obligations on top of a full-time academic schedule can be such a challenge.
- *Number of work hours.* If you will not be working next semester, you can skip this section. However, even if you are only working a few hours a week, you will need to schedule your work hours so that they do not overlap with the times you are in class. You also need to allow plenty of time to get to and from work and school and, if necessary, to eat a nutritious meal before class. Be realistic when calculating this time and plan for delays. Building adequate margins in your schedule will help keep your stress levels at a minimum.

- *Amount of learning support and learning opportunities.* If you know or antici-pate a need for learning assistance or tutoring, be sure to build that time into your schedule. You may also need to see each of your professors on a regular basis, some more than others, which should also be a consideration when creat-ing a schedule. If you leave little time for meeting with your instructors, it will be difficult to get the help and advice you need. Good time management and a flexible schedule will allow plenty of time for visits to the computer lab to get help with sending an attachment to an email, to the library for assistance in using the databases, and to the tutoring lab at the hours and locations that are most convenient to you.

- *Other obligations.* Working, going to school, exercising, taking care of a family, and participating in social and community activities all require your time and energy. To balance all your activities, you will need to keep an eye on upcom-ing events and make sure you plan accordingly. For example, if you are think-ing about registering for the fall semester and you know that you must take a weeklong trip for work in October, you should contact potential instructors to see what their policies are for missing class. Likewise, if you like to participate in your child's school activities, you will need to consider how much time you can give if you are also studying for classes. You may find that you need to cut back on social and volunteer commitments, or at least postpone them until after the semester.

- *Stress levels.* Your work schedule, course load, and other responsibilities can lead to high levels of stress. For example, if you have to take 15 hours of courses to maintain your financial aid and you have to work 40 hours to pay your bills, and you feel overwhelmed and anxious about balancing it all, then you are not likely to handle both well. If you find yourself in this situation, you will need to reconsider your plans before you get in over your head. Getting locked into a rigid schedule that doesn't allow you to drop a course that is too difficult or to decrease your hours at work will lead to frustration and high levels of negative stress.

On the other hand, you may thrive on such a schedule because you work better when you have to manage your time carefully. You may be the type of person who cannot study well if you have unlimited amounts of time to do it. If this is the case, you may feel excited about having so much activity in your schedule. Still, you could encounter a problem in which having flexibility (being able to drop a class or reducing your work hours) will help you cope. If you don't have this flexibility, then you need to pay extra attention to staying on top of your work. For example, if you find on the first day of the semester that one of your classes will be much more demanding than you had anticipated, you will need to be more careful about keeping up with assignments and managing your stress effectively. Planning ahead and managing your time will help you cope with a stressful schedule.

What should you do if you cannot work your schedule out despite your efforts to make it all fit together? There may be a semester that a course you need is not offered or the class is filled before you can register. Take advantage of the relationships you have cultivated at college to develop alternative solutions. Now is the time to talk with fellow students, professors, and advisors. They may be able to offer solutions that you have not considered. If there is an academic need for you to get into a class or rearrange your schedule, schedule time with the professor who teaches the class or a school official, such as a department chair or associate dean, to discuss your situation and make your case for a seat in the class. Professors and school officials sometimes have flexibility to add a few more students to a class, but only for compelling academic reasons.

Based on your experiences in college so far, what adjustments do you think you should make to your schedule next semester to better match your learning preferences and individual circumstances?

YOU HAVE OPTIONS FOR PAYING FOR COLLEGE

When thinking about your financial future, paying for college will most likely be at the top of your list. Even if you have a solid plan for paying tuition, fees, and books, it will be worth your time to investigate other methods in case your current plan falls through. Regardless of where you choose to go to school, you'll need to identify your different options and select the alternatives that work best for you, both short-term and long-term.

Scholarships

Winning a scholarship is by far the most rewarding (financially and psychologically) way to pay for college because it is literally free money—you don't have to pay it back. There are thousands of scholarships available for needy and accomplished students, but you often have to work hard to find them. To find the ones that match your profile, you will need to get the word out that you are looking. Talking with friends, family, employers, and college officials is a great way to start the process. They may know of obscure scholarships that will fit your needs perfectly.

Another way to get information about scholarships is to talk with the financial aid officers and counselors at your college. They have access to and knowledge of scholarships that fit the college's student profiles, such as single-parent and transfer scholarships that will pay your tuition and fees at a four-year college. Other effective methods for finding scholarships are to investigate sources at your library and search the Internet. Searching print and Web-based databases will provide you with more than enough information, but you'll need to narrow your focus so you can locate the options that best fit your qualities and circumstances.

Whatever information about scholarships you find—whether it's in books, in counselors' offices, or on the Internet—don't pay for it. There are services that claim to match your qualifications with scholarship qualifications but charge a fee to do so. You can get free help from high school and college counselors, as well as libraries and Internet searches. No reputable scholarship will require that you pay a fee to apply, and very few scholarship services will require payment. There are legitimate scholarship searching services out there, but be careful. The website FinAid! (www.finaid.org) provides information about different types of financial aid for college students, as well as tips for avoiding scholarship services scams. According to this site, any service that guarantees to match you with a scholarship or that offers you an award that you did not apply for is likely to be a scam. Many colleges recommend www.fastweb.com as a great starting point for finding scholarships that match your accomplishments.

Grants

By definition, grants are a form of financial assistance that does not need to be paid back. A common federal grant is the Pell Grant, which can be awarded for full-time or part-time enrollment. To determine your eligibility, talk with your financial aid counselor or visit any of the various websites that provide governmental information about financial aid. When you research Pell Grants, you will find that there is a maximum to the amount of the award ($5,500 for 2011–2012) and that your college will receive the money and then disburse it to you once classes start. Because of recent federal requirements about grants and student loans, colleges may wait several weeks before paying students. If you are expecting to receive your grant the first day or week of classes, you should make alternative arrangements to pay bills (including your bookstore bill).

Another type of grant that a student can receive is the Federal Supplemental Educational Opportunity Grant (FSEOG), which is available to those who demonstrate an exceptional need. According to the U.S. Department of Education (2011), the difference between a Pell Grant and an FSEOG is that "each participating school will receive enough money to pay the Federal Pell Grants of its eligible students. There's no guarantee every eligible student will be able to receive an FSEOG." The procedure for receiving an FSEOG is similar to that for receiving a Pell Grant; your eligibility will determine the amount that you receive, and your college will disburse the money to you after the semester begins.

You will need to maintain good academic standing at your college to remain eligible for a grant, so be sure to make note of the minimum GPA that you must maintain to receive future grant money. One last tip for continuing to receive grant funding: Make sure that you adhere to the college's attendance policy. You may be penalized (and lose your grant funding or have to pay it back) for missing too many classes or for dropping a course. As always, check with your financial aid officer to make sure that you clearly understand the expectations for receiving grants.

Student Loans

In the event that you are not eligible for grants, or if they aren't enough to cover all your costs, you should investigate student loans. The idea of taking out a loan to attend college makes many students shudder with fear because they don't want the added pressure that they must pay back what they borrow. If you can avoid a student loan, then by all means do so. However, receiving a student loan sometimes makes more financial sense in the long run, if the alternative is to forego college.

Federal student loans are typically low interest and can be paid back over 10 years. For families that would otherwise have to deplete their savings or borrow against retirement or their mortgages to pay for college, a low-interest student loan is a good option. Most loan programs allow you to defer (which means to delay) payment until after you graduate, or you can sometimes defer payment if you remain unemployed after you graduate. However, these loans may accumulate interest during this deferral period, so be sure to know the specific terms of your loan before making decisions.

One type of loan is the Stafford Loan, which comes in subsidized and unsubsidized versions. A subsidized loan is one in which the government pays the interest for you while you are in college. Once you graduate and start making payments on your loan, you will accrue interest as well. The government does not make interest payments for an unsubsidized loan, so you would need to decide whether to pay the interest while you are in college (usually a small amount), or allow the interest to be added (or capitalized) to the overall loan amount and wait until after you graduate to make any payments. This is a classic "pay now or pay more later" type of decision that you need to carefully evaluate.

A federal Perkins Loan is a loan between you and your college. The Perkins Loan currently allows you to borrow $5,500 per year, up to $27,500 for five years, and you don't have to start to repay it until nine months after you graduate or drop below at least part-time status (Student Aid on the Web, 2009). One benefit of a Perkins Loan is that you may be able to cancel up to 100% of the debt if you meet certain criteria. For example, upon graduation, if you choose to teach in a "teacher shortage" area, or if you serve as a full-time nurse, you may be eligible for cancellation of your loan. As you would for any type of federal financial aid, check out their websites (they usually end in ".gov") for the most current information.

PLUS, which stands for Parent Loan for Undergraduate Students, is another method for receiving money to help pay for college. If you are fortunate enough to have parents willing to take out a loan to help you pay for college, a PLUS is a possible option. To qualify, you must be a dependent student, which means your parents support you financially. A PLUS can be provided by the government or by private lenders. Parents who take out a PLUS are usually trying to make up the difference between the cost of tuition and the financial aid package that their children receive. Nonetheless, it is the parents who are ultimately responsible for repaying the loan, which can begin as early as 60 days after they receive it. See Exhibit 11.6 for repayment calculations for both a subsidized and an unsubsidized loan.

Military and Veterans Financial Aid

Being a member of the military can be especially helpful when you are paying for college. There are numerous benefits for active members and veterans, as well as their dependents, one of which is the Montgomery G.I. Bill. To find out about military benefits, talk with a financial aid officer, or a special counselor at your college or at a Veterans Affairs office for specific information. According to the United States Department of Veterans Affairs website (2011), the Post-9/11 G.I. Bill, which went into effect on August 1, 2009, provides benefits for qualified applicants to help students pay for tuition and some expenses related to attending an accredited and approved institution of higher education. There are differences between the Montgomery G.I. Bill and the Post-9/11 G.I. Bill, and you can find a benefits comparison, as well as a form to complete, on the website http://www.gibill.va.gov.

EXHIBIT **11.6** Loan Payment Recalculation

	Stafford Loan Subsidized	Stafford Loan Unsubsidized
Loan Amount	$5,000.00	$5,000.00
Interest Rate	4.500%	6.800%
Fees	1.500%	1.500%
Payment Term	10 years	10 years
Estimated Monthly Payment	$51.82	$74.17
Total Amount of Repayment	$6,128.30	$8,900.31

As you evaluate your different options for financing college (grants, loans, work), be sure to include potential military support as an option. The Army, Navy, and Air Force offer ROTC programs (Reserve Officer Training Corps; http://www.rotc.com) at thousands of campuses nationwide. These programs provide additional scholarship support for students who are interested and willing to commit to a specified period of military service during and after graduation.

Work Study

Work study is a program that allows students to earn money while they work on campus. The reason it is called "work study" is that the job may allow you to study when you work, though most work study positions are similar to office assistants and will keep you busy for the majority of the time you work. To work in such a program, you must be eligible for federal work study money, and you will be limited to a certain number of hours you can work per week. Not everyone who is eligible for work study will be able to find a position on campus, however. Each department and area of the college advertises, hires, and manages work study positions; sometimes, hiring can be competitive. There may be specific requirements (such as computer skills) that a candidate must meet before being hired. Since some positions require working with students' personal information, work study students must also abide by the college's privacy standards.

The benefits of participating in work study are that you can earn some money that will help pay your expenses and you will be able to work closely with college employees. By getting to know professors and administrators better—and by working for them— you may have access to valuable advice and information. To investigate whether or not work study is available for you, talk with your financial aid officer. He or she will review your eligibility and help you apply for on-campus employment.

Internships and Part- and Full-Time Jobs

For many college students, working during college will be an important and necessary part of their plan for paying for college. Having a job while attending college can be demanding, particularly because of the heavier schedule that it requires, so if you plan to work during college, you'll need to be especially mindful of how you manage your time. However, students who work also have an opportunity to develop an exceptional degree of discipline and time management skills that will serve them well when they are pursuing full-time careers after college. Like student athletes, students who work their way through college are a special group of individuals who have a demonstrated capability to endure challenges and succeed.

If you're working during college, you may need to reduce the number of credit units you enroll in during each semester. With experience, you'll get a better sense of your capacity for classes and work hours. The tradeoff of working while in college is that it can provide the financial support you need to pay for college, but it may also cause you to take longer to finish college, which can lead to higher educational costs and a delayed time to graduation, when you can transition to a full-time career. Take time to compare your options for financing college, and seek input from advisors, professors, and family members to help you make this important decision.

If you do decide to work while you're in college—either during the regular academic year or the summer—look for internship opportunities. Internships are jobs that provide job experience that is directly related to your academic interests, and in some cases, you can earn academic credit for your job. For example, a student majoring in

Recreation, Parks, and Tourism might work for the city parks department during the year or the summer, organizing youth programs and other community activities, and earn credit toward his or her major for doing so. Check your college catalog and your major requirements to determine if internships are a possible option. Internships can sometimes offer the dual benefit of helping you earn money for college while earning academic credit; however, some internships may be unpaid, which means that you earn credit for completing them, but you won't be paid an income. Talk to your professors and advisors to find out about the options available at your school.

Tuition Waivers for Employees

Another source of financial help is your employer. Large corporations sometimes offer financial assistance for employees, although there may be stipulations that you work for a certain amount of time after graduation. If your employer doesn't offer scholarships to employees, you should still ask if he or she is interested in doing so; employers will benefit from employees who further their education. Finally, your college may offer tuition waivers for its full-time employees. Some students take jobs offered at colleges so that they can take classes for free or at a reduced cost. If you need a part-time or full-time job while you are in school, you may want to check out the openings at your college.

Applying for Financial Aid

Each college is different in how it handles the application process, but it is worth talking generally about what to expect when applying for financial aid. Even if you have applied and received financial aid for this academic year, there may be some information that you need to know before applying again. The first step in the process is obtaining a Free Application for Federal Student Aid (FAFSA), which can be picked up from the financial aid office of your college or can be accessed online at http://www.fafsa.ed.gov. This website provides particularly helpful information that is broken down in steps, which can make the process less intimidating.

Be sure to remember that financial aid applications must be renewed each academic year; the timeline for receiving aid for a year starts in August and ends in July. Thus, if you applied for financial aid in November and received it for classes that started in January, you will have until July to use that aid; then, you will need to reapply for aid for the fall semester.

As part of the FAFSA application process, you will need to determine whether you are considered "independent" or "dependent." The federal government defines a student as independent if they meet certain criteria, such as being married, being 25 years or older, or both parents are deceased. Students who fit the definition for dependent status, or those who do not meet any of the criteria for being independent but who have extenuating circumstances, may be able to file an appeal to request that their status be changed to independent. In addition to determining your ability to pay for college, you will also be asked to provide an Estimated Family Contribution (EFC) amount; for example, if you

Planning for next semester includes taking into account how you will pay for both college and living expenses.

©THINKSTOCK

receive child support payments or Social Security payments, you will have to report that income as part of your EFC. One other consideration when applying for financial aid is that each year, a certain percentage of loan applications get identified for verification. This means that a number of student financial aid applications may take longer to process because of the requirements of verification.

Renewing Financial Aid and Paying It Back

In order to continue to receive financial aid, you will need to make sure that you understand and follow the requirements of your college. Many colleges maintain a satisfactory academic policy that states you will need to stay enrolled in a certain number of credit hours and maintain a certain grade point average (GPA) to continue to receive grants and loans. Sometimes, the required GPA is higher than the GPA to remain in college. For example, you may have to maintain a 2.7 GPA to continue to receive financial aid, whereas you may have to maintain a 2.0 GPA to stay in college. If you do not meet the requirements for a semester, your college may place you on financial aid probation, which means you must meet the college's requirements for the next semester to be removed from probation. The next step after probation can be suspension from financial aid. This means that you may not be able to receive financial aid, but you may still be able to enroll in classes as long as you pay for them yourself. Just in case your suspension is the result of extenuating circumstances, some colleges have an appeals process for financial aid suspension. This means you may file an appeal and meet before a group of people who will determine if you can reapply for financial aid.

Whenever you apply for loans, you will need to consider how you will pay them back after you complete your degree or when you stop attending college. Student loan default is a common problem nationwide, and there are stiff penalties for failing to pay back the federal government. On the other hand, loan forgiveness programs are often available for students who major in fields that are in high demand in their community. To find out more about these types of programs, be sure to talk to someone in the financial aid office at your college. The following are some useful resources that you can consult for guidance about financial aid and borrowing:

- The Free Application for Federal Student Aid (FAFSA) site (http://www.fafsa.ed.gov) provides extensive information about the FAFSA itself and the various forms of federal student aid.
- The Human Capital Score website (http://humancapitalscore.com) generates a custom calculation of your future income that can help you determine the maximum amount of money you should borrow through student loans.
- The College Board (http://www.collegeboard.com/student/pay/index.html) provides a number of resources, including a scholarship search tool and a net price calculator for estimating the total cost of attending college.

60-second PAUSE

From memory, write down the list of all the possible methods for financing your college education that were just covered in this section. For each, identify at least one advantage and one disadvantage. Which sources do you intend to use to finance your own education?

There is tremendous pressure to obtain a higher degree. Frequently, high school students hear this pitch from parents, counselors, and teachers: Success in life is dependent on obtaining a college degree. People who have been in the workforce know, as well, that a college degree can be the difference between doing the same job until retirement and being promoted.

But does everyone need to go to college? College is a great place to continue your education and to make your career dreams a reality. There are also indirect benefits to pursuing higher education, such as improving your health and financial well-being because you know more about yourself and the world around you. Nonetheless, going to college is not the only key to success. There are many vibrant, intelligent, successful people who have not completed a college degree.

College Should Be Right for You

How will you know if college is not right for you? It may be difficult to tell, but you shouldn't quit going just because you are unsure. The best way to discover how you feel about being in college is to ask yourself a series of questions. Then, talk about your responses with a college counselor, advisor, or trusted friend who can give you good advice.

- Who wants me to be in college?
- Do *I* want to be in college?
- How do I feel when I am in class?
- How do I feel when I am studying?
- How do I feel after I take an exam?
- What do I want to major in? Why?
- What do I want to do with my life? Do I need a college degree to do it?
- What do I value about higher education? What can it do for me?
- What is my passion?
- Am I doing everything I can to be successful in college?

Achieving your goal degree will be a proud moment for you and your family.

© SHUTTERSTOCK

Take your time answering these questions. You may find that your discomfort about being in college is really a fear about a new beginning and the unknown. Being apprehensive about a new program or a new environment is perfectly normal and does not necessarily indicate that you are not right for college. Also, if you find yourself struggling in your classes or with your schedule, there may be some specific strategies you could implement, such as joining a study group, to get you back on track for success. On the other hand, you may know very clearly that you do not want to be in college at this point in your life. College may not be right for you *right now*, which means that you should consider returning when you are certain it will be your top priority.

Benefits of Continuing Your Education

If you are considering whether or not to continue your education next semester, it may be helpful to think about the benefits of going on. First, you will be that much closer to finishing a degree. More completed classes mean more degree requirements checked off the list. Second, if you have to take courses in a sequence (e.g., Writing I and Writing II), then you are more likely to remember what you learned in the first course. Staying out too long between courses that need to be taken close together may mean you will forget important concepts, which could make that second course more difficult for you. Finally, staying in college now will mean you are more likely to stay friends with classmates. Even taking a semester break may mean that you lose touch with people you know and rely on now.

Benefits of Taking a Break

If you decide you need a break before you complete your degree, be sure you make the most of the time away from college. Some students use that time to earn extra money, take care of personal issues, or work on their academic skills outside of college. A much-needed break can help you stay focused; instead of burning out by continuing a stressful pace, you may find yourself able to re-energize yourself so that you can return with more focus and enthusiasm. A break can help you clarify your goals, and it can also help you recommit to the degree path you started on. Of course, during your break, if you decide to change degrees or career directions, you can return with a renewed sense of purpose.

If you do decide to take a break, be sure to meet with an academic advisor and make a plan that you can follow. Colleges have specific requirements for students who don't enroll every semester, and if your admission to the college was through a competitive process, it may not hold your spot open for re-enrollment unless you have a specific re-entry plan in place. Remember that your advisors and professors and other staff at your college are there for your success, so talk with them about your plans and stay in touch with them even while you're gone.

Consider Your Life Without College Before Choosing That Path

If you're uncertain at this point whether you can or want to continue with your college degree, and you're giving some consideration to dropping out, take some time to consider what your life will be like—both short-term and long-term—without a college degree. Consider these facts:

- In 2008, the average income for someone with an advanced degree (master's, professional, or doctoral) was $83,144; for someone with a bachelor's degree, it was $58,613; for someone with only a high school education, it was $31,283 (Menand, 2011).

BUZz

Q I have had many challenges this semester and am considering taking a semester off until I can get some bills paid and come back with the right mindset for completing my degree. Am I making a mistake by stopping for a while?

A There is no reason you have to complete college in four consecutive years, and there are many students who take a little time off while working toward a degree. Here are some tips to keep you on track if you do decide to stop:

- Make a plan for the time you are taking off and for getting back to your college.

- Talk with professors, advisors, financial aid officers, and counselors before leaving.

- Stay connected with friends and college personnel while you are gone.

- Stay informed about deadlines and due dates for registration and tuition payment.

Student loans, because they are low interest and have a long-term payment plan, are often a good way to pay for college. However, there are serious consequences if you do not pay them back whenever you are required to do so. Defaulting on student loans can make you ineligible for future federal aid and can have negative consequences on your credit rating.

If you find yourself unable to make a payment after your loan payments become due, notify your lender immediately. The lender may work out a repayment plan for you.

YOUR TURN

In approximately 250 words, discuss your concerns about paying for college. Describe what your plan would be for repaying a loan, if you were to take out one.

- The unemployment rate for workers 25 and older with a bachelor's degree or higher was 4.6% in August 2010, compared to 10.3% for those with just a high school diploma. That 5.7% gap compares to a 2.6% gap in December 2007, when the recession began (Dougherty, 2010).
- College grads generally show higher rates of civic participation, engage in volunteer work, and donate blood at more than twice the rate of high school graduates (Shellenbarger, 2009).
- College-educated adults are less likely than others to be obese, and children living in households with more educated parents are less likely than other children to be obese (Baum, Ma, & Payea, 2010).

There are many very successful and happy people who do not have a college degree, and you, too, could have a successful life if you choose not to complete your degree. However, you should weigh this decision carefully, knowing that the odds for success would be more in your favor if you stuck with it and finished your degree. It's not easy, especially if you're the first person in your family to go to college, you face significant financial challenges, or you have a lot of work or family responsibilities. But, there are many who have gone before you who faced similar challenges and who succeeded in college and in life, and you have what it takes to follow in their footsteps. Depending on your circumstances, taking a break from college may be a good choice; but don't write yourself off as a future college graduate. A college degree can still be in your future.

60-second PAUSE

Write yourself a letter, and put a date on it, then keep it somewhere and read it when you graduate. Give yourself encouragement to stick with college and finish your degree, and list the reasons why college is important to you.

from COLLEGE

Preparing for Unexpected Higher Costs

It is very likely that you will see a change in college costs when you transfer to a university. You may be paying twice as much for tuition at the four-year school as you did at your local community college. In addition to tuition, you may see added fees that you didn't have at your community college: fees for athletic facility use, sporting events, campus organizations, and labs are possible additional expenses. Be sure to read the college catalog carefully, and add the fees to the cost per credit hour to get an accurate picture of what you will be spending per class.

Despite the increase in tuition and fees, you may notice that your bookstore expenses stay the same. Although the price of books can be a significant portion of your overall college expenses, it is unlikely that you will experience an increase in cost. However, upper-level science and computer classes require weighty textbooks and additional software. These books can cost as much as $100. Multiply that by four classes, and you will be paying at least $400 for the semester. An advantage, however, to transferring to a larger school is that there are more people from whom you can buy used books. Take notice of special discounts for used books in the bookstore, and look for flyers on bulletin boards that announce books for sale.

© ISTOCKPHOTO

from COLLEGE
to CAREER

Make a Financial Plan If You Decide to Take a Break from College

There may be a time when you must interrupt your college career to return to your job full-time. Balancing financial and educational goals may be too difficult to handle at the moment, which may mean that your financial needs take precedence. If this happens to you, there are some ways of dealing with the transition back to the world of work while still keeping your eye on returning to college.

First, realize that going back to work doesn't have to be forever. Just because you are unable to return for more than one semester doesn't mean you never will. Be sure to talk with your employer about your desire to get a degree. There may even be financial assistance for employees who take college classes. Remember to talk with your family and friends about your need to further your education as well. Someone may be willing to help you with finances, scheduling, and family duties. Set a timeline for returning to college. If you need to work a semester to earn more money to pay for tuition, then be sure to keep up with registration periods and college announcements.

© ALAMY

Even if expenses were not the reason you returned to work, putting aside money in a "college fund" will make it easier to re-enroll in college. Also, look for scholarships and financial aid for working adults. Some states are creating grant programs for nontraditional students who work full-time. Finally, keep connected with former classmates and instructors.

UNDERSTAND & REMEMBER

Review Questions

1. What do you need to consider before registering for next semester?

2. What are the process and considerations for planning your degree?

3. What are four ways a student can pay for college? What are the benefits of each method?

4. Why would a student choose not to continue her education? What are the benefits if a student does choose to continue?

Create

Evaluate

Analyze

Apply

Understand

Remember

APPLY & ANALYZE

Critical Thinking

1. Choose two degree plans that you are considering and write down the benefits and drawbacks to each for you. Which one seems, for now, the better choice?

2. What has been the most challenging part of your class schedule this semester? What can you do next semester to make it less challenging?

3. What would it take for you to consider postponing your degree or stopping altogether? What can you do now to ensure that you stay on course to complete your degree?

EVALUATE

Case Scenarios

1. Carissa is starting a new job next semester to have some extra money to pay for the student activities she wants to participate in. She is also taking 18 credit hours again, even though she was stressed out by the end of this semester. She passed all her classes, but she could have done better in her chemistry class. Carissa's degree plan requires 150 hours, and if she is going to graduate in four years, she needs to take at least 18 hours each semester. Her new job will have her working nights and weekends so that she can take all of her classes during the day. The only problem at this point is that she has to attend a required orientation for her job (she cannot work if she doesn't attend) the first week of classes, which means she will miss the first few days. She has already contacted her professors to let them know she is enrolled in the classes, but won't be there the first week, and she has asked to complete any assignments ahead of time or when she returns.

   Use the following scale to rate the decision that has been made (1 = Poor Decision, 5 = Excellent Decision). Be prepared to explain your answer.

   Poor Decision ← ①——②——③——④——⑤ → Excellent Decision

2. Ramielle has paid for her first semester of tuition from her savings, but she is looking for other ways to pay for the rest of her college. She doesn't qualify for any grants and is not sure what her options are. A classmate suggests that she check out a website that lists all kinds of scholarships, some of which she should qualify for. In fact, Ramielle does find out that she can apply for scholarships for being left-handed, a first-generation college student, a competitive runner, and a twin. The website says that for a $19.99 application fee she can be guaranteed to receive at least one of the scholarships for which she applies. Ramielle submits her payment and completes the application form.

Use the following scale to rate the decision that has been made (1 = Poor Decision, 5 = Excellent Decision). Be prepared to explain your answer.

Poor Decision ← ─ 1 ─── 2 ─── 3 ─── 4 ─── 5 → Excellent Decision

3. Carlos has had a difficult time getting used to the expectations in college. He has not had a successful semester so far, and he is getting pressure at work to quit college and take a promotion. The promotion means more money, but no extra time to get the degree that he wants. He could always come back, he knows, but at 25 years old, he is afraid that if he doesn't go to college now, it will be even harder when he earns a bigger paycheck. Despite his difficulties in adjusting to college, he decides to give it one more try, and if he still does not feel comfortable—and continues to feel the pressures at work—he will quit. He believes at least some college credits are better than none.

Use the following scale to rate the decision that has been made (1 = Poor Decision, 5 = Excellent Decision). Be prepared to explain your answer.

Poor Decision ← ─ 1 ─── 2 ─── 3 ─── 4 ─── 5 → Excellent Decision

CREATE

Research It Further

1. Research the qualifications and requirements for the different loans and grants that your college offers. With the information, create a one-page handout for each type of financial aid that can help students remember the differences between each type. Be sure to provide any workshops or resources on financial aid that your college offers for students.

2. Survey your fellow classmates about their plans for continuing their degrees. How many plan to take a break before finishing? How many plan to graduate early? How many are unsure of what they will be doing next semester? Report your results to your class.

3. Using the Internet or another available source, research the most popular degrees and how much they may cost a student to complete at your college or at a local institution that offers those degrees. Be sure to determine, if it is not obvious, what kinds of careers are connected to those degree plans. Report the top five most popular degrees, and include the costs and the potential careers associated with each degree.

TAKE THIS WITH YOU

Based on the goals we set at the beginning of this chapter, here's how you can take this learning with you toward college success:

▪ Identify the required steps to complete your degree and what documents you need.

▪ Create a plan of action for the last few weeks of the semester, including completing course evaluations and talking to professors whose classes you may want to take next semester.

▪ Evaluate your methods of paying for college next semester and beyond. Be sure to determine if there are any other options for you.

▪ Make a list of the benefits of both staying in college and returning after a break as a reminder to complete your goals.

REFERENCES AND RECOMMENDED READINGS

Baum, S., Ma, J., & Payea, K. (2010). *Education pays 2010: The benefits of higher education for individuals and society.* Plano, TX: College Board.

College Board. (2009). *Getting financial aid 2010.* Plano, TX: Author.

Cress, C. M., Collier, P. J., & Reitenauer, V. L. (2005). *Learning through serving: A student guidebook for service-learning across the disciplines.* Sterling, VA: Stylus.

Dougherty, C. (2010, Sept. 20). College grads expand lead in job security. *The Wall Street Journal,* A1.

Lipphardt, D. (2008). *The scholarship and financial aid solution: How to go to college for next to nothing with short cuts, tricks, and tips from start to finish.* Ocala, FL: Atlantic Publishing Group.

Menand, L. (2011, June 6). Live and learn. *The New Yorker,* 74–79.

Schlacther, G., & Weber, R. D. (2009). *Kaplan Scholarships 2010: Billions of dollars in free money for college.* New York, NY: Kaplan Publishing.

Perkins Loans. (2011). Student Aid on the Web. Retrieved from http://studentaid .ed.gov/PORTALSWebApp/students/english/campusaid.jsp

Shellenbarger, S. (2009, Dec. 16). Weighing the value of that college diploma. *The Wall Street Journal,* D1.

U.S. Department of Education. (2011). Types of Federal Student Aid. Retrieved from http://studentaid.ed.gov/students/publications/student_guide/2006-2007/english/ typesofFSA_grants.htm

U.S. Department of Veterans Affairs. (2011). What Is the Post-9/11 G.I. Bill? Retrieved from http://www.gibill.va.gov/benefits/post_911_gibill/index.html

MyStudentSuccessLab

MyStudentSuccessLab (www.mystudentsuccesslab.com) is an online solution designed to help you 'Start strong, Finish stronger' by building skills for ongoing personal and professional development.

12 Preparing for a Career and a Life

The big red arrow points to the ballroom. There are dozens of booths inviting students to leave their resumes and learn more about a variety of local and national businesses and industries.

Fresh from class, in jeans and his old college sweatshirt, Evan stops to pick up a piece of candy. "I'm planning on going to all the booths. Are you?" Evan asks.

Michael has done a little research and knows the two booths he wants to visit. He runs his fingers down his pressed khakis and checks his crisp, white dress shirt for any spots.

"No," he says, "I plan on finding the two companies I checked out on the Internet last night, telling them what I know about the open positions, and leaving my resume."

"Aren't you *afraid* you will be cutting yourself short? Shouldn't you hit every one of the booths, just in case?" Evan asks.

"I don't know. I guess with all my time in the military, I have a lot of experience doing different jobs. I definitely know what I *don't* want to do," Michael replies.

"But there are so many options," Evan says.

"Well, what degree can you earn that will get you a job that pays well?" asks Michael.

"That's my problem. I don't quite know," Evan says.

"I am certain you won't be landing any jobs like that the way you are dressed today!" Michael says.

Evan pulls out 30 copies of his resume from his backpack. He strolls to the first table and introduces himself.

"I'm Evan. It is a pleasure to meet you," he says to the woman representing an aeronautics firm. "So, tell me what your company does and what I would do if I worked for you," Evan says.

Michael walks straight to one of the two healthcare companies at the fair. He already knows what he needs to do to get a good entry-level job.

 YOUR GOALS FOR THIS CHAPTER

Deciding where you want to go and what you want to do can be characterized by uncertainty, as both Michael and Evan demonstrate. Once you complete this chapter, you should be able to:

- Identify the tools and methods available for career exploration
- Develop an effective resume and cover letter
- Engage in networking activities that help you build important relationships
- Develop a plan for your life beyond college

MyStudentSuccessLab (www.mystudentsuccesslab.com) is an online solution designed to help you 'Start strong, Finish stronger' by building skills for ongoing personal and professional development.

Whether you know exactly what career you want, or whether you are still exploring the possibilities, your college experience can help you focus on what you want out of your professional life. After reading the following section about getting ready for a career, remember that the people you meet at your college can help you in many ways: they can help you decide what career is a best fit for you, and they can help you prepare to find and secure that job. Although it may seem like your career won't start until you're done with college in four years, the exciting reality is that the decisions you are making today are already starting to form your career. College is the time for exploring and preparing for a career, and the first step is to know your goals and what values you want to uphold.

Career Values and Goals Set the Course for Your Journey

Before you begin delving into the resources and services available at your college, take some time to reflect on what your career values and goals are. Values are personal and professional qualities and principles that are deeply important to you. For example, you

Your Terms for SUCCESS

WHEN YOU SEE . . .	IT MEANS . . .
Career fair	An event that brings various employers together into one place
Cover letter	A letter that "covers" a resume and provides a more detailed description of a job applicant's qualifications
Internship	A supervised position that allows a student to receive on-the-job training
Mentor	A person who provides advice and guidance to another person
Networking	Creating connections among people for the purpose of helping them or having them help you
Objective	A statement in a resume that explains your career goals
Recommendation letter	A letter written to provide a recommendation of your abilities and skills
References	People listed on a resume who can provide a recommendation of your abilities and skills
Resume	A document that provides information about you, your education, and your work experience
Resume padding	The act of exaggerating or lying about educational or work experience on a resume
Social networking	Creating connections, usually through websites, for the purpose of communicating with others

may have a passionate interest in working for a company that produces products or services that have a positive social impact on society or the environment. Or, it may be critically important to you that you work for an organization that is honest and ethical. A sample list of values is provided in Exhibit 12.1, just to give you a starting point for identifying your own.

In addition to considering your values as they relate to your career, you may also want to consider what your goals are. Goals are tangible outcomes that you want to achieve in your personal and professional life. For example, is one of your goals to move up quickly in a company, or to find a business that will allow you to indulge in one of your values—to travel and meet a diverse group of people? When you get to the point that you will be creating clear, realistic, and reachable career goals, your values will inform what you write down or tell others. Your values and goals will also help you with talking with a career counselor, searching for a job, and interviewing. You may have a goal of earning a salary that will allow you to pay off your student loan debt within three years of graduating, or providing enough income to support your parents. Your goals may also relate to a specific job title or position, such as becoming a partner in a law firm or accounting firm. Or, you may have goals about your contributions to society, such as having a career that allows you to contribute at least 10% of your time and money to charitable causes.

In addition to your personal values and goals, it is worth considering what you value in a career and what kinds of experiences you want to have. For example, do you value working with others in projects with strict deadlines, or would you prefer to work alone with little supervision? Your answer to that question and others can help you determine what you value and what careers work best for you. If, for instance, you have a strong interest in writing, but you prefer working with others, you may decide to choose a career that has many opportunities for collaboration when writing. Look at Exhibit 12.2 for other ways to consider what kind of career culture or environment you will most likely enjoy.

If you are not sure where to start when considering your career values and goals, then you may want to check out the various career assessment programs, such as DISCOVER or Kuder, at your career counseling center. There are also a number of

---

EXHIBIT 12.1 Career Values

Advancement	Excitement	Learning	Security
Authority	Family	Money	Social status
Beauty	Fast pace	People	Solitude
Challenge	Financial stability	Physical challenge	Spirituality
Creativity	Friendship	Power	Structure
Community	Helping others	Pressure	Teamwork
Competence	Independence	Recognition	Tranquility
Decision-making	Influence	Relationships	Travel
Education	Knowledge	Safety	Variety

EXHIBIT **12.2** Career Interest Questions

Do you like working in a team?	Yes	No
Do you like working on your own?	Yes	No
Do you want to work in a predictable, structured environment?	Yes	No
Do you prefer more spontaneity and ambiguity?	Yes	No
Do you prefer a steady, predictable paycheck?	Yes	No
Do you prefer the opportunity and risk of getting paid in proportion to your success and effort?	Yes	No
Do you want to work primarily in an office environment?	Yes	No
Do you want to travel and/or live internationally?	Yes	No
Do you prefer to work on quantitative and analytical projects?	Yes	No
Do you prefer to work on social and creative activities?	Yes	No
Do you want to work for an established firm with a well-defined organizational structure?	Yes	No
Do you want to run or own your own business some day?	Yes	No

books, such as Richard N. Bolles's *What Color Is Your Parachute?* (2011), and websites that offer helpful guidance for identifying your career interests, even at the early stages of your college career.

The career landscape can seem daunting and complex, especially because technology seems to cause careers to change so quickly. Careers that existed 10 years ago may not exist four years from now, and careers that didn't exist a few years ago are now emerging. For that reason, don't put pressure on yourself to identify a specific company and job title for your career goal. Instead, keep your focus on the kind of career you want to have in terms of its general characteristics—work environment, type of industry, technical requirements, individual versus team environment, highly structured versus unstructured organizational structure and job functions, and so on. Take time to browse career listings on websites such as careerbuilder.com, and save a copy of the posts that capture your interest. These will help you paint a picture that captures both your values and goals as they emerge and develop over time. It's OK if your interests change over time; this will happen as you take more classes and gain new perspective from your college experience. In fact, in today's work environment, the average individual will have several careers over their lifetime. What you're developing in college is the ability to identify your interests and abilities and match them with the career

It's in the SYLLABUS

Your syllabus may help you in your career exploration. Look at what you are covering during the semester.

- Do any topics really interest you?
- Do you find yourself drawn to certain subjects? What are they?
- Which instructors do you have now who will be helpful to you in the future if you need a recommendation for a job?

opportunities in the marketplace. You may not want to face this reality now, but you may very well find yourself back in college later in your life to pursue an advanced degree or certificate or a second bachelor's degree as you recreate yourself throughout your lifetime. As you learn to use the tools and resources we'll discuss in this next section, you'll be encouraged to know that they can serve you well repeatedly throughout your career journey.

Career Counselors Can Be Your Best Supporters

Long before you think about graduating and finding a career, you should visit the career counselors at your college. Preparing for a career takes longer than a few weeks, and the more planning you do, the smoother the process will be. Even though you won't pursue a full-time career until you graduate, commit yourself to meeting with a counselor your freshman year so you can put an effective plan in place for both internships and your career. Each college offers different services in its career center, but most provide access to interest inventories, which can help you pinpoint which careers you are best suited for. Most career services also provide "career libraries" that include information about different types of careers, their responsibilities, and their pay potentials. In addition, career centers may offer help with writing a cover letter and resume and tips for interviewing for a job. Evan should spend some time in his college's career library to learn more about careers before he hits all of the employers at the career fair.

Don't forget that your professors can also be great career counselors because they often have connections with people in the field (or have friends or relatives working in different industries). You never know when your sociology professor may have a contact at an accounting firm or your biology professor may have a connection with the human resources department at an advertising firm. Tell professors what you want to do as a career whenever you have a chance. They may be likely to remember you and your goals when they meet someone in your field of study.

Career Fairs Offer an Ideal Forum for Personal Contacts

Career fairs are another way to get information about jobs and employers in your area. If your college sponsors a fair off campus or provides one to students on campus, be sure to take advantage of it. Whether you are graduating next month or next year, it will pay to approach a career fair with the goal of making contacts and learning more about area businesses.

BUZZ

Q My professors talk about internships for chemistry majors and how important they are for getting a good job after graduation. Because I have to work and support myself through college, I cannot afford to take an internship, no matter how great the experience. Is there anything I can do?

A You are right: Internships are a great way to gain real-world experience in a career field, but they are often without pay. Here are some tips to take advantage of the opportunity:

- Talk to your professors about how you can get that experience without sacrificing your income.

- Talk to businesses that offer entry-level positions so that you can work there, while also learning from a mentor about the industry.

- Consider shadowing a person for a day, or several people at different companies over a series of days.

When you attend a career fair, there are several steps you can follow to make the most of your visits with potential employers. The following list is just a start; you can get even more tips from your college counselors about how to maximize your time at a career fair.

Use career fairs or on-campus events to network and put your best face forward to potential employers.

©THINKSTOCK

- Dress professionally. Also, carry a professional-looking bag (no backpacks!) and a folder with copies of your resume. Neatness counts.
- Do your homework. Find out what companies will be present at the fair, and research the ones that interest you. You can find out more about them through their websites or by visiting retailers or other locations where their products or services are sold.
- Avoid asking "And what does your company do?" Your research should tell you what the company does. Asking that question gives an immediate clue to the recruiter that you haven't taken the initiative to learn about the company.
- Choose a few booths to attend. Instead of blanketing the fair and hitting every representative, be selective and limit yourself only to companies that you would like to work for.
- Write a standard introduction, practice it, and then use it when you meet someone at the fair. Make sure the introduction is brief (state your name, your interests, and any relevant experience you may have) so that you maximize your time at the fair. A 30–60 second "elevator pitch" (the average length of a ride in an elevator) is a good standard to meet.
- Be energetic and positive. Recruiters and employers want to meet eager, exciting potential employees.
- Be clear and unapologetic about what you want. If you're an underclassman, you are probably trying to get an interview for an internship or you're just trying to get an informational interview (more on this concept later). If you're a senior, you want an interview for a full-time position. In either case, try to learn as much as you can beforehand about the positions available so you can clearly specify your interest. Company representatives who come to career fairs are expecting this from students, so you don't have to hesitate or apologize for asking for an interview.

If you cannot make your college's career fair, you may be able to participate in a virtual career fair, which allows job seekers to "meet" participating companies and send resumes. Virtual career fairs are usually linked to a college's website and coincide with the actual fair. For example, the Virtual Career Fair link may only be available while the on-campus fair is open. Some colleges and organizations, however, provide a perpetual Virtual Career Fair so that students can investigate potential careers and companies at any time. One such website is http://www.careersinoilandgas.com, which offers an abundance of information and resources for anyone interested in a career in the oil or gas industries. Other sites, such as http://www.collegegrad.com/careers, offer more general information about careers, as well as advice and preparation for job seekers.

Internships Give You and Your Employer a Chance for a Test Drive

Another work option for college students is an internship. This is a supervised position that allows a student to work for an organization before they graduate. Some internships are unpaid, which makes them less attractive to students who need to work. However, you may be able to earn academic credit for a paid or unpaid internship, so check with your advisor well in advance about this possibility. Internships are a great way to make progress toward your degree *and* explore careers. Another idea is to volunteer once or twice a week at a place of business. If you have a few extra hours a week or can trade college credit for an internship, then you should investigate the benefits of interning.

Why are internships such a good opportunity for college students? One reason is that they allow you to work closely in a field that you may be interested in. In addition, internships can help you explore different ways that a major can be used in the workforce. For example, an English or journalism major may want to participate in an internship at a newspaper or as a technical editor at a company. A computer science major may want to intern at a small business to get practical experience with computer networking issues on a small scale. These opportunities can give you firsthand experience with using what you're learning in your degree.

Internships also allow you to network with others who can help you find a job once you graduate. Even if you decide that you don't want to work in the same area as your internship, you will have contacts who may help you find a job in another field. If you decide to intern, you should treat it as a career. Some employers rely on interns to complete certain projects each year, and they will expect that you be serious about the position, even if you don't get paid. Keeping a good attitude and being self-motivated are excellent ways to shine during your internship. In addition, you should meet regularly with your supervisor to ask questions and get guidance on projects. Most of all, make the best of your unique opportunity, and add that experience to your resume.

Briefly describe the kind of career you want to pursue when you graduate. Then, identify two or three tangible action items you could commit to now to put you on a path toward that career.

YOUR RESUME AND COVER LETTER ESTABLISH YOUR PERSONAL BRAND

In addition to educating or training you for a career, your college may also offer services that help you land the job you want. Many specialized programs, such as nursing, business, engineering, and journalism, provide job placement services as well as a degree or minor. Other degree programs, such as psychology or health sciences, may provide fewer career services, but the professors and advisors in those programs can still be valuable resources as you prepare for the workforce. At the very least, you will need to know the basics for finding a job after you graduate. Writing resumes and cover letters, as well as polishing your interviewing skills, will be necessary for you to move into your career of choice. As you progress through your degree, your resume and cover letter will serve as a tangible representation of your personal brand—who you are, what you know, what you can do, and how you're different from your peers and other individuals competing for the same jobs. Just as McDonald's, Buick, Lenova, and Siemen's invest significant effort and resources in defining themselves through a distinctive brand, you also need to establish a distinctive personal brand that makes you recognizable and relevant to organizations who need a talented workforce. If you'd like to learn more about developing your personal brand, Tim O'Brien's book, *The Power of Personal Branding* (2007), is a great resource (http://www.thepersonalbrandinggroup.com).

Your Resume Puts Your Life on Paper

Learning to write a resume is an essential skill for new graduates, and there is no time like the present to begin honing that skill. A resume is no place to be modest, but neither is it a place to embellish or misrepresent your skills or experience. Prospective employers and recruiters will be looking for action verbs that describe your experience and abilities, and they'll be looking for evidence that you have something unique and valuable to contribute to their organization. All graduates have something, whether it's the classes they've taken, the projects they've completed, or the hardships they've overcome in their personal lives, that makes them special and gives them experience and personal qualities that are important for an employer. The challenge is to describe these qualities in a resume and to do it in no more than a page for most job applications.

When writing a resume, the first thing you will include is your name and contact information, including your address, phone number, and email address. Make sure your voicemail has an appropriate message on it, and that your email is professional as well: ejcantu@abcmail.com is preferred over bananafreak72@chunkymonkey.com. Double check that there are no errors in your address, phone number, or email address—one mistake can cost you an interview because a recruiter won't be able to contact you. Juanita's resume (see Exhibit 12.4 on p. 262) contains a new email address to replace her more personal one that she uses for friends and family, because she wants to separate career email from more casual correspondence.

A successful resume will also contain a clear objective, or statement that tells others your career goals—think of it as a mini mission statement for your career! Objectives are not always written in complete sentences. For example, your objective may be "To join an aircraft maintenance team at a highly rewarding company" or "To use my knowledge and skills to effectively manage employees in the retail industry." Writing a good objective takes time and consideration, and you may need to develop more than one if you plan to apply for different types of jobs or jobs in different industries. At a minimum, be sure that your objective matches the job for which you are applying. If, for example, your objective says that you want "To have a fulfilling career working with infants and toddlers in an accredited daycare," and you are applying to teach classes at a nursing home, then you may not get a second glance, much less an interview. Counselors and professors can help you craft an appropriate objective as you build your resume. You may also want to develop versions of your resume with different purpose statements so that you can personalize what you send to different companies in different industries.

Once you have an appropriate objective, you will need to include information about your educational accomplishments and job history. If you have not completed your degree at this point, you can write down the anticipated date: "Bachelor of Arts, May 2014." Be sure to include any other certificates or degrees that you have earned. The most recently earned certificate or degree should be listed first, and the rest of your academic accomplishments should be listed in reverse-chronological order. Information about your work history may be placed either before or after the information about your education. Again, list your most recent job first, and include the dates you worked, your position title, the name of the company and location, and a bulleted list of job responsibilities, written with action verbs such as "organized," "developed," "implemented," and "managed." Exhibit 12.3 is a very basic format for reporting your work experience on a resume. Depending on what kind of format you use, the order of the information may vary.

Depending on how much experience you have had, the first few parts of a resume may be easy to complete. Many students have previous or current work experience and know what educational experiences they have. However, a part of the resume that is sometimes more difficult is coming up with the section that contains extracurricular activities, organizations, and awards. If you are early in your college career, you may not feel as though you have been able to participate in extracurricular activities that would help you add to your list of accomplishments. Nonetheless, with just a little creative thinking, you may be able to create a list of activities and endeavors. For instance, if you received a college scholarship, you can list it as an award. If you volunteer regularly with your child's school, you can list it. If you have participated in a fundraising event, organized a community meeting, coached a sport, or sat on a committee at your church or synagogue, you can list it. You may not realize all the ways you have been involved with others that can show that you have interests other than college and work.

Your college will also provide you with future opportunities to add to a resume, so be sure to keep your eyes and ears open for chances to participate in a one-day event or a semester-long program. The key is to get involved at any level and record your involvement so that you can remember it when you need to develop your resume. Here are just a few opportunities that colleges often provide for students to get involved:

- Dean's List or President's List for specified grade point averages
- Student ambassador organization for promoting the college in the community
- Student Government Association for representing the voice of the students
- Honor societies, such as Phi Theta Kappa, as well as honor societies for specific disciplines, such as Sigma Kappa Delta, an English honor society
- Special events such as fundraisers, cultural events, political or community rallies, and celebrations

EXHIBIT 12.3 Example of Work Experience on a Resume

2008–2012   Dental Assistant   No Worry Dental Group   Tacoma, WA

- Cleaned clients' teeth and identified problem areas
- Took x-rays of clients' teeth and updated their charts
- Provided guidance for preventing tooth decay and improving gum health

One last part of the resume that you will want to include is a list of references, or a statement that says references are available upon request. As you meet people in college, you may want to create a list of potential references. A professor whom you got to know well, your advisor whom you see each semester as you plan your degree, or a campus official with whom you have worked closely on a project are good candidates for letters of recommendation or references. People you have worked with—either on the job or through a community project—are other excellent possibilities for references. Make sure these people know you well enough to speak of your strengths and potential in the workplace. Getting their permission before you list them is essential to getting a good reference.

Exhibit 12.4 is an example of a resume showing you one way you can list the necessary information. There are many ways to grab an employer's attention, and resume books will provide you with examples of the various formats. However, a format that is concise, easy to read, and professional is usually best.

EXHIBIT 12.4 Sample Resume

Juanita Cook
1234 Broadway Street
Anyplace, US 01234
555-555-1234
jrcook@anyplace.edu

Objective: To use my experience and education to work as an accounting manager.

Education

Associate of Applied Science in Accounting, Juno College, May 2013

Experience

Bookkeeper, Mays and Associates, August 2010–present
- Send invoices to clients
- Pay invoices from clients
- Maintain general ledger
- Supervise one staff member

Work Study, Financial Aid Office, Juno College, January 2009–July 2010
- Filed financial aid applications
- Maintained communication with students through newsletter

Honors and Awards

Accounting Award for Outstanding Student, May 2013

President's Scholarship, August 2010–May 2013

Volunteer of the Year, Humane Society, October 2009

References Available Upon Request

As you consider what content to include in your resume, think of it as body of evidence to support every claim you would want to make about yourself in an interview. If you believe that you are a hardworking person, then your resume might illustrate how you've managed to work during college. If you're an effective communicator, the resume itself should be very well-written, and you could reference the high grades you've received in your composition and technical writing classes, or that you've participated in a high school debate team. If you want to support your claim that you have strong computer skills, your resume can list the types of software programs that you use regularly and some of the technical features of these programs that you have used, such as mail merge in Microsoft Word or animated graphics with Java. Picture yourself in an interview, making each claim and then pointing to a particular line in your resume as the evidence. A resume that can serve this purpose in an interview is in good shape to be sent to prospective employers.

One last point about resumes: A curriculum vitae (CV, for short) is another form of a resume that allows you to be more descriptive in your experience, education, and special skills. A CV is usually used in certain fields, such as education, when the applicant has considerable experience that is directly related to the job posting. As you build on your education, experience, and skill sets, you will have more to include in a resume or CV, but always be sure to ask which is preferred when applying for a job.

Your Cover Letter Is Your Personal Introduction to Each Employer

A cover letter accompanies a resume and explains in detail how your qualifications match what the employer is looking for. As with a resume, keep a cover letter brief and to the point, usually no more than a page, unless you have more work experience that you believe needs to be detailed in the letter. The reason that cover letters should be short and to the point is that many employers simply scan these documents to see if candidates meet the minimum qualifications and then decide, pretty quickly, whether to interview them. The more concise your resume and cover letter, the easier it will be for potential employers to determine whether you are right for the job.

When writing a cover letter, be sure to address a specific person. Avoid starting your letter with "Dear Sir or Madam" or "To Whom It May Concern." If you do not know to whom you should address the letter, call the company and ask for the appropriate person's name, along with the correct spelling. If you are responding to several different job advertisements, double-check that you have correctly matched each letter with its corresponding addressed envelope. Also be sure that you have not made any references to people or companies other than to whom you are sending the cover letter.

The basic format of a cover letter is simple. Once you type in your address, the date, and the potential employer's name, company name, and address, you can follow this format:

1. Introduction Paragraph
   a. Introduce yourself
   b. Describe the specific job title or position you are seeking within the organization
   c. Tell where you learned about the job (Internet, newspaper, person at the company)

EXHIBIT 12.5 Sample Cover Letter

1234 Broadway Street
Anyplace, US 01234

June 1, 2011

Dr. Judy Pile
Ingram Enterprises
6789 Levi Lane
Anyplace, US 09876

Dear Dr. Pile,

I am responding to your advertisement in the *Tonitown Times* for an accounting specialist at your company, Ingram Enterprises. As you will see from my resume, I have earned an Associate of Arts degree in accounting from Juno Community College, and I have experience working as a bookkeeper for a local company.

My additional work study experience in the financial aid office at Juno has allowed me to improve my people skills as well as understand how an organized and efficient office works. I have also learned to use the following computer programs effectively: Microsoft Word, Microsoft Excel, and QuickBooks.

I am sure that you will find both my education and experience fit the position that was advertised. If you would like to interview me, I can be reached during the day at 555-555-1234. I look forward to hearing from you.

Sincerely,

Juanita Cook

2. Background Paragraph
   a. Tell more about yourself and how you are qualified
   b. Relate your education and skills to those the company is looking for

3. Closing Paragraph
   a. Tell the potential employer how to contact you
   b. Thank the person for her time and say you are looking forward to hearing from her

Exhibit 12.5 is an example of an effective cover letter that could accompany the resume in Exhibit 12.4.

The Interview Is Your Chance to Shine

Another important component to a successful career search, if not the most important, is interviewing for a job. If your winning resume gets you an interview, you are about halfway to getting a job. Consider the following tips to maximize your performance at the interview. Do a little research by checking out the company's website or search for other company information that may have appeared with the job advertisement. The goal is to find out what the company does and where it is going. Exhibit 12.6 provides the top five tips for preparing to interview with a company.

EXHIBIT 12.6 Top Five Tips to Prepare for an Interview

1. Know the company: what it does or sells, how big it is, how successful it is. If it's a company whose shares are publicly traded (i.e., you can buy its stock as investor), find the most recent annual report and read it, especially the CEO's introductory comments. If it's a privately held company, check with your reference librarian to get help in obtaining more information beyond the company website.

2. Know the industry: who are the competitors and who is winning and losing in the industry, what major trends or environmental forces are affecting the industry. Your reference librarian can help you find resources to do this research.

3. Know the job: you may have a job description from the job posting to help you, or you can poke around on the company website to see if it lists an employee directory or organizational chart.

4. Rehearse your 30–60 second "elevator speech" about yourself and practice using your resume to cite evidence for every claim you make about yourself.

5. Prepare for the famous behavioral questions. Employers who are looking for employees with specific qualities will often ask you to "Give me an example of a time when you demonstrated perseverance" (or any other personal quality or experience). Prepare for these questions by generating a list of the qualities and experiences that the recruiter might want for the position. Then, identify specific life events you've experienced that demonstrate that quality. These events don't all have to be from college. In fact, some of the most powerful testaments of your creativity, work ethic, problem-solving ability, and communication skills might involve experiences from your earlier life and the challenges and failures you've overcome.

Practice interviewing with a fellow student or a career counselor before going out there for real.

©RUBBERBALL/GETTY IMAGES

Don't forget to practice interview questions with your friends or family. Try to simulate the interview process by sitting across from the person who is practicing with you. Ask that person to make note of any fidgety habits and unclear answers. When you interview, you will want to dress professionally and pay attention to the details. Keep your fingernails clean and short. Check out hems and cuffs for tears. Make sure your clothes are clean and pressed and your shoes are polished. For women, be sure that there are no runs in your hose and that your heels are not scuffed.

When you score an interview, be sure to arrive early. Introduce yourself to the receptionist and prepare to wait. During the interview, listen carefully to the interviewer's questions, pause before answering, and speak slowly and carefully. Be sure, too, to look all of the interviewers in the eye when speaking, sit up, and lean forward slightly. Show by your body language that you are interested and relaxed, even if you are nervous. And speaking of nervous, it is normal if you are, but be sure to avoid fidgeting with a pencil or paper or tapping your fingers or feet. Some degree of nervousness is a good thing, because it demonstrates to the recruiter that this interview is really important to you.

When you are speaking about what you can do, be sure to highlight your strengths. Even if you don't meet all of the job's qualifications, you may be able to persuade the employer that you can do it. It's generally a good idea to avoid asking about the salary at the beginning of the interview. Instead, ask about the job responsibilities and benefits—the interviewer may provide a salary range as part of the information. As a last question, you may want to ask what the next step is in the interviewing process and what the timeline is for filling the position. Knowing when the company will be making the final decision will help you prepare for the next step.

As you leave, thank everyone you have met, shake their hands, and follow up with a thank you letter to each interviewer (see Exhibit 12.7). If you do not know how to spell their names, call the receptionist the next day to get the correct spellings. Although email is widely used for thank you letters and provides timely communication, also consider the possibility of accompanying the email with a handwritten personalized thank you letter to each interviewer. Such a practice may seem unusual, but it's the kind of effort and courtesy that will differentiate you from the other prospects who either don't send a thank you letter at all, or who choose to write a very brief, informal email that reads more like a text message than a carefully written letter. Every opportunity you have to make contact with a prospective employer is another chance to build and reinforce your personal brand and distinctive qualities.

If a question was raised in an interview that you weren't able to answer, or a topic came up that you know something about or later read something related to it, use the follow-up correspondence as an opportunity to share that information. For example, if one

EXHIBIT  **12.7** **Sample Thank You Letter**

Juanita Cook
1234 Broadway Street
Anyplace, US 01234
555-555-1234
jrcook@anyplace.edu

July 12, 2011

Dr. Judy Pile
Ingram Enterprises
6789 Levi Lane
Anyplace, US 09876

Dear Dr. Pile,

Thank you for interviewing me yesterday. I enjoyed meeting you and your colleagues and learning more about how your company works.

After speaking with you, I am more firmly convinced that I would be a good person for the job. My education and experience would be a great match for what the position demands. I enjoy professional challenges, and I think your company provides the type of opportunities I am looking for.

Please feel free to contact me at 555-555-1234 or jrcook@anyplace.edu. I look forward to hearing from you.

Sincerely,

Juanita Cook

---

of the interviewers seemed to be particularly interested in one of your class projects, in which you developed an idea for helping senior citizens navigate the Internet, follow up by sending a copy of the project to them or providing a more detailed description. This is an example of an opportunity to move yourself from a recruiter's short-term memory to long-term memory. Interviewers want to hire people who are energetic, polite, professional, and appreciative. Put your best face forward and try to relax and enjoy the process.

Informational Interviews Get Your Foot in the Door

Traditional job interviews are arranged when employers have specific job openings and they are evaluating potential candidates for hire. Sometimes, however, you may have a strong interest in working for a particular company, even if there aren't job openings available at the time. For example, after conducting a lot of research about different careers and industries, you may discover during your second year that you really want to be a veterinary tech, but the company you're interested in doesn't have any openings at the time. An option to consider is an informational interview. In an informational interview, you arrange to meet with one or more employees in the organization who have positions that are similar to the career you want to pursue. Your purpose is to learn more about their day-to-day responsibilities and what it's like to work at the company.

Because you aren't directly seeking a job, like in a traditional interview, you can often convince someone in an organization to schedule an informational interview with you, even when the organization isn't hiring. An informational interview gives you a chance to really learn about a particular position, what it takes to be successful in that position, and where that position might lead in the future of a long-term career path. You can also gain insights about how the person presently in that position secured the job in the first place. All of this information can help you develop your own career strategy. A side benefit of an informational interview is that it helps you create a relational network within that organization so that when you are in the job search mode, you have a specific person to contact who knows about you and your interests.

The Internet Offers Great Opportunities—and Potential Pitfalls—for Your Career Search

The Internet has made it so much easier to find and apply for jobs, communicate with potential employers, and network to improve your contacts and connections. However, it can also be a potential hazard if it is not used appropriately and professionally. Most people are aware that posting messages, information, and photos can be risky—even dangerous—to your professional "health," but they may not be aware how much potential employers look for—and find—before they interview candidates. Many employers and company recruiters search for potential candidates online to see what kinds of information and images are out there. In some career fields, the more a candidate exposes (literally and figuratively) himself, the less likely he is to get the job.

What can you do to protect yourself? Deleting your accounts can be your best defense, but you may also change your account settings to private. Be aware, though, that if you have a large network of "friends," people who want to find out about you may still be able to do so. It is best not to post or put into writing anything that you think may be questionable to a potential employer, and if you have posted anything, delete it if you feel it may jeopardize your ability to get the job you want. Also, keep in mind that your friends may have posted photos on their Facebook pages or other sites and tagged you in them. As you consider the digital footprint that you've created to date and are practicing daily, carefully consider the reality that this content could very well emerge in the public arena and stay there for a long time. Chances are you're reading this book at an early stage in your college career, and this gives you a great opportunity to establish online habits that can give you a positive, public personal brand.

Your Career Plan Should Include a Contingency Plan

All college career counselors want students to walk into high-paying jobs the day after graduation, but the reality is much different. Students who major in sought-after fields, such as information technology and health services, sometimes do not find the jobs that they thought were plentiful. Fluctuations in the economy are usually the cause for

changes in the job market. Being prepared in case the job market has changed is your best defense.

To keep yourself grounded, formulate a plan for what you will do if you don't waltz into a dream job immediately. When writing your plan, be sure to answer the following questions:

- Are you willing to take less money if the opportunity is good?
- Are you willing to relocate for a better job?
- Are you willing to take a job in a different field from what you expected?
- Are you willing to repackage your skills and knowledge to be considered for different types of work?

These are all questions that both Evan and Michael would do well to ask themselves. Even though Michael is very sure of the kind of job he wants, he may want to have an alternate plan in case those jobs are not readily available when he graduates. Evan can ask himself these questions, too, to help him focus on what is most important to him in a job.

In addition, start building up your network of friends, family, coworkers, classmates, and acquaintances, if you have not already been working on it. Let them know that you are about to graduate and will be looking for a job.

Finally, consider the process that you must go through if you are to be successful in finding the right job for you. Getting a job requires that you:

- Consider what field best suits your skills, personality, and dreams
- Attend workshops and information sessions that provide assistance with resume writing, interviewing, and networking
- Prepare a solid resume
- Network with friends, family, and acquaintances
- Actively look for work
- Respond to job advertisements by sending out your resume and cover letter
- Follow up each job interview with a thank you letter
- Remain positive and flexible, but stick to your goals

TECHNOLOGY *Tips*

USING TECHNOLOGY TO GET AHEAD

There are numerous resources on the Internet that can help you prepare for stepping out into the workforce, including resume writing sites and professional networking sites.

RECOMMENDED SITES

- http://career-advice.monster.com: Monster's career advice site provides numerous links to job search tips, including how to highlight military service and how to show holes in work experience.
- http://www.bestcoverletters.com: This site provides over 40 examples of cover letters to suit any field, any situation.
- http://www.symsdress.com: The Dress to Achieve site gives college graduates the basic information they need to make the best first impression.

60-second PAUSE

Briefly describe an action plan that you can implement to develop a high-quality resume that you can use to secure a job or an internship during college, or a full-time career after college.

Networking is defined as the "sharing of knowledge and contacts; getting the help you need when you need it from those from whom you need it . . . ; [and] building relationships *before* you need them" (Darling, 2003, p. 16). Now, more than ever, networking is an essential part of an effective career search. If you ask 10 recent college graduates who have full-time careers how they landed their jobs, chances are that at least six of them will tell a story about how someone they knew helped them meet someone in the organization to get a first interview. If you establish good relationships with a variety of individuals across multiple companies and industries throughout your college experience—including your freshman year—these individuals will be your primary gateway to those initial interviews.

It's important to establish what networking can and cannot do for your career search. Effective networking throughout your college years can help you get your foot in the door at various organizations, and may help you land that first interview. At that point, however, it's all up to you. Someone else's referral on your behalf is often enough for a recruiter to take time to give you an interview, but it's not enough for them to hire you. You have to prove yourself in the interview process and, once you're hired, you have to prove yourself on the job. In a competitive job market in which hundreds of people are applying for a single position, landing that first interview is a crucial step, and networking can help you get there.

Q I have heard that employers search for information about you on the Internet. What do I do if I have posted things I don't want them to see?

A The truth of the matter is that anything you place on the Internet can be seen by someone at some point, even material you may think is "private." Here are some tips for minimizing this issue:

- If there is anything out there you don't want people to see, delete it.

- Live by the philosophy "If you don't want to see it on the front page of the newspaper, don't put it on the Internet."

- Periodically check for your name on Google by typing it in, clicking the search button, clicking on the "more" link, and then clicking on "real time."

- If there is anything out there that may jeopardize a job, be prepared to bring it up or explain it.

Networking Is More Than Exchanging Business Cards

When you see the word "networking," what scene or activities do you picture in your mind? The stereotypical perception of networking is a bunch of people introducing themselves to each other and chit-chatting with each other at a social or business function. Some people think they've done a good job of networking if they come home from an event with a lot of business cards in their pockets. Networking is a lot more than that. It certainly begins with an initial point of contact, and for that you need to make a professional first impression. How you dress, what you say, and how you act during the initial social exchange will be important. But once you've made that initial contact with someone, how you follow up with them and maintain contact with them really determines the value of your network.

Let's say that you're at a relative's wedding and you meet someone who has a highly successful career at an accounting firm. At the time, you have no interest in accounting, nor do you know much about the company he works for, but you take time to ask questions about his career and organization, and you

politely ask his for his business card or contact information. Was that networking? Yes, but you're just getting started. It's what happens after the introduction that matters most. When you get home, you need to add that person's contact information to a database, and then compose a follow-up email or personal letter expressing your sentiments that you enjoyed meeting him and learning about his career, and that you'd like to stay in touch with him as your college career progresses. If you have a current resume prepared, you could send that to him, even if you don't have a present interest in a career at his organization.

In the months and years to follow, you can use a calendaring system to remind yourself to touch base with that person. You can update him on your own accomplishments in college, ask him about his career accomplishments, ask him questions about how they chose his career, arrange an informational interview at his firm, and share any news articles that you read that have something to do with his industry or company. As you invest in this relationship over time, you're building a connection that is far more extensive than what you had when you first met that person. Then, when you really need the individuals in your network to help you secure that first interview, they know you well enough to trust in your personal qualities and professionalism. When someone takes the risk of recommending you to one of his friends or associates for a job interview, he is putting his own reputation at risk on your behalf. This is a significant request! Successful networking—over time—establishes a range of personal and professional relationships that can help you make the right connection at the right time when your career search gets into full swing. If you wait until late in your college career to start networking, it will be far more difficult for you to prove your sincerity and professionalism through the test of time. Start networking early, and build a broad network, because you never know where your interests may take you in the future.

Networking Face to Face

The most effective method of networking is by building relationships through face-to-face interactions. There are a number of specific activities you can pursue that will help you form broad, long-term connections:

- Look for clubs on campus that share your interests. Even if they are not career-related, such as a drama club, you will meet people who may be future contacts for jobs.
- Scan your school newspaper and announcements for events, such as guest speakers and discussion panels. Colleges often host influential experts and industry leaders for speaking engagements. Attend these events when you can, not only to learn new perspectives, but also in an effort to meet these individuals and introduce yourself.
- Join a college ambassador club or other host-related student organization. Many colleges have a student ambassador group that plays a lead role in hosting distinguished college guests, provides campus tours for visitors, and represents the college at community events, such as Chamber of Commerce meetings and special task forces and committees.
- Consider a student leadership position on your campus. Student leaders, such as the members of the student council, often have special access to college administrators and community leaders.

- Get involved in community service and philanthropic activities. Industry and community leaders—the kinds of people who are ideal to have in your personal network—are often actively engaged in nonprofit organizations, community service activities, and philanthropy. By committing your own time to these types of activities, you are not only giving back to your community and society, but you might also have a chance to network with individuals who have a relatively exclusive and high-profile network of their own. You probably wouldn't bump into the CEO of a large organization in your daily life as a college student, but if you invest yourself in community service and philanthropy, you might find yourself working next to someone who could eventually become a valuable member of your network.

As you pursue these networking opportunities, it's important that you carry them out with a genuine interest in making a contribution to these organizations, and that you aren't simply participating just to meet people. Before you commit to any club, organization, community event, or philanthropic cause, be sure that it's something you really believe in and are willing to support. Otherwise, your lack of sincerity and commitment will affect your reputation, and you'll do more harm than good. However, if you get involved in something that you really believe in and support, the personal network of relationships you establish will open doors for you in your career that you never could have imagined for yourself.

Networking Online

One of the largest trends in networking is using online websites, such as LinkedIn and Facebook, to create networks of friends, family, and special interest groups. The possibilities seem endless as to how you can use the Internet to connect with others who have special interests and activities or problems to solve. With this said, if you decide to join a network that focuses on an interest of yours, such as computer programming, be sure to investigate who runs the group, what kinds of information are shared, and how active the group is. Some networks will be more active than others, which will make it easier to connect with others and get involved; other networks or groups may be less active, which won't help you if you are using it to get to know others as potential contacts in the future. Because creating networks of your own is so easy, you may want to consider creating an interest group if you cannot find one relating to your career of interest. Networking sites such as Facebook allow you to set up groups that can be used for professional, educational, or social purposes.

If you decide to set up a profile on a social network site like LinkedIn, take time to establish a profile that is well-written, professional, and informative. These sites often allow you to post a photo, so provide one that shows you dressed professionally, as you would appear for a job interview. Upload your entire resume or the contents of the resume, and make sure that all of your contact information is current, accurate, and professional. These types of sites often have a mechanism for you to connect with others, and in most cases this requires the other person to accept your invitation. Be sure to initiate these invitations with a courteous, respectful approach, recognizing that if they choose to connect with you, it's comparable to the risk they face when recommending you to others. This is not a trivial decision on someone's part, so be sure that your profile and your request are presented in a manner that gives them confidence that you will represent yourself—and their reputation—well.

Recommendation Letters

Recommendation letters and letters of reference are an important part of the career search process. Some individuals prefer to write letters of recommendation on your behalf that you can send to prospective employers, and sometimes employers require these letters. In other circumstances, the individuals you select to serve as references will simply want you to share their contact information so that the employer can contact them to discuss their recommendation in person.

Employers will often call or contact references as one of the final steps in the hiring process, and if an employer detects any type of concern or unfamiliarity from the reference during that call, it could bring the hiring process to an end. Conversely, if the employer receives a lot of positive feedback from your references and your references know you well, those recommendations could propel you to the next step in the hiring process. If you have taken the time to build an extensive network, you will have an easier time asking for and receiving a recommendation letter or reference that is full of specific information about the quality of your work and your character.

© DAVID YOUNG-WOLFF/PHOTOEDIT

Developing faculty relationships is essential before you ask for letters of recommendation.

When considering who to ask, choose a person who has had the chance to see you at your best. If you worked closely with a professor or spent many hours talking with a counselor, ask him or her to write a recommendation letter for you. The better the person knows you, the better the recommendation letter will be. In addition, give this person plenty of time to think about the quality of your work, recall specific examples, and write a polished letter. If you are on a tight deadline, such as a week, be honest with the person and give him or her a chance to decline the opportunity. If the person does agree to write a recommendation letter on such short notice, be sure to provide him or her with all the necessary materials to complete it properly, including an addressed, stamped envelope and the correct forms. You also want to provide them with your resume so that the person can speak specifically about your accomplishments.

Once your recommendation letter has been written, write a thank you note and show your appreciation for the favor. Consider a handwritten note that expresses your gratitude, rather than a verbal or email message of thanks. Finally, when requesting a recommendation, you should take the necessary steps to ensure that you do not read the recommendation letter. If you must hand-deliver the letter, ask that it be sealed in an envelope first. The reason that you should not request a copy or attempt to read it is that doing so jeopardizes the honesty of the individual who is writing it. Committees that evaluate recommendation letters want truthful descriptions of your abilities and strengths; if they know that you have seen the recommendation letter, they may doubt the accuracy of the description.

60-second **PAUSE**

Generate a list of all the people you would count as part of your network. What specific activities are you going to implement to maintain and develop your relationships with them over time?

It is now a cliché to say that "commencement"—the ceremony you participate in when you graduate—means "a beginning" rather than "an ending." Many graduation speakers address this point each year: when you graduate from college, you are not just ending your academic career, but you are beginning the rest of your life.

What will be left for you once you graduate? You may be on track to pursue a full-time career. Or, the career you've chosen may require you to pursue an advanced degree or professional education, such as law or medicine. Other students have the opportunity to explore the world through travel or volunteer work after graduation before they step into the full-time career world. Or, because of challenging economic conditions, perhaps you're not able to find a full-time career in your chosen field, and you have to pursue your contingency plan of finding other employment that can serve as a stepping stone to a future career. Whichever options are available to you, don't overlook the importance of celebrating your accomplishment of completing your degree and preparing yourself for the future. Also, seek the advice and support of your family, friends, and networking contacts to help you choose the alternative that is best for you.

The competencies that you have developed in college, such as information literacy, critical thinking skills, and cultural competency, will serve you well in your pursuit of lifelong learning. To be a lifelong learner acknowledges the reality that even when you've completed your degree, you will have an opportunity to continue to learn throughout your lifetime. You may find yourself in several different careers throughout your life, each one requiring you to reinvent yourself and develop new skills. The changing cultural, social, economic, and technological environment of our society and our globe will also challenge you to be a lifelong learner and adapt to changing conditions. Once you have graduated from your college, you now enjoy all the benefits of being an alumnus, which gives you such privileges as access to the library resources and career services, invitations to college events and programs, and lifetime connections with your professors, advisors, fellow alumni, and other individuals in your network of relationships. Your relationship with your college is a permanent bond that is established when you graduate, and it provides tremendous value for your lifelong success.

Your Mission, Values, and Goals Are Your "True North"

In a previous chapter, you wrote down your values, goals, and mission statement. Do you still have that information in a convenient location? If so, get it out and reflect on how well you have met your original short-term goals and how far you have come toward reaching your long-term goals. Have your values changed? Or have they been strengthened by your achievements? Have you followed your mission statement? Is there anything that you would change about your mission statement?

To answer these questions, you will need to reflect on your achievements over the past semester. Your mission and values should not have changed much in the past weeks, but if they have, you can make a new list of values and rewrite your mission statement. Most definitely, some of your short-term goals should be met, and you have no doubt moved on to a new list as you make your way toward your long-term goals. Now is the time, then, to revisit your long-range plans and make any necessary adjustments. Also, you should keep a record of the short-term goals you have reached and create a new list. Keeping up with what you have accomplished will serve as a reminder of your success if you ever feel unsure about your progress. Exhibit 12.8 is an example of a new list you can make.

EXHIBIT  **12.8**   Goal Achievement and Goal Setting

Goals I Have Met:

1. Completed my courses with above average grades
2. Created a study group with classmates
3. Kept up with my commitments on the job
4. Paid my tuition

New Short-Term Goals:

1. Get registered for next semester
2. Speak with a counselor about career possibilities
3. Make at least two A's in my classes
4. Take more time to relax

Once you revise your short-term goals, you may notice that your timeline for reaching your long-term goals needs adjusting as well. Keeping your list in a convenient location and looking at it every day or week will help you stay on track.

You Serve an Important Role in Your Community

Although most of your focus during college will be on yourself and either moving on to complete a higher degree or to a new job, consider looking for opportunities to improve your community. One of the purposes of higher education is to improve the lives of individuals so that the community benefits as well, and it is essential that educated community members give back and make improvements.

Professional clubs, social and civic groups, churches, and volunteer organizations offer opportunities for you to get involved in the community after college, if you have not done so already. The people you meet in these groups and the connections you make, both professional and personal, can enrich your life and your career. If you are not part of a community group, seek out one whose interests are similar to yours; also, look for ways to participate in events in your community, whether a 5K run or a recycling drive. Participating in strengthening your community will allow you to give back to those in need, improve your community, and gain friendships and business connections that may last a long time.

Now may not be the time to encourage you to help your college financially, but think about how you can continue to support your school after you have left. In order for a college—or any educational institution—to be successful in improving the lives of the people in its community, it must depend in part on its graduates to make a good name for themselves and to give back with their time, talent, and financial resources. There are a variety of ways that you can

© BOB DAEMMRICH/PHOTOEDIT

Giving back to the community is one way you can serve as a role model for others.

contribute to the education of those who will surely follow in your footsteps. If you ever have a chance to talk with someone who has made a significant gift to their college, you'll realize that they received as much satisfaction and reward from the experience as their college did from the gift.

By being a productive, educated member of society, you are already giving back to your college. Because higher education's mission is to improve a community by increasing the knowledge and enhancing the values of its population, we all benefit from students who complete graduation requirements for degree and certificate programs and continue to lead productive, happy lives. The skills and knowledge you have obtained in college are a good advertisement for the school. Alumni who make a difference in the lives of others through their jobs and community service fulfill the college's mission to not only provide education to strengthen the local economy, but to also graduate people who demonstrate the ideals of an educated society.

Briefly describe the life you would like to have after you graduate. How will you exemplify the ideals of a lifelong learner?

from COLLEGE

Hold Off on Starting Your Career Until You Have Met Your Educational Goals

It will be very tempting to head back to work before you have completed your certificate or degree because of changes in your family or financial situation. However, remember that if you can hang in there, the further you go toward your ultimate education goal, the better opportunities you will have in the workforce, and you will have an easier time going back if you find yourself "stopping out" of college for awhile as you work.

Another idea for helping you stay in college before returning to work is to look for ways to break your ultimate educational goal into achievable, realistic shorter-term goals that will move you in the right direction. For example, if you need to return to work before completing your Registered Nursing (RN) degree, which is often a two-year degree, you may be able to complete a Licensed Practical Nursing (LPN) program in a shorter amount of time. Completing a shorter program first, working in the field, and then returning to complete a longer program may be a good fit for your educational and financial needs. Be sure, though, that you speak with an advisor to make sure that your plans keep you from taking too many classes that will not fit into your longer-term educational goal.

© SHUTTERSTOCK

from COLLEGE

to CAREER

Strong Academic Skills Can Translate to On-the-Job Success

Time management, goal setting, and long-term planning are all skills that you have learned during your college career, and these skills will take you far in the workplace. If anything, knowing that you can juggle multiple responsibilities, such as taking care of yourself, your family, a job, and college responsibilities, should give you the confidence to tackle other challenges that you will face in the workforce. Practice these skills on the job, but also know that you may need to improve on these skills as you complete new tasks and take on more projects at work or change positions.

Don't forget that your college, even long after you have graduated, can help you while you are in the workplace. You may still have, for example, access to their career services as a graduate of the college. You may also be able to use the library to do research. For sure, you will have the connections that you made while in college, people you can call on for advice and friendship. Look into what services your college offers for you before you graduate, services that you can utilize as a successful graduate.

© DENNIS MCDONALD/PHOTOEDIT

UNDERSTAND & REMEMBER

Review Questions

1. How can you explore different kinds of careers?

2. What are the differences and similarities between a cover letter and a resume?

3. What are the different types of networking, and what are the costs and benefits of each?

4. In what ways can you build a life beyond college?

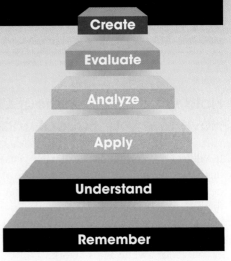

APPLY & ANALYZE

Critical Thinking

1. At your college and in your community, what kinds of resources are available for you to explore careers? Which ones are you planning to use? Which do you think will be most helpful to you as you search for a career—face-to-face resources or online? Why?

2. What are the biggest mistakes that college students make when creating an online presence, whether it is through a social networking account or a professional networking account? Do you think that the norms of what should be private or acceptable to share have changed in the last 10 years? Why or why not?

3. In what ways have you already mentored others who want to attend college or who are just starting their college careers? How have you influenced others to value education and a college degree?

EVALUATE

Case Scenarios

1. Rudy is getting a degree in business management, but doesn't have any idea how to look for a good job. He is not really even sure if that is what he needs to break into financial planning, which is a career that he believes will give him the financial stability that he values. He has decided to use his connections with his classmates and his professors to meet with a dozen different people at banks and financial institutions to find out what it will take to get a job and succeed. While it will take him a few weeks to complete the interviews, he knows he will have time after he graduates and before he really gets serious about looking for a job to take the time to do the interviews.

   Use the following scale to rate the decision that has been made (1 = Poor Decision, 5 = Excellent Decision). Be prepared to explain your answer.

   Poor Decision ← —①——②——③——④——⑤→ Excellent Decision

2. Brian's dream is to own a horse farm, but he doesn't think he can afford his dream, so he is in his second semester as a radiology technician because it is a job with a steady income. Also, Brian doesn't want to quit school to follow his dream because he values an education. He realizes that as a radiology technician he can make enough money to save up to purchase a horse farm on his own, but it will be at least 10 years of saving and planning before it can happen. Brian thinks he can endure the long hours and stressful work to make his dream eventually come true.

   Use the following scale to rate the decision that has been made (1 = Poor Decision, 5 = Excellent Decision). Be prepared to explain your answer.

   Poor Decision ← 1 ——— 2 ——— 3 ——— 4 ——— 5 → Excellent Decision

3. Lakeshia is ready to graduate with a degree in networking, and she has been circulating her resume with the hope that she can roll right into a job after graduation. Because Lakeshia lacks experience in the field, she has decided to elaborate on some of her responsibilities as a work study student in the Information Technology Department and as an intern at a local advertising company. While she did provide assistance in both roles, she had little responsibility and did not complete the kinds of projects she has listed. She decides to send out her resume with the exaggerations because she is looking for out-of-state jobs, and she believes no one will find out.

   Use the following scale to rate the decision that has been made (1 = Poor Decision, 5 = Excellent Decision). Be prepared to explain your answer.

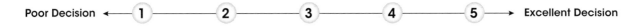

   Poor Decision ← 1 ——— 2 ——— 3 ——— 4 ——— 5 → Excellent Decision

CREATE

Research It Further

1. Using the Internet, find three articles or websites that discuss social networking guidelines for professionals. Create a list from your research that can provide important tips for your classmates as they transition from college students to professionals. Share your list with your class.

2. What job seeking services does your college provide? Investigate the resources provided by the library, career counseling and placement (if available), advising, and financial aid. Think beyond the obvious departments that can provide job assistance. Then, create a one-page list of the resources available, where to find them, and how they can help students.

3. Interview your classmates about their questions and concerns regarding finding a job. Make a list of the top 10 issues related to their potential (or current) job searches and report your results to the class.

TAKE THIS WITH YOU

Based on the goals we set at the beginning of this chapter, here's how you can take this learning with you toward college success:

■ Find career counselors, career fairs, and internships to help you explore career options and learn about yourself.

■ Begin to explore specific employers and use what you have learned about the key elements of an effective resume and how to use a cover letter to introduce yourself to a specific employer.

■ Get started developing a broad network of personal and professional relationships that you can maintain throughout your college career and beyond.

■ Start thinking about the stepping stones for your career plan, whether graduate school or an advanced professional degree, a full-time career, travel, or volunteer work.

REFERENCES AND RECOMMENDED READINGS

Bolles, R. (2011). *What color is your parachute 2011?: A practical manual for job-hunters and career-changers*. Berkeley, CA: Ten Speed Press.

Darling, D. (2003). *The networking survival guide: Get the success you want by tapping into the people you know*. New York, NY: McGraw-Hill.

Farr, M. J. (2004). *Same-day resume: Write an effective resume in an hour*. Indianapolis, IN: Jist Publishing.

Leider, R. J. (2005). *The power of purpose: Creating meaning in your life and work*. San Francisco, CA: Berrett-Koehler Publishers.

Marcus, J. J. (2003). *The resume makeover: 50 common resume and cover letter problems—and how to fix them*. New York, NY: McGraw-Hill.

O'Brien, T. (2007), *The power of personal branding*. Los Angeles, CA: Mendham Publishing.

Safko, L., & Brake, D. (2009). *The social media bible: Tactics, tools, and strategies for business success*. Hoboken, NJ: Wiley & Sons.

MyStudentSuccessLab

MyStudentSuccessLab (www.mystudentsuccesslab.com) is an online solution designed to help you 'Start strong, Finish stronger' by building skills for ongoing personal and professional development.

Academic calendar—A list of important dates. Included are vacation breaks, registration periods, and deadlines for certain forms.

Academic probation—A student whose GPA falls below a designated number can be placed on academic probation. If the GPA does not *improve*, then the student may be prohibited from registering for classes for a designated number of semesters.

Adjunct instructor—An instructor who is not employed full-time with the college. An adjunct instructor usually teaches one or two courses at the college.

Articulation agreement—A signed document stating that one college will accept credit for the courses from another college.

Asynchronous communication—When two or more people do not have to be communicating at the same time. Email and discussion boards are asynchronous communication methods.

Audience—In essay writing and presentations, the audience is the person or persons whom you are addressing.

Bursar—The person at your college who handles payments for tuition and fees.

Catalog—A book that provides students with information about the college's academic calendar, tuition and fees, and degree/certificate programs.

Chat room—An electronic method of communicating with other people in real time.

Corequisite—A course that you can take at the same time as another course. For example, if intermediate algebra is a corequisite for physical science, then you will take both courses during the same semester.

Cornell System—A note-taking system in which a student draws an upside-down "T" on a sheet of paper and uses the space to the right for taking notes, the space to the left for adding questions and highlighting important points, and the space at the bottom for summarizing the material; also called the T system.

Course objective—A goal that the instructor has identified for the student to meet once the course is completed. For example, a course objective could be to use MLA documentation properly.

Cover letter—A letter accompanying a résumé that describes how a person's qualifications match the advertised requirements for the job.

Critical thinking—The ability to use specific criteria to evaluate reasoning and make a decision.

Curriculum—A term used to refer to the courses that a student must take in a particular field, or it can refer to all the classes that the college offers.

Dean—An administrator who is in charge of faculty or a division in the college.

Developmental classes—Sometimes referred to as remedial classes, developmental classes focus on basic college-level skills, such as reading, writing, and math. Students who earn a lower than a set score on standardized tests, such as the ACT and COMPASS exams, may be required to take developmental classes before enrolling in college-level courses.

Discussion board—An electronic method of interacting with other people by posting messages and reading postings from other people.

Family Educational Rights and Privacy Act (FERPA)—A federal law that ensures that a student's educational records, including test grades and transcripts, are not accessed or viewed by anyone who is not authorized by the student to do so.

Full-time student—A student who is taking at least 12 credit hours of courses per semester.

Full-time worker—A person who is working at least 40 hours per week.

Grade point average (GPA)—The number that is used to determine a student's progress in college. It refers to the number of quality points divided by the number of hours a student has taken.

Information literacy—A set of abilities requiring individuals to "recognize when information is needed and have the ability to locate, evaluate, and use effectively the needed information."

Knowledge—This comes from taking in information, thinking about it critically, and synthesizing one's own ideas about what one has read or seen.

Long-term goal—A goal that takes a long time to complete (a year or more).

Major—The area that a student is focusing on for his or her degree. If a student wants to teach third grade, his or her major can be elementary education. (*See also* Minor.)

Matching question—A test question that provides one column of descriptors and another column of words that must be matched with the appropriate descriptor.

Minor—A second area that a student can emphasize in his or her degree. A minor usually requires fewer classes and is not as intensive as a major. For example, if a student majors in marketing but also wants to learn more about running his or her own business, the student may want to minor in business or accounting.

Mission statement—A declaration of what a person or an institution believes in and what that person or institution hopes to accomplish.

Multiple-choice question—A type of test question in which an incomplete sentence or a question is given and the correct response must be chosen from a list of possibilities.

Objective question—A question that presents a limited number of possible answers.

OK5R—A reading strategy that was developed by Dr. Walter Pauk and stands for Overview, Key Ideas, Read, Record, Recite, Review, and Reflect.

Part-time student—A student who is taking less than 12 credit hours per semester.

Prerequisite—A required course or score that must be completed or achieved before enrolling in a course.

Priority—Something that is important at that moment.

Provost—A high-ranking college administrator.

Purpose—What a student hopes to accomplish with his or her writing assignment or presentation.

Quality points—The number that is assigned each grade. For example, an A is worth four quality points and a B is worth three quality points.

Registrar—The official record keeper at the college.

Remedial classes—*See* Developmental classes.

Résumé—A page or two that provides a person's educational and work experience, career objective, and contact information.

Short-term goal—A goal that can be accomplished in a short period of time (within a week or a few months).

Stress—A physical and psychological response to outside stimuli.

Student handbook—A publication of the college that outlines what the college expects of the student.

Subjective question—A test question that requires a student to provide a personal answer. Usually, there are no "wrong" answers to subjective questions.

Syllabus—A document that contains an overview of the course, including objectives, assignments, and required materials, as well as the instructor's policies for attendance, exams, and grading. It may also contain the college's policies on disability accommodations and academic dishonesty.

Synchronous communication—When two or more people have to be communicating at the same time. Internet-based synchronous communication includes chat rooms.

Time management—Strategies for using time effectively.

Topic—The subject of a piece of writing or presentation.

Transcript—A record of the courses a student has taken and the grades the student has earned. Transcripts also note the student's grade point average.

Transfer—Refers to moving from one school to another. Students who transfer must apply for admissions to the second school and must request that their transcript(s) be sent to the new school.

T system—*See* Cornell System.

Values—Part of a person's belief system that provides the foundation of what the person does and what the person wants to become. If a person values financial stability, then the person will look for opportunities to earn money and provide a secure future.

Work study—A federal program that allows students to work at their college and earn money while taking classes. Students must qualify for work study money and must meet college department requirements for work.